A
GUIDE
TO THE
MERCHANT
SHIPPING ACTS
VOLUME II

BY

L. F. H. STANTON
F.C.I.T.

GLASGOW
BROWN, SON & FERGUSON, LTD.
52 DARNLEY STREET, G41 2SG

A*

First Edition - - 1980

ISBN 0 85174 365 X

© 1980 Brown, Son & Ferguson, Ltd., Glasgow G41 2SG
Printed and Made in Great Britain

A GUIDE
TO THE MERCHANT SHIPPING ACTS
VOLUME II

A

FOREWORD

THE presentation of this volume is accompanied with the same thoughts as guided my approach in Volume 1, namely that I owe a great debt to those who, in the past, have sought by their endeavours in this field to bring such knowledge to their fellow-men, and further, to present such a work in an easily assimilable manner.

Once again I owe my grateful thanks to Alfred C. Hedges, Esq., one-time Librarian and Curator to the Great Yarmouth Borough Council, for his meticulous proof-reading and general assistance in the compilation of the work. My special thanks also to Mrs. Suzanne Wright, whose assistance was of great help in the compilation of the Index.

Hethersett,   L.F.H.S.
   Norwich, 1980.

v

PREFACE

'To be construed as one.'

Throughout the ambit of the Merchant Shipping Acts, reference is made in the individual Act to the effect it be construed as one with the Merchant Shipping Acts.

This collective title includes the following Acts, which range at the time of going to press, from the Merchant Shipping Act of 1974.

The following are the unrepealed Acts included within the range:—

The Merchant Shipping Act 1894, also referred to as 'the Principal Act'.

The Merchant Shipping Act 1897.

The Merchant Shipping (Mercantile Marine Fund) Act 1898.

The Merchant Shipping (Liability of Shipowners and Others) Act 1900.

The Merchant Shipping Act 1906.

The Merchant Shipping Act 1911.

The Maritime Conventions Act 1911.

The Pilotage Act 1913.

The Merchant Shipping (Certificates) Act 1914.

The Merchant Shipping (Amendment) Act 1920.

The Merchant Shipping (Scottish Fishing Boats) Act 1920.

The Merchant Shipping Act 1921.

The Fees Increase Act 1923 (insofar as it amends the Merchant Shipping Acts 1894–1921).

The Merchant Shipping (Equivalent Provisions) Act 1925.

The Merchant Shipping (International Labour Conventions) Act 1925 (prospectively repealed).

The Merchant Shipping (Safety and Load Line Convention) Act 1932.

The Merchant Shipping Act 1948.

The Merchant Shipping (Safety Convention) Act 1949.

The Merchant Shipping Act 1950.

The Merchant Shipping Act 1952.

A**

The Merchant Shipping (Liability of Shipowners and Others) Act 1958.

The Merchant Shipping (Minicoy Lighthouse) Act 1960.

The Merchant Shipping Act 1964.

The Merchant Shipping Act 1965.

The Merchant Shipping Act 1967.

The Merchant Shipping (Load Lines) Act 1967.

The Fishing Vessels (Safety Provisions) Act 1970.

The Merchant Shipping Act 1970.

The Merchant Shipping (Oil Pollution) Act 1971.

The Merchant Shipping Act 1974.

Attention is also directed to section 29, sub-section *b* of the Prevention of Oil Pollution Act 1971, viz.:

'Subject to the preceeding sub-sections, expressions used in this Act and in the Merchant Shipping Act 1894, have the same meanings in this Act as in that Act.

The meaning of the phrase:

It means that every part of each of the Acts has to be construed as if it had been contained in one Act. Unless there is some manifest discrepancy making it necessary to hold that the later Act has to some extent modified something found in the earlier Act: per Earl of Selbourne L.C. in

Canada Southern Railway Co. *v.* International Bridge Co. 1883.

This principle has applied in Hart *v.* Hudson Bros. Ltd. 1928, and Phillips *v.* Parnaby 1934.

See also and compare:

Kirkness *v.* John Hudson & Co. Ltd. 1955.

Crowe *v.* Lloyd's British Testing Co. Ltd. 1960.

CONTENTS

CONTENTS xiii

CONTENTS

TABLE OF CASES CITED

A GUIDE TO THE MERCHANT SHIPPING ACTS

Merchant Shipping Act 1897

1 (1) Section four hundred and fifty-nine of the Merchant Shipping Act, 1894 (which gives power to detain unsafe ships), shall apply in the case of undermanning, and accordingly that section shall be construed as if the words 'or by reason of undermanning' were inserted therein after the word 'machinery', and as if the words 'or for ascertaining the sufficiency of her crew' were inserted after the word 'surveyed', and as if the words 'or the manning of the ship' were inserted therein after the words 'reloading of cargo', and the powers exerciseable under or for the purposes of that section shall include power to muster the crew. Extension of powers of detention for unsafety to under-manning.

(2) Section four hundred and sixty-two of the Merchant Shipping Act 1894 (which relates to foreign ships), shall also apply in the case of undermanning, and accordingly that section shall be construed as if the words 'or by reason of undermanning' were inserted therein after the words 'improper loading'.

2 This Act may be cited as the Merchant Shipping Act 1897.

COMMENTS:

Consult also the Merchant Shipping Act 1894, sections 459, 462 and 732.

⚓   ⚓   ⚓   ⚓

Merchant Shipping (Exemption from Pilotage) Act 1897
Repealed by Pilotage Act 1913, section 60 and Schedule 2

⚓   ⚓   ⚓   ⚓

Merchant Shipping (Liability of Shipowners) Act 1898

Repealed by
Merchant Shipping (Liability of Shipowners and Others)
Act 1958, section 8, sub-section 6, and Schedule

For provisions regarding Limitation of Liability,
consult the appropriate section in Volume One of this work

⚓   ⚓   ⚓   ⚓

Merchant Shipping (Mercantile Marine Fund) Act 1898

Abolition of
Mercantile
Marine Fund
and consti-
tution of
General
Lighthouse
Fund.

1 (1) As from the commencement of this Act—

(a) All sums accounted for and paid to the Mercantile Marine Fund, except the light dues or other sums mentioned in paragraph (i) of section six hundred and seventy-six of the Merchant Shipping Act 1894, shall be paid into the Exchequer:

(b) All expenses charged on and payable out of the Mercantile Marine Fund, except the expenses relating to lighthouses, buoys and beacons mentioned in paragraph (i) of section six hundred and seventy-seven of the same Act, and except also any expenses incurred by a general lighthouse authority under section five hundred and thirty-one of the same Act, shall, so far as they are not paid by any private person, be paid out of moneys provided by Parliament:

(c) The said excepted sums shall be accounted for and paid to, and the said excepted expenses shall be charged on and payable out of, a fund which shall be called the General Lighthouse Fund, and references in Part XI and in sections five hundred and thirty-one and six hundred and seventy-nine of the Merchant Shipping Act 1894, to the Mercantile Marine Fund shall be construed as references to the General Lighthouse Fund.

(2) The General Lighthouse Fund shall be applied to the payment of the expenses by this Act charged thereon, and to no other purpose whatever.

(3) The amount standing at the commencement of this Act to the credit of the Mercantile Marine Fund shall be carried to the credit of the General Lighthouse Fund and the liabilities of the Mercantile Marine Fund existing at the commencement of this Act shall be discharged out of the General Lighthouse Fund.

An additional section has been inserted, for details consult COMMENTS to this section.

COMMENTS:

The words underlined repealed as spent by the Statute Law Revision Act 1908.

In respect to the payment of sums into the Exchequer, it does not apply to fees payable under section 83 of the Merchant Shipping Act 1894.

Consult also the Merchant Shipping (Ministry Lighthouse) Act 1960, section 1, sub-section 3.

ADDITIONAL SECTION:

Pension Rights of Certain Employees.

(i) There shall be payable to, or in respect of, persons whose salaries are paid out of the General Lighthouse Fund, such pensions, allowances or gratuities as may be determined in accordance with, or in the case of such of those persons as are employed by the Secretary of State, arrangements made by him and, in the case of other such persons, arrangements made by a general lighthouse authority and approved by the Secretary of State, and those benefits shall be charged on and payable out of that fund.

Comments referring to this section which was inserted as a result of section 17, sub-section 1 of the Superannuation Act 1972. The direct result of this was that the power of general lighthouse authority to grant pensions in accord with section 665 of the Merchant Shipping Act 1894 ceased.

A sub-section 1A (2) had been inserted but this in turn has been repealed by the Finance Act 1972, section 134, sub-section 7 and Schedule 28, Part IV.

⚓   ⚓   ⚓   ⚓

2 (1) All colonial light dues shall, after the commencement of this Act, be carried to the General Lighthouse Fund, subject to the prior payment thereout of any sums payable on account of money secured on those dues at the commencement of this Act in accordance with the conditions on which the money is secured. *Transfer of certain light dues and charges to General Lighthouse Fund.*

(2) All sums which, at the commencement of this Act, are standing to the credit of the accounts kept by the Board of Trade with respect to colonial light dues (including any sum standing to the credit of the Basses Lights Fund), shall be transferred and paid to the General Lighthouse Fund, but shall remain subject to any existing charges thereon.

(3) All expenses incurred in constructing or maintaining any colonial lights, and the contributions made by Her

Majesty's Government in respect of the lighthouse on Cape Spartel, Morocco, shall, after the commencement of this Act, be paid out of the General Lighthouse Fund.

(4) Sections six hundred and sixty-one, six hundred and sixty-two, and six hundred and sixty-three of the Merchant Shipping Act, 1894 (which relate to the advance and borrowing of money for the purpose of the construction and repair of lighthouses) shall apply in the case of colonial lights as they apply in the case of other lighthouses, buoys, or beacons.

(5) All expenses incurred after the commencement of this Act by the Board of Trade or any of the general lighthouse authorities in making and maintaining communication between lighthouses and the shore shall be paid out of the General Lighthouse Fund.   Provided that such communication shall be available for private messages at reasonable charges, so far as may be compatible with the efficiency and safety of the lighthouse service, and all sums received in respect thereof shall be paid to the General Lighthouse Fund.

COMMENTS:

Colonial Light Dues.
See Merchant Shipping Act 1894, section 670 to 675.   Consult also the Colonial Light Dues (Revocation) Order 1960, Statutory Instrument 1960, No. 471.

Colonial Lights.
See section 7.

Repeal.
The words underlined repealed as spent by the Statute Law Revision Act 1908.

The words 'six hundred and sixty-one', underlined with double lines, were repealed by the National Loans Act 1968, section 24, sub-sub-section 2.

⚓   ⚓   ⚓   ⚓

Fees for registration, transfer, &c. of ships.

3 Such fees shall be paid in respect of the registration, transfer (including transmission), and mortgage of British ships as the Board of Trade, with the consent of the Treasury, determine, not exceeding those specified in the First Schedule to this Act, and all such fees shall be paid into the Exchequer.

Provided that fees shall not be payable under this section in respect of vessels solely employed in fishing or sailing ships of under one hundred tons.

COMMENTS.

Fees.

For the fees at present in force, *see* the Merchant Shipping (fees) Regulations 1977, S.I. 1977, No. 2049.

Substitution.

The words underlined with double lines have been replaced by 'not exceeding 10 tons gross register employed solely in fishing'.

See Fees (Increase) Act 1923, section 1, sub-section 1.

The words underlined with a single line were repealed as from November 19th, 1952 by the Merchant Shipping (Safety Convention) Act 1949, section 37, sub-section 5 and the Third Schedule.

Mortgage.

Fees are payable under this section to the registrar on the transfer of a mortgage of a British ship.

Consult Re New Zealand Shipping Co. Ltd. 1918.

⚓   ⚓   ⚓   ⚓

Merchant Shipping (Mercantile Marine Fund) Act 1898

Section 4
Repealed by Merchant Shipping Act 1906

Section 85 and 2nd Schedule

5 (1) On and after the commencement of this Act the general lighthouse authorities shall levy light dues with respect to the voyages made by ships or by way of periodical payment, and not with respect to the lights which a ship passes or from which it derives benefit, and the dues so levied shall take the place of the dues now levied by those authorities. *Scale of light dues.*

(2) The scale and rules set out in the Second Schedule to this Act shall have effect for the purpose of the levying of light dues in pursuance of this Act, but Her Majesty may, by Order in Council, alter, either generally or with respect to particular classes of cases, the scale or rules and the exemptions therefrom.

(3) Before any Order in Council is made under this section, the draft thereof shall be laid before each House of Parliament for not less than thirty days on which that House is sitting, and if either House, before the expiration of the thirty days during which the draft has been laid before it, presents an address to Her Majesty against the draft, or any part thereof, no further proceedings shall be taken thereon, but this shall be without prejudice to the making of any new draft Order.

COMMENTS.

The words underlined were repealed as spent S.L.R. Act 1908.

General Lighthouse Authorities.

See section 634 of the Merchant Shipping Act 1894.

Laid Before Parliament.

The making of orders in Council under this section is now subject to the Statutory Instruments Act 1946.

Levying of Light Dues.

The original scale of light dues was contained in the second schedule of the Merchant Shipping (Mercantile Marine Fund) Act 1898.

Over the years the rate has been increased and the position is now as contained in the Merchant Shipping (Light Dues) (No. 2) Order 1975, S.I. 1975 No. 2194.

⚓   ⚓   ⚓   ⚓

Merchant Shipping (Mercantile Marine Fund) Act 1898

Section 6

Repealed as spent

S.L.R. Act 1908

Definitions.   **7** In this Act, unless the context otherwise requires—
The expression 'colonial lights' means any lighthouses, buoys or beacons on or near the coast of a British possession and maintained by the Board of Trade out of moneys provided by Parliament or out of colonial light dues, and includes the lighthouses mentioned in the Third Schedule to this Act.

The expression 'Basses Lights Fund' means the fund

referred to in section five of the Public Works Loans Act 1887, formed by the dues levied in respect of the Basses lights.

Other expressions have the same meaning as in the Merchant Shipping Act 1894.

COMMENTS.

Colonial Light Dues.

See Merchant Shipping Act 1894, sections 670–675.

Definitions.

See Merchant Shipping Act 1894, section 742.

Public Works Loans Act 1887, Section 5.

Repealed by section 8 of, and the Fourth Schedule to this Act.

⚓   ⚓   ⚓   ⚓

Merchant Shipping (Mercantile Marine Fund) Act 1898

Section 8

Repealed by the S.L.R. Act 1908

9 (1) This Act may be cited as the Merchant Shipping (Mercantile Marine Fund) Act 1898. *Short title, construction, and commencement.*

(2) This Act shall be construed as one with the Merchant Shipping Act 1894, and that Act and the Merchant Shipping Act 1897, the Merchant Shipping (Exemption from Pilotage) Act 1897, and this Act may be cited together as the Merchant Shipping Acts 1894 to 1898.

(3) This Act shall come into operation on the first day of April, one thousand eight hundred and ninety-nine.

COMMENTS.

Sub-section (3) of this section repealed by the Statute Law Revision Act 1908.

Construed as One.

This means that every part of each Act is to be construed as if contained in one Act unless there is some manifest reason making it necessary to hold that the later Act has to some extent modified something found in the earlier Act.

This was enacted by the Earl of Selbourne L.C. in: Canada Southern

Railway Co. *v.* International Bridge Co. 1883, followed in: Phillips *v.* Barnaby 1934.

This Act may be cited, together as the Merchant Shipping Acts 1894–1975.

⚓ ⚓ ⚓ ⚓

Merchant Shipping (Mercantile Marine Fund) Act 1898

First Schedule

Repealed by Merchant Shipping (Safety Convention) Act 1949

Section 37, sub-section 5, and Third Schedule

Scale of Fees

Consult Merchant Shipping (Fees) Regulations 1977 S.I. 1977 No. 2049 made under section 33, sub-section 2 of the Merchant Shipping (Safety Convention) Act 1949

⚓ ⚓ ⚓ ⚓

Second Schedule

Substitution

COMMENTS.

This Schedule was substituted by the Merchant Shipping (Light Dues) Order 1972

See now the Merchant Shipping (Light Dues) (No. 2) Order 1975, S.I. 1975 No. 2194.

Third Schedule

(i) Lighthouses maintained by the (Department of Trade) out of money voted by Parliament.

Bahamas—11 lighthouses as follows:—Gun lay, Abaco, Cay Sal, Great Isaacs, Cay Lobes, Elbow Cay, Great Stirrup Cay, Castle Island, Inagua, Bird Rock, Watling Island.

On Sombrero, one of the Leeward Islands, Cape Pembroke, Falkland Islands.

COMMENT.

The necessity for the maintenance of the lighthouses was repealed by the Bahamas Independence Act 1973.

(ii) Lighthouses maintained by the (Department of Trade) out of Colonial Light Dues, levied under the Merchant Shipping Act 1894.

Off the Coast of Ceylon.
Great Basses
Little Basses.

On the Coast of Ceylon.
Barberyn
Dondra Head.

⚓ ⚓ ⚓ ⚓

Minicoy Island, between the Laccadore and Maldive Islands—

The words underlined above . . . Minicoy . . . Islands, were repealed by the Merchant Shipping (Minicoy Lighthouse Act 1960.

COMMENTS.

On an agreed date, the Minicoy Lighthouse and sums in the General Lighthouse fund in connection with the Minicoy Lighthouse are to be transferred to the Government of India. Also, the light ceased to be a Colonial Light within the meaning of the Merchant Shipping Act.

Consult Merchant Shipping (Minicoy Lighthouse) Act 1960, section 1, sub-section 2.

⚓ ⚓ ⚓ ⚓

Fourth Schedule

Repealed by Statute Law Revision Act 1908

⚓ ⚓ ⚓ ⚓

The Anchors and Chain Cable Act 1899

Repealed

This Act has been repealed by the Anchors and Chain Cables Act 1967 q.v., operative as from 19th October, 1967

The Anchors and Chain Cables Act 1967 (Commencement) Order 1970 S.I. 1970, No. 1443 (s. 35)

⚓   ⚓   ⚓   ⚓

Merchant Shipping (Liability of Shipowners & Others) Act 1900

The provisions relating to 'Limitation of Liability' have been taken out of their chronological order and grouped together

See Volume 1, page 209 *et seq.*

⚓   ⚓   ⚓   ⚓

Shipowners' Negligence (Remedies) Act 1905

Repealed

Administration of Justice Act 1956, section 7, sub-section 1

Section 55, sub-section 1, Section 57, sub-section 2

Schedule 1, Part 1, paragraph 7, Part 3, Schedule 2

⚓   ⚓   ⚓   ⚓

Merchant Shipping Act 1906

Part One—Safety

Section 1 Repealed

Merchant Shipping (Safety and Load Lines Conventions) Act 1932

Section 67, sub-section 2, and Fourth Schedule, Part 2

2 Section four hundred and sixty-two of the principal Act (which relates to the detention of foreign ships)— *Detention of foreign ships when unsafe owing to defective equipment, &c.*

(1) shall apply in the case of a ship which is unsafe by reason of the defective condition of her hull, equipments, or machinery, and accordingly that section shall be construed as if the words 'by reason of the defective condition of her hull, equipments, or' 'machinery, or' were inserted before the words 'by reason of overloading or improper loading'; and

(2) shall apply with respect to any foreign ships being at any port in the United Kingdom, whether those ships take on board any cargo at that port or not.

COMMENTS.

Exceptions.

See section 6 of this Act.

United Kingdom.

Consult Merchant Shipping Act 1894, section 3 and comments thereto.

⚓   ⚓   ⚓   ⚓

Merchant Shipping Act 1906

Sections 3 and 4

Repealed

Merchant Shipping (Safety Convention) Act 1949

Section 37, sub section 5, and Third Schedule

⚓   ⚓   ⚓   ⚓

Merchant Shipping Act 1906
Section 5
Repealed

Statute Law Revision Act 1927

Saving for ship
coming in
under stress of
weather etc.

6 Nothing in the foregoing provisions of this Part of this Act shall affect any foreign ship not bound to a port of the United Kingdom which comes into any port of the United Kingdom for any purpose other than the purpose of embarking or landing passengers, or taking in or discharging cargo or taking in bunker coal.

COMMENTS.

United Kingdom.

Consult Merchant Shipping Act 1894, section 3, and comments thereto.

Passengers.

See generally section 267 of the Merchant Shipping Act 1894.

⚓   ⚓   ⚓   ⚓

Merchant Shipping Act 1906
Sections 7 and 8
Repealed

Merchant Shipping (Safety and Load Lines Conventions) Act 1932
Section 67, sub-section 2 and Fourth Schedule, Part 2

⚓   ⚓   ⚓   ⚓

Merchant Shipping Act 1906
Section 9
Repealed

The Merchant Shipping Act 1970 (Commencement No. 1)
Order 1972 as from 1st January, 1973

⚓   ⚓   ⚓   ⚓

Merchant Shipping Act 1906
Section 10
Repealed

Merchant Shipping (Safety and Load Line Conventions) Act 1932
Section 67, sub-section 2 and Fourth Schedule, Part 2

⚓   ⚓   ⚓   ⚓

Merchant Shipping Act 1906

Section 11

Repealed

Merchant Shipping (Safety Convention) Act 1949
Section 37, sub-section 5 and Third Schedule

⚓   ⚓   ⚓   ⚓

Merchant Shipping Act 1906

Section 12

Repealed

The Merchant Shipping Act 1970 (Commencement No. 1) Order 1972
as from 1st January, 1973

PART II

PASSENGER AND EMIGRANT SHIPS

13 The definition of 'passenger steamer' in section *Inclusion of foreign steam-* two hundred and sixty-seven of the principal Act shall be *ships as* amended so as to include every foreign steamship (whether *passenger steamers.* originally proceeding from a port in the United Kingdom or from a port out of the United Kingdom) which carries passengers to or from any place, or between any places, in the United Kingdom.

COMMENTS.

United Kingdom.

Consult Merchant Shipping Act 1894, section 3, and comments thereto.

Passenger Steamer.

Consult section 267 of the Merchant Shipping Act 1894, section 26 of the Merchant Shipping (Safety Convention) Act 1949.

Section 17, sub-section 2 of the Merchant Shipping Act 1964.

⚓   ⚓   ⚓   ⚓

Merchant Shipping Act 1906
Section 14
Repealed

The Merchant Shipping Act 1970 (Commencement No. 1) Order 1972
As from 1st January, 1973

Passengers landed or embarked by means of tenders.

15 Where a passenger steamer takes on board passengers from a tender, or lands passengers by means of a tender, she shall be deemed to be taking the passengers on board from, or landing the passengers at, the port from or to which the tender comes or goes, and passengers conveyed in a tender to or from a ship from or to a place in the United Kingdom shall for the purposes of Part III of the principal Act, and for the purposes of any returns to be made under the Merchant Shipping Acts, be deemed to be passengers carried from or to a place in the United Kingdom.

COMMENTS.

Passenger Steamer; Passenger.

Consult Merchant Shipping Act 1894, section 267, Merchant Shipping (Safety Convention) Act 1949, section 26.

United Kingdom.

See Merchant Shipping Act 1894, section 3, and notes thereto.

⚓   ⚓   ⚓   ⚓

Restriction as to the decks on which passengers may be carried.

16 (1) A ship shall not carry passengers, whether cabin or steerage passengers, on more than one deck below the water-line.

(2) If this section is not complied with in the case of any ship the master of the ship shall for each offence be liable to a fine not exceeding five hundred pounds.

COMMENTS.

The words underlined 'whether . . . passenger' repealed; Merchant Shipping Act 1970 (Commencement No. 1) Order 1972, as from 1st January, 1973.

Fine.

The procedure for the recovery of this fine, is, it is submitted, prosecution by indictment. The Merchant Shipping Act 1894, section 680, provides only for the summary recovery of fines, not exceeding one hundred pounds.

⚓   ⚓   ⚓   ⚓

Merchant Shipping Act 1906

Sections 17–20

Repealed

Merchant Shipping Act 1970 (Commencement No. 1) Order 1972

As from 1st January, 1973

21 If the provisions of the Merchant Shipping Acts which require a passenger steamer to be surveyed and to have a passenger steamer's certificate are not complied with in the case of any such steamer, the master or owner of the steamer shall, without prejudice to any other remedy or penalty under the Merchant Shipping Acts, be liable on summary conviction to a fine not exceeding ten pounds for every passenger carried from or to any place in the United Kingdom, and the master or owner of any tender by means of which passengers are taken on board or landed from any such steamer shall be liable to a like penalty for every passenger so taken on board or landed. *A.D. 1906. Penalty on master or owner for non-compliance with provisions as to passenger steamers.*

Per Merchant Shipping Act (Load Lines) Act 1967, new penalty substituted.

Old Penalty, £10 for each passenger carried.

New Penalty, irrespective of the number of passengers, on summary conviction, a fine not exceeding £400; and, on conviction on indictment, a fine.

COMMENTS:

Provisions.

Consult sections 271 and 272 of the Merchant Shipping Act 1894.

Merchant Shipping Acts, Remedy and Penalty.

Consult sections 271 and 284 of the Merchant Shipping Act 1894.

⚓   ⚓   ⚓   ⚓

22 If a passenger steamer has on board at any place a number of passengers which, having regard to the time, occasion, and circumstances of the case, is greater than the *Overcrowding of passenger steamers.*

number allowed by the passenger steamer's certificate, the owner or master of the steamer shall, for the purposes of section two hundred and eighty-three of the principal Act, be deemed to have received those passengers on board at that place.

COMMENTS.

General.

There is an offence, under this section, not only to receive on board, but to have on board. It would thus appear that a conviction could be obtained under section 283 of the Merchant Shipping Act 1894 in respect of an illegal number on board, at each port of call.

⚓   ⚓   ⚓   ⚓

Merchant Shipping Act 1906

Section 23

Repealed

Merchant Shipping Act 1970

Section 100, sub-section 3, Schedule 5

The Merchant Shipping Act 1970
(Commencement No. 1) Order 1972, S.I. 1972, No. 1977,
Operative as from 1st January, 1975

⚓   ⚓   ⚓   ⚓

Merchant Shipping Act 1906

Section 24

Repealed
Merchant Shipping Act 1970

Section 100, sub-section 3, Schedule 5

The Merchant Shipping Act 1970 (Commencement No. 1) Order 1972

S.I. 1972, No. 1977

Operative as from 1st January, 1973

⚓   ⚓   ⚓   ⚓

Merchant Shipping Act 1906
Section 25
Repealed

Merchant Shipping Act, 1970, section 100, sub-section 3, Schedule 5

The Merchant Shipping Act 1970 (Commencement No. 1) Order 1972
S.I. 1972, No. 1977

Operative as from 1st January, 1973

⚓   ⚓   ⚓   ⚓

Merchant Shipping Act 1906
Section 26
Repealed

Merchant Shipping Act 1970, section 100, sub-section 3, Schedule 5

The Merchant Shipping Act 1970 (Commencement No. 1) Order 1972
S.I. 1972, No. 1977

Operative as from 1st January, 1973

⚓   ⚓   ⚓   ⚓

27 (1) After the thirtieth day of June nineteen hundred and eight, every British foreign-going ship of a thousand tons and upwards gross tonnage, going to sea from any place in the British Islands or on the continent of Europe between the River Elbe and Brest inclusive, shall be provided with and carry a duly certificated cook who is able to prove one month's service at sea in some capacity. *Certificated cooks for foreign-going ships.*

(2) A cook shall not be deemed to be duly certificated within the meaning of this section unless he is the holder of a certificate of competency in cooking granted by the Board of Trade or by some school of cookery or other institution approved for the purpose by that Board, or is the holder of certificates of discharge showing at least two year's service as cook previously to the said thirtieth day of June, nineteen hundred and eight.

(3) The cook shall be rated in the ship's articles as ship's cook, or in the case of ships of not more than two thousand tons gross tonnage, or ships in which the crew, or the majority of the crew, provide their own provisions, either as ship's cook or as cook and steward.

(4) In the case of an emigrant ship, the ship's cook shall be in addition to the cook required by section three hundred and four of the principal Act.

(5) If the requirements of this section are not complied with in the case of any ship, the master or owner of the ship shall, if there is no sufficient reason for the failure to comply with the requirements, for each offence be liable on summary conviction to a fine not exceeding twenty-five pounds.

COMMENTS.

This section is repealed by the Merchant Shipping Act 1970, section 100, sub-section 3, as from a date to be appointed.

British Foreign-going Ship.

See Merchant Shipping Act 1894, section 742.

Agreement with Crew.

Consult Merchant Shipping Act 1970, section 1.

Emigrant Ships.

Provisions relating to emigrant ships are repealed by the Merchant Shipping Act 1970.

For 'Board of Trade' *read* 'Secretary of State for Trade'.

⚓ ⚓ ⚓ ⚓

Merchant Shipping Act 1906
Sections 28 to 42 inclusive
Repealed

These sections which were substituted for sections 186 to 193 of the Merchant Shipping Act 1894, and repealed by the 1906 Act, have in turn been repealed by the Merchant Shipping Act 1970, section 100, sub-section 3, Schedule 5, S.I.

The Merchant Shipping Act 1970 (Commencement No. 1) Order 1972 No. 1977, operative as from 1st January, 1973

⚓ ⚓ ⚓ ⚓

Deduction from wages and payment to superintendents, &c., of fines.

44 (1) Every fine imposed on a seaman for any act of misconduct for which his agreement imposes a fine shall be deducted as follows (that is to say)—

(a) if the offender is discharged in the United Kingdom, and the offence, and the entry in the log-book required by the Merchant Shipping Acts in respect thereof, are proved to the satisfaction, in the case of a foreign-going ship of the superintendent before whom the offender is discharged, and in the case of a home-trade ship of the superintendent at or nearest the port at which the crew are discharged, the master or owner shall deduct the fine from the wages of the offender;

(b) if the offender enters His Majesty's naval service or is discharged abroad, and the offence and the entry as aforesaid are proved to the satisfaction of the officer in command of the ship he so enters, or of the proper authority by whose sanction he is discharged, as the case may be, the fine shall be deducted as aforesaid and an entry made in the official log-book of the ship and signed by the officer or authority to whose satisfaction the offence is proved.

(2) Every fine so deducted shall be paid—

(a) if the offender is discharged in the United Kingdom, to the superintendent;

(b) if the offender enters His Majesty's naval service, on the return of the ship to its port of destination, if that port is in the United Kingdom, to the superintendent before whom the crew is discharged, or in the case of a home-trade ship, to the superintendent at or nearest to the port at which the crew is discharged, and, if the port of destination is not in the United Kingdom, to the proper authority as defined for the purpose of this Part of this Act;

(c) if the offender is discharged at any place out of the United Kingdom, to the proper authority.

(3) A proper authority shall remit any amounts received by them under this section at such times and in such manner, and render such accounts in respect thereof, as the Board of Trade require.

(4) If a master or owner fails without reasonable cause to pay any fine as required by this section, he shall for each offence be liable on summary conviction to a fine not exceeding six times the amount of the fine not so paid.

(5) An act of misconduct for which any fine has been inflicted and paid by, or deducted from the wages of, the

seaman, shall not be otherwise punished under the Merchant Shipping Acts.

COMMENTS.

The words underlined above have been repealed by the Merchant Shipping Act 1970, section 100, sub-section 3, Schedule 5 S.I. The Merchant Shipping Act 1970 (Commencement No. I) Order 1972, Bo. 1977.

It is anticipated that the whole of this section will be repealed by the Merchant Shipping Act 1970, section 100, sub-section 3, Schedule 5, as from a date to be appointed.

Disciplinary Offences.

See section 34 *et seq.*, Merchant Shipping Act 1970.

⚓   ⚓   ⚓   ⚓

Merchant Shipping Act 1906

Sections 45–48 inclusive

Repealed

Merchant Shipping Act 1970, section 100, sub-section 3, Schedule 5

The Merchant Shipping Act 1970 (Commencement No. 1) Order 1972

S.I. 1972, No. 1977

Operative as from 1st January, 1973

⚓   ⚓   ⚓   ⚓

Definitions of 'proper authority' and 'seamen.'   **49** For the purposes of this Part of this Act, unless the context otherwise requires,—

(1) The expression 'proper authority' means—

(*a*) as respects a place out of His Majesty's dominions, the British consular officer, or, if there is no such officer in the place, any two British merchants resident at or near the place, or, if there is only one British merchant so resident, that British merchant; and

(*b*) as respects a place in a British possession—

(i) in relation to the discharge or leaving behind of seamen, or the payment of fines, a superintendent, or, in the absence of any such superintendent, the chief officer of customs at or near the place; and

(ii) in relation to distressed seamen the governor of the possession, or any person acting under his authority; and

(2) The expression 'seamen' includes not only seamen as defined by the principal Act, but also apprentices to the sea service:

(3) The provisions of this Part of this Act shall, for the purpose of sections two hundred and sixty to two hundred and sixty-six of the principal Act (which relate to the application of Part II of that Act), be construed as if they were contained in Part II of that Act.

COMMENTS.

This section is to be repealed as from a day to be appointed by the Merchant Shipping Act 1970, section 100, sub-section 3, Schedule 5.

Apprenticeship.

The provisions relating to apprenticeship to the sea service, section 463, Merchant Shipping Act 1894, have been repealed by the Merchant Shipping Act 1970, section 100, sub-section 3, Schedule 5, S.I. The Merchant Shipping Act 1970 (Commencement No. 1) Order 1972, No. 1977.

⚓   ⚓   ⚓   ⚓

PART V

MISCELLANEOUS

50 (1) The Board of Trade, in conjunction with the Commissioners of Customs, may make regulations enabling the Board of Trade to refuse the registry of any ship by the name by which it is proposed to register that ship if it is already the name of a registered British ship or a name so similar as to be calculated to deceive, and may by those regulations require notice to be given in such manner as may be directed by the regulations before the name of the ship is marked on the ship, or before the name of the ship is entered in the register. *Ships' Names.*

(2) If the registry of a ship by the name by which it is proposed to register that ship is refused by the Board of Trade, or if any requirements of the regulations are not complied with in the case of any ship which it is proposed to register, that ship shall not be registered under the name proposed or until the regulations are complied with, as the case may be.

COMMENTS.

Commissioner of Customs.

Now Commissioners of Customs and Excise. *See* S.R. & O. 1909, No. 197.

Registrations of Ships' Names.

Consult Merchant Shipping (Ships' Names) Amendment Regulations S.R. & O., 1936, No. 390.

⚓ ⚓ ⚓ ⚓

Power to inquire into the title of a registered ship to be registered.

51 (1) Where it appears to the Commissioners of Customs that there is any doubt as to the title of any ship registered as a British ship to be so registered, they may direct the registrar of the port of registry of the ship to require evidence to be given to his satisfaction that the ship is entitled to be registered as a British ship.

(2) If within such time, not less than thirty days, as the Commissioners fix, satisfactory evidence of the title of the ship to be registered is not so given, the ship shall be subject to forfeiture under Part I of the principal Act.

(3) In the application of this section to a port in a British possession, the Governor of the British possession, and, in the application of this section to foreign ports of registry, the Board of Trade, shall be substituted for the Commissioners of Customs.

COMMENTS.

Commissioners of Customs.

Now Commissioners of Customs and Excise.

See S.R. & O. 1909, No. 197.

Ownership.

The main element given by this section is that it enables the Commissioners of Customs and Excise to enquire whether persons owing a beneficial interest in the ship or share thereof, have the capacity to own such property. Consult section 71 of the Merchant Shipping Act 1894 as to forfeiture.

⚓ ⚓ ⚓ ⚓

Provisions with respect to mortgages of ships sold to foreigners.

52 (1) Subsection one of section twenty-one of the principal Act shall be read as if the following words were inserted at the end of that subsection, 'and the registry of the ship in that book shall be considered as closed except so far as relates to any unsatisfied mortgages or existing certificates of mortgage entered therein'.

(2) It is hereby declared that where the registry of a ship is considered as closed under subsection (1) of section twenty-one of the principal Act as amended by this section, or under subsection (10) of section forty-four of that Act, on account of a transfer to persons not qualified to be owners of British ships, any unsatisfied registered mortgage (including mortgages made under a certificate of mortgage) may, if the ship comes within the jurisdiction of any court in His Majesty's dominions which has jurisdiction to enforce the mortgage, or would have had such jurisdiction if the transfer had not been made, be enforced by that court notwithstanding the transfer, without prejudice, in cases where the ship has been sold under a judgment of a court, to the effect of that judgment.

COMMENTS:

Owners of British Ships.

Consult Merchant Shipping Act 1894, section 1.

⚓ ⚓ ⚓ ⚓

53 The following sub-section shall be substituted for sub-section (2) of section forty-eight of the principal Act:— Amendmen to 57 & 58 Vict. c. 60. s. 48.

'(2) If default is made in registering anew a ship, or in registering an alteration of a ship so altered as aforesaid, the owner of the ship shall be liable on summary conviction to a fine not exceeding one hundred pounds, and in addition to a fine not exceeding five pounds for every day during which the offence continues after conviction.'

COMMENTS.

This section amended section 48 of the Merchant Shipping Act 1894.

Prior to this amendment, an unregistered alteration of a British ship, affecting the tonnage, caused her not to be recognised as a British ship. This deprived her owners, amongst other things, of the right to limit liability in case of collision, section 503 Merchant Shipping Act 1894 refers.

This new subsection amending the Principal Act allows her rights to continue as a recognised British ship subject to the penalties contained herein.

⚓ ⚓ ⚓ ⚓

Merchant Shipping Acts 1906

Section 54

Repealed

Merchant Shipping Acts 1965, section 7, sub-section 2, Schedule 2

Consult now Merchant Shipping Acts 1965, section 1

⚓   ⚓   ⚓   ⚓

Merchant Shipping Acts 1906

Section 55

Repealed

Merchant Shipping Act 1965, section 7, sub-section 2, Schedule 2

Consult now, Merchant Shipping Act 1965, section 1

⚓   ⚓   ⚓   ⚓

Second mate certificates allowed in small foreign-going sailing ships. **56** The following paragraph shall be substituted for paragraph (b) of sub-section (1) of section ninety-two of the principal Act (which relates to the certificates of competency to be held by officers of ships):—

'(b) If the ship is of one hundred tons burden or upwards with at least one officer besides the master holding a certificate not lower than that of—

   (i) mate in the case of a home trade passenger ship;

   (ii) second mate in the case of a foreign-going sailing ship of not more than two hunred tons burden; and

   (iii) only mate in the case of any other foreign-going ship.'

COMMENTS.

As from a day to be appointed, this section is to be repealed by the Merchant Shipping Act 1970, section 100, sub-section 3.

Tons Burden.

Consult Merchant Shipping Act 1894, section 3, *The Brunel*, 1900.

⚓   ⚓   ⚓   ⚓

Merchant Shipping Act 1906

Section 57

Repealed

Merchant Shipping Act 1970, section 100, sub-section 3, Schedule 5

As from 1st January, 1973

The Merchant Shipping Act 1970 (Commencement No. 1) Order, 1972, No. 1977

⚓   ⚓   ⚓   ⚓

58 (1) For the purpose of reducing the period of service required as a qualification for the rating of A.B., the period of 'three years before the mast' shall be substituted for the period of 'four years before the mast', and 'two years of that employment' shall be substituted for 'three years of that employment', and 'two or more years sea service' shall be substituted for 'three or more years sea service', in section one hundred and twenty-six of the principal Act. *Title to be rated as A.B.*

(2) Any superintendent or other officer before whom a seaman is engaged shall refuse to enter the seaman as A.B. on the agreement with the crew unless the seaman gives such satisfactory proof as is required by section one hundred and twenty-six of the principal Act of his title to be so rated; and if any seaman, for the purpose of obtaining a rating as A.B., makes any false statement or false representation, he shall be liable on summary conviction in respect of each offence to a fine not exceeding five pounds.

COMMENTS.

As from a day to be appointed, it is anticipated that this section will be repealed by the Merchant Shipping Act 1970, section 100, sub-section 3, Schedule 5.

Certification of Seamen Engaged in a British Ship Registered in the United Kingdom.

As from 1st May, 1953, this section does not apply.

Consult Merchant Shipping Act 1948, section 5, sub-section 6, Merchant Shipping (Certificates of Competency as AB) Regulations, 1959. S.I. 1959, No. 2148.

Merchant Shipping (Certificates of Competency as AB) 1962, S.I. 1962, No. 579.

Merchant Shipping (Certificates of Competency as AB) 1975, S.I. 1975, No. 341.

Fees.

See The Merchant Shipping (Fees) Regulations 1977, S.I. 1977, No. 2049.

⚓   ⚓   ⚓   ⚓

Merchant Shipping Act 1906

Sections 59–63 inclusive

Repealed

Merchant Shipping Act 1970, section 100, sub-section 3, Schedule 5

The Merchant Shipping Act 1970 (Commencement No. 1) Order 1972

S.I. 1972, No. 1977

Operative as from 1st January, 1973

⚓   ⚓   ⚓   ⚓

Increase of crew space.

64 (1) Sub-section (1) of section two hundred and ten of the principal Act (which provides for the space required for each seaman or apprentice in any place in a British ship occupied by seamen or apprentices and appropriated to their use) shall be construed as if a space of not less than one hundred and twenty cubic feet and of not less than fifteen superficial feet measured on the deck or floor of that place were substituted for a space of not less than seventy-two cubic feet and of not less than twelve superficial feet measured on the deck or floor of that place.

(2) In estimating the space available for the proper accommodation of seamen and apprentices, there may be taken into account the space occupied by any mess rooms, bath rooms, or washing places appropriated exclusively to the use of those seamen and apprentices, so, however, that the space in any place appropriated to the use of seamen or apprentices in which they sleep is not less than seventy-two cubic feet and twelve superficial feet for each seaman or apprentice.

(3) Nothing in this section shall affect—

(*a*) any ship registered before the passing of this Act or which was in course of construction on the first day of January nineteen hundred and seven; or

(*b*) any ship of not more than three hundred tons burden; or

(*c*) any fishing boat within the meaning of Part IV of the principal Act,

or require any additional space to be given in the case of places occupied solely by lascars and appropriated to their use.

COMMENTS.

Repeal.

As from a date to be appointed, it is anticipated that this sectio n will be repealed, Merchant Shipping Act 1970, section 100, sub-secti on 3, Schedule 5.

Consult Merchant Shipping Act 1948, section 1, Merchant Shipping Act 1948, section 4, sub-section 5.

N.B.

This section, i.e. section 64 of the 1906 Act, does not apply to any ship to which regulations made under the 1948 Act, apply.

⚓   ⚓   ⚓   ⚓

Merchant Shipping Act 1906

Section 65

Repealed

Merchant Shipping Act 1970, section 100, sub-section 3, Schedule 5

The Merchant Shipping Act 1970 (Commencement No. 1) Order 1972

S.I. 1972, No. 1977

Operative as from 1st January, 1973

⚓   ⚓   ⚓   ⚓

66   Where, on any investigation or inquiry under the provisions of Part VI of the principal Act, the court find that a shipping casualty has been caused or contributed to by the wrongful act or default of any person, and an application for

Appeal from decision on investigation as to shipping casualties.

rehearing has not been made under section four hundred and seventy-five or section four hundred and seventy-eight of the principal Act, or has been refused, the owner of the ship, or any other person who, having an interest in the investigation or inquiry, has appeared at the hearing and is affected by the decision of the court, may appeal from that decision in the same manner and subject to the same conditions in and subject to which a master may appeal under those sections against a decision with respect to the cancelling or suspension of his certificate.

COMMENTS.

As from a day to be appointed it is anticipated that this section will be repealed, Merchant Shipping Act 1970, section 100, sub-section 3, Schedule 5.

Hovercraft.

Applications to:

Consult Hovercraft (Applications of Enactments) Order 1972, S.I. 1972, No. 971. The Hovercraft (Application of enactments) (Amendment Order) 1977. S.I. 1977, No. 1257.

Diving Operations.

Consult the Merchant Shipping (Diving Operations) Regulations 1975, S.I. 1975, No. 116 as Amended. S.I. 1975, No. 2062.

Power of naval court to send a person sentenced to imprisonment home to undergo sentence.

67 (1) The powers of a naval court under section four hundred and eighty-three of the principal Act (which deals with those powers) shall include a power to send an offender sentenced by the Court to imprisonment either to the United Kingdom or to any British possession to which His Majesty by Order in Council has applied this section, as appears to them most convenient for the purpose of being imprisoned, and the court may take the same steps, and for that purpose shall have the same powers, as respects the orders which may be given to masters of ships as a consular officer has for the purpose of sending an offender for trial under section six hundred and eighty-nine of the principal Act, and sub-sections (2), (4), and (5) of that section shall apply with the necessary modification.

(2) Any master of a ship to whose charge an offender is committed under this section shall, on his ship's arrival in the United Kingdom or in a British Possession, as the case may be, give the offender into the custody of some police officer or

constable, and the offender shall be dealt with as if he had been convicted and sentenced to imprisonment by a court of competent jurisdiction in the United Kingdom or in the British possession, as the case may be.

(3) His Majesty may by Order in Council apply this section to any British possession the Legislature of which consents to that application.

COMMENTS.

As from a day to be appointed, it is anticipated that this section will be repealed. Merchant Shipping Act 1970, section 100, sub-section 3, Schedule 5.

Direction of Naval Court.

Consult Merchant Shipping Act 1950, section 3, sub-section 4 (Direction may be revoked by a reviewing officer).

⚓   ⚓   ⚓   ⚓

68 (1) Any person aggrieved by an order of a naval court ordering the forfeiture of wages, or by a decision of a naval court of a question as to wages, fines, or forfeitures, may appeal to the High Court in such manner and subject to such conditions and provisions as may be provided by rules of court, and on any such appeal the High Court may confirm, quash, or vary the order or decision appealed against as they think just. *Appeal from naval courts.*

(2) Sub-section (2) of section four hundred and eighty-three of the principal Act shall not have effect with respect to any order of a naval court which is quashed on an appeal under this section, and, where an order of a naval court is varied on appeal, shall apply as if the order as so varied were the order originally made by the naval court.

COMMENTS.

As from a day to be appointed, it is anticipated that this section will be repealed. Merchant Shipping Act 1970, section 100, sub-section 3, Schedule 5.

See Hutton *v.* Ras S.S. Co., 1907, where an action by crew members for wages was dismissed. It being held that the finding of the Naval Court was conclusive.

⚓   ⚓   ⚓   ⚓

Calculation of tonnage of steamship for the purpose of limitation of liability.

69   For the purpose of the limitation under the Merchant Shipping Acts of the liability of owners of ships, docks, or canals, and of harbour authorities and conservancy authorities, the tonnage of a steamship shall be her registered tonnage, with the addition of any engine-room space deducted for the purpose of ascertaining that tonnage, and the words 'registered tonnage with the addition of any engine-room space deducted for the purpose of ascertaining that tonnage' shall accordingly be substituted in paragraph (*a*) of sub-section (2) of section five hundred and three of the principal Act for 'gross tonnage without deduction on account of engine-room'.

COMMENTS.

Crew Space(s).

This can now be deducted in respect of steamships for the purpose of tonnage calculations in regard to limitation of liability actions. *See* generally Merchant Shipping (Liability of Shipowners and Others) Act 1900 *et seq.*, fully contained in Volume One of this work.

Tonnage Measurement.

Consult Merchant Shipping Act 1965, section 1.

⚓   ⚓   ⚓   ⚓

Merchant Shipping Act 1906

Sections 70 and 71

Repealed

Merchant Ship (Liability of Shipowners and Others) Act 1958

Section 8, sub-section 6, and A Schedule

Consult now, section 3, sub-section 1, and section 4 of the same Act

⚓   ⚓   ⚓   ⚓

Delivery of wreck to receiver.

72   Section five hundred and eighteen of the principal Act shall apply to wreck found or taken possession of outside the limits of the United Kingdom, and brought within the limits of the United Kingdom, as it applies to wreck found or taken possession of within the limits of the United Kingdom.

COMMENTS.

Wreck.

Consult Merchant Shipping Act 1894, section 510.

Hovercraft.

Application to:

Consult Hovercraft (Application of Enactments) Order 1972, S.I. 1972, No. 971.

⚓   ⚓   ⚓   ⚓

73 After the date of the passing of this Act a pilotage Alien pilotage certificate shall not be granted to the master or mate of a ship certificates. unless he is a British subject, but nothing in this section shall affect the renewal of a pilotage certificate granted before the first day of June, nineteen hundred and six to a master or mate who is not a British subject.

A pilotage certificate includes not only a certificate which may be granted under sections five hundred and ninety-nine and six hundred of the principal Act, but also the certificate which may be granted under section six hundred and four of that Act.

⚓   ⚓   ⚓   ⚓

Merchant Shipping Act 1906

Section 73

Repealed

Pilotage Act 1913, section 60, and Schedule 11

Consult now, section 24 of this Act

⚓   ⚓   ⚓   ⚓

Merchant Shipping Act 1906

Section 74

Repealed

C

Merchant Shipping Act 1970, section 100, sub-section 3, Schedule 5

The Merchant Shipping Act 1970 (Commencement No. 1) order 1972

S.I. 1972, No. 1977

Operative as from 1st January, 1973

⚓   ⚓   ⚓   ⚓

Substitution of ship surveyor for shipwright surveyor.

75 (1) Any person appointed to be a surveyor of ships under section seven hundred and twenty-four of the principal Act may be appointed either as a ship surveyor or as an engineer surveyor, or as both, and any reference in that section or in any other section of the principal Act to a shipwright surveyor shall be construed as a reference to a ship surveyor.

(2) Any surveyor of ships who before the passing of this Act has been appointed as a shipwright surveyor, or both as a shipwright surveyor and an engineer surveyor, shall be deemed to have been appointed as a ship surveyor, or both as a ship surveyor and an engineer surveyor, as the case may be.

(3) The surveys required to be made under section two hundred and seventy-two of the principal Act by a ship surveyor and by an engineer surveyor may be made by the same person if that person has been appointed both as a ship surveyor and as an engineer surveyor, and that section shall be construed accordingly.

(4) The Board of Trade may, under sub-section (2) of section seven hundred and twenty-four of the principal Act, in addition to appointing a surveyor-general of ships, appoint such other principal officers in connection with the survey of ships and other matters incidental thereto, as the Board think fit.

COMMENTS.

Powers of Surveyors of Ships.

Consult Merchant Shipping Act, section 76 1970.

For 'Board of Trade' *read* 'Secretary of State for Trade'.

⚓   ⚓   ⚓   ⚓

Return to be furnished by masters of ships as to passengers.

76 (1) The master of every ship, whether a British or foreign ship, which carries any passenger to a place in the United Kingdom from any place out of the United Kingdom, or from any place in the United Kingdom to any place out of the United Kingdom, shall furnish to such person and in such manner as the Board of Trade direct a return giving the total number of any passengers so carried, distinguishing, if so directed by the Board, the total number of any class of passengers so carried, and giving, if the Board of Trade so direct, such particulars with respect to passengers as may be for the time being required by the Board.

(2) Any passenger shall furnish the master of the ship with any information required by him for the purpose of the return.

(3) If the master of a ship fails to make a return as required by this section, or makes a false return, and if any passenger refuses to give any information required by the master of the ship for the purpose of the return required by this section, or gives any false information for the purpose, the master or passenger shall be liable for each offence on summary conviction to a fine not exceeding twenty pounds.

COMMENTS.

Passenger—Meaning of.

Consult Merchant Shipping Act 1894, section 267, and Comments, Merchant Shipping (Safety Convention) Act 1949, section 26, also; section 15 of this Act, relating to passengers conveyed to and from a ship in a tender.

Rules and Regulations.

Consult Merchant Shipping (Passenger Returns) Regulations 1960, S.I. 1960, No. 1477.

For 'Board of Trade' read 'Secretary of State for Trade'.

⚓   ⚓   ⚓   ⚓

77 (1) The master of every ship which carries any cattlemen to any port in the United Kingdom from any port out of the United Kingdom shall furnish to such person and in such manner as the Secretary of State directs a return giving such particulars with respect to any cattlemen so carried as may be required for the time being by order of the Secretary of State, and every such cattleman shall furnish the master of the ship with any information required by him for the purpose of the return. *Return as to cattlemen brought to the United Kingdom.*

(2) If the master of a ship fails to make the return required

by this section, or makes a false return, he shall be liable on summary conviction to a fine not exceeding one hundred pounds, and if any cattleman refuses to give information required by the master for the purpose of the return under this section, or gives any false information for the purpose, he shall be liable on summary conviction to imprisonment with hard labour for a term not exceeding three months.

(3) For the purpose of this section the expression 'cattleman' means any person who is engaged or employed to attend during the voyage of the ship on any cattle carried therein as cargo.

COMMENTS.

Return of Cattlemen.

Consult S.R. & O. 1923, No. 876.

Hard Labour.

Imprisonment with hard labour now abolished, Criminal Justice Act 1948.

⚓   ⚓   ⚓   ⚓

Dispensing powers of the Board of Trade. **78** (1) The Board of Trade may, if they think fit, and upon such conditions (if any) as they think fit to impose, exempt any ship from any specified requirement contained in, or prescribed in pursuance of, the Merchant Shipping Acts, or dispense with the observance of any such requirement in the case of any ship, if they are satisfied that that requirement has been substantially complied with in the case of that ship, or that compliance with the requirement is unnecessary in the circumstances of the case, and that the action taken or provision made as respects the subject-matter of the requirement in the case of the ship is as effective as, or more effective than, actual compliance with the requirement.

(2) The Board of Trade shall annually lay before both Houses of Parliament a special report stating the cases in which they have exercised their powers under this section during the preceding year, and the grounds upon which they have acted in each case.

For 'Board of Trade' *read* 'Secretary of State for Trade'.

⚓   ⚓   ⚓   ⚓

Power to appoint advisory committees. **79** (1) The Board of Trade may, if they think fit, appoint committees for the purpose of advising them when considering the making or alteration of any rules, regulations, or scales for the purpose of the Merchant Shipping Acts, consisting of such persons as they may appoint representing the interests principally affected, or having special knowledge of the subject matter.

(2) There shall be paid to the members of any such committee, out of moneys provided by Parliament, such travelling and other allowances as the Board of Trade fix with the consent of the Treasury.

(3) Committees may be appointed under this section to advise the Board of Trade specially as regards any special rules, regulations, or scales, or generally as regards any class or classes of rules, regulations, or scales which the Board may assign to them.

COMMENTS.

For 'Board of Trade' *read* 'Secretary of State for Trade'.

⚓   ⚓   ⚓   ⚓

80 (1) His Majesty may by Order in Council make regulations with respect to the manner in which Government ships may be registered as British ships for the purpose of the Merchant Shipping Acts, and those Acts, subject to any exceptions and modifications which may be made by Order in Council, either generally or as respects any special class of Government ships, shall apply to Government ships registered in accordance with those regulations as if they were registered in manner provided by those Acts.

Power to register Government ships under the Merchant Shipping Acts.

(2) Nothing in this Act shall affect the powers of the Legislature of any British possession to regulate any Government ships under the control of the Government of that possession.

(3) In this section the expression 'Government ships' means ships not forming part of His Majesty's Navy which belong to His Majesty, or are held by any person on behalf of or for the benefit of the Crown, and for that reason cannot be registered under the principal Act.

COMMENTS.

The Merchant Shipping Acts do not, except where specifically noted, apply to ships belonging to Her Majesty. Merchant Shipping Act 1894, section 741.

⚓   ⚓   ⚓   ⚓

Application of certain sections of principal Act to Scotland.

81 (1) Sections four hundred and thirteen to four hundred and sixteen of the principal Act (which relate to certificates of skippers and second hands on trawlers) shall apply to fishing boats being trawlers of twenty-five tons tonnage and upwards going to sea from any port of Scotland in like manner as they apply to such fishing boats going to sea from any port of England or Ireland, except that in section four hundred and fifteen the date of the commencement of this Act shall be substituted for the dates mentioned in that section, and Part IV of the principal Act shall be construed accordingly.

(2) The sections aforesaid as hereby applied to Scotland shall, notwithstanding anything contained in Part IV of the principal Act, be deemed to be portions or provisions of Part IV, referred to in section three hundred and sixty-nine of the principal Act (conferring power on the Board of Trade to make exempting or extending orders), and that section (with the substitution of the *Edinburgh Gazette* for the *London Gazette*) and Part IV shall be construed accordingly: Provided that any Order to be published in the *Edinburgh Gazette* under that section shall be subject to the consent of the Secretary for Scotland.

COMMENTS.

See Merchant Shipping (Scottish Fishing Boats) Act 1920.

For 'Board of Trade' *read* 'Secretary of State for Trade'.

⚓   ⚓   ⚓   ⚓

Amendment of procedure in Scotland.

82 The principal Act in its application to Scotland, is amended as follows:—

(1) Sub-section one of section two hundred and thirty-seven of the principal Act is hereby amended by the addition thereto of the following words: 'And such person found on board without consent as aforesaid may be taken before any sheriff or justice of the peace without warrant, and such sheriff or justice may summarily hear the case, and, on proof of the offence, convict such offender as aforesaid.'

(2) The provisions of section six hundred and eighty of the principal Act shall apply to Scotland.

(3) Section seven hundred and two of the principal Act shall be amended by the deletion of the words 'by criminal libel at the instance of the procurator fiscal of the county before the sheriff', and every offence referred to in section

seven hundred and two of the principal Act may be prosecuted by indictment.

(4) The words 'or misdemeanours' in section seven hundred and three of the principal Act are hereby repealed.

COMMENTS.
Repeal.
The whole of sub-section 1 repealed. Merchant Shipping Act 1970, section 100, sub-section 3, Schedule 5.

The words underlined in sub-sections 3 and 4 repealed as spent. S.L.R. Act 1927.

⚓   ⚓   ⚓   ⚓

83 Section seven hundred and forty-four of the principal Act (which relates to the application of that Act to certain fishing vessels) shall not apply to ships engaged in the whale fisheries off the coast of Scotland and registered at ports in Scotland, and accordingly there shall be added at the end of that section the words 'and of ships engaged in the whale 'fisheries off the coast of Scotland and registered at ports in Scotland'.

Amendment of s. 744 of 57 & 58 Vict. c. 60, as respects Scottish whalers.

⚓   ⚓   ⚓   ⚓

PART VI

SUPPLEMENTAL

84 (1) In this Act the expression 'principal Act' means the Merchant Shipping Act 1894, and the expression 'Merchant Shipping Acts' means the Merchant Shipping Acts 1894 to 1900, and this Act.

Construction of references to Merchant Shipping Acts.

(2) Any reference in this Act to any provision of the Merchant Shipping Acts 1894 to 1900, which has been amended by any subsequent Act or is amended by this Act, shall be construed as a reference to the provision as so amended.

⚓   ⚓   ⚓   ⚓

85 The enactments mentioned in the Second Schedule to this Act are hereby repealed to the extent specified in the third column of that Schedule.

Repeal.

COMMENTS.

This section repealed as spent.
S.L.R. Act 1927.

⚓   ⚓   ⚓   ⚓

Short title and commencement.
86   (1) This Act may be cited as the Merchant Shipping Act 1906, and shall be construed as one with the principal Act, and the Merchant Shipping Acts 1894 to 1900, and this Act may be cited together as the Merchant Shipping Acts 1894 to 1906.

COMMENTS.

Sub-section 2 repealed as spent.   S.L.R. Act 1927.

⚓   ⚓   ⚓   ⚓

Merchant Shipping Act 1906

Section 86, sub-section 2

Repealed

S.L.R. Act 1927

Instead of the Merchant Shipping Acts 1894 to 1906, read: The Merchant Shipping Acts 1894 to 1974.

⚓   ⚓   ⚓   ⚓

Merchant Shipping Act 1906

Schedules

Repeal

First Schedule Merchant Shipping Act 1970, section 100, sub-section 3

The Merchant Shipping Act 1970 (Commencement No. 1) Order 1972

Operative as from 1st January 1973

Second Schedule

Repealed as spent

S.L.R. Act 1927

⚓   ⚓   ⚓   ⚓

Merchant Shipping Act 1907

Repealed

Merchant Shipping Act 1965, section 5, sub-section 1, section 7, sub-section 2, Schedule 11

Consult now section 1 of that Act

⚓   ⚓   ⚓   ⚓

Merchant Shipping (Seamens Allotment) Act 1911

Repealed

Merchant Shipping Act 1970, Section 100, sub-section 3
The Merchant Shipping Act 1970 (Commencement No. 1) Order 1972
S.I. 1972, No. 1977
Operative as from 1st January, 1973
Consult now section 13 of the 1970 Act

⚓   ⚓   ⚓   ⚓

Merchant Shipping (Stevedores and Trimmers) Act 1911

Repealed

Administration of Justice Act 1956
Section   7, sub-section 1
Section 55, sub-section 1
Section 57, sub-section 2
Schedule 1, Part 3, paragraph 7, sub-section 1
Schedule 2, Part 3

⚓   ⚓   ⚓   ⚓

Merchant Shipping Act 1911

Author's note:—

This Act was passed as the result of the decision in the s.s. *Maori King* 1909, where it was held that a British Court in Shanghai had no jurisdiction regarding a case of forfeiture.

The Act is not now so important although there are still British Courts in various parts of the world, which as a result of this Act, obtain jurisdiction over forfeiture.

⚓   ⚓   ⚓   ⚓

Extension of jurisdiction under s. 76 and Part VIII of 57 & 58 Vict. c. 60 to certain British Courts in foreign countries.

1 (1) Among the courts before which a ship may be brought for adjudication under section seventy-six of the Merchant Shipping Act 1894 (which relates to proceedings on forfeiture of a ship), there shall be included any British Court in a foreign country, being a court having Admiralty jurisdiction, as if such a court were included among the courts specified in that section, and that section shall be construed and have effect accordingly.

(2) Any such British Court shall also have jurisdiction to entertain any proceedings under Part VIII of the Merchant Shipping Act 1894, and accordingly section five hundred and four of that Act (which relates to the power of courts to consolidate claims against owners) shall be construed and have effect as if such a court were included among the courts to which an application under that section may be made.

(3) In this Act the expression 'British Court in a foreign country' means any British Court having jurisdiction out of His Majesty's Dominions in pursuance of an Order in Council whether made under any Act or otherwise.

⚓   ⚓   ⚓   ⚓

Short title and construction.

2 This Act may be cited as the Merchant Shipping Act 1911, and shall be construed as one with the Merchant Shipping Act 1894, and the Merchant Shipping Acts 1894 to 1907, and this Act may be cited together as the Merchant Shipping Acts 1894 to 1911.

COMMENTS.

This Act may be cited:—

Construed as one with the Merchant Shipping Act 1894 and together as the Merchant Shipping Acts 1894–1974.

⚓　　　　⚓　　　　⚓　　　　⚓

Maritime Conventions Act 1911

Author's Note:—

This Act brings the English Law as to division of loss in collision actions and salvage in accord with the practice of most maritime nations.

In this country the statutory presumption of fault arising in proof of a breach of the Collision Regulations, or of failure to stand by after collision, were of an arbitrary nature, and led to inequitable results. This, conjoined with the old Admiralty rule of equal division of loss, even though the colliding vessels were in fault in different degrees, brought additional hardship.

In the year nineteen hundred and ten, two conventions, dealing with collisions between vessels, and with salvage, were signed on behalf of His Majesty and ratified by the signatory Powers.

Resulting from this convention, English law was altered, resulting in the enactment of the Maritime Conventions Act of 1911. It was only necessary for minor amendments in the law of salvage in order to give effect to the Salvage Convention. The alterations in the law in regard to proof of liability and division of loss were extensive.

In the event of the words of the stature being ambiguous, reference may be made to the Conventions in order to arrive at the true intention of the contracting parties.

Consider the words of Sir S. Evans P in *The Cairnbahn* 1914—'If the words in the section which I have to construe were ambiguous, I think I should be entitled to look at the conventions referred to in the preamble in order to see whether a reasonable construction could be given to the section which would carry out what was agreed by the high contracting parties to the conventions. It is not necessary to do this, because the words appear to be unambiguous and clear . . .'

⚓   ⚓   ⚓   ⚓

Provisions as to Collisions, &c.

Rule as to division of loss.
1 (1) Where, by the fault of two or more vessels, damage or loss is caused to one or more of those vessels, to their cargoes or freight, or to any property on board, the liability to make good the damage or loss shall be in proportion to the degree in which each vessel was in fault.

Provided that—

(a) if, having regard to all the circumstances of the case, it is not possible to establish different degrees of fault, the liability shall be apportioned equally; and

(b) nothing in this section shall operate so as to render any vessel liable for any loss or damage to which her fault has not contributed; and

(c) nothing in this section shall affect the liability of any person under a contract of carriage or any contract, or shall be construed as imposing any liability upon any person from which he is exempted by any contract or by any provision of law, or as affecting the right of any person to limit his liability in the manner provided by law.

(2) For the purposes of this Act, the expression 'freight' includes passage money and hire, and references to damage or loss caused by the fault of a vessel shall be construed as including references to any salvage or other expenses consequent upon that fault, recoverable at law by way of damages.

COMMENTS.

Application of Section.

This section appllies to Crown ships.   Crown Proceedings Act 1947.

The Law Reform (Contributory Negligence) Act 1945 does not apply to any claim to which this section applies and this Act has effect as if that Act had not been passed.   As the intention of the two Acts is the same, similar principles should be applied by both the Common Law Courts and the Admiralty Courts.

Definition of Vessel.

Consult Merchant Shipping Act 1894, section 742.   No craft propelled by oars is a 'vessel' within the meaning of this Act.   Edwards v. Quickenden & Forester 1939.   A wreck and a wreck-marking vessel were held to be vessels within this section, for the purpose of apportioning blame.   *The Manobier Castle* 1922.

Fault of Vessels.

For treatment of the term 'vessel' for the purpose of this Act, and for the position when a third (innocent) vessel is involved, *see The Cairnbahn* 1914 and *The Omona* 1914.   For distinction between fault of vessel and individuals, with consequent exclusion of this Act, *see The Rockabill* 1937 and *The Sobieski* 1949.

See generally—*Marsden on Collisions at Sea*, 2nd Edition, Part II;

Damage or Loss.

British Shipping Laws, Volume 4. The words 'damage and loss' include the words 'damages and losses'. Thus, a court can make different apportionments of liability for different heads of damage or loss resulting from the same event. *The Calliope* 1970.

Damages for Personal Injuries.

See section 2 of this Act.

Limitation of Actions.

See section 8 of this Act.

Proof of 'Fault'.

The onus is on the party claiming negligence to prove both the breach of duty and the consequence of damage: s.s. *Heranger* (Owners) *v.* s.s. *Diamond* (Owners) 1939.

Compare. *The Mimosa* 1944 . . . 'The fact that one ship does not allege any fault against the other seems to me to be quite immaterial if the court, after inquiring into all the facts, find that such fault exists. I think, therefore, that this is a case in which liability should be apportioned . . .' per Pilches, J.

No Actual Contact.

This section applies to cases where the vessels in fault have not been in actual contact. *The Batavier III* 1925.

Cargo or Freight or Property on Board.

Where cargo is damaged in a collision due to the fault of both vessels, the cargo owner is only entitled to recover such proportion as the carrying ship is entitled to receive. *The Umona* 1914, *Tongariro* (Cargo Owners) *v. Drum Canrig* (Owners), *The Drum Canrig* 1911.

Liability . . . in Proportion.

The words 'the liability to make good the damage or loss shall be in proportion to the degree in which each vessel was in fault' must be construed as meaning in which each vessel was in fault, causing or contributing to the collision. *The Peter Bendit* 1915. Due note should, however, be taken of the decision reached in *The Margaret* 1881, where it was held that liability attaches to acts of negligence causing or contributing to the loss.

Only one liability arises, and not cross liabilities, in the case of division of loss. Stoomvaart Matschappy Nederland *v.* P. & O. Steam Navigation Co. 1882: This liability, upon the owners of the vessel that had done the greater damage, is to pay the owners of the vessel that had done the lesser damage, the difference. This case is distinguished in that the owners of the first-named vessel were able to limit their liability under the Merchant Shipping Act, and further, that the owners of the last-named vessel were only entitled to prove against the fund for this difference. As to when the appelate tribunal will interfere with the judge's apportionment of blame, *see The Karamea* 1922 and *The Clara Camus* 1926. However, in *The Testbank* 1942, the Court of Appeal regarded the principles laid down in *The Karamea* as placing too strict a limitation on the discretion of the Court of Appeal. It should be noted in *The MacGregor* 1943, the House of Lords approved *The Karamea* and disapproved the statement of principle enunciated in *The Testbank*.

Costs.

The practice generally followed that where each vessel had been to blame, the court would apply the old rule of making each vessel pay her own costs, even though there were different degrees of fault. *The Rosalia* 1912 and *The Bravo* 1912.

However, in *The Modica* 1926, Hill, J., laid down the principle that the court was at liberty to give to the party least in fault such proportion of the cost as appeared just and the modern practice is that an order apportioning such costs is frequently made. It is, however a matter of pure discretion and not of legal right, and unless the judge can be shown to have considered matters immaterial to the particular issue, his decision as to costs is unappealable. *The Young Sid* 1929.

Salvage.

For general provisions as to salvage, *see* the Merchant Shipping Act 1894, sections 544 *et seq.*

⚓   ⚓   ⚓   ⚓

2   Where loss of life or personal injuries are suffered by any person on board a vessel owing to the fault of that vessel and of any other vessel or vessels, the liability of the owners of the vessels shall be joint and several: *Damages for personal injuries.*

Provided that nothing in this section shall be construed as depriving any person of any right of defence on which, independently of this section, he might have relied in an action brought against him by the person injured, or any person or persons entitled to sue in respect of such loss of life, or shall affect the right of any person to limit his liability in cases to which this section relates in the manner provided by law.

COMMENTS:

Application.

See comments to section 1. This section now applies to vessels belonging to Her Majesty. (*See* section 38, sub-section 2, Crown Proceedings Act 1947) as it applies in the case of other vessels.

Loss of Life or Personal Injuries.

Proceedings in respect of such damages may now be brought *in rem* or *in personam*. *See* section 5 of this Act.

Fault of Vessel.

See comments to section 1.

Liability of Owners.

For persons included in the expression 'owners', *see* section 9.

A passenger or member of the crew who has not, by his own negligence caused or contributed to the collision, can recover damages in full from the other party to the collision. Mills *v.* Armstrong—*The Bernina* 1888. However, if the defendants can prove contributory negligence, this right of defence is preserved to them, but is now subject to the Law Reform (Contributory Negligence) Act 1945.

Limit His Liability.

Consult Merchant Shipping Act 1894, sections 502 to 509, and succeeding Limitation Acts, in Volume 1 of this work.

⚓   ⚓   ⚓   ⚓

Right of contribution.

3 (1) Where loss of life or personal injuries are suffered by any person on board a vessel owing to the fault of that vessel and any other vessel or vessels, and a proportion of the damages is recovered against the owners of one of the vessels which exceeds the proportion in which she was in fault, they may recover by way of contribution the amount of the excess from the owners of the other vessel or vessels to the extent to which those vessels were respectively in fault:

Provided that no amount shall be so recovered which could not, by reason of any statutory or contractual limitation of, or exemption from, liability, or which could not for any other reason, have been recovered in the first instance as damages by the persons entitled to sue therefor.

(2) In addition to any other remedy provided by law, the persons entitled to any such contribution as aforesaid shall, for the purpose of recovering the same, have, subject to the provisions of this Act, the same rights and powers as the persons entitled to sue for damages in the first instance.

Comments.

Application of Section.

See comments to section 1. This section now applies to vessels belonging to Her Majesty (*see* section 38, sub-section 2, Crown Proceedings Act) 1947.

Fault of Vessel.

See comments to section 1.

Damages.

This section only applies to damages recoverable by action and not to claims for compensation arising out of a particular statute and independently of fault on the part of the shipowner. *The Moliere* 1925.

The costs of unsuccessfully disputing liability cannot be recovered. *The Cairnbahn* (No. 2) 1914—*See* also *The Napier Star* 1939.

Statutory or Contractual Limitation.

No recovery of contribution against owners of French vessel when protected by French law. *The Cedric* 1920.

⚓   ⚓   ⚓   ⚓

4 (1) Sub-section (4) of section four hundred and nineteen of the Merchant Shipping Act 1894 (which provides that a ship shall be deemed in fault in a case of collision where any of the collision regulations have been infringed by that ship), is hereby repealed.

Abolition of statutory presumptions of fault.

(2) The failure of the master or person in charge of a vessel to comply with the provisions of section four hundred and twenty-two of the Merchant Shipping Act 1894 (which imposes a duty upon masters and persons in charge of vessels after a collision to stand by and assist the other vessel) shall not raise any presumption of law that the collision was caused by his wrongful act, neglect, or default, and accordingly sub-section (2) of that section shall be repealed.

Comments.

Repeal.

Sub-section 1 above, repealed as spent. Statute Law Revision Act 1927.

Although this statutory presumption of fault no longer exists, failure to assist and stand by after a collision may still render the master or person in charge liable for a misdemeanour unless he can show reasonable cause.   Merchant Shipping Act 1894, section 422.

⚓   ⚓   ⚓   ⚓

Jurisdiction in cases of loss of life.

5   Any enactment which confers on any court Admiralty jurisdiction in respect of damage shall have effect although references to such damage included references to damages for loss of life or personal injury, and accordingly, proceedings in respect of such damages may be brought *in rem* or *in personam*.

COMMENTS.

This section was repealed so far as it relates to the High Court, by the Supreme Court of Judicature (Consolation) Act 1925, section 226, and Sixth Schedule, being replaced by sections 22 and 33 of that Act.   These sections have in turn been repealed by the Administration of Justice Act 1956, section 57, sub-section 2, Schedule 2, and replaced by sections 1 and 3 of the 1956 Act.

This section was also repealed so far as it relates to County Courts (Amendment) Act 1934, being replaced by sections 56 and 57 of that Act. These sections have in turn been repealed by the County Courts Act 1959 section 204, Schedule 3, and replaced by section 56 of the 1959 Act.

An Admiralty County Court, has for this purpose the same Admiralty jurisdiction as the High Court subject to that the amount of claim does not exceed £1000.   Section 57 allows a similar provision for actions *in personam* or *in rem*.

For the arrest of ships in Scotland, *see* Administration of Justice Act 1956 (Part V) sections 45–46.

In regard to Northern Ireland, *see* the Administration of Justice Act 1956, section 55, sub-section 1, Schedule 1, Part 3.

⚓   ⚓   ⚓   ⚓

Provisions as to Salvage

General duty to render assistance to persons in danger at sea.

6   (1) The master or person in charge of a vessel shall, so far as he can do so without serious danger to his own vessel, her crew and passengers (if any), render asistance to every person, even if such person be a subject of a foreign State at war with His Majesty, who is found at sea in danger of being lost, and, if he fails to do so, he shall be guilty of a misdemeanour.

(2) Compliance by the master or person in charge of a

vessel with the provisions of this section shall not affect his right or the right of any other person to salvage.

COMMENTS.

Rendering Assistance.

The duty of rendering assistance in answer to a distress call is contained in the Merchant Shipping (Safety Convention) Act 1949, section 22.

A duty is owed by the assisting vessel, she not being a volunteer, so the doctrine of assumption of risk does not apply. *The Gusty v The Daniel M* 1940.

The Right of Salvage.

See The Tower Bridge 1956, where salvage was awarded in such circumstances.

⚓   ⚓   ⚓   ⚓

7   Where any dispute arises as to the apportionment of any amount of salvage among the owners, master, pilot, crew, and other persons in the service of any foreign vessel, the amount shall be apportioned by the court or person making the apportionment in accordance with the law of the country to which the vessel belongs.

Apportionment of salvage amongst owners, &c., of foreign ship

COMMENTS.

Consult the Merchant Shipping Act 1894, sections 555 and 556 as to apportionment of salvage summarily, and by Admiralty Courts.

⚓   ⚓   ⚓   ⚓

General Provisions

8   No action shall be maintainable to enforce any claim or lien against a vessel or her owners in respect of any damage or loss to another vessel, her cargo or freight, or any property on board her, or damages for loss of life or personal injuries suffered by any person on board her, caused by the fault of the former vessel, whether such vessel be wholly or partly in fault, or in respect of any salvage services, unless proceedings therein are commenced within two years from the date when the damage or loss or injury was caused or the salvage services were rendered, and an action shall not be maintainable under this Act to enforce any contribution in respect of an overpaid proportion of any damages for loss of life or personal injuries

Limitation of actions.

unless proceedings therein are commenced within one year from the date of payment:

Provided that any court having jurisdiction to deal with an action to which this section relates may, in accordance with the rules of court, extend any such period, to such extent and on such conditions as it thinks fit, and shall, if satisfied that there has not during such period been any reasonable opportunity of arresting the defendant vessel within the jurisdiction of the court, or within the territorial waters of the country to which the plaintiff's ship belongs or in which the plaintiff resides or has his principal place of business, extend any such period to an extent sufficient to give such reasonable opportunity.

COMMENTS.

General Comments and Application.

This section is only applicable in respect of:—

    (*a*) Damage or loss to cargo;

    (*b*) Damage or loss of property;

    (*c*) Loss of life;

    (*d*) Personal Injury,

which lie against the other vessel.

Such claims, which are concerned against the carrying vessel, are not affected by this section. Whilst it is clear that the limitation period of two years applies in respect of actions which come within the terms of this section, there appears to be doubt as to what period of limitation applies generally to claims within Admiralty jurisdiction of the High Court, enforceable *in rem*.

Section 2, sub-section (*b*) of the Limitation Act 1939 excludes such actions in Admiralty, from the provisions of the Limitation Act, except claims for the recovery of seamen's wages. Thus, the succeeding Law Reform (Limitation of Actions) Act 1954, amending the 1939 Limitation Act, providing a three-year limitation period, does not apply to such actions in Admiralty.

The period of limitation was extended in relation to enemies, and persons detained in enemy territory, by the Limitation (Enemies and War Prisoners) Act 1945.

By entering an unconditional appearance to a writ issued outside the limitation period, defendants do not waive the right of pleading the protection of the Statute of Limitations, i.e. this section. *The Llandovery Castle* 1920.

Her Majesty's ships are now in the same position as other ships, for the purposes of this section. The Crown Proceedings Act 1947, section 30.

Commencement of Proceedings.

A claim may be brought under the Fatal Accidents Act 1846, within two years—(under this section) even though the Fatal Accidents Act of 1846 expressly provides that the action must be brought within 12 months after the death of the deceased person. *The Caliph* 1912.

The limitation period of one year, provided by Fatal Accidents Act 1846, has now been extended to three years by the Law Reform (Limitation of Actions) Act 1954, section 3. There is some doubt with the enactment of this statute, whether in the case of a claim for loss of life, which is within the provisions of section 8 of the 1911 Act, whether the two-year or the three-year period is applicable. Lord Merriman, P. *in obiter dietum The Vadne* 1959, said he thought the two-year period applied.

Extension of Period.

As to extension of time for the renewal of an unserved writ, *see The Espanoleto* 1920. *See* also, as to the extension of time: Re Dorie S.S. Co. Ltd. 1923, *The James Westoll* 1923, *The Fairplay XIV* 1939.

For a case where the reason for delay in issuing a writ was held insufficient, *see The Kashmir* 1923. The proviso is applicable to action *in rem* and *in personam The Airaiz* 1924.

Rules of Court.

No rules of court have been made under this section, but the court's discretion is not thereby affected, H.M.S. *Archer* 1919.

Reasonable Opportunity.

This proviso is considered effective with regard to any 'sister' vessels named in the writ. Consult Administration of Justice Act 1956, section 3, sub-section 4, and *see The Preveze* 1973. *See* also *The Largo Law* 1920, where it was held that the fact that the vessel has been within the jurisdiction for a few days within the period, does not necessarily disprove lack of reasonable opportunity to arrest.

9 (1) This Act shall extend throughout His Majesty's dominions and to any territories under his protection, and to Cyprus: *Application of Act.*

Provided that it shall not extend to the Dominion of Canada, the Commonwealth of Australia, the Dominion of New Zealand, the Union of South Africa, and Newfoundland.

(3) The provisions of this Act shall be applied in all cases heard and determined in any court having jurisdiction to deal with the case and in whatever waters the damage or loss in question was caused or the salvage services in question were rendered, and sub-section (9) of section twenty-five of the Supreme Court of Judicature Act 1873, shall cease to have effect.

(4) This Act shall apply to any persons other than the owners responsible for the fault of the vessel as though the expression 'owners' included such persons, and in any case where, by virtue of any charter or demise, or for any other reason, the owners are not responsible for the navigation and management of the vessel, this Act shall be read as though for references to the owners there were substituted references to the charterers or other persons for the time being so responsible.

COMMENTS.

Repeal.

The words underlined in sub-section 1 above were repealed, in the case of South Africa, by the South Africa Act 1962, and in the case of Newfoundland, by the Newfoundland (Consequential Provisions) Act 1950.

Sub-section 2 Repealed as spent.   S.L.R. Act 1927.

Persons Other than Owners.

This expression includes the responsible officer of a Queen's ship. H.M.S. *Archer* 1919.   Any liability of an officer on board a ship which is not at fault in navigation for a failure of his own, is his personal liability, and he cannot be held liable under this Act.   *See The Sobieski* 1949. (Senior escort officer of a convoy aboard an innocent vessel negligently fails to give information to another ship.)

Supreme Court of Judicature Act 1873, Section 25, Sub-section 9.

That sub-section provided that the Admiralty rule of division of loss should prevail over the common law rule of contributory negligence.

⚓   ⚓   ⚓   ⚓

10   This Act may be cited as the Maritime Conventions Act 1911, and shall be construed as one with the Merchant Shipping Acts 1894 to 1907.   Short title connection.

COMMENTS.

Construed as One.

For the meaning and effect of this provision, *see* Merchant Shipping (Safety Convention) Act 1949, section 37 and comment thereto.

Merchant Shipping Act 1894 to 1907.

Now Merchant Shipping Acts 1894 to 1974. *See* the Merchant Shipping Act 1974, section 24, sub-section 1.

Pilotage Act 1913

PART I

REVISION OF PILOTAGE ORGANISATION

Improvement
of pilotage
organisation.

1 The Board of Trade shall take steps to obtain information with respect to pilotage organisation at the various ports in the United Kingdom, and, by the exercise of their powers under this Act to make Pilotage Orders, shall carry into effect any re-organisation or improvement of organisation which the Board may consider necessary or expedient at any port, and shall also at any port deal by Pilotage Order with any Act, order, charter, custom, byelaw, regulation, or provision in force at the port with a view to rendering the law relating to pilotage at the various ports in the United Kingdom accessible and, so far as possible, uniform.

COMMENTS.

Board of Trade.

Read now: 'Secretary of State for Trade.'

United Kingdom.

See Merchant Shipping Act 1894, section 3, for meaning.

⚓   ⚓   ⚓   ⚓

Recommenda-
tions with
respect to
pilotage bye-
laws.

2 (1) The Board of Trade shall also take steps to obtain information with respect to the byelaws as to pilotage in force at the various ports in the United Kingdom, and, after consulting with the pilotage authority at the port and considering any byelaws proposed by that authority, shall, when necessary or expedient and with a view to securing, so far as practicable, uniformity of administration and to carrying out any changes consequent on the passing of this Act, make recommendations for the substitution of new byelaws for those in force at the port, or in case there are no such byelaws in force, for the making of such byelaws as may be required at the port.

(2) If a pilotage authority fail to submit byelaws in accordance with the recommendations for confirmation by the Board of Trade under this Act, the Board may treat the byelaws recommended by the Board as if they were byelaws submitted to them by the pilotage authority for confirmation,

and those byelaws, when confirmed by the Board of Trade in accordance with this Act, shall have the same effect as if they had been so submitted.

COMMENTS.

See comments to section 1 of this Act.

⚓   ⚓   ⚓   ⚓

Sections 3 to 5 inclusive

Repealed

Statute Law Revision Act 1927

⚓   ⚓   ⚓   ⚓

6 The Board of Trade, before making recommendations to a pilotage authority under this Act for the substitution of new byelaws for those in force in any port, and a pilotage authority, before submitting any scheme to the Board for the re-organisation or improvement of organisation of pilotage at their port shall, unless pilots are directly represented on the authority or on a pilotage committee of the authority, take steps to ascertain the opinion of the pilots at the port with respect to the matter in question. *Consultation with pilots as to bye-laws and schemes.*

COMMENTS.

Board of Trade.

Read now: Secretary of State for Trade.

⚓   ⚓   ⚓   ⚓

PART II

GENERAL PILOTAGE LAW

Pilotage Orders

7 (1) The Board of Trade may, by Order made under this Act (in this Act referred to as a Pilotage Order)— *Power of Board of Trade to make Pilotage Orders.*

(*a*) make such rearrangement of pilotage districts and pilotage authorities as the Board think necessary or expedient; and

(*b*) establish new pilotage districts and new pilotage authorities and abolish existing pilotage districts and existing pilotage authorities in cases where it appears to the Board necessary or expedient; and

(c) define the limits of pilotage districts, distinguishing as respects any pilotage district in part of which pilotage is compulsory and in part of which pilotage is not compulsory, the part of the district in which pilotage is compulsory; and

(d) provide for the incorporation of any pilotage authority, and make such alteration in the constitution of any pilotage authority with reference to their powers and duties as pilotage authority, and such provisions as to the appointment of committees (including, if it is thought fit, persons not members of the authority), and as to the relations between the authority and the committee, as the Board think necessary or expedient; and

(e) empower a pilotage authority to delegate to a committee thereof any of its powers and duties, and provide, if it seems necessary or desirable, that the decisions of the committee on questions so delegated shall not require confirmation by the pilotage authority; and

(f) make such provision for the direct representation of pilots and shipowners on any pilotage authority or committee of a pilotage authority as the Board think necessary or expedient; and

(g) in cases where a pilotage authority have powers and duties as to other matters as well as pilotage, provide for their accounts as pilotage authority being kept separate from their accounts in relation to other matters; and

(h) provide that pilotage shall be compulsory in any area where it has previously not been compulsory, or provide, in connection with any rearrangement of a pilotage district, that pilotage shall be non-compulsory in any area where it has been compulsory, subject to provision being also made for the payment of compensation to the pilots concerned for any loss or damage which may be incurred by them in consequence of such rearrangement; and

(i) authorise, where it appears expedient, any pilotage authority to make byelaws providing for the grant of certificates (in this Act referred to as deep-sea certificates) certifying that persons are qualified to act as pilots of ships for any part of the sea or channels outside the district of any pilotage authority, so, however, that a pilot holding such a certificate shall not be entitled to supersede any other person as pilot of a ship; and (*j*) provide that any Act (other than this Act), order, charter, custom, byelaw, regulation, or provision shall, so far as it relates to pilotage, cease to have effect within any pilotage district or as respects any pilotage authority, but may re-enact the whole or any part thereof so far as is not inconsistent with the provisions of this Act; and

(*k*) provide for compensation being paid to any pilots for any loss or damage which may be incurred by them in consequence of any Order abolishing or rearranging any pilotage districts; and

(*l*) make any provisions which appear necessary or expedient for the purpose of giving full effect to the Order.

(2) Provision shall be made by Pilotage Order for the direct representation of pilots either on the pilotage authority or on the committee of the pilotage authority of any district where there are not less than six licensed pilots if a majority of the pilots licensed for the district signify in writing to the Board of Trade that they desire such representation, and, where such provision is made, provision shall also be made for the representation of shipowners on the authority or committee, as the case may be.

(3) A Pilotage Order establishing a pilotage authority for any pilotage district shall provide for the representation on the pilotage authority of any dock or harbour authority having jurisdiction within the district which was represented on the pilotage authority for the district at the time of the passing of this Act, and which desires to be so represented.

(4) A Pilotage Order shall not be made by the Board of Trade except—

(*a*) for any of the purposes of Part I of this Act; or

(*b*) on the application in writing of any person interested in the pilotage of any pilotage district or in the operation of the laws relating to pilotage in that district or the administration of those laws.

(5) A Pilotage Order shall require confirmation by Parliament—

(*a*) if it is an Order made for any of the purposes of Part I of this Act; and

(*b*) if, whatever the purpose for which it is made, a petition is presented to the Board of Trade against the Order by

> any person appearing to the Board of Trade to be interested in the administration of pilotage in the district within six weeks after the Order is published and the petition is not withdrawn.
>
> (6) A Pilotage Order which does not require confirmation by Parliament shall have effect as if enacted in this Act.
>
> (7) The provisions contained in the First Schedule to this Act shall have effect with respect to Pilotage Orders.

COMMENTS.

Board of Trade.

Read now: Secretary of State for Trade.

Pilotage District.

For meaning, *see* section 8.

Accounts.

Consult section 21 of this Act.

Supersede . . . as Pilot.

For the rights of licenced pilots to supersede unlicenced persons within a pilotage district, *see* section 30.

Apply Money.

As to receipts and expenses of pilotage authorities, *see* section 21. If on the coming into operation of this Act, a Pilotage Authority had power under statute to receive moneys in the name of pilotage, and to apply them for purposes other than those authorised by this Act, an order made under this section may provide for the apportionment of such moneys between the pilotage fund or account, and such other purposes. *See* section 58.

Confirmed by Parliament.

Provisional orders confirmed by Parliament are statutory instruments. A list of the Acts in force confirming Pilotage Orders may be found in the 'List of the Principal Acts of Parliament, Regulations, Orders, Instruments and Notices relating to Merchant Shipping issued annually by the Department of Trade.

Pilotage Orders, not requiring confirmation by Parliament, have been made for various districts, and are printed as S.R. & O., or Statutory Instruments. Some of these Pilotage Orders have the effect of amending the Confirmation Act for the Pilotage District covered by such Order. Accordingly, therefore, the Confirmation Acts themselves should always be considered with reference with the Pilotage Orders, for the Pilotage district concerned.

Limitation of Liability.

The liability of Pilotage Authorities is limited by the Pilotage Authorities (Limitation of Liability) Act 1936.

Trinity House.

For the powers and duties of the Trinity House (Deptford Stroud) in Trinity House outpost districts, *see* section 52.

⚓   ⚓   ⚓   ⚓

Pilotage Districts and Authorities

8 (1) For the purposes of this Act the districts estab- Pilotage dis-
lished as pilotage districts under Pilotage Orders made under pilotage
this Act shall be pilotage districts, and the pilotage authorities authorities.
shall be the pilotage authorities as constituted by Pilotage
Orders made under this Act.

(2) Until otherwise provided by Pilotage Order made under this Act, every pilotage district which is, at the time of the passing of this Act, a pilotage district shall continue to be a pilotage district, and every pilotage authority which is a pilotage authority at the time of the passing of this Act shall continue to be a pilotage authority.

⚓   ⚓   ⚓   ⚓

Advisory Committee

9 (1) The Board of Trade may appoint an advisory Power to
committee for the purpose of advising them with reference to advisory com-
the exercise of their powers or the performance of their duties mittee.
under this Act, consisting of such persons as they may appoint,
being pilots, shipowners, representatives of pilotage authorities, representatives of dock and harbour authorities, or other
persons representing the interests principally affected, or having
special knowledge of the subject-matter.

(2) There shall be paid to the members of any such committee out of moneys provided by Parliament such allowances
and expenses as the Board of Trade may fix with the consent
of the Treasury.

COMMENTS.

For Board of Trade, read now: Secretary of State for Trade.

Pilotage Authority.

For meaning, *see* section 8.

⚓   ⚓   ⚓   ⚓

Compulsory Pilotage

Continuation of existing compulsory districts and abolition of existing exemptions.

10 (1) Subject to the provisions of any Pilotage Order, pilotage shall continue to be compulsory in every pilotage district in which it was compulsory at the time of the passing of this Act, and shall continue not to be compulsory in every pilotage district in which it was not compulsory at the time of the passing of this Act, and subject to the provisions of this Act all exemptions from compulsory pilotage in force at the date of the passing of this Act shall cease to have effect.

(2) Any reference in this Act to a pilotage district in which pilotage is compulsory shall, in the case of a district in which pilotage is compulsory only in part of the district, be construed, if the context so requires, as a reference to that part of the district only.

COMMENTS.

Pilotage District.

See section 8 for meaning.

Docks.

This section would seem to be qualified in respect of docks in a compulsory pilotage area. *See* section 32, sub-section 2.

Compulsory Pilotage.

As to when pilotage is considered compulsory, *see The Maria* 1839. Beechgrove S.S. Co. Ltd. *v.* Akt Fjord of Kristiana 1916.

As regards payment for pilotage where both compulsory and non-compulsory areas are involved, *see* Arnold Malabre & Co. *v.* Kingston Pilotage Authority 1972.

It is generally accepted that the term 'compulsory pilotage' implies that a charge for pilotage can be recovered, whether or not a pilot is employed.

⚓   ⚓   ⚓   ⚓

Obligations where pilotage is compulsory.

11 (1) Every ship (other than an excepted ship) while navigating in a pilotage district in which pilotage is compulsory for the purpose of entering, leaving, or making use of any port in the district, and every ship carrying passengers (other than an excepted ship), while navigating for any such purpose as aforesaid in any pilotage district (whether pilotage is compulsory or not compulsory in that district) shall be either—

(*a*) under the pilotage of a licensed pilot of the district; or (*b*) under the pilotage of a master or mate possessing a pilotage certificate for the district who is bona fide acting as master or mate of the ship.

(2) If any ship (other than an excepted ship) in circumstances in which pilotage is compulsory under this section, is not under pilotage as required by this section, after a licensed pilot of the district has offered to take charge of the ship, the master of that ship shall be liable in respect of each offence to a fine not exceeding double the amount of the pilotage dues that could be demanded for the conduct of the ship.

(3) For the purposes of this Act the following ships are excepted ships:—

(*a*) Ships belonging to His Majesty;

(*b*) Pleasure yachts;

(*c*) Fishing vessels;

(*d*) Ferry boats plying as such exclusively within the limits of a harbour authority;

(*e*) Ships of less than fifty tons gross tonnage;

(*f*) Ships exempted from compulsory pilotage by bye laws hereinafter provided in this section.

(4) A pilotage authority may by byelaw made under this Act exempt from compulsory pilotage in their district any of the following classes of ships, if not carrying passengers, up to such limit of gross tonnage in each case as may be fixed by the byelaw, that is to say:—

   (i) Ships trading coastwise;

  (ii) Home trade ships trading otherwise than coastwise;

 (iii) Ships whose ordinary course of navigation does not extend beyond the seaward limits of a harbour authority, whilst navigating within those limits or within such parts thereof as may be specified in the byelaw:

Provided that, if any such byelaw appears to the Board of Trade to exempt from compulsory pilotage ships of any class or description which were not at the date of the passing of this Act in practice exempted in the district to which the byelaw relates, the Board shall not confirm the byelaw, but may, if they think fit, submit to Parliament a Bill confirming the byelaw with or without modifications, and such Bill shall

D

be treated as if it were a Bill confirming a Pilotage Order, and the provisions of this Act with respect to such Bills shall apply accordingly.

(5) For the purposes of this section, a ship which habitually trades to or from any port or ports outside the British Islands shall not be deemed to be trading coastwise, and a ship which habitually trades to or from any port outside the home trade limits shall not be deemed to be a home trade ship, by reason only that she is for the time being engaged on a voyage between ports in the British Islands, or within the home trade limits, as the case may be.

COMMENTS.

Compulsory Pilotage.

See generally section 10, and for the exemption of certain ships belonging to local authorities, see section 12. The 'excepted ships' under this Act are contained in section 3. See section 32 for instance, where the provisions of compulsory pilotage do not apply. Consult also section 8. See also McMillan v. Crouch 1972.

Leaving or Making Use of Any Port.

'Port' includes place. See Merchant Shipping Act 1894, section 742 'Place' must be interpreted generally as a 'port' when it has some or many of the characteristics of a port, though by reason of the absence of charter or other reasons, one would not speak of it as a port. Humber Conservancy Board v. Federated Coal & Shipping Co. 1928. In Cannell & Trinity House Corporation v. Lantler Latter & Co. 1914, it was held that a ship was 'making use of a port' when she approached a port, and in order to receive orders from a motor-boat, sent out from a port.

In Humber Conservancy Board v. Federated Coal & Shipping Co. 1928, referred to above, Scrution L. J. intimated that he would require liberty, should circumstances arise, to examine this decision. The words, however, exclude the case of a ship merely passing through a compulsory pilotage district. The Stranton 1917.

Taking or Landing Pilot.

A ship calling at a port for the purpose of taking or landing a pilot belonging to another district, is not deemed to be navigating in the district of that port for the purpose of the provisions of this Act relating to compulsory pilotage. See section 13.

Passenger.

Generally, see Merchant Shipping Act 1894, section 267. However, a passenger ship, when not carrying passengers, does not come within this section. Note that any ship (other than an excepted ship) actually carrying passengers, is within this section. Furthermore, the carriage of even one passenger is sufficient to invoke the section.

See The Lion 1869 and *The Hanna* 1866, where it was held that a relative of the master in the first case and a friend of the master in the second, were not passengers within this section. It was further held in *The Lion* 1869, that payment of a fare is necessary to constitute a passenger within the provisions as to pilotage. However, a more recent case, Clayton v. Albertsen 1972, when it was held that lorry drivers on board a Roll-on/Roll-off vessel, were passengers even though no fares were paid. This would appear to throw some doubt upon the decision reached in Hay v. Corporation of Trinity House 1895 (persons given passage on payment for food only are not passengers).

Defence of Compulsory Pilotage.

For the abolition of the defence of compulsory pilotage, *see* section 15.

Pilotage Dues.

Sub-section 1 of this section does not create a debt for pilotage dues when no pilot offers his services . . . 'The true construction is not that no vessel shall navigate unless she has a licenced pilot on board, but that she is under a continuing obligation to fly the pilot flag, and must take a pilot on board if he offer.' *See* Mallis & Co. v. Trinity House (Deptford Strond) 1925. But *see* comments to section 10. A vessel has no need to go out of her way to search for a pilot boat—Rindby v. Brewis 1926.

It should be noted that there is no power given by this section to charge double pilotage dues if the provisions as to compulsory pilotage are not observed. The method for the pilotage authority to adopt to prosecute under sections 680–681 of the Merchant Shipping Act 1894 bv the authority of Section 62.

Trading Coastwise.

A vessel which enters a United Kingdom port from a foreign port, and after discharging some of her cargo proceeds to another United Kingdom port to discharge the rest of her cargo, is not trading coastwise. *The Glanystwyth* 1899. *See* also *The Lloyds* or *Sea Queen* 1863, Phillips v. Born 1905. Compare also *The Winestead* 1895 (a vessel making regular voyages coastwise to complete loading, then proceeding foreign).

Home Trade Ship.

See definition in section 742, Merchant Shipping Act 1894. Where a vessel regularly trades within the home trade limits, i.e. within the limits of Brest in the south, and the Elbe in the north, and then proceeds from a port in the U.K. to a port outside of the home trade limits, she ceases to be a home trade ship, and is required to engage a pilot. Smith v. Veen 1955.

Bye-Laws.

Powers to make bye-laws are given to Pilotage Authorities by section 17. If no such bye-law is made, application may be made to the Secretary of State. Consult section 18.

⚓   ⚓   ⚓   ⚓

Exemption from compulsory pilotage of ships belonging to certain public authorities.

12 The provisions of this Act with respect to compulsory pilotage shall not apply to tugs, dredgers, sludge-vessels, barges, and other similar craft—

(a) belonging to or hired by a dock, harbour or river authority whilst employed in the exercise of the statutory powers or duties of the authority and navigating within any pilotage district which includes within its limits the whole or any part of the area of the authority; or

(b) belonging to a local authority whilst employed in the exercise of the statutory powers or duties of the authority and navigating within the pilotage district within which the port to which they belong is situate:

Provided that, where in any pilotage district any of the classes of vessels aforesaid were at the time of the passing of this Act in practice subject to compulsory pilotage, the pilotage authority may by bye-law provide that any of such classes of vessels shall continue to be so subject.

COMMENTS.

Compulsory Pilotage.

Consult sections 10, 11, 13 and 15 of this Act.

Harbour Authority.

Defined in section 742, Merchant Shipping Act 1894.

Pilotage District; Pilotage Authority.

See section 8.

Bye-law.

For powers relating to the making of bye-laws, *see* sections 17 and 18.

⚓   ⚓   ⚓   ⚓

Provision with respect to ships calling at a port for the purpose only of taking pilot.

13 A ship calling at a port in a pilotage district for the purpose only of taking on board or landing a pilot belonging to some other pilotage district shall not, for the purpose of the provisions of this Act relating to compulsory pilotage, be deemed to be navigating in the first-mentioned district for the purpose of entering, leaving, or making use of that port.

COMMENTS.

Pilotage District.

Consult also section 8.

Pilot; Port; Ship.

See section 742 of the Merchant Shipping Act 1894.

⚓   ⚓   ⚓   ⚓

14 Notwithstanding anything in any Pilotage Order made under this Act, any area in which pilotage was not compulsory at the date of the passing of this Act shall be deemed to be an area in which pilotage is not compulsory for the purpose of determining the liability of the owner or master of a ship being navigated in the area for any loss or damage occasioned by or arising out of the navigation of such ship. *Provision against extension of defence of compulsory pilotage.*

COMMENTS.

General.

It is submitted that in view that section 15 is now operative, whether this section has any force.

It would appear that its purpose is to prevent the extension of the defence of compulsory pilotage during this period, which might be made by Pilotage Order under section 7, sub-section 1.

See the judgement of Warrington L.J. in *The Mickleham* 1918.

Defence of Compulsory Pilotage.

Sub-section 1 of this section does not limit the abolition of the defence of compulsory pilotage, where it rested on a local or public Act. *The Chyebassa* 1919. *See* also *The Nord* 1916.

Sub-section 1 applies to a claim by shipowners for negligence or breach of contract. (*N.B.* This decision reached before the effective date of the Law Reform (Contributory Negligence) Act 1945). The word 'answerable' in sub-section 1, means 'responsible'. Workington Harbour & Dock Board *v.* Towerfield (Owners) 1950.

This Act extends to the United Kingdom, and the Isle of Man only. The defence of compulsory pilotage was consequently successfully raised, when damage was caused at Gibraltar, where by the existing common law, the defendants would not have been liable for the negligence of a pilot, put on board by compulsion of law. *The Arum* 1921. *See* also *The Halley* 1868, *The Dallington v. The Socotra* 1903, *The Waziristan* 1953, *The City of Philadelphia* 1921 (American territorial waters).

Relationship between Master and Pilot Compulsorily Employed.

See The Tactician 1907 and compare *The Hans Hotl* 1952. Consult also sections 10–14 of this Act.

⚓   ⚓   ⚓   ⚓

Liability of owner or master in the case of a vessel under pilotage.

15 (1) Notwithstanding anything in any public or local Act, the owner or master of a vessel navigating under circumstances in which pilotage is compulsory shall be answerable for any loss or damage caused by the vessel or by any fault of the navigation of the vessel in the same manner as he would if pilotage were not compulsory.

(2) and (3) Repealed as Spent

Statute Law Revision Act 1927

⚓   ⚓   ⚓   ⚓

Power of Pilotage Authorities to License Pilots and make Bye-laws

Powers of Pilotage authorities to license pilots for their district.

16 Subject to the provisions of this Act, a pilotage authority may license pilots for their district, and do all such things as may be necessary or expedient for carrying into effect their powers and duties.

COMMENTS.

Pilot.

See Merchant Shipping Act 1894 for definition.

Liability.

The issuing or renewal of a pilot's licence does not impose any liability on the pilotage authority for any loss occasioned by his acts or default.

Licence.

See section 20 as to the form of a pilot's licence, its production, and return to the pilotage authority. A Pilot, must, on request, produce his licence to any person by whom he is employed.

Pilotage Authority.

See section 8.

Pilotage Certificates.

Pilotage certificates may be granted to masters and mates under sections 23 and 24.

⚓   ⚓   ⚓   ⚓

17 (1) A pilotage authority may by bye-laws made under this Act— *Power of pilotage authorities to make bye-laws.*

(a) determine the qualification in respect of age, physical fitness, time of service, local knowledge, skill, character, and otherwise to be required from persons applying to be licensed by them as pilots, provide for the examination of such persons, and fix the term for which a licence is to be in force, and the conditions under which a licence may be renewed; and

(b) fix the limit (if any) on the number of pilots to be licensed, and provide for the method in which and the conditions under which the list of pilots is to be filled; and

(c) provide generally for the good government of pilots licensed by the authority, and of apprentices, and in particular for ensuring their good conduct and constant attendance to and effectual performance of their duties, whether at sea or on shore; and

(d) determine the system to be adopted with respect to the supply and employment of pilots, and provide, so far as necessary, for the approval, licensing, and working of pilot boats in the district, and for the establishment and regulation of pilot boat companies; and

(e) provide for the punishment of any breach of any bye-laws made by them for the good government of pilots or apprentices by the infliction of fines not exceeding twenty pounds (to be recoverable as fines are recoverable under the Merchant Shipping Acts, 1894 to 1907), without prejudice to their powers under this Act to revoke or suspend the licence in the case of any such breach of bye-law; and

(f) fix for the district the rates of payments to be made in respect of the services of a licensed pilot (in this Act referred to as pilotage dues), and define the circumstances and conditions under which pilotage dues may be payable on different scales and provide for the collection and distribution of pilotage dues; and

(g) if and so far as it appears to the authority to be generally desired by the pilots concerned, provide for the pooling of pilotage dues earned by the licensed pilots or by any class of pilots in the district; and

(*h*) provide for a deduction being made from any sums received by pilots of any sums required for meeting the administrative expenses of the authority, or any contributions required for any fund established for the payment of pensions or other benefits to pilots, their widows or children (in this Act referred to as a pilots' benefit fund); and

(*i*) provide, if and so far as it appears to the authority to be generally desired by the pilots, for bonds (the penalty of which shall not in any case exceed one hnudred pounds) being given by pilots for the purpose of the provisions of this Act limiting pilots' liability; and

(*j*) establish, either alone or in conjunction with any other pilotage authority, pilots' benefit funds, and provide for the direct payment to any such fund of any contributions by pilots towards the fund, or of any part of the ordinary receipts of the pilotage authority, and also for the administration of any such fund and for the conditions of participation in any such fund; and

(*k*) provide for the method of conducting the examination of masters and mates applying for pilotage certificates so as to maintain a proper standard of efficiency; and

(*l*) prohibit the grant of pilotage certificates to masters or mates who do not hold at least a mate's certificate of competency recognised under Part II of the Merchant Shipping Act 1894; and

(*m*) provide that a pilotage certificate shall not be renewed without re-examination unless the master or mate has made not less than a specified number of visits to the port as master or mate of any ship in respect of which the certificate is granted; and

(*n*) if the pilotage authority are an authority authorised to grant deep-sea certificates by virtue of a Pilotage Order made with reference to that authority, provide for the grant of deep-sea certificates; and

(*o*) apply any bye-laws made under this section for the good government of pilots and the punishment of any breach of any such bye-law, with any necessary modifications, to masters and mates holding pilotage certificates; and (*p*) require the owners of ships, whose masters or mates hold pilotage certificates, to contribute towards the pilot fund or account of the pilotage district, and require the holders of such certificates to make a periodical return to them of the pilotage services rendered by them; provided that the contribution so required from an owner shall not exceed such proportion of the pilotage dues which would have been payable in respect of the ship if the master or mate had not held a pilotage certificate, as may be fixed by the Board of Trade; and

(*q*) provide for any matter for which provision is to be made or may be made under this Act by bye-law.

(2) A bye-law shall not take effect unless it has been submitted to the Board of Trade and confirmed by them with or without modifications.

(3) Notice of any bye-law proposed to be submitted for confirmation under this section shall, before it is so submitted, be published in such manner as the Board of Trade direct.

COMMENTS.

General.
Under this Act, the system of the supply and employment of Pilots must be regulated by bye-laws. It should be noted that in the event of failure by a pilotage authority to maintain an adequate pilotage service, they, i.e. the pilotage authority may be liable to the shipowner if his ship suffers damage. Anchor Line *v*. Dundee Harbour Trustees 1922.

Prospective Repeal.
It is indicated by the Merchant Shipping Act 1970, section 100, sub-section 1, Schedule 3, paragraph 5, that as from a day to be appointed, the words underlined in sub-section 1, paragraph (*l*) above, will be substituted by the following . . . 'such certificate issued under the Merchant Shipping Act 1970 as may be specified in such bye-laws' . . .

Confirmation of Bye-law.
There is no need for unanimous agreement by the constituent parties before a bye-law should be confirmed. Forth (Trinity House of Leith) Pilotage Authority *v*. Lord Advocate and Others 1949.

Fines.
Fines are recovered in accord with the Merchant Shipping Act 1894, section 681, as applied by section 62.

Pilots Benefit Fund.

These funds may not be charged, attached, or taken in execution or otherwise made available for meeting any liability of, or claim against a pilotage authority. *See* Pilotage Authorities (Limitation of Liability) Act 1936, section 5.

Masters' and Mates' Certificates.

Pilotage certificates may be granted to masters and mates under sections 23, 24, 25 and 27. The word 'master' is defined in section 742, Merchant Shipping Act 1894. Mates certificates of competency are granted under section 92 to 104, Merchant Shipping Act 1894.

As to foreign certificates approved by the Secretary of State for Trade, *see* section 25 of the Pilotage Act 1913.

Bonds.

A Pilot may limit his liability where a bond is given. *See* section 35 of this Act.

⚓   ⚓   ⚓   ⚓

Power of Board of Trade on representation to revoke or vary bye-laws or require pilotage authority to make bye-laws.

18 (1) If at any port either—

(*a*) a majority of the licensed pilots belonging to the port; or

(*b*) any number of persons, not less than six, being masters, owners, or insurers of vessels using the port; or

(*c*) a dock or harbour authority not being the pilotage authority;

object to any bye-law in force at the port, or desire that any bye-law should be in force at the port which is not in force therein, they may make a representation to the Board of Trade to that effect, and the Board of Trade if the representation appears to them reasonable after giving the pilotage authority, and, if they think fit, any other persons, an opportunity of making representations on the subject, may, by order, revoke, vary, or add to any bye-law to which objection is made, or require the pilotage authority to submit to them for confirmation a bye-law for the purpose of giving effect to the representation.

(2) Any bye-law revoked by any such order shall cease to have effect, and any bye-law to which additions are made or which is varied or added to, shall have effect with the variations or additions made by the order.

(3) If a pilotage authority fail to submit to the Board of Trade for confirmation a bye-law in accordance with an order

made under this section, the Board of Trade may treat the bye-law which they have required the pilotage authority to submit to them as a bye-law submitted to them by the authority, and confirm it accordingly, and the bye-law so confirmed shall have effect as if it had been made and confirmed in accordance with this Act.

COMMENTS.

Harbour Authority: Master, Pilot, Port.

For definitions *see* Merchant Shipping Act 1894, section 742.

Licence.

For power to licence pilots, *see* section 16.

Bye-Laws.

For power to make bye-laws, *see* section 17.

Pilotage Authority.

For meaning, *see* section 8.

For 'Board of Trade' *read* 'Secretary of State for Trade'.

⚓   ⚓   ⚓   ⚓

19 The grant or renewal of a licence to a pilot by a pilotage authority under the powers given to them by this Act does not impose any liability on the authority for any loss occasioned by any act or default of the pilot.

Licensing of pilots by pilotage authority not to involve any liability.

COMMENTS.

Liability.

The liability of pilotage authorities are further limited by the Pilotage Authorities (Limitation of Liability) Act 1936.

There would appear to be some doubt as to the position where a pilotage authority pay pilots a fixed wage. In such an instance, it may be difficult to place responsibility for the pilot's negligence on the pilotage authority. *See The Bearn* 1906, and compare Fowles *v.* Eastern and Australian S.S. Co. Ltd. 1916, where it was held that a Queensland Government's sole duties were to provide a qualified man.

Licence.

Pilots are licenced by pilotage authorities under section 16.

Pilot.

Defined in section 742 of the Merchant Shipping Act 1894.

Pilotage Authority.

For meaning, *see* section 8.

⚓   ⚓   ⚓   ⚓

Form of pilot's licence, and production and return of pilot's licence to pilotage authority.

20 (1) A pilot's licence shall be in a form approved for the time being by the Board of Trade.

(2) A licensed pilot shall, when required by the pilotage authority by whom the licence has been granted, produce his licence to the authority, and, in case his licence is revoked or suspended, shall deliver up his licence to the authority.

(3) On the death of a licensed pilot, the person into whose hands his licence comes shall without delay transmit it to the pilotage authority by whom it was granted.

(4) If any licensed pilot or other person fails to comply with the requirements of this section, he shall be liable in respect of each offence to a fine not exceeding ten pounds.

COMMENTS.

Licence.

Licences are granted by pilotage authorities under section 16. For power to revoke or suspend, *see* sections 26 and 27.

Pilotage Authority.

See section 8.

Recovery of Fines.

See Merchant Shipping Act 1896, section 680 and section 62.

For 'Board of Trade' *read* 'Secretary of State for Trade'.

⚓   ⚓   ⚓   ⚓

Receipts and expenses of pilotage authority.

21 (1) All receipts of a pilotage authority in their capacity as such (other than any money received by them on behalf of and paid over to any pilot, or if the authority administer a pilots' benefit fund, any sums received by them as direct payments for that fund), shall be paid into a separate fund or account, to be called the pilot fund or account of the pilotage district.

(2) All expenses incurred by a pilotage authority in the exercise of their powers or performance of their duties as such authority shall be paid out of their pilot fund or account, and,

except so far as may be provided to the contrary by bye-law, subject to the payment of those expenses, the balance shall in each year be applied for the purposes of any pilots' benefit fund established in the district, and so far as not required for that purpose shall be applied for the benefit of pilots in such manner as may be determined by the pilotage authority with the approval of the Board of Trade.

(3) A separate account shall be kept by any pilotage authority who administer a pilots' benefit fund of all moneys received by them as payments to that fund, or for the benefit of that fund, and money standing to the credit of that account shall not be applicable to any purpose other than the purposes of the fund.

(4) Nothing in this section shall prevent a pilotage authority which owns or hires the pilot boats for the district from keeping a separate account in respect of such boats.

COMMENTS.

Pilotage Authority Pilotage District.

For meanings, *see* section 8.

Pilot.

Defined in section 742, Merchant Shipping Act 1894, as applied by section 62.

Pilots' Benefit Fund.

See generally under section 17. *See* also Pilotage Authority (Limitation of Liability) Act 1936, section 5, as to non-availability for such fund to meet any liability of claim.

Board of Trade.

Read now: Secretary of State for Trade.

⚓   ⚓   ⚓   ⚓

22 (1) Every pilotage authority shall deliver triennially, or, if the Board of Trade so direct, at shorter intervals, to the Board, in the form and at the time required by the Board, returns giving such particulars as the Board may by order prescribe with respect to pilotage in their district, and any returns so delivered shall, as soon as may be, be laid before both Houses of Parliament. _{Returns to be furnished and statements of accounts to be sent to Board of Trade by pilotage authorities.}

(2) Every pilotage authority shall in addition furnish annually to the Board of Trade, at such time as the Board

direct, a statement of their accounts in the form prescribed by the Board, duly audited, including a statement of the average gross and net earnings of pilots during the past year, and, where the authority administer a pilots' benefit fund, the separate accounts of that fund, including particulars of the investments if any.

(3) Every pilotage authority shall allow the Board of Trade, or any person appointed by the Board for the purpose, to inspect any books or documents in the possession of that authority relating to any matter in respect of which a return is required to be delivered or a statement is required to be furnished under this section.

(4) If a pilotage authority refuse or fail without reasonable cause to deliver any return or furnish any statement to the Board of Trade in accordance with this section, His Majesty may by Order in Council suspend the pilotage authority for such time as His Majesty may direct, and thereupon the Board of Trade shall by order direct that, in the meantime, the powers of the authority shall be exercised, and the duties of the authority shall be performed, by such person as they may appoint for the purpose, and any such order shall take effect as if it were enacted in this Act.

COMMENTS.

Board of Trade.

Read now: Secretary of State for Trade.

Board.

Read now: Secretary of State.

Pilotage Authority.

For meaning, *see* section 8.

Pilots' Benefit Fund.

Pilotage Authorities have power by bye-laws under the provisions of section 17.

Pilotage Returns.

See now: Pilotage Authorities (Returns) Order 1965, S.I. 1965, No. 170.

⚓   ⚓   ⚓   ⚓

Masters' and Mates' Certificates

23 (1) A pilotage authority may grant a certificate (in this Act referred to as a pilotage certificate) to any person who is bona fide the master or mate of any ship if that person applies for such a certificate, and if, after examination, they are satisfied that, having regard to his skill, experience, and local knowledge, he is capable of piloting the ship of which he is master or mate within their district: *Grant of masters' and mates' certificates by pilotage authorities.*

Provided that—

(*a*) A pilotage certificate shall not be granted to the master or mate of a ship unless he is a British subject, except in the cases for which special provision is made by this Act; and

(*b*) In any district where a bye-law is in force prohibiting the grant of pilotage certificates to masters or mates who do not hold at least a mate's certificate of competency recognised under Part II of the Merchant Shipping Act 1894, the pilotage authority shall not grant a certificate except to a master or mate holding such a certificate of competency.

(2) A pilotage certificate shall be in a form approved for the time being by the Board of Trade, and shall contain (in addition to any other particulars which may be prescribed) the name of the person to whom the certificate is granted, the name and draught of water of the ship or ships in respect of which it is granted, the limits of the district in respect of which the certificate is granted, and the date on which it was granted.

(3) A pilotage certificate shall not be in force for more than a year from the date on which it is granted, but may be renewed annually by the pilotage authority, subject to the provisions of any bye-law made by that authority as to re-examination.

(4) A pilotage certificate may be granted so as to extend to more than one ship belonging to the same owner, while the master or mate is bona fide acting as master or mate of any such ship, provided that they are ships of substantially the same class.

(5) A pilotage authority may, on the application of the master or mate of a ship, alter his pilotage certificate so as to relate to any other ship or ships of a not substantially greater draught of water or tonnage than that to which the certificate

formerly related, to which the master or mate may be transferred, or so as to cover any ships of substantially the same class and belonging to the same owner as the ships to which the certificate already relates.

(6) A pilotage authority may, for the purposes of this section, treat ships which are shown to their satisfaction to be bona fide under the management of the same person as manager, managing owner, demisee, or time charterer, as being ships owned by that person.

COMMENTS.

It is anticipated that the words underlined in this section will be, as from a day to be appointed, substituted by:
'such certificate issued under the Merchant Shipping Act 1970, as is specified in the bye-law' and 'a certificate so specified', Merchant Shipping Act 1970, section 100, sub-section 1, Schedule 3, paragraph 6.

Board of Trade.
Read now: Secretary of State for Trade.

Mate of Any Ship.
This has been held to be any mate on the ship and not just the first mate. *The Empire Jamaica* 1957.

Pilotage Authority.
For meaning, *see* section 8.

Certificates.
Pilotage certificates may be revoked or suspended, *see* section 26.

British Subject.
For persons who now have the status of 'British Subjects', *see* British Nationality Act 1948.

Fee.
The fee payable on the grant or renewal of a certificate is fixed by bye-law.

Special Provision.
See section 24, where power is given to grant certificates to masters and mates who are aliens.

⚓   ⚓   ⚓   ⚓

24 (1) Notwithstanding anything in this Act, the provisions of this Act as to the renewal of a pilotage certificate shall apply, with respect to the renewal of a pilotage certificate granted before the first day of June, nineteen hundred and six, to a master or mate who is not a British subject in the same manner as they apply to a pilotage certificate granted to a master or mate who is a British subject.

Power to grant certificate to a master or mate, not being a British subject, under special circumstances.

(2) If any master or mate who is not a British subject shows to the satisfaction of the Board of Trade that he is the master or mate of a ship which is of substantially the same class, and is trading regularly between the same ports as a foreign ship which, on the first day of June, nineteen hundred and six, was exempt from the obligation to carry a licensed pilot, or had habitually been piloted by a master or mate of the ship who held a pilotage certificate, the Board of Trade may authorise the master or mate to apply to the pilotage authority for a pilotage certificate under this Act, and the provisions of this Act as to the granting of a pilotage certificate shall, notwithstanding anything in this Act, extend to a master or mate so applying for a certificate, although he is not a British subject, as they extend to a master or mate who is a British subject:

Provided that if the Admiralty at any time consider that, on the grounds of public safety, the provisions of this subsection should not be applicable with respect to any pilotage district or part of a pilotage district, they may make an order excluding that district or part of a district from the operation of those provisions; and while any such order is in force with respect to any such district or part of a district, a certificate granted under those provisions shall not be of any effect within that district or part of a district.

COMMENTS.

Board of Trade.
Read now: Secretary of State for Trade.

General.
The Aliens Restriction Act 1919, section 4, modifies this section, viz.: 'No alien should hold a pilotage certificate for any pilotage district in the United Kingdom, except that the provisions of section 24 of the Pilotage Act 1913, shall continue to apply to the renewal and issue of certificates entitling a master or mate of French nationality to navigate his ship into the ports of Newhaven or Grimsby.

⚓ ⚓ ⚓ ⚓

Provision with respect to foreign certificates of competency.

25 For the purposes of this Act, references to certificates of competency recognised under Part II of the Merchant Shipping Act 1894, shall be deemed to include references to any certificate of competency granted by the government of a foreign country, being a certificate of a class approved by the Board of Trade for the purpose.

COMMENTS.

Board of Trade.

Read now: Secretary of State for Trade.

It is anticipated that the words underlined in this section will be, as from a day to be appointed, be substituted by 'certificates issued under the Merchant Shipping Act 1970.'

⚓   ⚓   ⚓   ⚓

Supplementary Provisions as to Licences and Certificates

Suspension or revocation of a pilot's licence or a pilotage certificate.

26 A pilotage authority may suspend or revoke any pilot's licence or any pilotage certificate granted by them if it appears to them, after giving the holder thereof an opportunity of being heard, that he has been guilty of any offence under this Act or of any breach of any bye-law made by the authority, or of any other misconduct affecting his capability as a pilot, or that he has failed in or neglected his duty as a pilot, or that he has become incompetent to act as pilot; and a licence or certificate, if so revoked, shall cease to have effect, and, if so suspended, shall cease to have effect for the period for which it is suspended:

Provided that in any case where pilots are directly represented on a committee of a pilotage authority, that committee may, until a Pilotage Order is made regulating the relations between the authority and the committee, exercise the powers conferred on a pilotage authority by this section with respect to pilots' licences as though they were the pilotage authority.

COMMENTS.

Pilot.

For meaning, *see* section 742 of the Merchant Shipping Act 1894.

Licence and Certificate.

Licences are granted under section 16, and pilotage certificates are granted to masters and mates under sections 23 and 24.

Offences.

For offences under this Act, *see* sections 46 and 48.

Opportunity to be Heard.

The holder of a pilots licence has the opportunity to be heard under this sub-section. *See* Moore *v.* Clyde Pilotage Authority 1943; Conway *v.* Clyde Pilotage Authority 1951.

Appeals.

As to appeals against the revocation or suspension of licences or certificates, *see* sections 27 and 28.

⚓   ⚓   ⚓   ⚓

27 (1) If a complaint is made to the Board of Trade that a pilotage authority have—

(*a*) without reasonable cause refused or failed to examine any candidate for a pilot's licence, or a master or mate for a pilotage certificate, or to grant such a licence or certificate after examination; or

(*b*) conducted any examination for a pilot's licence or a pilotage certificate improperly or unfairly; or

(*c*) imposed conditions on the granting of a pilot's licence or a pilotage certificate which they have no power to impose or which are unreasonable; or

(*d*) without reasonable cause refused or failed to renew a pilotage certificate, or, having obtained possession of any such certificate, refused or failed to return it; or

(*e*) without reasonable cause suspended or revoked a pilotage certificate; or

(*f*) in any other manner failed properly to perform their duties under this Act with respect to the matters above-mentioned in this section, or improperly exercised any of their powers under this Act with respect to those matters;

the Board of Trade shall consider the complaint, and, if they are of opinion that the complaint is in any respect wellfounded, shall make such order as they think fit for the purpose of redressing the matter complained of, and the pilotage authority shall give effect to any order so made by the Board of Trade.

(2) If a pilotage authority refuse or fail to give effect to any such order of the Board of Trade, the Board of Trade may, for the purpose of giving effect to the order, exercise any powers of

Appeal by pilot, master, or mate, against action of pilotage authority with respect to pilot's licence or pilotage certificate.

the pilotage authority, and anything done by the Board of Trade in the exercise of those powers shall have the same effect as if it had been done by the pilotage authority.

COMMENTS.

Pilotage Authority.

For definition, *see* section 8.

Licence.

Pilots' licences are granted under section 16.

Certificate.

Pilotage certificates are granted to masters and mates under sections 23 and 24.

Suspension.

A right to appeal is given to a pilot against the suspension or revocation of licences under section 28.

For 'Board of Trade' *read* 'Secretary of State for Trade'.

⚓   ⚓   ⚓   ⚓

Appeal by pilot against action of pilotage authority in suspending, &c., pilot's licence.

28 (1) If a pilot is aggrieved by the suspension or revocation by the pilotage authority of his licence, or by the refusal or failure of the pilotage authority to renew his licence, or by the refusal or failure of the pilotage authority who have obtained possession of his licence to return it to him, or by the imposition upon him by the pilotage authority of a fine exceeding two pounds, he may either appeal to a judge of county courts having jurisdiction within the port for which the pilot is licensed, or to a metropolitan police magistrate or stipendiary magistrate having jurisdiction within that port.

(2) For the purpose of hearing the appeal, the judge or magistrate shall sit with an assessor of nautical and pilotage experience selected and summoned by the judge or magistrate.

(3) Objection may be taken to any person proposed to be summoned as an assessor, either personally or in respect of his qualification, and by either party to the appeal.

(4) The judge or magistrate may confirm or reverse the suspension or revocation of the licence, or make such order in the case as may seem just, and his decision shall be final,unless special leave to appeal from the same to the High Court on a question of law or a question of mixed law and fact is given by the judge or magistrate, or by the High Court, and in such case the decision of the High Court shall be final.

(5) The costs incurred by a pilotage authority under this section shall be payable out of any fund applicable to the general expenses of the pilotage authority.

(6) Rules with respect to the procedure under this section (including costs and the remuneration of assessors) may be made, as respects county court judges, by the authority having power to make rules of practice under the County Courts Act, 1888, and as respects metropolitan police and stipendiary magistrates by a Secretary of State, but in either case with the concurrence of the Treasury as to fees.

(7) In Scotland the appeal under this section shall be to the sheriff having jurisdiction at the port where the decision is given, and may be heard by the sheriff sitting with an assessor as provided in this section, and rules may be made by the Court of Session by Acts of sederunt with respect to the procedure in case of those appeals in Scotland (including costs and the remuneration of assessors), subject to the concurrence of the Treasury as to fees. In the application of this section to Scotland, references to the Court of Session shall be substituted for references to the High Court.

(8) In the application of this section to Ireland—

(*a*) The expression 'judge of county courts' and 'judge' shall respectively mean a county court judge and chairman of quarter sessions, and include recorder;

(*b*) The expressions 'stipendiary magistrate' and 'magistrate' shall respectively mean a magistrate appointed under the Constabulary (Ireland) Act 1836;

(*c*) Rules with respect to the procedure in case of appeals under this section (including costs and the remuneration of assessors) may from time to time be made, as respects county court judges and chairmen of quarter sessions, by the authority having power to make rules and orders for regulating the practice under the County Officers and Courts (Ireland) Act 1877, and as respects stipendiary magistrates, by the Lord Lieutenant of Ireland in Council, but in either case with the concurrence of the Treasury as to fees.

COMMENTS.

Assessor.

The judge or magistrate must sit with an assessor whatever the circumstances. Soames *v.* Corporation of Trinity House 1950.

Rules.

The Secretary of State has made rules dated 16th January, 1916, S.R. & O., 1916, No. 62.

The rules regulating appeals to county courts are contained in the County Court Rules 1936, in accord with the County Courts Act 1959, section 52.

The words underlined in sub-section 8, paragraph (*c*) repealed. County Courts Act (Northern Ireland) 1959.

Fees in respect of pilots' licences and pilotage certificates.

29 Such fees shall be payable on the examination for a pilot's licence, or for a pilotage certificate, and on the grant, renewal, or alteration of any such licence or certificate, as may be fixed by bye-law made under this Act.

COMMENTS.

Licence.

Pilots' licences are granted under section 16.

Certificate.

Pilotage certificates are granted under sections 23 and 24.

Bye-Law.

For the power of Pilotage authorities and the Secretary of State for Trade, *see* sections 17 and 18.

Rights and Obligations of Licensed Pilots

Right of licensed pilot to supersede unlicensed persons.

30 (1) A pilot licensed for a district may supersede any pilot not so licensed who is employed to pilot a ship in the district.

(2) Where a licensed pilot supersedes an unlicensed pilot the master of the ship shall pay to the latter a proportionate sum for his services, and shall be entitled to deduct the sum so paid from the sum payable in respect of the services of the licensed pilot.

Any question as to the proportion payable to the licensed pilot and to the person whom the licensed pilot has superseded shall be referred to the pilotage authority by whom the licensed pilot has been licensed, and their decision on the question shall be final.

(3) If in any pilotage district a pilot not licensed for the district pilots or attempts to pilot a ship after a pilot licensed for that district has offered to pilot the ship, he shall be liable in respect of each offence to a fine not exceeding fifty pounds.

(4) If the master of a ship knowingly employs or continues to employ a pilot not licensed for the district to pilot the ship within any pilotage district after a pilot licensed for that district has offered to pilot the ship, or, in the case of an outward-bound ship, without having taken reasonable steps (proof whereof shall lie on the master) to obtain a licensed pilot, he shall be liable in respect of each offence to a fine not exceeding fifty pounds.

(5) If any person other than the master or a seaman being bona fide one of the crew of the ship is on the bridge of a ship, or in any other position (whether on board the ship or elsewhere) from which the ship is navigated, that person shall, for the purposes of this section, be deemed to be piloting the ship unless the contrary is proved.

COMMENTS.

Licenced.

See section 16 for licensing of pilots. The holder of a deep-sea certificate is not entitled to supersede any other person as pilot of a ship.

May Supersede.

It would appear that a pilot qualified to pilot deep-draught vessels would have a right to supersede the pilot in charge who was not so qualified, the latter would however be entitled to a fair proportion of the fees. *The Carl XV* 1892. There is no right to supersede if the vessel is not being navigated in accordance with a bye-law made under section 32. McMillan *v.* Crouch 1972.

Master; Pilot; Seaman; Ship.

See section 742 of the Merchant Shipping Act 1894

Pilotage District; Pilotage Authority

Defined in section 8.

Sum Payable.

Pilotage dues are fixed by bye-law made by the pilotage authority, *see* section 17.

Offered to Pilot a Ship.

The offer must be made to the ship in question. In *Babbs v*. Press 1971, it was held that a pilot flag displayed at a pilot station was insufficient and did not constitute an offer. *See* also Montague *v. Babbs* 1972.

Note also that where a licensed pilot offers his services, which was refused within the hearing of an unlicensed pilot in charge of a vessel, who subsequently completed the pilotage, it was held that the unlicensed pilot had committed an offence. Smith *v*. Cocking 1959.

⚓   ⚓   ⚓   ⚓

Declaration as to draught of ship.

31 (1) A licensed pilot may require the master of any ship which he is piloting to declare her draught of water, length and beam, and the master shall comply with any such request.

(2) If the master of a ship refuses to comply with any such request of a pilot, or makes or is privy to any other person making any false statement to the pilot in answer to the request, he shall be liable in respect of each offence to a fine not exceeding fifty pounds.

COMMENTS.

Licensed.

See section 16.

Recovery of Fines.

Consult Merchant Shipping Act 1894, sections 680 to 682.

Master; Pilot; Ship.

See definitions in section 742, Merchant Shipping Act 1894.

⚓   ⚓   ⚓   ⚓

Provision as to ships within a harbour, dock, &c.

32 (1) A ship while being moved within a harbour which forms part of a pilotage district shall be deemed to be a ship navigating in a pilotage district, except so far as may be provided by bye-law in the case of ships being so moved for the purpose of changing from one mooring to another mooring or of being taken into or out of any dock:

Provided that a bye-law shall in every case be made for the

purpose aforesaid in any pilotage district where any class of persons other than licensed pilots were in practice employed at the date of the passing of this Act for the purpose of changing the moorings of ships or of taking ships into or out of dock.

(2) A ship whilst being navigated within any closed dock, lock, or other closed work in a pilotage district shall notwithstanding anything in this Act be deemed to be navigating in a district in which pilotage is not compulsory.

COMMENTS.

Pilotage is Not Compulsory.

Sub-section 2 does not affect section 59, i.e. where any local Act, giving compulsory pilotage remains in force until it has been superseded in accordance with that section. *The Port Hunter* 1915.

Pilotage District.

See section 8.

Compulsory Pilotage.

See generally, sections 10 to 15.

⚓   ⚓   ⚓   ⚓

33 (1) The pilotage authority shall cause every pilot licensed by them to be furnished with a copy of this Act as amended for the time being, and with a copy of any Pilotage Order for the time being in force in the district, and of any bye-laws so in force. *Copies of pilotage provisions to be furnished to pilots.*

(2) A licensed pilot shall produce any copy so furnished to him to the master of any ship or other person employing him when required to do so, and if he fails without reasonable cause to do so, he shall be liable in respect of each offence to a fine not exceeding five pounds.

COMMENTS.

Pilotage Authority.

See section 8.

Master; Pilot; Ship.

See section 742, Merchant Shipping Act 1894.

Licensed Pilot.

See section 16

Recovery of Fines.

See section 680, Merchant Shipping Act 1894.

⚓   ⚓   ⚓   ⚓

Allowance to
licensed pilot
taken out of
his district.

34 (1) A master of a ship shall not, except under circumstances of unavoidable necessity, take a licensed pilot without his consent beyond the district for which he is licensed, or beyond the point up to which he has been engaged to pilot the ship, and if a master of a ship acts in contravention of this section, he shall be liable in respect of each offence to a fine not exceeding twenty pounds.

(2) Where a pilot is taken beyond the district for which he is licensed, or beyond the point up to which he is engaged to pilot the ship, either without his consent or under circumstances of unavoidable necessity, he shall be entitled, over and above his pilotage dues, to maintenance and to the sum of ten shillings and sixpence a day, recoverable in the same manner as the pilotage dues.

(3) The sum so paid shall be computed from and inclusive of the day on which the ship passes beyond the district for which the pilot is licensed, or the point up to which the pilot was engaged to pilot her, and up to and inclusive of either the day of his being returned in the said ship to the place where he was taken on board, or, if he is discharged from the ship at a distance from that place, such day as will allow him sufficient time to return thereto; and in the last-mentioned case he shall be entitled to his reasonable travelling expenses.

COMMENTS.

Recovery of Dues.

See section 49.   Also, consult the Pilotage Authorities (Limitation of Liability) Act 1936, section 3, which apply to the consolidation of claims against pilotage authorities.

Recovery of Fines.

See section 680, Merchant Shipping Act 1894.

Master; Pilot; Ship.

Defined in section 742, Merchant Shipping Act 1894.

⚓   ⚓   ⚓   ⚓

Licensed.

For power to license Pilots, *see* section 16.

⚓　　　　⚓　　　　⚓　　　　⚓

35 (1) A licensed pilot, who has given a bond in conformity with bye-laws made for the purpose under this Act, shall not be liable for neglect or want of skill beyond the penalty of the bond and the amount payable to him on account of pilotage in respect of the voyage in which he was engaged when he became so liable.

(2) Any bond given by a pilot in conformity with bye-laws made for the purpose under this Act shall not be liable to stamp duty, and a pilot shall not be called upon to pay any expenses in relation to the bond other than the actual expense of preparing the same.

(3) Where any proceedings are taken against a pilot for any neglect or want of skill in respect of which his liability is limited as provided by this section, and other claims are made or apprehended in respect of the same neglect or want of skill, the court in which the proceedings are taken may determine the amount of the pilot's liability, and, upon payment by the pilot of that amount into court, may distribute that amount rateably among the several claimants, and may stay any proceedings pending in any other court in relation to the same matter, and may proceed in such manner and subject to such regulations as to making persons interested parties to the proceedings, and as to the exclusion of any claimants who do not come in within a certain time, and as to requiring security from the pilot, and as to payment of any costs as the court thinks just.

Comments.

Repeal.

The words underlined in sub-section 2, Repealed, Finance Act 1971, section 69, Schedule 14, Part VI, for Northern Ireland, by The Finance Act (Northern Ireland) 1971, section 9, Schedule 3, Part 1.

Bond.

Pilotage authorities have power under section 17, sub-section 1, to provide by bye-law for the giving of bonds by pilots.

Licensed Pilot.

The power to license pilots is given under section 16.

(margin note beside section 35: Limitation of pilots' liability where bond is given.*)*

Pilot.

Defined in section 742, Merchant Shipping Act 1894.

⚓   ⚓   ⚓   ⚓

Obligation on
licensed pilot
to produce his
licence to
employer.

36 (1) Every licensed pilot when acting as such shall be provided with his licence, and shall, if requested, produce it to any person by whom he is employed, or to whom he offers his services as pilot.

(2) If a licensed pilot refuses to produce his licence in accordance with this section, he shall be liable, in respect of each offence, to a fine not exceeding ten pounds.

COMMENTS.

Licensed Pilots.

Pilots are licensed under section 16.

Pilot.

Defined in Merchant Shipping Act 1894, section 742.

Fine.

Summary proceedings for the recovery of fines are contained in the Merchant Shipping Act 1894, sections 680 to 683.

⚓   ⚓   ⚓   ⚓

Penalty on
fraudulent use
of licence.

37 If any person not being a licensed pilot for a district falsely represents himself to be a licensed pilot for that district, either by means of using a licence which he is not entitled to use or by any other means, he shall be liable in respect of each offence to a fine not exceeding twenty pounds.

COMMENTS.
See comments to section 36.

⚓   ⚓   ⚓   ⚓

Approval of
pilot boats.

38 All vessels regularly employed in the pilotage service of any pilotage district (in this Act referred to as 'pilot boats') shall be approved and licensed by the pilotage authority of the district, and that authority may, at their discretion, appoint and remove the masters of those pilot boats.

COMMENTS.

Pilotage District; Pilotage Authority.

See section 8.

Master.

For definition, *see* Merchant Shipping Act 1894, section 742.

⚓   ⚓   ⚓   ⚓

39 (1) Every pilot boat shall be distinguished by the following characteristics, namely:— *Characteristics of pilot boats.*

(*a*) On her stern the name of her owner and the port to which she belongs, painted in white letters at least one inch broad and three inches long, and on each bow the number of her licence:

(*b*) In all other parts a black colour, painted or tarred outside, or such other colour or colours as the pilotage authority of the district, with the consent of the Board of Trade, direct:

(*c*) When afloat a flag (in this Act called a pilot flag) of large dimensions compared with the size of the pilot boat, and of two colours, the upper horizontal half white, and the lower horizontal half red, to be placed at the mast head, or on a sprit or staff, or in some equally conspicuous situation.

(2) It shall be the duty of the master of the pilot boat to see that the pilot boat possesses all theabove characteristics, and that the pilot flag is kept clean and distinct, so as to be easily discerned at a reasonable distance; and also that the names and numbers aforesaid are not at any time concealed; and if a master fails, without reasonable cause, to comply with the requirements of this section, he shall be liable in respect of each offence to a fine not exceeding twenty pounds.

COMMENTS.

Lights.

For the lights to be exhibited at night by pilot boats when engaged on their station, *see* the Collision Regulations and Distress Signals Order 1977, S.I. 1977, No. 982.

Pilot Flag.

The master of a vessel not a pilot boat displaying a pilot flag, is liable to a penalty. *See* section 42.

Pilot Boat.

For meaning, *see* section 38.

⚓   ⚓   ⚓   ⚓

Pilotage order not to diminish powers of pilotage authorities as to pilot boats. **40** A Pilotage Order in dealing with any Act, order, charter, custom, bye-law, regulation, or provision shall not provide for abolishing or diminishing any power of a pilotage authority to acquire, own, hire, build, renew, maintain, or work pilot boats.

COMMENTS.

Pilotage Order.

See section 7, sub-section 1, paragraph 'j', which provides that any Act, Order, Charter, Custom, Bye-Law, Regulation or provision so far as it relates to pilotage, ceases to have effect if a Pilotage Order is made for the District.

Separate Account in Respect of Pilot Boats.

See section 21, sub-section 4.

Provision of Pilot Boats.

See section 17, sub-section 1, paragraph 'd'.

⚓   ⚓   ⚓   ⚓

Display of pilot flag when pilot is on board ship. **41** (1) When a ship is navigating in a pilotage district, and has on board a pilot licensed for that district, or a master or mate holding a pilotage certificate for that district, the master of the ship shall cause a pilot flag to be exhibited; and if he fails, without reasonable cause, to do so, he shall be liable in respect of each offence to a fine not exceeding fifty pounds.

COMMENTS.

Recovery of Fines.

See Merchant Shipping Act 1894, section 680 to 685.

Pilot Flag.

See section 39, sub-section 1, for meaning.

⚓   ⚓   ⚓   ⚓

Penalty on ordinary boat displaying pilot flag. **42** A pilot flag, or a flag so nearly resembling a pilot flag as to be likely to deceive, shall not be displayed on any ship or boat not having a licensed pilot or a master or mate holding a pilotage certificate on board, and, if any such flag is displayed on any such ship or boat, the master of that vessel shall, unless in the case of the display of a flag likely to deceive he proves that he had no intention to deceive, be liable for each offence to a fine not exceeding fifty pounds.

COMMENTS.

Pilot Flag.

See section 39, sub-section 1.

Recovery of Fines.

See Merchant Shipping Act 1894, sections 680 to 683.

⚓   ⚓   ⚓   ⚓

43 (1) The master of a ship (other than an excepted ship) shall when navigating in circumstances in which pilotage is compulsory under this Act, display a pilot signal, and keep the signal displayed until a licensed pilot comes on board. *Obligation to display signal for pilot in certain circumstances.*

(2) The master of a ship, whether navigating in circumstances in which pilotage is compulsory or not, which is being piloted in a pilotage district by a pilot not licensed for the district, shall display a pilot signal and keep the signal displayed until a licensed pilot comes on board.

(3) If the master of any ship fails to comply with this section, he shall be liable in respect of each offence to a fine not exceeding twenty pounds.

COMMENTS:

Excepted Ship.

The ships which are excepted from compulsory pilotage are specified in section 11, sub-section 3. Consult also, sections 12 and 13.

Pilot Signal.

See section 45 for meaning.

Compulsory Pilotage.

See generally, as to compulsory pilotage, sections 10 to 15.

Offence.

It is an offence for a master to employ or continue to employ a pilot who is not licensed for a district if a pilot for that district offers his services.

⚓   ⚓   ⚓   ⚓

Facilities to
be given for
pilot getting
on board ship.

44 (1) The master of a ship (other than an excepted ship) which, in circumstances in which pilotage is compulsory under this Act, is not under pilotage as required in these circumstances, shall, if a licensed pilot of the district makes a signal for the purpose of offering his services as pilot, by any practical means consistent with the safety of his ship, facilitate the pilot getting on board the ship, and shall give the charge of piloting the ship to that pilot, or, if there are two or more licensed pilots offering at the same time, to such one of them as may, according to any bye-laws for the time being in force in the district, be entitled or required to take charge of the ship.

(2) Where the master of a ship, whether in circumstances in which pilotage is compulsory or not, accepts the services of a licensed pilot, he shall, by any practical means consistent with the safety of his ship, facilitate the pilot getting on board the ship.

(3) If the master of any ship fails to comply with the provisions of this section, he shall be liable in respect of each offence to a fine not exceeding double the amount of pilotage dues that could be demanded for the conduct of the ship.

⚓   ⚓   ⚓   ⚓

COMMENTS.

Master; Pilot; Ship.

For definition, *see* Merchant Shipping Act 1894, section 742.

Excepted Ship.

Ships excepted from compulsory pilotage are specified in section 11, sub-sections 3 and 4. Consult also sections 12 and 13.

Compulsory Pilotage.

Consult generally, sections 10 to 15.

Bye-Laws.

For the powers of pilotage authorities and the Secretary of State for Trade, relating to the making of bye-laws, *see* sections 17 and 18.

Pilotage Dues.

These are fixed by bye-laws. *See* section 17.

Fine.

Proceedings for recovery of fines are contained in Merchant Shipping Act 1894, sections 680 to 683.

Facilities to be given for Pilot Getting on Board Ship.

See now, the Merchant Shipping (Pilot Ladders) Rules 1965, S.I. 1965, No. 1046, as amended S.I. 1971, No. 724, S.I. 1972, No. 531. *See* also Merchant Shipping (Smooth and Partially Smooth Waters) Rules 1977, S.I. 1977, No. 252 as amended by S.I. 1977, No. 632.

These rules supersede the Merchant Shipping (Pilot Ladders) Rules 1952 and require the provision of a pilot ladder in ships of certain classes, and implement the relevant provisions of the International Convention for the Safety of Life at Sea 1960. The principal change by the amending Statutory Instrument of 1971 is the imposition of new requirements as to the means to be provided to enable pilots to pass safely between the head of the pilot ladder and the ship. Other amendments relate to the construction of pilot ladders, and the position in which they are to be secured when in use. The statutory instrument of 1972 revokes the Merchant Shipping (Pilot Ladders) (Amendment) Rules 1971, and amends the Merchant Shipping (Pilot Ladders) Rules 1965.

The principal changes made by these rules are:

(i) additional requirements relating to the steps and ropes of pilot ladders, and to the material of which battens are made, and:

(ii) the introduction of new requirements for the securing of bulwark ladders and the fitting of stanchions, and for the provision of a lifebuoy at the position where pilots board the ship.

Dimensions are also expressed in metric units.

⚓   ⚓   ⚓   ⚓

45 (1) His Majesty may by Order in Council make rules as to the signals to be used or displayed where the services of a pilot are required on any vessel, and those signals are in this Act referred to as pilot signals.

Signals to be displayed by ships requiring a pilot.

(2) If a vessel requires the services of a pilot, the master of that vessel shall use or display the pilot signals.

(3) If a master of a vessel uses or displays, or causes or permits any person under his authority to use or display, any of the pilot signals for any other purpose than that of summoning a pilot, or uses or causes or permits any person under his authority to use any other signal for a pilot, he shall be liable in respect of each offence to a fine not exceeding twenty pounds.

COMMENTS.

Master; Pilot; Vessel.

See Merchant Shipping Act 1894, section 742 for meaning.

E

Rules Under this Section.

See now, the Merchant Shipping (Pilot Signals) Order 1970, S.I. 1970, No. 1952.

This order replaces S.R. & O., 1933, No. 976, and specifies that the signals to be used or displayed where the services of a pilot are required (referred to in this section, sub-section 1, as 'pilot signals') on any vessel are to be given by use of the single letter 'G' in the International Code of Signals 1969.

⚓   ⚓   ⚓   ⚓

Penalty on pilot endangering ship, life, or limb.

46 If any pilot, when piloting a ship, by wilful breach of duty or by neglect of duty, or by reason of drunkenness—

(*a*) does any act tending to the immediate loss, destruction, or serious damage of the ship, or tending immediately to endanger the life or limb of any person on board the ship; or

(*b*) refuses or omits to do any lawful act proper and requisite to be done by him for preserving the ship from loss, destruction, or serious damage, or for preserving any person belonging to or on board the ship from danger to life or limb;

that pilot shall in respect of each offence be guilty of a misdemeanour.

Comments.

Compare the Merchant Shipping Act 1970, section 27, which relates to misconduct relating to the endangering of ship, or persons on board ship.

Pilot; ship.

For definitions, *see* Merchant Shipping Act 1894, section 742.

Misdemeanour.

These are punishable under Merchant Shipping Act 1894, section 680, as applied by section 62.

⚓   ⚓   ⚓   ⚓

Penalty on person obtaining charge of a ship by misrepresentation.

47 If any person, by wilful misrepresentation of circumstances upon which the safety of a ship may depend, obtains, or endeavours to obtain, the charge of that ship, that person and every person procuring, abetting, or conniving at the commission of the offence shall, in addition to any liability for damages, be liable in respect of each offence to a fine not exceeding one hundred pounds.

COMMENTS.

Ship.

See Merchant Shipping Act 1894, section 742.

Fine.

As to recovery, *see* Merchant Shipping Act 1894, section 680.

⚓   ⚓   ⚓   ⚓

48   (1) If a licensed pilot, either within or without the district for which he is licensed,— *Offences by pilots.*

(*a*) himself keeps, or is interested in keeping by any agent, servant, or other person, any premises licensed for the sale of intoxicating liquors, or sells or is interested in selling any intoxicating liquors, tobacco, or tea;

(*b*) is in any way directly or indirectly concerned in any corrupt practices relating to ships, their tackle, furniture, cargoes, crews, or passengers, or to persons in distress at sea or by shipwreck, or to their moneys, goods, or chattels;

(*c*) lends his licence;

(*d*) acts as pilot whilst suspended;

(*e*) acts as pilot when in a state of intoxication;

(*f*) employs, or causes to be employed, on board any ship which he is piloting any boat, anchor, cable, or other store, matter, or thing beyond what is necessary for the service of that ship, with intent to enhance the expenses of pilotage for his own gain or for the gain of any other person;

(*g*) refuses or wilfully delays, when not prevented by illness or other reasonable cause, to pilot any ship within the district for which he is licensed, upon the signal for a pilot being made by that ship, or upon being required to do so by the master, owner, agent, or consignee thereof, or by any officer of the pilotage authority by whom the pilot is licensed, or by any chief officer of Customs and Excise;

(*h*) unnecessarily cuts or slips, or causes to be cut or slipped, any cable belonging to any ship;

(*i*) refuses, otherwise than on reasonable ground of danger to the ship, when requested by the master, to conduct the ship which he is piloting into any port or place within the district for which he is licensed; or

(*k*) quits the ship, which he is piloting, before the service for which he was engaged has been performed and without the consent of the master of the ship;

that pilot shall, in addition to any liability for damages, be liable in respect of each offence to a fine not exceeding one hundred pounds.

(2) If any person procures, aids, abets, or connives at the commission of any offence under this section, he shall, in addition to any liability for damages, be liable to a fine not exceeding one hundred pounds.

(3) The provisions of the law relating to Customs with respect to the recovery of penalties under that law, and the application of such penalties, shall apply in the case of any prosecution by any officer of Customs and Excise for the recovery of a fine in respect of any offence against this section.

COMMENTS.

Master; Pilot; Ship.

See Merchant Shipping Act 1894, section 742 for meaning.

Licensing of Pilots.

See section 16.

Signal.

See section 43, and comments thereto.

Suspension of Licenses.

See section 26.

Reasonable Cause.

See The Frederick 1838, where it was held that a pilot is not bound to board a damaged vessel solely for pilotage reward, if the circumstances were such that he would be entitled to salvage.

Quits the Ship . . . Without Consent of Master.

See The Saratoga 1861, where it would appear that a pilot is not entitled to leave a ship because his services have changed from mere pilotage to those that would rank as salvage. *See* also *The Santiago*, 1900, when it was held that it was his duty to stand by the ship he was piloting, even though his services could be regarded as salvage.

⚓   ⚓   ⚓   ⚓

Recovery, &c. of Pilotage Dues

49 (1) The following persons shall be liable to pay pilotage dues for any ship for which the services of a licensed pilot are obtained, namely:— *Recovery of pilotage dues.*

(*a*) the owner or master;

(*b*) as to pilotage inwards, such consignees or agents as have paid or made themselves liable to pay any other charge on account of the ship in the port of her arrival or discharge;

(*c*) as to pilotage outwards, such consignees or agents as have paid or made themselves liable to pay any other charge on account of the ship in the port of her departure.

and those dues may be recovered in the same manner as fines of like amount under the Merchant Shipping Act 1894, but that recovery shall not take place until a previous demand has been made in writing.

(2) Any consignee or agent (not being the owner or master of the ship) who is hereby made liable for the payment of pilotage dues in respect of any ship may, out of any moneys received by him on account of that ship or belonging to the owner thereof, retain the amount of all dues paid by him, together with any reasonable expenses he may have incurred by reason of the payment of the dues or his liability to pay the dues.

COMMENTS.

Pilotage Dues.

See section 17 as to meaning. An action *in rem* or *in personam* may be instituted for the recovery of pilotage dues, and the pilot is not restricted to this right under this section of taking proceedings in a court of summary jurisdiction. Indeed, unless the ship is already under arrest or is not a British ship, the latter course may well be advisable. *See The Ambatielos and The Cephalonia* 1923.

It is doubtful whether a maritime lien exists in respect of pilotage dues. Consult the same case, at page 75, where the matter was discussed but left undecided.

Recovery of Fines.

See Merchant Shipping Act 1894, sections 680 to 682.

Allowance.

See section 34 as to recovery.

Port of London.

In the Port of London, pilotage dues are collected by Officers of the Customs and Excise. *See* section 55.

⚓   ⚓   ⚓   ⚓

Receiving or offering im-proper rates of pilotage.

50   A licensed pilot shall not demand or receive, and a master shall not offer or pay to any licensed pilot, dues in respect of pilotage services at any other rates, whether greater or less, than the rates which may be demanded by law, and, if a pilot or master acts in contravention of this enactment, he shall be liable in respect of each offence to a fine not exceeding ten pounds.

COMMENTS.

Licensed.

Pilots are licensed under section 16 q.v.

Pilotage Services/Salvage.

Where the services may be considered outside of the scope of his pilotage duty, he may be entitled to salvage reward from the ship he is piloting, or indeed, from a ship salved by her.

See The Aeolus 1873; Akerblom *v.* Price 1881; *The Santiago* 1900.

⚓   ⚓   ⚓   ⚓

Pilotage rate for leading ships.

51   If any boat or ship, having on board a licensed pilot, leads any ship which has not a licensed pilot on board when the last-mentioned ship cannot, from particular circumstances, be boarded, the pilot so leading the last-mentioned ship shall be entitled to the full pilotage rate for the distance run as if he had actually been on board and had charge of that ship.

COMMENTS.

Last-Mentioned Ship.

For circumstances in which pilotage duties are turned into Salvage from 'the last-mentioned ship', consult *The Santiago* 1900.

Pilot; Ship.

See Merchant Shipping Act 1894, section 742, as to meaning.

Licensed.

Pilots are licensed under section 16.

Pilotage Rate.

Pilotage dues are fixed by bye-law, under section 17.

⚓   ⚓   ⚓   ⚓

Special Provisions as to the Trinity House

52   (1) For the purposes of this Act, any district which Trinity House at the time of the passing of this Act is under the authority of tricts. sub-commissioners appointed by the Trinity House and any pilotage district which may be declared after the passing of this Act to be a Trinity House outport district, shall be deemed to be a Trinity House outport district.

(2) The powers and duties of the Trinity House under this Act as the pilotage authority of an outport district shall be exercised and performed through a committee appointed for the district in such manner and subject to such conditions as may be determined by a Pilotage Order, under the name of Sub-Commissioners or such other name as may be fixed by the Order, and any such Order may be made so as to apply to all or any one or more of the outport districts.

COMMENTS.

The Trinity House.

As to meaning, *see* Merchant Shipping Act 1894, section 742.

Pilotage Districts; Pilotage Authorities.

See generally, section 8.

⚓   ⚓   ⚓   ⚓

53   Nothing in this Act shall oblige the Trinity House to Trinity House maintain separate pilot funds for each of the pilotage districts Pilot Fund. of which they are the authority, and, if they maintain a single pilot fund for all those districts, the provisions of this Act as to pilot funds shall apply as if all the districts of which they are the pilotage authority were a single pilotage district.

COMMENTS.

Pilotage Funds.

As to pilotage funds, *see* section 21.

The Trinity House.

As to meaning, *see* Merchant Shipping Act 1894, section 742.

⚓   ⚓   ⚓   ⚓

Power of
Trinity House
to make pro-
visions as to
exempt pilots.

54 Notwithstanding anything in this Act, the Trinity House may permit any person who, at the date of the passing of this Act, was licensed to pilot an exempted vessel in the Thames or Medway, to continue to pilot any vessel in those rivers belonging to a class which, at the date of the passing of this Act, were exempted vessels, and were, in the opinion of the Trinity House, in practice piloted by such persons, and any such person while so acting shall be deemed, for the purposes of this Act, to be a licensed pilot.

COMMENTS.

To Pilot an Exempted Vessel.

By this section, certain persons are licensed to pilot the various vessels, normally exempted from compulsory pilotage under Merchant Shipping Act 1894, section 625. They are in such circumstances, deemed to be a Licensed Pilot.

⚓   ⚓   ⚓   ⚓

Collection of
pilotage dues
in Port of
London by
officers of
Customs and
Excise.

55 (1) The following pilotage dues in respect of foreign ships, not being excepted ships, trading to and from the port of London, namely:—

(*a*) as to ships inwards, the full amount of pilotage dues for the distance piloted; and

(*b*) as to ships outwards, the full amount of dues for the distance required by law;

shall be paid to the chief officer of Customs and Excise in the port of London by the master, or by any consignees or agents of the ship who have paid, or made themselves liable to pay, any other charge for the ship in the port of London.

(2) The chief officer of Customs and Excise, on receiving any pilotage dues in respect of foreign ships, shall give to the person paying the dues a receipt in writing for the dues, and

in the port of London the ship may be detained until the receipt is produced to the proper officer of Customs and Excise of the port.

(3) The chief officer of Customs and Excise shall pay over to the Trinity House the pilotage dues received by him under this section, and the Trinity House shall apply the dues so received—

(*a*) in paying to any licensed pilot who produces to them sufficient proof of his having piloted the ship such dues as would have been payable to him for pilotage services if the ship had been a British ship, after making any deductions which they are authorised to make by bye-law under this Act; and

(*b*) in paying to any person not being a licensed pilot who produces to them sufficient proof of his having, in the absence of a licensed pilot, piloted the ship, such amount as the Trinity House think proper, not exceeding the amount which would, under similar circumstances, have been payable to a licensed pilot after making the said deductions; and

(*c*) in paying over to the Trinity House pilot fund the residue, together with the amount of any deductions made as aforesaid.

(4) Nothing in this section shall affect the application of the provisions of this Act as to the recovery of pilotage dues.

COMMENTS.

Pilotage Dues.
See section 17, sub-section 1, as to meaning.

Exempted Ships.
For ships which are excepted from compulsory pilotage, *see* section 11, sub-sections 3 and 4. Consult also, section 12 as to the exemption of certain ships belonging to public authorities.

Detained.
Procedure for enforcement of detention, *see* section 692 of the Principal Act.

British Ship.
See Merchant Shipping Act 1894, section 1.

The Trinity House Pilot Fund.
The Trinity House need not keep a separate fund for each of the districts of which they are the pilotage authority.

⚓   ⚓   ⚓   ⚓

Miscellaneous and General Provisions

Limit on
expenditure.

56   The expenditure under this Act out of money provided by Parliament shall not exceed six thousand pounds in any one year.

⚓   ⚓   ⚓   ⚓

Application of
37 & 38 Vict.
c. 40.

57   The Board of Trade Arbitrations, &c. Act 1874, shall apply as if this Act were a special Act within the meaning of the first-mentioned Act.

⚓   ⚓   ⚓   ⚓

Saving for
pilotage autho-
rities having
power to apply
money received
in name of
pilotage to
other purposes.

58   Notwithstanding anything in this Act, where a pilotage authority is entitled by statute at the time of the passing of this Act to receive moneys in the name of pilotage and to apply part of such moneys to purposes other than those authorised under this Act, a Pilotage Order made under Part I of this Act in respect of that authority may provide for the apportionment of the moneys so received as between the pilot fund or account and such other purposes.

COMMENTS.

Pilotage Authority.
   See section 8.

Pilotage Order.
   Secretary of State for Trade has powers under section 7.

Pilot Fund or Account.
   For meaning, *see* section 21, sub-section 1.

⚓   ⚓   ⚓   ⚓

A.D. 1913.

Commence-
ment of Act.

59   This Act shall (except as expressly provided) come into operation on the first day of April nineteen hundred and thirteen: Provided that Any enactment, order, charter, custom, bye-law, regulation, or provision with reference to pilotage affecting any pilotage district in particular, and in force at the time of the passing of this Act, including any exemptions from compulsory pilotage taking effect thereunder, shall remain in force notwithstanding anything in this Act or any repeal effected by this Act, until provision is made by Pilotage Order, or in the case of a bye-law by bye-law, made under this Act superseding any such enactment, order, charter, custom, bye-law, regulation, or provision.

COMMENTS.

Repeal.

The words underlined were repealed as spent by the S.L.R. Act 1927.

Pilotage Order.

The Secretary of State has power under section 7 to make Pilotage Orders by sub-section 1, paragraph 'j' of that section, a Pilotage Order may provide for the repeal of Acts, charters, etc.

Custom.

It would appear that a custom, may under section 17, be superseded as a result of a Pilotage Order, and bye-law. *See*, however, Thames Launches Ltd. *v*. Trinity House Corporation 1962, where it was held that a custom was not superseded by a Pilotage Order.

See also Muller *v*. Trinity House 1925, where it was held that past agreement by shipowners to the payment of certain dues by Trinity House which no longer had any legal basis, does not constitute a custom as referred to by this section.

Enactment . . . in Particular.

See The Port Hunter 1915, where it was held that a previous Act remained in force until a Pilotage Order or new bye-law was made.

⚓   ⚓   ⚓   ⚓

60 (1) The enactments mentioned in the Second Schedule to this Act are hereby repealed to the extent specified in the third column of that schedule.

Provided that—

(*a*) Any order in council, licence, certificate, bye-law, rule, or regulation made or granted under any enactment hereby repealed or in pursuance of any power which ceases in consequence of this Act, shall, subject to the provisions of this Act, continue in force as if it had been made or granted under this Act; and

(*b*) Any officer appointed, any body elected or constituted, and any office established under any enactment hereby repealed shall continue and be deemed to have been appointed, elected, constituted, or established, as the case may be, under this Act;

(*c*) Any document referring to any Act or enactment hereby repealed shall be construed to refer to this Act or to the corresponding enactment of this Act.

(2) The mention of particular matters in this section shall not be held to prejudice or affect the general application of section thirty-eight of the Interpretation Act 1889, as regards the effect of repeals.

COMMENTS.

Repeal.

The words underlined, which provided for the repeal of the enactments specified in the Second Schedule (also repealed) were repealed as spent by the Statute Law Revision Act 1927.

⚓   ⚓   ⚓   ⚓

Extent of Act.   **61** This Act extends to the United Kingdom and the Isle of Man, and applies to all ships, British and foreign.

COMMENTS.

British Ship.

See Merchant Shipping Act 1894, section 1.

⚓   ⚓   ⚓   ⚓

Short title.   **62** This Act may be cited as the Pilotage Act 1913, and shall be construed as one with the Merchant Shipping Act 1894, and the Acts amending the same; and the Merchant Shipping Acts 1894 to 1907, and this Act may be cited together as the Merchant Shipping Acts 1894 to 1913.

COMMENTS.

Merchant Shipping Acts.

Now the Merchant Shipping Acts 1894 to 1974.

⚓   ⚓   ⚓   ⚓

FIRST SCHEDULE

PROVISIONS AS TO PILOTAGE ORDERS

1. Subject to the provisions of this schedule, the Board of Trade may make rules in relation to applications for Pilotage Orders, and to the payments to be made in respect thereof,

and to the publication of notices and advertisements, and the manner in which and the time within which representations or objections with reference to any application are to be made, and as to the publication of Pilotage Orders.

2. Notice of an application for an Order shall be published once at least in each of two successive weeks in the month immediately succeeding the date of the application in such manner as may be prescribed by the rules made by the Board of Trade.

3. The notice shall state the object which it is proposed to effect by the Order.

4. The Board of Trade on receiving any application for an Order shall refer the application to the pilotage authority of the district, if the authority are not themselves the applicants, and shall consider any objections which may be made to the proposed Order whether by the pilotage authority or by other persons appearing to the Board of Trade to be interested, and for that purpose shall allow at least six weeks to elapse between the date on which the application is referred to the authority and that on which the Order is made.

5. The Board of Trade may submit to Parliament for confirmation any Order which requires confirmation by Parliament.

6. If and when a Bill confirming any such Order is pending in either House of Parliament, a petition is presented against any Order comprised therein, the Bill, so far as it relates to that Order, may be referred to a Select Committee, or, if the two Houses of Parliament think fit so to order, to a Joint Committee of those Houses, and the petitioner shall be allowed to appear and oppose as in the case of private Bills.

7. Any Act confirming an Order under this Act may be repealed, altered, or amended by any subsequent Order made under this Act.

8. The Board of Trade may revoke, either wholly or partially, any Order made by them before the Order is confirmed by Parliament, but such revocation shall not be made whilst the Bill confirming the Order is pending in either House of Parliament.

9. The making of an Order shall be prima facie evidence that all the requirements of this Act in respect of proceedings required to be taken previously to the making of the Order have been complied with.

COMMENTS.

See now for rules at present in force, Pilotage Orders (Application) Rules 1964, S.I. No. 1467.

Board of Trade.

Read now: 'Secretary of State for Trade.'

Pilotage Orders.

See section 7.

Pilotage Authorities.

For meaning, *see* section 8.

⚓   ⚓   ⚓   ⚓

SECOND SCHEDULE

Repealed

Statute Law Revision Act 1927

⚓   ⚓   ⚓   ⚓

Merchant Shipping (Certificates) Act 1914.

1. Examinations for Certificates of Competency as Masters or Mates.

(i) For the purpose of granting certificates of competency as masters or mates to persons desirous of obtaining such certificates, examinations shall be held at such places as the Secretary of State for Trade directs.

(ii) The Secretary of State for Trade may appoint times for the examinations, and may appoint, remove and reappoint examiners to conduct the examinations, and determine the remuneration of those examiners, and may regulate the conduct of the examinations and the qualification of the applicants, and may do all such acts and things as he thinks expedient for the purpose of the examinations.

(iii) This sub-section repealed by the Statute Law Revision Act 1927.

Short Title and Construction.

2. This Act may be cited as the Merchant Shipping (Certificates) Act 1914, and the provisions of this Act shall be construed as if they were contained in Part II of the Merchant Shipping Acts 1894 to 1913, and this Act may be cited together as the Merchant Shipping Acts 1894 to 1974.

Note.

It is anticipated that this Act will be repealed as from a day to be appointed. *See* Merchant Shipping Act 1970, section 100, sub-section 3, Schedule 5.

COMMENTS.

Consult The Merchant Shipping (Certification of Deck Officers) Regulations 1977, S.I. 1977, No. 1152 and *see* 'Comments' under Section 43 of the Merchant Shipping Act 1970.

⚓   ⚓   ⚓   ⚓

Merchant Shipping (Convention) Act 1914

Repealed

Merchant Shipping (Safety and Load Line Conventions) Act 1932

Section 74, sub-section 2, Schedule IV, Part 3

⚓   ⚓   ⚓   ⚓

The Merchant Shipping (Wireless Telegraphy) Act 1919

Repealed

Merchant Shipping (Safety Convention) Act 1949, section 37
Sub-section 5

See now section 3 of the 1949 Act

⚓   ⚓   ⚓   ⚓

Merchant Shipping (Amendment) Act 1920.

Amendment of section 659 of 57 & 58 Vict. c. 60.

1. The power of His Majesty, under section six hundred and fifty-nine of the Merchant Shipping Act 1894 as amended by subsequent enactments, by Order in Council, to fix the annual or other sums to be paid out of the General Lighthouse Fund, in respect of the establishment of the general lighthouse authority, shall extend to the fixing of the annual or other sums to be paid out of that fund to members of the general lighthouse authority for England and Wales, and the sums so fixed shall have effect notwithstanding anything in any Act, limiting the amount thereof.

Short Title.

2. This Act may be cited as the Merchant Shipping (Amendment) Act 1920, and shall be included amongst the Acts which may be cited together as the Merchant Shipping Acts 1894 to 1974.

Merchant Shipping (Scottish Fishing Boats) Act 1920

Author's Note:

As a result of this Act, the provisions of Part IV (Fishing Boats) of the Principal Act and section 81 of the Merchant Shipping Act 1906 are of general application.   Before the enactment of this Act the provisions of Part IV only partially applied.   It is included amongst the Acts which may be cited as the Merchant Shipping Acts 1894–1974.

Merchant Shipping Act 1921

This Act extended the protection enjoyed by shipowners under Part VIII of the Principal Act, and has been included in the Liability of Shipowners' section, page 209 *et seq.* of Vol. I of this series q.v.

    ⚓   ⚓   ⚓   ⚓

Oil in Navigable Waters Act 1922

Repealed

See now the Prevention of Oil Pollution Act 1971

⚓   ⚓   ⚓   ⚓

Fees (Increase) Act 1923

An Act to provide for the increase of certain fees and the imposition of certain new fees in respect of various services, and for purposes connected therewith.

⚓   ⚓   ⚓   ⚓

Increase of Certain Fees Under Merchant Shipping Acts

1 (1) The provisions of . . . the Merchant Shipping (Mercantile Marine Fund) Act 1898, specified in the first column of Part I of the First Schedule to this Act, so far as they . . . grant exemptions from any . . . fees, shall have effect subject to the amendments mentioned in the third column of that part of the Schedule. Provided that no fees shall be payable under section 3 of the Merchant Shipping (Mercantile Marine Fund) Act 1898 in respect of vessels not exceeding ten tons gross register employed solely in fishing.

(2) *Charge of new fees for certain services under the Merchant Shipping Acts.*

COMMENTS.

The words omitted in section 1 sub-section (1), and the whole of sub-section (2), were repealed, Merchant Shipping (Safety Convention) Act 1949, section 37 sub-section 5, and Third Schedule.

⚓   ⚓   ⚓   ⚓

2 (1) Where:
The words omitted in section 1, sub-section (1). and the whole of sub-section (2) were repealed, Merchant Shipping (Safety Convention) Act 1949, section 37, sub-section 5, and Third Schedule.

> (*a*) under section nineteen of the Merchant Shipping Act 1894, a Registrar of Shipping endorses and signs on the certificate of registry of a ship a memorandum of the change of the master;
>   or
>
> (*b*) a certificate of service is granted in pursuance of section ninety-nine of the Merchant Shipping Act 1894, or
>
> (*c*) an indenture of apprenticeship to the sea service is recorded by a Superintendent or by the Registrar-General of Shipping and Seamen;

there shall be payable such fees as the Secretary of State for Trade may determine . . .

(2) There shall be payable upon all engagements and discharges of seamen effected in the presence of a superintendent under section one hundred and fifteen, sub-section (2) of section one hundred and sixteen, and section one hundred and twenty-seven of the Merchant Shipping Act 1894, such fees as may be fixed by the Secretary of State for Trade . . . and the superintendent may refuse to proceed with any engagement or discharge unless the fees payable have been first paid by the master or owner of the ship.

(3) On the inspection of a ship:—

(a) Under section four hundred and thirty-one of the Merchant Shipping Act 1894, either during the construction of the ship or otherwise, for the purpose of seeing that the ship is properly provided, in accordance with the provisions of the Merchant Shipping Acts 1894 to 1921, or any rules made thereunder, with life-saving appliances;

(b) . . . there shall be paid in respect of the inspection such fees as the Secretary of State may determine . . .

(4) Where under section two hundred and six of the Merchant Shipping Act 1894, or section twenty-six of the Merchant Shipping Act 1906, any provisions are inspected, either before shipment or on board a ship, there shall be payable in respect of such inspection, such fees as the Secretary of State for Trade may determine, not exceeding those specified in Part IV of the Second Schedule to this Act; but it shall not be obligatory that such an inspection should be made, and accordingly, in sub-section 1 of the first-mentioned section for the words 'shall be inspected' there shall be substituted the words 'May be inspected', and for the words 'shall certify' there shall be substituted the words 'may certify' and sub-section 3 of the same section shall be repealed:

Provided that where provisions which have been inspected and sealed by an inspecting officer, are found on board any ship within such time as may be prescribed by the Secretary of State for Trade as the time for which the seals are to hold good, no fee shall be charged for the verification of the seals.

COMMENTS.

Fees.

The fees at present in force are contained in The Merchant Shipping (Fees) Regulations 1977, S.I. 1977, No. 2049.

Section 2, Sub-section (1), Paragraph (b).

It is anticipated that the words underlined will be repealed as from a day to be appointed. Merchant Shipping Act 1970, section 100, sub-section 3, Schedule V.

Paragraph (c).

The words in the paragraph double-underlined—Repealed Merchant Shipping Act 1970, section 100, sub-section 3, Schedule V as from the 1st January, 1973.

The words omitted at the end of this paragraph have been repealed as from the 19th November, 1952. Merchant Shipping (Safety Convention) Act 1949, section 37, sub-section 5, Third Schedule.

Sub-section 2.

The words omitted in this sub-section have been repealed. Merchant Shipping (Safety Convention) Act 1949, section 37, sub-section 5 and Third Schedule. It is anticipated that the remainder of the sub-section, underlined, will be repealed as from a day to be appointed. Merchant Shipping Act, 1970, section 100, sub-section 3, Schedule V.

Sub-section 3, Paragraph (b).

This paragraph has been repealed. Merchant Shipping (Safety Convention) Act 1949, section 37, sub-sections and Third Schedule.

The words omitted after 'determine'—repealed. Merchant Shipping (Safety Convention) Act 1949, section 37, sub-section 5 and Third Schedule.

Sub-Section 4.

The words double underlined repealed, Merchant Shipping (Safety Convention) Act 1949, section 37, sub-section 5, and Third Schedule. The remainder of the sub-section underlined is due to be repealed as from a day to be appointed, Merchant Shipping Act 1970, section 100, sub-section 3, Schedule 5.

⚓   ⚓   ⚓   ⚓

Section 3.

Repealed, Economy (Miscellaneous Provisions) Act 1926, section 19, sub-section 2, and Fourth Schedule.

Sections 4-9.

These sections have been repealed by various subsequent Acts, but as they do not affect the Merchant Shipping Acts, they have not been included.

Section 10.

Repealed as spent.   Statute Law Revision Act 1950.

Section 11.

(i) This Act may be cited as the Fees (Increase) Act 1923.

(ii) This Act, so far as it amends the Merchant Shipping Acts 1894 to 1921, shall be construed as one with those Acts, and Those Acts, and this Act, so far as it amends those Acts, may be cited together as the Merchant Shipping Acts 1894 to 1923.   (Read now 1894 to 1974.)

(iii) This Act, so far as it relates to matters with respect to which the Parliament of Northern Ireland has not power to make laws, shall extend to Northern Ireland.

First Schedule, Part 1.

Repealed, Merchant Shipping (Safety Convention) Act 1949, section 37, sub-section 5, and Third Schedule.

Part II.

Repealed, Merchant Shipping (Safety Convention) Act 1949, section 37, sub-section 5, and Third Schedule.

Second Schedule.

Repealed, Merchant Shipping (Safety Convention) Act 1949, section 37, sub-section 5, and Third Schedule.

For fees at present in force, *see* Merchant Shipping (Fees) Regulations 197, S.I. 197, No. 2049.

Third Schedule.

Repealed as spent.   Statute Law Revision Act 1950.

⚓   ⚓   ⚓   ⚓

Merchant Shipping Acts (Amendment) Act 1923

Repealed

Merchant Shipping Act 1970, S.I. 1972, No. 1977

⚓   ⚓   ⚓   ⚓

Merchant Shipping (International Labour Conventions) Act 1925

As from a day to be appointed, the whole of this Act will be
Repealed.   Merchant Shipping Act 1970, section 100,
sub-section 3, Schedule V

⚓   ⚓   ⚓   ⚓

Merchant Shipping (Equivalent Provisions) Act 1925

Power to exempt foreign ships from certain provisions of Merchant Shipping Acts.

1 Where His Majesty is satisfied that:—

(a) ships of a foreign country are required by the law of that country to comply with any provisions which are substantially the same as or equally effective with any provisions of the Merchant Shipping Acts which apply to foreign ships while they are within a port of the United Kingdom; and

(b) that country has made or has undertaken to make provision for the exemption of British ships, while they are within a port of that country, from the corresponding requirement of the law of that country;

His Majesty may, by Order in Council, direct that any such provisions of the Merchant Shipping Acts as aforesaid shall not apply to any ship of that country within a port of the United Kingdom if it is proved that the ship complies with the corresponding provision of the law of that country applicable to that ship.

COMMENTS.

Orders Under this Section.

Merchant Shipping (Wireless Telegraphy) French Ships Order 1926, S.R. & O. 1926, No. 218 (Exempting French ships in the United Kingdom Ports from Wireless Telegraphy provisions, on compliance with French provisions).

Merchant Shipping (Passenger Steamer and Emigrant Ships) Italian Ships Order 1929, S.R. & O. 1929, No. 1154. This allows Italian ships, whilst in the U.K. to be exempted from certain provisions of the Merchant Shipping Acts, relating to passenger steamers, and emigrant ships, on compliance with the corresponding provisions of the law of Italy.

See, however, section 21, sub-section 2 of the Merchant Shipping (Safety and Load Line Conventions) Act 1932, now repealed by the Merchant Shipping (Safety Convention) Act 1949, section 37, sub-section 37, and Third Schedule. The exemption of certain ships from the effect of this 1925 Act, is still considered effective, although repealed by reason of the Interpretation Act 1889, section 38, sub-section 2.

Consult section 734, Merchant Shipping Act 1894, for application by

Orders in Council, of provisions of the Merchant Shipping Acts to foreign ships.

⚓ ⚓ ⚓ ⚓

2 Where His Majesty is satisfied that British Ships registered in a part of His Majesty's dominions outside the United Kingdom, or ships registered in a port of a territory over which His Majesty exercises jurisdiction, are required by the law of that part of His Majesty's dominions or the law in force in that territory to comply with any provisions which are substantially the same as, or equally effective with, any of the provisions of the Merchant Shipping Acts which apply to such ships if, but only if, they are within a port of the United Kingdom, His Majesty may, by Order in Council, direct that any such provisions of the Merchant Shipping Acts as aforesaid shall not apply to any ship registered in that part of His Majesty's dominions, or in that territory, whilst within a port in the United Kingdom, if it is proved that the ship complies with the corresponding provision of the law of the part of His Majesty's dominions or territory in which the ship is registered. *Power to exempt British ships registered out of the United Kingdom from certain provisions of Merchant Shipping Acts.*

⚓ ⚓ ⚓ ⚓

3 (1) This Act may be cited as the Merchant Shipping (Equivalent Provisions) Act 1925, and shall be construed as one with the Merchant Shipping Acts 1894 to 1923, and those Acts and this Act may be cited together as the Merchant Shipping Acts 1894 to 1925. *Short title, construction, etc.*

(2) In this Act, the expression 'the Merchant Shipping Acts' means the Merchant Shipping Acts 1894 to 1923, and includes any Orders in Council, rules and regulations made thereunder, and the expression 'United Kingdom' means Great Britain and Northern Ireland.

COMMENTS.

Merchant Shipping Acts 1894 to 1925—Read now 1894 to 1974.

⚓ ⚓ ⚓ ⚓

Merchant Shipping (Safety and Load Line Conventions) Act 1932

An Act to give effect to an International Convention for the Safety of Life at Sea, signed in London on the thirty-first day of May, nineteen hundred and twenty-nine, to give effect to an International Load Line Convention signed in London on the fifth day of July, nineteen hundred and thirty, and to amend the provisions of the Merchant Shipping Acts 1894 to 1928, relating to passenger steamers, life-saving appliances, wireless telegraphy, load lines, timber cargoes, and other matters affected by the said Conventions.   [17th March 1932.]

Whereas a Convention (in this Act referred to as 'the Safety Convention') which is set out in the First Schedule to this Act, was signed on behalf of the Government of the United Kingdom in London on the thirty-first day of May, nineteen hundred and twenty-nine, for promoting safety of life at sea by establishing in common agreement uniform principles and rules directed thereto:

And whereas a Convention (in this Act referred to as 'the Load Line Convention') which is set out in the Second Schedule to this Act, was signed on behalf of the Government of the United Kingdom in London on the fifth day of July, nineteen hundred and thirty, for promoting safety of life and property at sea, by establishing in common agreement uniform principles and rules with regard to the limits to which ships on international voyages may be loaded:

And whereas it is expedient to give effect to the said Conventions and to amend the provisions of the Merchant Shipping Acts, 1894 to 1928, relating to passenger steamers, life-saving appliances, wireless telegraphy, load lines, timber cargoes and other matters affected by the said Conventions:

COMMENTS.

In the event that the words of the operative part of this Act are ambiguous, reference may be made to the Conventions in order to explain the ambiguity.

Part One

Safety of Life at Sea—Construction and Surveys

Section 1

Repealed Merchant Shipping (Safety Convention) Act 1949,
Section 37, sub-section 5, and Third Schedule
Consult now: That Act

⚓   ⚓   ⚓   ⚓

Section 2

Repealed Merchant Shipping (Safety Convention) Act 1949
Section 37, Sub-section 5, and Third Schedule
Consult now: That Act

⚓   ⚓   ⚓   ⚓

Section 3

Repealed

Merchant Shipping (Safety Convention) Act 1949, section 37
sub-section 5, and Third Schedule
Consult now: That Act

⚓   ⚓   ⚓   ⚓

Section 4

Life-saving Appliances

Repealed

Merchant Shipping (Safety Convention) Act 1949, section 37
sub-section 5, and Third Schedule
Consult now: That Act, and section 427 of the M.S.A. 1894

⚓   ⚓   ⚓   ⚓

5 (1) *See* 'Comments'.

Amendments
of Merchant
Shipping Acts
as to life-saving
appliances.

(2) Subsection (1) of section four hundred and thirty of
the principal Act (which imposes penalties for failure to

comply with the rules for life-saving appliances) shall be amended by inserting after paragraph (*d*) thereof the following paragraph:—

'(*e*) if any provision of the rules for life-saving appliances applicable to the ship is contravened or not complied with.'

(3) The following section shall be substituted for section four hundred and thirty-one of the principal Act:—

'431.—(1) A surveyor of ships may inspect any ship for the purpose of seeing that the rules for life-saving appliances have been complied with in her case, and for the purpose of any such inspection shall have all the powers of a Department of Trade Inspector under this Act.

(2) If the surveyor finds that the rules for life-saving appliances have not been complied with, he shall give written notice to the owner or master stating in what respect the said rules have not been complied with, and what, in his opinion, is required to rectify the matter.

(3) Every notice so given shall be communicated in manner directed by the Department of Trade to the Chief Officer of Customs of any port at which the ship may seek to obtain a clearance or transire, and a clearance or transire shall not be granted to the ship and the ship shall be detained until a certificate under the hand of a surveyor of ships is produced to the effect that the matter has been rectified.'

(4) *See* 'Comments'.

(5) *See* 'Comments'.

COMMENTS.

Section 5.   Sub-section 1: Repealed.

Merchant Shipping (Safety Convention) Act 1949, section 37, sub-section 5, and Third Schedule.

Sub-section 4: Repealed.

Merchant Shipping (Safety Convention) Act 1949, section 37, sub-section 5, and Third Schedule.

Sub-section 5: Repealed.

Merchant Shipping (Safety Convention) Act 1949, section 37, sub-section 5, and Third Schedule.

Sections 6 and 7.   Wireless Telegraphy: Repealed.

Merchant Shipping (Safety Convention) Act 1949, section 37
Sub-section 5, and Third Schedule
Consult now: That Act

⚓   ⚓   ⚓   ⚓

8   A person appointed to be a surveyor of ships under ^Appointment of wireless^ section seven hundred and twenty-four of the principal Act ^telegraphy surveyors.^ may be appointed as a wireless telegraphy surveyor:

Provided that the functions of the Board of Trade under the said section with respect to surveyors of ships shall not be exercised with respect to wireless telegraphy surveyors except with the approval of the Postmaster-General.

COMMENTS.

The words underlined repealed.

Post Office Act 1969, section 137, sub-section 1 and Schedule 8, Part 2.

Wireless Telegraphy Surveyor.

Read now: 'Radio surveyors' Merchant Shipping (Safety Convention) Act 1949, section 4.

⚓   ⚓   ⚓   ⚓

9   (1) The surveys of a passenger steamer required by ^Survey of passenger^ the principal Act shall, in the case of every survey made after ^steamers by^ the commencement of this Part of this Act in respect of a ^wireless telegraphy^ sea-going steamer which is not exempt under the Merchant ^surveyors.^ Shipping (Wireless Telegraphy) Act, 1919, from the obligations imposed by that Act, include a survey by a wireless telegraphy surveyor, and accordingly subsection (1) of section two hundred and seventy-two of that Act shall be amended by inserting after the words 'engineer surveyor of ships' the words 'and, in the case of a sea-going passenger steamer required to be provided with a wireless telegraph installation' by a wireless telegraphy surveyor.'

(3) Section two hundred and seventy-five of the principal Act (which provides for appeals to a court of survey by persons aggrieved by the declaration of survey of a ship or engineer surveyor) shall be amended by inserting the words

F

'or wireless telegraphy surveyor' after the words 'engineer surveyor' in both places where they occur.

COMMENTS.

Wireless Telegraphy Surveyors.

Now to be known as 'radio surveyors'.

Sub-section 2.

Repealed Merchant Shipping (Safety Convention) Act 1949, section 37, sub-section 5 and Third Schedule.

⚓   ⚓   ⚓   ⚓

Section 10

Repealed

Merchant Shipping (Safety Convention) Act 1949, section 37 sub-section 5, and Third Schedule

⚓   ⚓   ⚓   ⚓

Section 11

Certificates

Repealed

Merchant Shipping (Safety Convention) Act 1949, section 37, Sub-section 5, and Third Schedule

Consult now: That Act

⚓   ⚓   ⚓   ⚓

Modification of safety certificates as respects life-saving appliances.

12 (1) If, on any international voyage, a British passenger steamer registered in the United Kingdom in respect of which a safety certificate is in force has on board a total number of persons less than the number stated in that certificate to be the number for which the life-saving appliances on the steamer provide, the Secretary of State, or any person authorised by them for the purpose, may, at the request of the master of the steamer, issue a memorandum stating the total number of persons carried on the steamer on that voyage, and the consequent modifications which may be made for the purpose of that voyage in the particulars with respect to life-saving appliances stated in the certificate, and that memorandum shall be annexed to the certificate.

(2) Every such memorandum shall be returned to the Secretary of State at the end of the voyage to which it relates, and, if it is not so returned, the master of the steamer shall be liable to a fine not exceeding twenty pounds.

COMMENTS.

Life-saving Appliances.

Consult Merchant Shipping Act 1894, section 427.

Recovery of Fines.

Consult Merchant Shipping Act 1894, section 680 *et seq.*

General.

Consult Generally, Merchant Shipping (Safety Convention) Act 1949.

⚓   ⚓   ⚓   ⚓

Sections 13, 14 and 15

These sections Repealed

Merchant Shipping (Safety Convention) Act 1949, section 37 sub section 5, and Third Schedule q.v.

⚓   ⚓   ⚓   ⚓

Sections 16, 17, 18, 19, 20 and 21

Provisions as to Safety Convention ships Not Registered in the United Kingdom

These sections Repealed

Merchant Shipping (Safety Convention) Act 1949, section 37, sub-section 5, and Third Schedule

⚓   ⚓   ⚓   ⚓

Section 22

Miscellaneous Provisions for furthering Safety of Life at Sea

Repealed

Merchant Shipping (Safety Convention) Act 1949, section 37, sub-section 5, and Third Schedule

⚓   ⚓   ⚓   ⚓

Section 23

Repealed

Merchant Shipping (Load Lines) Act 1967, section 33
sub-section 1, and Schedule 2
Consult now: That Act

⚓   ⚓   ⚓   ⚓

Report of
dangers to
navigation.

24 (1) The master of any British ship registered in the United Kingdom, on meeting with dangerous ice, a dangerous derelict, a tropical storm or any other direct danger to navigation, shall send information accordingly, by all means of communication at his disposal and in accordance with rules to be made for the purposes of this section, to ships in the vicinity and to such authorities on shore as may be prescribed by those rules.

(2) Rules for the purposes of this section shall be made by the Board of Trade and shall make such provision as appears to the Board to be necessary for the purpose of giving effect to the provisions of Article forty-four (so far as it relates to safety signals) and of Regulation XLVI of the Safety Convention.

(3) If the master of a ship fails to comply with the provisions of this section, he shall for each offence be liable to a fine not exceeding fifty pounds.

(4) Every person in charge of a wireless telegraph station which is under the control of the Postmaster General, or which is established or installed under licence of the Postmaster General, shall, on receiving the signal prescribed by the said rules for indicating that a message is about to be sent under this section, refrain from sending messages for a time sufficient to allow other stations to receive the message, and, if so required by the Board of Trade, shall transmit the message in such manner as may be required by the Board, and compliance with this subsection shall be deemed to be a condition of every licence granted by the Postmaster General under the Wireless Telegraphy Act, 1904:

Provided that nothing in this subsection shall interfere with the transmission by wireless telegraphy of any signal of

<u>distress or urgency prescribed under the next following section of this Act.</u>

(5) For the purposes of this section, the expression 'tropical storm' means a hurricane, typhoon, cyclone, or other storm of a similar nature, and the master of a ship shall be deemed to have met with a tropical storm if he has reason to believe that there is such a storm in his vicinity.

(6) The Derelict Vessels (Report) Act 1896, shall cease to have effect.

COMMENTS.

For 'Board of Trade' read Secretary of State for Trade, and for 'Board' read Secretary of State.

Repeal.

The words underlined were repealed by the Merchant Shipping (Safety Convention) Act 1949, sub-section 6, 'The Derelict Vessels', etc., repealed as spent.

Statute Law Revision Act 1950.

Rules for the Purposes of this Section.

Consult Merchant Shipping (Navigational Warnings) Rules 1965, S.I. 1965, No. 1051.

⚓   ⚓   ⚓   ⚓

Section 25

Repealed

Merchant Shipping (Safety Convention) Act 1949, section 37, sub-section 5, and Third Schedule.
See now Section 21 of that Act

⚓   ⚓   ⚓   ⚓

Section 26

Repealed

Merchant Shipping (Safety Convention) Act 1949, section 37 sub-section 5, and Third Schedule

⚓   ⚓   ⚓   ⚓

Signalling
lamps.

27 No British ship registered in the United Kingdom being a ship of over one hundred and fifty tons gross tonnage shall proceed to sea on an international voyage, unless the ship is provided with a signalling lamp of a type approved by the Board of Trade, and if any ship proceeds or attempts to proceed to sea in contravention of this section, the owner or master thereof shall for each offence be liable to a fine not exceeding twenty pounds.

COMMENTS.

International Voyage.

Consult Merchant Shipping (Safety Convention) Act 1949, section 36.

Recovery of Fines.

Consult Merchant Shipping Acts 1894, section 680 to 682.

For 'Board of Trade' *read* 'Secretary of State for Trade'.

⚓   ⚓   ⚓   ⚓

Section 28

Repealed

Merchant Shipping (Safety Convention) Act 1949, section 37
sub-section 5, and Third Schedule
For provisions now in force, consult section 23 of that Act

⚓   ⚓   ⚓   ⚓

Method of
giving helm
orders.

29 (1) No person on any British ship registered in the United Kingdom shall when the ship is going ahead give a helm or steering order containing the word 'starboard' or 'right' or any equivalent of 'starboard' or 'right', unless he intends that the head of the ship shall move to the right, or give a helm or steering order containing the word 'port' or 'left', or any equivalent of 'port' or 'left', unless he intends that the head of the ship shall move to the left.

(2) Any person who contravenes the provisions of this section shall for each offence be liable to a fine not exceeding fifty pounds.

COMMENTS.

This section is applicable to British Ships registered in any of the following countries:

The Channel Islands, Isle of Man, Colonies and Countries in which Her Majesty exercises jurisdiction.

Merchant Shipping (Helm Orders) Order in Council 1935, S.R. & O. 1935, No. 837.

⚓ ⚓ ⚓ ⚓

30 (1) The master of a British ship registered in the United Kingdom, when ice is reported on or near his course, shall at night either proceed at a moderate speed or change his course so as to keep amply clear of the ice reported and of the area of danger. *Careful navigation near ice.*

(2) If the master of any such ship fails to comply with this section, he shall for each offence be liable to a fine not exceeding one hundred pounds.

COMMENTS.

For the position in regard to British Ships registered outside the United Kingdom, consult section 36, sub-section 3 of this Act.

⚓ ⚓ ⚓ ⚓

31 (1) The owner of any line of passenger steamers crossing the North Atlantic from or to any port in the United Kingdom by regular routes shall give public notice, in such manner as may be directed by the Board of Trade, of the routes which it is proposed that the ships belonging to the line should follow, and of any changes which may be made in those routes. *Notice of Atlantic routes.*

(2) If the owner of any such line of passenger steamers fails to comply with this section, he shall for each offence be liable to a fine not exceeding twenty pounds.

COMMENTS.

Passenger Steamer.

For definition, for the purposes of this Act, consult Merchant Shipping (Safety Convention) Act 1949, section 26, sub-section 2.

⚓ ⚓ ⚓ ⚓

Section 32

Repealed

Merchant Shipping (Safety Convention) Act 1949, section 37
sub-section 5, and Third Schedule

⚓   ⚓   ⚓   ⚓

Section 33

Repealed

Merchant Shipping (Safety Convention) Act 1949, section 37
sub-section 5, and Third Schedule

⚓   ⚓   ⚓   ⚓

Section 34

Repealed

Merchant Shipping (Safety Convention) Act 1949, section 37
sub-section 5, and Third Schedule

⚓   ⚓   ⚓   ⚓

Section 35

Repealed

Merchant Shipping (Safety Convention) Act 1949, section 37
sub-section 5, and Third Schedule

⚓   ⚓   ⚓   ⚓

Application of Part 1 to British possessions, protectorates and mandated territories

Application of Part I to British possessions, protectorates and mandated territories.

36 (1) His Majesty may by Order in Council direct that the provisions of this Part of this Act and (so far as may appear to His Majesty to be expedient for the purpose of giving effect to the provisions of this Part of this Act) the provisions of any other Act relating to Merchant Shipping, including any enactments for the time being in force amending or substituted for the provisions of this Part of this Act or any other such Act, shall extend, with such exceptions, adaptations or modifications (if any) as may be specified in the Order, to the Isle of Man, any of the Channel Islands and any colony.

(2) The Foreign Jurisdiction Act 1890, shall have effect as if the provisions of this Part of this Act were included among the enactments which, by virtue of section five of that Act, may be extended by Order in Council to foreign countries in which for the time being His Majesty has jurisdiction.

(3) His Majesty may by Order in Council direct—

(a) that any provision of this Part of this Act, which is expressed to apply only to British ships or passenger steamers registered in the United Kingdom, shall apply to British ships or passenger steamers, as the case may be, registered in any country or part of His Majesty's dominions to which the provisions of this Part of this Act can be extended by virtue of the foregoing provisions of this section;

(b) that any reference in this Part of this Act to a port in the United Kingdom shall be construed as including a reference to a port in any such country or part of His Majesty's dominions as aforesaid.

COMMENTS.

The references contained in this section relating to Part 1 of this Act also include reference to Merchant Shipping (Safety Convention) Act 1949, the Merchant Shipping Act 1964, and section 3, sub-sections 3–5 of the Post Office Act 1969.

Sub-section 2 above.

Consult the Merchant Shipping (Helm Orders) Order 1935, S.R. & O., No. 837, as amended by S.I. 1975, No. 388.

Passenger Steamer.

Consult Merchant Shipping (Safety Convention) Act 1949, section 26, sub-section 2.

⚓   ⚓   ⚓   ⚓

Section 37

Repealed

Merchant Shipping (Safety Convention) Act 1949, section 37
sub-section 5, and Third Schedule

⚓ ⚓ ⚓ ⚓

Section 38

Repealed

Merchant Shipping (Safety Convention) Act 1949, section 37
sub-section 5, and Third Schedule

⚓ ⚓ ⚓ ⚓

Section 39

Repealed as spent

Statute Law Revision Act 1950

⚓ ⚓ ⚓ ⚓

PART TWO

Sections 40 to 61 (inclusive)

Repealed and replaced by the provisions of the
Merchant Shipping (Load Lines) Act 1967 q.v.

⚓ ⚓ ⚓ ⚓

Supplemental

Amendment of
ss. 436 and 454
of the principal
Act.

62 (1) In subsections (1) and (3) of section four hundred
and thirty-six and in subsection (1) of section four hundred
and fifty-four of the principal Act the expression 'freeboard'
hall be substituted for the expression 'clear side'.

(2) Subsection (3) of the said section four hundred and
thirty-six shall cease to have effect with respect to load line
ships.

(3) The following subsection shall be substituted for sub-
section (5) of the said section four hundred and thirty-six,
namely—

'(5) In this section the expression 'freeboard' means, in the case of any ship which is marked with a deck-line, the height from the water to the upper edge of the deck-line, and, in the case of any other ship, the height amidships from the water to the upper edge of the deck from which the depth of hold as stated in the register is measured.'

COMMENTS.

The words underlined in sub-section 1, above Repealed.

Merchant Shipping (Safety Conventions) Act 1949, section 37, sub-section 5, and Third Schedule.

Sub-section 2.

Repealed—Merchant Shipping (Load Lines) Act 1967, Schedule 2.

⚓ ⚓ ⚓ ⚓

Sections 63 to 67 (inclusive)

Repealed and replaced
Merchant Shipping (Load Lines) Act 1967

⚓ ⚓ ⚓ ⚓

PART THREE

Section 68

Repealed

Merchant Shipping (Load Lines) Act 1967, Schedule 2

⚓ ⚓ ⚓ ⚓

69 Where any foreign ship is detained under this Act, and where any proceedings are taken under this Act against the master or owner of any such ship, notice shall forthwith be served on the Consular officer for the country to which the ship belongs at or nearest to the port where the ship is for the time being, and such notice shall specify the grounds on which the ship has been detained or the proceedings have been taken.

Notice to be given to Consular officer where proceedings taken in respect of foreign ships.

COMMENTS.

Consult section 4, Consular Relations Act 1968, in respect of Orders in Council, or limiting the jurisdiction of any court in the United Kingdom.

⚓   ⚓   ⚓   ⚓

Sections 70 to 72 (inclusive)

Repealed

Merchant Shipping (Load Lines) Act 1967, Schedule 2

⚓   ⚓   ⚓   ⚓

Interpretation and construction.   **73** (1) In this Act the following expressions have the meanings hereby respectively assigned to them, that is to say:—

     'Contravention' includes, in relation to any provision, failure to comply with that provision, and the expression 'contravenes' shall be construed accordingly;

     'The Merchant Shipping Acts' means the Merchant Shipping Acts, 1894 to 1928, and this Act;

     'Passenger' has the same meaning as it has for the purpose of Part III of the principal Act;

     'Passenger steamer' means a steamer carrying more than twelve passengers;

     'The principal Act' means the Merchant Shipping Act, 1894.

(2) In this Act references to a ship constructed before or after any date shall be construed as references to a ship the keel of which has been laid before or after that date, as the case may be.

(3) For the purpose of any provision of this Act relating to Safety Convention ships, Safety Convention passenger steamers or Load Line Convention ships not registered in the United Kingdom, a passenger steamer or other ship registered in any of the Channel Islands or in the Isle of Man shall be deemed to be registered in the United Kingdom.

(4) Any references in this Act to any provision of the Merchant Shipping Acts 1894 to 1928, which has been amended by any subsequent Act, including this Act, shall be construed as a reference to that provision as so amended.

COMMENTS.

Repeal.

The words underlined in this section repealed. Merchant Shipping (Safety Convention) Act 1949, section 37, sub-section 5, and Third Schedule.

The present definitions of 'passenger' and 'passenger steamer' are contained in section 26 of the Merchant Shipping (Safety Convention) Act 1949.

Safety Convention Ships.

Consult sections 14 to 17 of the Merchant Shipping (Safety Convention) Act 1949.

Load Line Convention Ships.

Consult Merchant Shipping (Load Lines) Act 1967.

74 (1) This Act may be cited as the Merchant Shipping (Safety and Load Line Conventions) Act 1932, and shall be construed as one with the Merchant Shipping Acts, 1894 to 1928, and those Acts and this Act may be cited together as the Merchant Shipping Acts, 1894 to 1932. *Short title, citation and repeal.*

(2) The enactments set out in Part III of the Fourth Schedule to this Act shall be repealed, to the extent specified in the third column of that Part of that Schedule, as from the passing of this Act.

COMMENTS.

Merchant Shipping Acts 1894 to 1928.

Read now Merchant Shipping Acts 1894 to 1974.

Sub-section 2.

Repealed as spent, Statute Law Revision Act 1950.

SCHEDULES.

First Schedule.

This Schedule, which came into being as a result of the 1929 Convention, was superseded by the 1948 Convention, and in turn was superseded by the 1960 Convention.

Second Schedule.

Repealed, Merchant Shipping (Load Lines) Act 1967, Schedule 2.

Third Schedule.

Repealed, Merchant Shipping (Safety Convention) Act 1949, section 37, sub-section 5, and Third Schedule.

Fourth Schedule.

Repealed as spent. Statute Law Revision Act 1950.

⚓ ⚓ ⚓ ⚓

Pilotage Authorities (Limitation of Liability) Act 1936

This Act has been taken out of its chronological order, and is included with the other Limitation Acts 1894–1958, pages 209 to 261, of Volume I of this work

⚓   ⚓   ⚓   ⚓

Merchant Shipping Act 1937

Repealed

(i) In relation to the submergence of load lines, repealed and replaced by Merchant Shipping (Load Lines) Act 1967, Second Schedule.

(ii) Section 2, Repealed, Statute Law Revision Act 1950

⚓   ⚓   ⚓   ⚓

Merchant Shipping (Superannuation Contributions) Act 1937

Repealed

Merchant Shipping Act 1970, section 100, sub-section 3
Fifth Schedule, as from 1st January 1973, S.I. 1972
No. 1977 refers

⚓   ⚓   ⚓   ⚓

Sea Fish Industry Act 1938

Part IV

Repealed

Merchant Shipping Act 1970, section 100, sub-section 3,
sub section 3, Fifth Schedule, as from 1st January, 1973
S.I. 1972, No. 1977

⚓   ⚓   ⚓   ⚓

Ships and Aircraft (Transfer Restrictions) Act 1939

This Act was passed on the outbreak of the 1939–45 War, and by the Defence Powers (Continuance) Order 1969, S.I. 1969 No. 1836 remained in force until 31st December, 1974.

⚓   ⚓   ⚓   ⚓

Merchant Shipping (Salvage) Act 1940

Repealed

Crown Proceedings Act 1947

⚓ ⚓ ⚓ ⚓

Statutory Instruments Act 1946

This Act is included in this work, to indicate how statutory powers to make orders, rules, regulations, and other subordinate legislation are exercised.

With the mass of legislation invoking these procedures, it is anticipated that the bald presentation of the Act itself will be of general and possibly specific interest to the reader.

⚓   ⚓   ⚓   ⚓

1 (1) Where by this Act or any Act passed after the commencement of this Act power to make, confirm or approve orders, rules, regulations or other subordinate legislation is conferred on His Majesty in Council or on any Minister of the Crown then, if the power is expressed— *Definition of 'Statutory Instrument'.*

(*a*) in the case of a power conferred on His Majesty, to be exercisable by Order in Council;

(*b*) in the case of a power conferred on a Minister of the

Crown, to be exercisable by statutory instrument, any document by which that power is exercised shall be known as a 'statutory instrument' and the provisions of this Act shall apply thereto accordingly.

(2) Where by any Act passed before the commencement of this Act power to make statutory rules within the meaning of the Rules Publication Act, 1893, was conferred on any rule-making authority within the meaning of that Act, any document by which that power is exercised after the commencement of this Act shall, save as is otherwise provided by regulations made under this Act, be known as a 'statutory instrument' and the provisions of this Act shall apply thereto accordingly.

2 (1) Immediately after the making of any statutory instrument, it shall be sent to the King's printer of Acts of Parliament and numbered in accordance with regulations made under this Act, and except in such cases as may be provided by any Act passed after the commencement of this Act or prescribed by regulations made under this Act, copies *Numbering, printing, publication and citation.*

thereof shall as soon as possible be printed and sold by the King's printer of Acts of Parliament.

(2) Any statutory instrument may, without prejudice to any other mode of citation, be cited by the number given to it in accordance with the provisions of this section, and the calendar year.

Supplementary provisions as to publication.

3 (1) Regulations made for the purposes of this Act shall make provision for the publication by His Majesty's Stationery Office of lists showing the date upon which every statutory instrument printed and sold by the King's printer of Acts of Parliament was first issued by that office; and in any legal proceedings a copy of any list so published purporting to bear the imprint of the King's printer shall be received in evidence as a true copy, and an entry therein shall be conclusive evidence of the date on which any statutory instrument was first issued by His Majesty's Stationery Office.

(2) In any proceedings against any person for an offence consisting of a contravention of any such statutory instrument, it shall be a defence to prove that the instrument had not been issued by His Majesty's Stationery Office at the date of the alleged contravention unless it is proved that at that date reasonable steps had been taken for the purpose of bringing the purport of the instrument to the notice of the public, or of persons likely to be affected by it, or of the person charged.

(3) Save as therein otherwise expressly provided, nothing in this section shall affect any enactment or rule of law relating to the time at which any statutory instrument comes into operation.

Statutory Instruments which are required to be laid before Parliament.

4 (1) Where by this Act or any Act passed after the commencement of this Act any statutory instrument is required to be laid before Parliament after being made, a copy of the instrument shall be laid before each House of Parliament and, subject as hereinafter provided, shall be so laid before the instrument comes into operation:

Provided that if it is essential that any such instrument should come into operation before copies thereof can be so laid as aforesaid, the instrument may be made so as to come into operation before it has been so laid; and where any statutory instrument comes into operation before it is laid before Parliament, notification shall forthwith be sent to the

Lord Chancellor and to the Speaker of the House of Commons drawing attention to the fact that copies of the instrument have yet to be laid before Parliament and explaining why such copies were not so laid before the instrument came into operation.

(2) Every copy of any such statutory instrument sold by the King's printer of Acts of Parliament shall bear on the face thereof—

(a) a statement showing the date on which the statutory instrument came or will come into operation; and

(b) either a statement showing the date on which copies thereof were laid before Parliament or a statement that such copies are to be laid before Parliament.

(3) Where any Act passed before the date of the commencement of this Act contains provisions requiring that any Order in Council or other document made in exercise of any power conferred by that or any other Act be laid before Parliament after being made, any statutory instrument made in exercise of that power shall by virtue of this Act be laid before Parliament and the foregoing provisions of this section shall apply thereto accordingly in substitution for any such provisions as aforesaid contained in the Act passed before the said date.

5 (1) Where by this Act or any Act passed after the commencement of this Act, it is provided that any statutory instrument shall be subject to annulment in pursuance of resolution of either House of Parliament, the instrument shall be laid before Parliament after being made and the provisions of the last foregoing section shall apply thereto accordingly, and if either House, within the period of forty days beginning with the day on which a copy thereof is laid before it, resolves that an Address be presented to His Majesty praying that the instrument be annulled, no further proceedings shall be taken thereunder after the date of the resolution, and His Majesty may by Order in Council revoke the instrument, so, however, that any such resolution and revocation shall be without prejudice to the validity of anything previously done under the instrument or to the making of a new statutory instrument. *Statutory Instruments which are subject to annulment by resolution of either House of Parliament.*

(2) Where any Act passed before the date of the commencement of this Act contains provisions requiring that any Order in Council or other document made in exercise of any

power conferred by that or any other Act shall be laid before Parliament after being made and shall cease to be in force or may be annulled, as the case may be, if within a specified period either House presents an address to His Majesty or passes a resolution to that effect, then, subject to the provisions of any Order in Council made under this Act, any statutory instrument made in exercise of the said power shall by virtue of this Act be subject to annulment in pursuance of a resolution of either House of Parliament and the provisions of the last foregoing subsection shall apply thereto accordingly in substitution for any such provisions as aforesaid contained in the Act passed before the said date.

Statutory
Instruments
of which drafts
are to be
laid before
Parliament.

6 (1) Where by this Act or any Act passed after the commencement of this Act it is provided that a draft of any statutory instrument shall be laid before Parliament, but the Act does not prohibit the making of the instrument without the approval of Parliament, then, in the case of an Order in Council the draft shall not be submitted to His Majesty in Council, and in any other case the statutory instrument shall not be made, until after the expiration of a period of forty days beginning with the day on which a copy of the draft is laid before each House of Parliament, or, if such copies are laid on different days, with the later of the two days, and if within that period either House resolves that the draft be not submitted to His Majesty or that the statutory instrument be not made, as the case may be, no further proceedings shall be taken thereon, but without prejudice to the laying before Parliament of a new draft.

(2) Where any Act passed before the date of the commencement of this Act contains provisions requiring that a draft of any Order in Council or other document to be made in exercise of any power conferred by that or any other Act shall be laid before Parliament before being submitted to His Majesty, or before being made, as the case may be, and that it shall not be so submitted or made if within a specified period either House presents an address to His Majesty or passes a resolution to that effect, then, subject to the provisions of any Order in Council made under this Act, a draft of any statutory instrument made in exercise of the said power shall by virtue of this Act be laid before Parliament and the provisions of the last foregoing subsection shall apply thereto accordingly in substitution for any such provisions as aforesaid contained in the Act passed before the said date.

7 (1) In reckoning for the purposes of either of the last Supplementary provisions as to ss. 4, 5 and 6. two foregoing sections any period of forty days, no account shall be taken of any time during which Parliament is dissolved or prorogued or during which both Houses are adjourned for more than four days.

(2) In relation to any instrument required by any Act, whether passed before or after the commencement of this Act, to be laid before the House of Commons only, the provisions of the last three foregoing sections shall have effect as if references to that House were therein substituted for references to Parliament and for references to either House and each House thereof.

(3) The provisions of sections four and five of this Act shall not apply to any statutory instrument being an order which is subject to special Parliamentary procedure, or to any other instrument which is required to be laid before Parliament, or before the House of Commons, for any period before it comes into operation.

8 (1) The Treasury may, with the concurrence of the Regulations. Lord Chancellor and the Speaker of the House of Commons, by statutory instrument make regulations for the purposes of this Act, and such regulations may, in particular:—

(*a*) provide for the different treatment of instruments which are of the nature of a public Act, and of those which are of the nature of a local and personal or private Act;

(*b*) make provision as to the numbering, printing, and publication of statutory instruments including provision for postponing the numbering of any such instrument which does not take effect until it has been approved by Parliament, or by the House of Commons, until the instrument has been so approved;

(*c*) provided with respect to any classes or descriptions of statutory instrument that they shall be exempt, either altogether or to such extent as may be determined by or under the regulations, from the requirement of being printed and of being sold by the King's printer of Acts of Parliament, or from either of those requirements;

(*d*) determine the classes of cases in which the exercise of a statutory power by any rule-making authority constitutes or does not constitute the making of such a statutory rule as is referred to in subsection (2) of section one of this

Act, and provide for the exclusion from that subsection of any such classes;

(e) provide for the determination by a person or persons nominated by the Lord Chancellor and the Speaker of the House of Commons of any question—

(i) as to the numbering, printing, or publication of any statutory instrument or class or description of such instruments:

(ii) whether or to what extent any statutory instrument or class or description of such instruments is, under the regulations, exempt from any such requirement as is mentioned in paragraph (c) of this subsection:

(iii) whether any statutory instrument or class or description of such instruments is in the nature of a public Act or of a local and personal or private Act:

(iv) whether the exercise of any power conferred by an Act passed before the commencement of this Act is or is not the exercise of a power to make a statutory rule.

(2) Every statutory instrument made under this section shall be subject to annulment in pursuance of a resolution of either House of Parliament.

Powers to extend Act to other orders, etc., and to modify applications of certain provisions thereof.

9 (1) If with respect to any power to confirm or approve orders, rules, regulations or other subordinate legislation conferred on a Minister of the Crown by any Act passed before the commencement of this Act, it appears to His Majesty in Council that, notwithstanding that the exercise of that power did not constitute the making of a statutory rule within the meaning of the Rules Publication Act, 1893, it is expedient that the provisions of this Act should apply to documents by which that power is exercised, His Majesty may by Order in Council direct that any document by which that power is exercised after such date as may be specified in the Order shall be known as a 'statutory instrument' and the provisions of this Act shall apply thereto accordingly.

(2) If with respect to any Act passed before the commencement of this Act it appears to His Majesty in Council that by reason of the exceptional nature of any provisions of that Act the application of subsection (2) of section five or subsection (2) of section six of this Act to statutory instruments made under any provisions of that Act would be inexpedient, His Majesty

may by Order in Council direct that those subsections shall not apply to statutory instruments made under those provisions, or shall apply thereto subject to such modifications as may be specified in the Order.

(3) A draft of any Order in Council proposed to be made under this section shall be laid before Parliament.

10 (1) This Act shall come into operation on such date as His Majesty may by Order in Council appoint: *Commencement of Act. 52 & 53 Vict. c. 63.*

Provided that, without prejudice to the provisions of section thirty-seven of the Interpretation Act, 1889, the last foregoing section and, in relation to any Order in Council made thereunder, the provisions of sections six and seven of this Act shall come into operation on the passing of this Act.

(2) The Order in Council made under this section shall be laid before Parliament after being made.

11 (1) For the purposes of this Act, any power to make, confirm or approve orders, rules, regulations or other subordinate legislation conferred on the Treasury, the Admiralty, the Board of Trade or any other government department shall be deemed to be conferred on the Minister of the Crown in charge of that department. *Interpretation.*

(2) If any question arises whether any board, commissioners or other body on whom any such power as aforesaid is conferred are a government department within the meaning of this section, or what Minister of the Crown is in charge of them, that question shall be referred to and determined by the Treasury.

12 (1) The Rules Publication Act, 1893, is hereby repealed. *Repeal of 56 & 57 Vict. c. 66 and re-enactment of s. 3 (3) thereof.*

(2) The publication in the London, Edinburgh or Belfast Gazette of a notice stating that a statutory instrument has been made, and specifying the place where copies thereof may be purchased, shall be sufficient compliance with the provisions of any enactment, whether passed before or after the commencement of this Act, requiring that instrument to be published or notified in that Gazette.

13 (1) This Act may be cited as the Statutory Instruments Act, 1946. *Short title and extent.*

(2) This Act shall apply to any statutory instrument made by His Majesty in Council or by any Minister of the Crown (not being a rule-making authority within the meaning of the Rules Publication Act (Northern Ireland), 1925) in so far as it extends to Northern Ireland, but except as aforesaid this Act shall not extend to Northern Ireland.

⚓   ⚓   ⚓   ⚓

Crown Proceedings Act 1947

General Note.

The provisions of this Act, and the purpose of its enactment, is to place the Crown in the same position of a private individual as regards legal liability for the acts of its servants, and the procedure for the enforcement of such liabilities.

Only the sections of the Act which are applicable to the Merchant Shipping Acts are set out below.

5 (1) The provisions of the Merchant Shipping Acts, 1894 to 1940, which limit the amount of the liability of the owners of ships shall, with any necessary modifications, apply for the purpose of limiting the liability of His Majesty in respect of His Majesty's ships; and any provision of the said Acts which relates to or is ancillary to or consequential on the provisions so applied shall have effect accordingly. Liability in respect of Crown ships, &c.

(2) Without prejudice to the provisions of the preceding subsection, where a ship is built at any port or place within His Majesty's dominions, and His Majesty is interested in her by reason of the fact that she is built by or on behalf of or to the order of His Majesty in right of His Government in the United Kingdom, the provisions of the Merchant Shipping Acts, 1894 to 1940, which limit the amount of the liability of the owners of ships shall, with any necessary modifications, apply for the purpose of limiting the liabilities in respect of that ship of His Majesty, her builders, her owners, and any other persons interested in her; and any provision of the said Acts which relates to or is ancillary to or consequential on the provisions so applied shall have effect accordingly.

This subsection shall have effect only in respect of the period from and including the launching of the ship until the time of her completion, and shall not in any event have effect in respect of any period during which His Majesty is not so interested in the ship as aforesaid. In relation to a ship built to the order of His Majesty in right of His Government in the United Kingdom, the time of her completion shall be taken for the purposes of this subsection to be the time when His Majesty, acting in His said right, finally takes delivery of her under the building contract.

(3) Where any ship has been demised or sub-demised by His Majesty acting in right of His Government in the United Kingdom, then, whether or not the ship is registered for the purposes of the Merchant Shipping Acts, 1894 to 1940, the provisions of those Acts which limit the amount of the liability of the owners of ships shall, in respect of the period for which the demise or sub-demise continues, apply, with any necessary modifications, for the purpose of limiting the liabilities in respect of the ship of any person entitled to her by demise or sub-demise; and any provision of the said Acts which relates to or is ancillary to or consequential on the provisions so applied shall have effect accordingly.

This subsection shall be deemed always to have had effect.

(4) Where by virtue of any arrangement between His Majesty and some other person (not being a servant of His Majesty) that other person (hereinafter referred to as 'the manager') is entrusted with the management of any of His Majesty's ships, the provisions of the Merchant Shipping Acts, 1894 to 1940, which limit the amount of the liability of the owners of ships shall apply for the purpose of limiting the manager's liability in respect of the ship while so entrusted; and any provision of the said Acts which relates to or is ancillary to or consequential on the provisions so applied shall have effect accordingly.

This subsection shall be deemed always to have had effect.

(5) Where for the purposes of any enactment as applied by this section it is necessary to ascertain the tonnage of any ship, and that ship is not registered for the purposes of the Merchant Shipping Acts, 1894 to 1940, the tonnage of the ship shall be taken for the purposes of that enactment to be the tonnage arrived at by:—

(*a*) ascertaining her tonnage in accordance with section seventy-seven of the Merchant Shipping Act, 1894, and the Rules contained in the Second Schedule to that Act, or those Rules as modified or altered from time to time under subsection (7) of the said section seventy-seven, and deducting from her tonnage as so ascertained ten per cent thereof; or

(*b*) where it is impossible to ascertain her tonnage as provided by paragraph (*a*) of this subsection, taking her estimated tonnage as certified for the purposes of this paragraph,—

and deducting from her estimated tonnage as so certified ten per cent thereof.

Where it is necessary to ascertain the tonnage of a ship in the manner provided by paragraph (*b*) of this subsection, the Chief Ships Surveyor of the Ministry of Transport, or the officer for the time being discharging the functions of the said Surveyor, shall, upon the direction of the court concerned, and after considering such evidence of the dimensions of the ship as it may be practicable to obtain, estimate what her tonnage would have been found to be if she could have been duly measured for the purpose, and issue a certificate stating her tonnage as so estimated by him.

(6) For the purposes of this section the expression 'ship' has the meaning assigned to it by section seven hundred and forty-two of the Merchant Shipping Act, 1894, but includes also:—

(*a*) any vessel which is a ship as defined by section four of the Merchant Shipping (Liability of Shipowners) Act, 1898; and

(*b*) every description of lighter, barge or like vessel used in navigation in Great Britain, however propelled, so, however, that a vessel used exclusively in non-tidal waters, other than harbours, shall not for the purposes of this paragraph be deemed to be used in navigation.

(7) Any reference in this section to the provisions of the Merchant Shipping Acts, 1894 to 1940, which limit the amount of the liability of the owners of ships shall be construed as including a reference to any provision of those Acts which negatives the liability of the owner of a ship, and accordingly any reference in this section to limiting the liability of any person shall be construed as including a reference to negativing his liability.

(8) Relief shall not be available by virtue of the Merchant Shipping (Liability of Shipowners) Act, 1898, in any case in which it is available by virtue of this section.

COMMENTS.

Deletion and Substitution:

Section 5, sub-section 5, para. (a).

The words underlined to be deleted in place thereof the following substituted:—'Regulations made under the Merchant Shipping Act, 1965' per Merchant Shipping Act 1965, section 6, para. (*a*).

Section 5, sub-section 6, para (a).

The words underlined to be deleted, and the following substituted:— 'any structure to which Part VIII of that Act is applied by section four of the Merchant Shipping (Liability of Shipowners and Others) Act, 1958' and 'per Merchant Shipping (Liability of Shipowners and Others) Act, section 8, sub-section 5.'

Section 5, sub-section 8.

The words underlined to be deleted, and the following substituted: 'Sections three and four of the Merchant Shipping (Liability of Shipowners and Others) Act, 1958' per Merchant Shipping (Liability of Shipowners and Others Act 1958, section 8, sub-section 5.

Ship—Definition of.

The definition of 'ship' per section 742 of the Merchant Shipping Act 1894, includes 'every description of vessel used in navigation, not propelled by oars'.

This definition has been extended by section 4, sub-section (i) of the Merchant Shipping (Liability of Shipowners and Others) Act 1958 q.v.

See also Merchant Shipping Act 1921, section 1, and note the definitions given in section 30, sub-section 3, of the Crown Proceedings Act 1947, which is also an extension of definition.

His Majesty's Ships.

For definition, *see* section 38, sub-section 2 of this Act. Note also *The Truculent*, 1952, where the effect of this provision was considered.

Merchant Shipping Acts 1894–1940.

Consult now Merchant Shipping (Liability of Shipowners and Others) Act 1958, section 4, section 8, sub-section 5.

Managing Owner.

Consult Merchant Shipping Act 1894, section 59.

Ascertainment of Tonnage of a Registered Ship.

Consult Merchant Shipping Act 1894, section 503, sub-section 2.

⚓   ⚓   ⚓   ⚓

Application to Crown ships of rules as to division of loss, &c.

6 The provisions of sections one, two and three of the Maritime Conventions Act, 1911 (which relate to the apportionment of damage or loss caused by vessels) shall apply in the case of vessels belonging to His Majesty as they apply in the case of other vessels.

7 (1) It is hereby declared that the provisions of the Merchant Shipping Acts, 1894 to 1940, which limit the amount of the liability of the owners of docks and canals, and of harbour and conservancy authorities, apply for the purpose of limiting the liability of His Majesty in His capacity as the owner of any dock or canal, or in His capacity as a harbour or conservancy authority, and that all the relevant provisions of the said Acts have effect in relation to His Majesty accordingly. *Liability in respect of Crown docks, harbours, &c.*

(2) In this section the expressions 'dock', 'harbour', 'owner', 'harbour authority' and 'conservancy authority' have respectively the same meanings as they have for the purposes of section two of the Merchant Shipping (Liability of Shipowners and Others) Act, 1900.

(3) In this section references to His Majesty include references to any Government department and to any officer of the Crown in his capacity as such.

COMMENTS.

Provisions of the Merchant Shipping Acts.

See Merchant Shipping (Liability of Shipowners and Others) Act 1900, section 2 as amended—Merchant Shipping (Liability of Shipowners and Others) Act 1958, section 1, sub-section 1.

Harbour Authority—Conservancy Authority.

For definitions, consult section 742, Merchant Shipping Act 1894.

⚓   ⚓   ⚓   ⚓

8 (1) Subject to the provisions of this Act, the law relating to civil salvage, whether of life or property, except sections five hundred and fifty-one to five hundred and fifty-four of the Merchant Shipping Act, 1894, or any corresponding provisions relating to aircraft, shall apply in relation to salvage services rendered after the commencement of this Act in assisting any of His Majesty's ships or aircraft, or in saving life therefrom, or in saving any cargo or apparel belonging to His Majesty in right of His Government in the United Kingdom, in the same manner as if the ship, aircraft, cargo or apparel belonged to a private person. *Salvage claims against the Crown and Crown rights to salvage.*

(2) Where after the commencement of this Act salvage services are rendered by or on behalf of His Majesty, whether in right of His Government in the United Kingdom or other-

G

wise, His Majesty shall be entitled to claim salvage in respect of those services to the same extent as any other salvor, and shall have the same rights and remedies in respect of those services as any other salvor.

COMMENTS.

Provisions as to Salvage; Definition of Salvage.

Consult Merchant Shipping Acts 1894, sections 544—571.

Merchant Shipping Act 1894, section 710, applicable to Scotland.

Merchant Shipping Act 1894, section 742.

See also, Maritime Conventions Act 1911, sections 6 and 7.

    ⚓   ⚓   ⚓   ⚓

Section 9

Repealed

Post Office Act 1969, section 141, Schedule 2, Part 2

    ⚓   ⚓   ⚓   ⚓

Transitional provisions.

12 (1) When this Act comes into operation, the preceding provisions of this Part of this Act (except subsections (3) and (4) of section five thereof and any provision which is expressly related to the commencement of this Act) shall be deemed to have had effect as from the beginning of the thirteenth day of February, nineteen hundred and forty-seven:

Provided that where by virtue of this subsection proceedings are brought against the Crown in respect of a tort alleged to have been committed on or after the said thirteenth day of February and before the commencement of this Act, the Crown may rely upon the appropriate provisions of the law relating to the limitation of time for bringing proceedings as if this Act had at all material times been in force.

(2) Where any civil proceedings brought before the commencement of this Act have not been finally determined, and the court for the time being seized of those proceedings is of opinion that having regard to the provisions of this section the Crown ought to be made a party to the proceedings for the purpose of disposing completely and effectually of the questions involved in the cause or matter before the court, the court may order that the Crown be made a party thereto upon such terms, if any, as the court thinks just, and may make such consequential orders as the court thinks expedient.

29 (1) Nothing in this Act shall authorise proceedings in rem in respect of any claim against the Crown, or the arrest, detention or sale of any of His Majesty's ships or aircraft, or of any cargo or other property belonging to the Crown, or give to any person any lien on any such ship, aircraft, cargo or other property.

(2) Where proceedings in rem have been instituted in the High Court or in a county court against any such ship, aircraft, cargo or other property, the court may, if satisfied, either on an application by the plaintiff for an order under this subsection or an application by the Crown to set aside the proceedings, that the proceedings were so instituted by the plaintiff in the reasonable belief that the ship, aircraft, cargo or other property did not belong to the Crown, order that the proceedings shall be treated as if they were in personam duly instituted against the Crown in accordance with the provisions of this Act, or duly instituted against any other person whom the court regards as the proper person to be sued in the circumstances, and that the proceedings shall continue accordingly.

Any such order may be made upon such terms, if any, as the court thinks just; and where the court makes any such order it may make such consequential orders as the court thinks expedient.

30 (1) Section eight of the Maritime Conventions Act, 1911 (which relates to the limitation of actions in respect of damage or loss caused to or by vessels and the limitation of actions in respect of salvage services) shall except in the case of proceedings in respect of any alleged fault of a ship of war or a ship for the time being appropriated to the service of the armed forces of the Crown or to the service of the Post Office, apply in the case of His Majesty's ships as it applies in the case of other vessels:

Provided that the said section eight, as applied by this section, shall have effect as if the words from 'and shall, if satisfied' to the end of the said section eight were omitted therefrom.

(2) Subject to the provisions of the preceding subsection, nothing in this Act shall prejudice the right of the Crown to rely upon the law relating to the limitation of time for bringing proceedings against public authorities.

(3) In this section the expression 'ship' includes any boat or other description of vessel used in navigation, and the expression 'His Majesty's ships' shall be construed accordingly.

COMMENTS:

Repeal.

The words underlined in sub-section 1 above, repealed. Law Reform (Limitation of Actions) Act 1954, section 5, sub-section 2, section 8, sub-section 3, and Schedule.

Sub-section 2.

The whole of this sub-section repealed. Law Reform (Limitation of Actions) Act 1954, section 8, sub-section 3, and Schedule.

⚓   ⚓   ⚓   ⚓

Interpretation.   **38** (1) Any reference in this Act to the provisions of this Act shall, unless the context otherwise requires, include a reference to rules of court or county court rules made for the purposes of this Act.

(2) In this Act, except in so far as the context otherwise requires or it is otherwise expressly provided, the following expressions have the meanings hereby respectively assigned to them, that is to say:—

'Agent', when used in relation to the Crown, includes an independent contractor employed by the Crown;

'Civil proceedings' includes proceedings in the High Court or the county court for the recovery of fines or penalties, but does not include proceedings on the Crown side of the King's Bench Division;

'His Majesty's aircraft' does not include aircraft belonging to His Majesty otherwise than in right of His Government in the United Kingdom;

'His Majesty's ships' means ships of which the beneficial interest is vested in His Majesty or which are registered as Government ships for the purposes of the Merchant Shipping Acts, 1894 to 1940, or which are for the time being demised or subdemised to or in the exclusive possession of the Crown, except that the said expression does not include any ship in which His Majesty is interested otherwise than in right of His Government in the United Kingdom unless that ship is for the time being demised or subdemised to His Majesty in right of His said Government or in the exclusive possession of His Majesty in that right;

'Officer', in relation to the Crown, includes any servant of His Majesty, and accordingly (but without prejudice to the generality of the foregoing provision) includes a Minister of the Crown;

'Order' includes a judgment, decree, rule, award or declaration;

'Prescribed' means prescribed by rules of court or county court rules, as the case may be;

'Proceedings against the Crown' includes a claim by way of set-off or counterclaim raised in proceedings by the Crown;

'Ship' has the meaning assigned to it by section seven hundred and forty-two of the Merchant Shipping Act, 1894:

'Statutory duty' means any duty imposed by or under any Act of Parliament.

(3) Any reference in this Act to His Majesty in His private capacity shall be construed as including a reference to His Majesty in right of His Duchy of Lancaster and to the Duke of Cornwall.

(4) Any reference in Parts III or IV of this Act to civil proceedings by or against the Crown, or to civil proceedings to which the Crown is a party, shall be construed as including a reference to civil proceedings to which the Attorney General, or any Government department, or any officer of the Crown as such is a party:

Provided that the Crown shall not for the purposes of Parts III and IV of this Act be deemed to be a party to any proceedings by reason only that they are brought by the Attorney General upon the relation of some other person.

(5) Any reference in this Act to the armed forces of the Crown shall be construed as including a reference to the following forces:—

(a) the Women's Royal Naval Service;

(b) the Queen Alexandra's Royal Naval Nursinng service; and

(c) any other organisation established under the control of the Admiralty, the Army Council or the Air Council.

(6) References in this Act to any enactment shall be construed as references to that enactment as amended by or under any other enactment, including this Act.

40 (1) Nothing in this Act shall apply to proceedings by or against, or authorise proceedings in tort to be brought against, His Majesty in His private capacity.

(2) Except as therein otherwise expressly provided, nothing in this Act shall:—

(a) affect the law relating to prize salvage, or apply to proceedings in causes or matters within the jurisdiction of the High Court as a prize court or to any criminal proceedings; or

(b) authorise proceedings to be taken against the Crown under or in accordance with this Act in respect of any alleged liability of the Crown arising otherwise than in respect of His Majesty's Government in the United Kingdom, or affect proceedings against the Crown in respect of any such alleged liability as aforesaid; or

(c) affect any proceedings by the Crown otherwise than in right of His Majesty's Government in the United Kingdom; or

(d) subject the Crown to any greater liabilities in respect of the acts or omissions of any independent contractor employed by the Crown than those to which the Crown would be subject in respect of such acts or omissions if it were a private person; or

(e) subject the Crown, in its capacity as a highway authority, to any greater liability than that to which a local authority is subject in that capacity; or

(f) affect any rules of evidence or any presumption relating to the extent to which the Crown is bound by any Act of Parliament; or

(g) affect any right of the Crown to demand a trial at bar or to control or otherwise intervene in proceedings affecting its rights, property or profits; or

(h) affect any liability imposed on the public trustee or on the Consolidated Fund of the United Kingdom by the Public Trustee Act, 1906;

and, without prejudice to the general effect of the foregoing provisions, Part III of this Act shall not apply to the Crown except in right of His Majesty's Government in the United Kingdom.

(3) A certificate of a Secretary of State:—

(*a*) to the effect that any alleged liability of the Crown arises otherwise than in respect of His Majesty's Government in the United Kingdom;

(*b*) to the effect that any proceedings by the Crown are proceedings otherwise than in right of His Majesty's Government in the United Kingdom;

shall, for the purposes of this Act, be conclusive as to the matter so certified.

(4) Where any property vests in the Crown by virtue of any rule of law which operates independently of the acts or the intentions of the Crown, the Crown shall not by virtue of this Act be subject to any liabilities in tort by reason only of the property being so vested; but the provisions of this subsection shall be without prejudice to the liabilities of the Crown under this Act in respect of any period after the Crown or any person acting for the Crown has in fact taken possession or control of any such property, or entered into occupation thereof.

(5) This Act shall not operate to limit the discretion of the court to grant relief by way of mandamus in cases in which such relief might have been granted before the commencement of this Act, notwithstanding that by reason of the provisions of this Act some other and further remedy is available.

COMMENTS.

Repeal.

Sub-section 2, para. (*e*), underlined, repealed Highways (Miscellaneous Provisions) Act 1961.

⚓   ⚓   ⚓   ⚓

PART VI

EXTENT, COMMENCEMENT, SHORT TITLE, &C.

52 Subject to the provisions hereinafter contained with Extent of Act. respect to Northern Ireland, this Act shall not affect the law enforced in courts elsewhere than in England and Scotland, or the procedure in any such courts.

⚓   ⚓   ⚓   ⚓

Provisions as
to Northern
Ireland.

53 (1) His Majesty may by Order in Council provide for extending this Act to Northern Ireland with such additions, exceptions and modifications as appear to His Majesty to be expedient.

(2) An Order in Council under this section may provide for amending the law both in its application to the Crown in right of His Majesty's Government in the United Kingdom and in its application to the Crown in right of His Majesty's Government in Northern Ireland.

(3) An Order in Council under this section may provide for amending the law:—

(*a*) with respect to the right of the Crown to sue in a county court in Northern Ireland; and

(*b*) with respect to the award of costs to or against the Crown in Northern Ireland.

(4) An Order in Council under this section may be varied or revoked by a further Order in Council made thereunder.

(5) An Order in Council under this section may include such provisions as appear to His Majesty to be incidental to or consequential on any provisions contained in such an Order by virtue of the preceding provisions of this section.

(6) So far as any provision contained in an Order in Council under this section deals with a matter with respect to which the Parliament of Northern Ireland has power to make laws, it shall, for the purposes of section six of the Government of Ireland Act, 1920 (which relates to the power of the Parliament of Northern Ireland), be deemed to be a provision of an Act passed before the appointed day.

(7) An Order in Council under this section shall be laid before Parliament as soon as may be after it is made, and, if either House of Parliament, within the next twenty-eight days on which that House has sat after such an Order is laid before it, resolves that the Order be annulled, the Order shall thereupon cease to have effect except as respects things previously done or omitted to be done, without prejudice, however, to the making of a new Order.

Notwithstanding anything in subsection (4) of section one of the Rules Publication Act, 1893, such an Order shall be deemed not to be a statutory rule to which that section applies.

COMMENTS.

Repeal.

Sub-section '6' underlined, repealed—Northern Ireland Constitution Act 1973.

The words underlined in sub-section 7, repealed Statute Law Revision Act 1953.

⚓   ⚓   ⚓   ⚓

54 (1) This Act may be cited as the Crown Proceedings Act 1947.

Short title and commencement.

(2) This Act shall come into operation on such day, not later than the first day of January, nineteen hundred and forty-eight, as His Majesty may by Order in Council appoint.

COMMENTS.

Sub-section 2, repealed as spent. Statute Law Revision Act 1950. The Act came into operation on the 1st January, 1948.

⚓   ⚓   ⚓   ⚓

Merchant Shipping Act 1948

INTRODUCTION.

This Act sought to amend the provisions of the Merchant Shipping Acts as a result of certain International Conventions adopted at Seattle in 1946, which dealt with crew accommodation on board ship, the certification of able seamen, food and catering for crews on board ship, the certificates of ships' cooks, and social security for seafarers.

When words of the operative part of the statute are ambiguous, recourse should be made to the text of the Conventions.

Section 7 of the Act was repealed on the 1st January, 1973, S.I. 1972, No. 1977, The Merchant Shipping Act 1970 (Commencement No. 1) Order 1972.

It is anticipated that the remainder of the Act will be repealed as from a day to be appointed. *See* Merchant Shipping Act 1970, section 100, sub-section 3, and Fifth Schedule.

Accordingly therefore, comments have been kept to an absolute minimum.

⚓   ⚓   ⚓   ⚓

Crew Accommodation and Food and Catering

Accommodation for seamen.

1 (1) The Minister may, after consultation with such organisation or organisations as appear to him to be representative both of owners of British ships and of seamen employed therein, make regulations with respect to the crew accommodation to be provided in ships of any class specified in the regulations, being ships in respect of which such regulations are authorised to be made by the next following section.

(2) Without prejudice to the generality of the foregoing sub-section, regulations made thereunder may, in particular—

(*a*) prescribe the minimum space per man which must be provided in any ship to which the regulations apply by way of sleeping accommodation for seamen and apprentices, and the maximum number of persons by whom any specified part of such sleeping accommodation may be used;

(*b*) regulate the position in any such ship in which the crew accommodation or any part thereof may be located, and the standards to be observed in the construction, equipment and furnishing of any such accommodation;

(*c*) require the submission to a surveyor of ships of plans and specifications of any works proposed to be carried out for the purpose of the provision or alteration of any such accommodation, and authorise the surveyor to inspect any such works;

(*d*) provide for the maintenance and repair of any such accommodation, and prohibit or restrict the use of such accommodation for purposes other than those for which it is designed;

and may make different provision in respect of different classes of ships and in respect of crew accommodation provided for different classes of persons.

(3) In this Act the expression 'crew accommodation' includes sleeping rooms, mess rooms, sanitary accommodation, hospital accommodation, recreation accommodation, store rooms and catering accommodation provided for the use of seamen and apprentices, not being accommodation which is also used by or provided for the use of passengers:

Provided that regulations made under this section may provide that any store rooms comprised in the crew accommodation of a ship shall, to such extent as may be prescribed by the regulations, be disregarded in estimating the space to be deducted from the tonnage of the ship under section seventy-nine of the principal Act in respect of crew accommodation.

(4) If the provisions of any regulations made under this section are contravened in the case of a ship, the owner or master of the ship shall be liable to a fine not exceeding one hundred pounds.

COMMENTS.

Minister of Transport.

Now read Secretary of State.

British Ship.

See Merchant Shipping Act 1894, section 1.

Regulations.

These are contained in the Merchant Shipping (Crew Accommodation) Regulations 1953, S.I. 1953, No. 1036, as amended S.I. 1954, No. 1660, S.I. 1961, No. 393, S.I. 1965, No. 1047, S.I. 1975, No. 341, S.I. 1977, No. 2049.

When this section is repealed, these regulations will have effect under section 20 of the Merchant Shipping Act 1970.

Additional sub-section.

The following sub-section was added by section 1, sub-section 1 of the Merchant Shipping Act 1952:

'2(*a*) The Secretary of State may exempt any ships or classes of ships from any requirements of regulations made under this section, either absolutely, or subject to such conditions as he thinks fit.'

Repeal.

Section 1, the proviso to sub-section 3 (omitted from text).

Section 4, sub-sections 1 and 2 (omitted from text).

⚓   ⚓   ⚓   ⚓

Application of section one.   **2** (1) Subject to the provisions of this section, regulations made under section one of this Act may apply—

(*a*) to any British ship for the time being registered in the United Kingdom, whether so registered before or after the date on which the regulations come into force; and

(*b*) to any ship which, at any time after that date, is being constructed to the order of a person qualified under the principal Act to be the owner of a British ship and has not been registered in the United Kingdom or elsewhere,

not being a fishing boat or a ship being constructed for use as a fishing boat:

Provided that, subject to the provisions of any Order in Council made under section nine of this Act, such regulations shall not apply to any ship under construction which is being constructed at any place in His Majesty's dominions outside the United Kingdom or in any foreign country or territory in which His Majesty has for the time being jurisdiction, or is intended on her first registration to be registered at any such place.

(2) Where any ship to which regulations made under section one of this Act apply was a British ship registered in the United Kingdom immediately before the date on which those regulations came into force, then, unless and until, after that date, the ship is re-registered in the United Kingdom or undergoes substantial structural alterations or repairs (not being repairs carried out in consequence of damage or in an emergency)—

(*a*) any requirements of the regulations (including any subsequent regulations amending or substituted for those regulations) relating to matters specified in paragraph (*a*) or paragraph (*b*) of subsection (2) of section one of this Act (in this section referred to as 'the construction requirements') shall be deemed to be complied with in the case of the ship if the corresponding requirements of the law in force immediately before that date are so complied with; and

(*b*) any requirements of any such regulations relating to matters specified in paragraph (*c*) of the said subsection (2) (in this section referred to as 'the survey requirements') shall not apply to any works other than works proposed to be carried out for the purpose of any such alterations or repairs as aforesaid.

(3) Where regulations made under section one of this Act become applicable—

(*a*) to a ship under construction of which the keel was laid before the date on which those regulations came into force;

(*b*) to a ship registered as a British ship in the United Kingdom after that date, not being a ship to which such regulations applied while she was under construction,

or where any such ship as is mentioned in the last foregoing subsection is re-registered, altered or repaired as mentioned in that subsection, then, if, upon application made to him by the owner of the ship, the Minister is satisfied, after consultation with the owner of the ship or an organisation which appears to him to be representative of owners of British ships, and with an organisation which appears to him to be representative of seamen employed in British ships, that such steps if any as are reasonable and practicable have been taken for securing compliance with the construction requirements of the regulations in the case of the ship, he shall certify accordingly.

(4) In determining for the purposes of the last foregoing subsection what steps for securing compliance with the construction requirements of any regulations are reasonable and practicable, the Minister shall have regard to the age of the ship, to the purpose for which she is or is intended to be used and to the nature of any alterations or repairs which are carried out, or to the extent to which the construction of the ship had been completed before the date on which the regulations came into force, as the case may be.

(5) Where any such certificate is issued by the Minister as aforesaid, then, subject to compliance with such conditions, if any, as may be specified in the certificate—

(*a*) the construction requirements of the regulations (including any subsequent regulations amending or substituted for those regulations) shall be deemed to be complied with in the case of the ship; and

(*b*) the survey requirements of any such regulations shall not apply to any works other than works proposed to be carried out for the purpose of any such alterations or repairs as are mentioned in subsection (2) of this section :

Provided that on the occurrence of any such event as is mentioned in the said sub-section (2), the provisions of this subsection shall cease to have effect in relation to the ship, but without prejudice to the issue of a further certificate under subsection (3) of this section.

COMMENTS.

British Ship.

Consult Merchant Shipping Act 1894, section 1.

Regulations.

Operative as from 1st January, 1954.

Re-registered:

It is submitted that this has the same meaning as 'registered anew', Merchant Shipping Act 1894, section 48, sub-section 1.

Minister.

For 'Minister' read 'Secretary of State'.

⚓   ⚓   ⚓   ⚓

Inspections of crew accommodation.

3 (1) Whenever a ship to which regulations made under section one of this Act apply is registered or re-registered in the United Kingdom, whenever a complaint in respect of the crew accommodation in any such ship is duly made in accordance with the regulations, and on such other occasions as may be prescribed by the regulations, a surveyor of ships shall inspect the crew accommodation.

(2) If, upon any such inspection, the surveyor is satisfied that the crew accommodation complies with the regulations, he shall (except where the inspection is made in consequence of a complaint) give to the registrar of British ships a certificate

specifying as space deductible under section seventy-nine of the principal Act the whole of the space comprised in that accommodation, except any part thereof required by the regulations to be disregarded in estimating the space so to be deducted.

(3) If, upon any such inspection, it appears to the surveyor that the accommodation does not comply in all respects with the regulations, he may give to the registrar a certificate specifying as space deductible as aforesaid such part of the space comprised in the accommodation as he considers appropriate having regard to the extent to which it complies with the regulations, but if he does not give such a certificate he shall report to the registrar that no space is deductible as aforesaid:

Provided that the surveyor shall not be required to make such a report as aforesaid—

(a) if the inspection is made on the occasion of the registration or re-registration of the ship; or

(b) if it appears to him that the failure to comply with the regulations is not substantial and will be remedied within a reasonable time.

(4) Where any certificate is given or report made under the foregoing provisions of this section in respect of a ship already registered any certificate previously given thereunder in respect of that ship shall cease to have effect, and the registered tonnage of the ship shall be altered accordingly.

(5) In respect of any inspection of a ship carried out by a surveyor for the purposes of this section, there shall be paid such fees as may be prescribed by regulations made under section one of this Act.

(6) Regulations made under section one of this Act may require the master of any ship to which the regulations apply, or any officer authorised by him for the purpose, to carry out such inspections of the crew accommodation as may be prescribed by the regulations, and to record in the official log such particulars of any such inspection as may be so prescribed.

COMMENTS.

Merchant Shipping Act 1894, section 79, Repealed.

Merchant Shipping Act 1965, section 5, sub-section 1, section 7, sub-section 1, 2nd Schedule.

Consult now: section 1 of the 1965 Act.

Entries in Official Log.

Consult now, Merchant Shipping Act 1970, section 68.

⚓   ⚓   ⚓   ⚓

4 (1) In relation to ships to which regulations made under section one of this Act apply, section seventy-nine of the principal Act (which authorises certain deductions in ascertaining the register tonnage of ships) shall have effect as if in sub-paragraph (*a*) (i) of subsection (1) for the words 'any space occupied by seamen or apprentices and appropriated to their use, which is certified under the regulations scheduled to this Act with regard thereto' there were substituted the words 'any space provided by way of crew accommodation which is certified under the Merchant Shipping Act, 1948, to be space deductible under this section'.

(2) In relation to a ship of any foreign country, being a ship to which regulations made under section one of this Act would apply if she were a British ship and were registered in the United Kingdom, subsection (1) of section eighty-four of the principal Act (which as amended by section fifty-five of the Merchant Shipping Act, 1906, provides for the ascertainment of the tonnage of certain foreign ships) shall have effect subject to the following modifications, that is to say:—

(*a*) for the words 'shall be deemed to have been certified under this Act and to comply with the provisions of this Act which apply to such a space in the case of British ships' there shall be substituted the words 'shall be deemed to have been specified in a certificate issued under the Merchant Shipping Act, 1948, and to comply with regulations made under section one of that Act';

(*b*) for the words 'the standard required under this Act in the case of a British ship' there shall be substituted the words 'the standard which would be required under or for the purposes of those regulations if she were a British ship registered in the United Kingdom'.

(3) Section two hundred and ten of the principal Act and the Sixth Schedule to that Act, and section sixty-four of the Merchant Shipping Act, 1906, shall not apply to any ship to which regulations made under section one of this Act apply (but without prejudice to the provisions of subsection (2) of section two of this Act); and the proviso to paragraph (*a*) of subsection (2) of section five hundred and three of the principal Act shall cease to have effect:

Provided that any certificate given in relation to any such ships as aforesaid, under paragraph (3) of the said Sixth Schedule before the date on which the regulations apply thereto shall have effect for the purposes of this Act and of the principal Act as if it had been given under the last foregoing section.

COMMENTS.

Repeal.

Sub-section 1 and 2 underlined above, Repealed Merchant Shipping Act 1965, section 7, sub-section 2, and 2nd Schedule.

⚓   ⚓   ⚓   ⚓

Certification of Able Seamen

5 (1) After such date as may be prescribed by regula- Rating of seamen. tions made under the following provisions of this section, a seaman engaged in any British ship registered in the United Kingdom shall not be rated as A.B. unless he is the holder of a certificate of competency granted in pursuance of those regulations.

(2) The Minister may make regulations providing for the grant of certificates of competency as A.B. for the purposes of this section; and such regulations shall in particular direct that no such certificate shall be granted to any person unless—

(*a*) he has reached such minimum age as may be prescribed by the regulations; and

(*b*) he has performed such qualifying service at sea as may be so prescribed; and

(*c*) he has passed such examination as may be so prescribed;
Provided that the regulations may authorise the grant of a certificate thereunder to any person, not withstanding that he has not complied with the conditions aforesaid, if he shows,

in such manner as may be prescribed by the regulations, that he was serving as A.B., or in an equivalent or superior deck rating, on the date on which the regulations came into force, or had so served at any time before that date.

(3) Regulations made under this section may make such consequential provisions as appear to the Minister to be necessary or expedient, including provision—

(a) for the payment of such fees as may be prescribed by the regulations in respect of any application for the grant or replacement of a certificate thereunder;

(b) for applying to certificates granted under the regulations, subject to such adaptations and modifications as may be so prescribed, the provisions of section one hundred and four of the principal Act (which relates to forgery and other offences relating to certificates of competency of ships' officers granted under that Act).

(4) Where provision is made by the law of any part of His Majesty's dominions outside the United Kingdom for the grant of certificates of competency as A.B., and the Minister reports to His Majesty that he is satisfied that the conditions under which such a certificate is granted require standards of competency not lower than those required for the grant of a certificate in pursuance of regulations made under this section, His Majesty may by Order in Council direct that certificates granted in that part of His Majesty's dominions shall have the same effect for the purposes of this section as if they had been granted in pursuance of such regulations as aforesaid; and any such Order may apply to any such certificate any of the provisions of the regulations relating to certificates granted thereunder.

(5) Any superintendent or other officer before whom, at any time after such date as may be prescribed by regulations made under this section, a seaman is engaged in any British ship registered in the United Kingdom, shall refuse to enter the seaman as A.B. on the agreement with the crew unless the seaman produces a certificate of competency granted in pursuance of the regulations or such other proof that he is the holder of such a certificate as may appear to the superintendent or other officer to be satisfactory.

(6) As from such date as may be prescribed by regulations made under this section, section one hundred and twenty-six of the principal Act and section fifty-eight of the Merchant

Shipping Act, 1906, shall cease to have effect in relation to any seamen for the time being engaged in a British ship registered in the United Kingdom.

COMMENTS.

Minister.

For 'Minister' read 'Secretary of State'.

Regulations.

See now Merchant Shipping (Certificates of Competency as A.B.) Regulations 1970, S.I. 1970, No. 294, as amended by The Merchant Shipping (Fees) Regulations 1977, S.I. 1977, No. 2049.

Superintendent.

Consult Merchant Shipping Act 1970, section 81.

Agreement with Crew.

Consult Merchant Shipping Act 1970, sections 1 and 2.

Orders in Council.

Comparable Certificates.

Orders in Council have been made in respect of the following countries:
New Zealand—S.I. 1956, No. 1895.
Barbados—S.I. 1957, No. 1371.
Republic of Ireland—S.I. 1958, No. 1048.
Canada—S.I. 1959, No. 2213.
Mauritius—S.I. 1960, No. 1662.
Trinidad and Tobago—S.I. 1960, No. 1663.
Ghana—S.I. 1963, No. 1316.
Nigeria—S.I. 1964, No. 700.
Gilbert and Ellice Islands—S.I. 1972, No. 1105.

⚓   ⚓   ⚓   ⚓

Certification of Ships' Cooks

6 (1) Where provision is made by the law of any part of His Majesty's dominions outside the United Kingdom for the issue of certificates of competency as ship's cook, and the Minister reports to His Majesty that he is satisfied that the conditions under which such certificates are granted require standards of competency not lower than those required for the grant of certificates of competency in cooking for the purposes of section twenty-seven of the Merchant Shipping Act, 1906, His Majesty may by Order in Council direct that the holders of such certificates granted in that part of His

Certificated cooks for foreign-going ships.

Majesty's dominions shall be deemed to be duly certificated within the meaning of the said section twenty-seven.

(2) If the Minister reports to His Majesty that he is satisfied that it is the wish of such organisation or organisations as appear to him to be representative both of owners of British ships and of seamen employed therein that the provisions of the said section twenty-seven should, with such exceptions, adaptations and modifications, if any, as may be specified in such report, apply—

(a) to such classes of British ships, other than the class mentioned in the said section, as may be specified in the report, or

(b) to British ships going to sea from such places, other than places mentioned in the said section, as may be so specified,

and that it is expedient that the provisions of the said section should so apply, His Majesty may by Order in Council direct that the said provisions shall, with such exceptions, adaptations and modifications as aforesaid, apply to that class of ships or to ships going to sea from those places:

Provided that nothing in this subsection shall authorise the said provisions to be applied to ships registered in any Dominion within the meaning of the Statute of Westminster, 1931 (other than Newfoundland) or in India, Pakistan or Ceylon.

(3) His Majesty may by Order in Council direct that the provisions of the said section twenty-seven shall extend, with such exceptions, adaptations and modifications, if any, as may be specified in the Order, to any country or territory to which, under the following provisions of this Act, any of the provisions of this Act can be extended.

COMMENTS.

This section, in common with the remainder of the Act (except section 7 repealed) will be repealed as from a day to be appointed, however, it has not yet come into operation.

Consult section 10 of this Act.

⚓   ⚓   ⚓   ⚓

Section 7
Repealed
See introduction to this Act

⚓   ⚓   ⚓   ⚓

Supplemental

8 Any fees received by the Minister under this Act or regulations made thereunder shall be paid into the Exchequer. *Payment of fees into the Exchequer.*

COMMENTS.

For 'Minister' read 'Secretary of State'.

⚓   ⚓   ⚓   ⚓

9 (1) His Majesty may by Order in Council direct that any of the provisions of this Act (including any enactments for the time being in force amending or substituted for the said provisions) shall extend, with such exceptions, adaptations and modifications, if any, as may be specified in the Order, to the Isle of Man, any of the Channel Islands, Newfoundland or any colony. *Application to British possessions etc.*

(2) The Foreign Jurisdiction Act, 1890, shall have effect as if the provisions of this Act were included among the enactments which, by virtue of section five of that Act, may be extended by Order in Council to foreign countries in which for the time being His Majesty has jurisdiction.

(3) His Majesty may by Order in Council direct that any provision of this Act shall apply, subject to such exceptions, adaptations and modifications, if any, as may be specified in the Order, to ships registered in any country or territory to which the provisions of this Act can be extended by virtue of subsection (1) or subsection (2) of this section, or under construction in any such country or territory, or to be registered on first registration in any such country or territory, as it applies to ships registered, under construction or to be registered on first registration, as the case may be, in the United Kingdom.

COMMENTS.

At present this is applied to fishing boats (with modifications).

Consult Merchant Shipping Act 1950, section 1, sub-section 5, and Schedule 1.

⚓   ⚓   ⚓   ⚓

Commence-
ment.
10 (1) This Act shall come into operation on such date as the Minister may by order appoint, and different dates may be appointed for the purposes of different provisions of this Act.

(2) The date or dates to be appointed for the purposes of the coming into operation of the provisions of this Act hereinafter mentioned shall be the date or dates on which the relevant Conventions come into force for the United Kingdom, that is to say—

(a) in respect of sections one to four of this Act, the Conventions dealing with crew accommodation on board ship and with food and catering for crews on board ship;

(b) in respect of section five, the Convention dealing with the certification of able seamen;

(c) in respect of section six, the Convention dealing with the certification of ships' cooks; and

(d) in respect of section seven, the Convention dealing with social security for seafarers:

Provided that if the Minister is satisfied that it is the wish of such organisation or organisations as appear to him to be representative both of owners of British ships and of seamen employed therein, that any such provision of this Act as aforesaid should come into operation on a date earlier than the date aforesaid, and that it is expedient that it should come into operation on that date, he may appoint that date as the date on which that provison is to come into operation.

COMMENTS.

For 'Minister' read 'Secretary of State'.

    ⚓   ⚓   ⚓   ⚓

Regulations
and orders.
11 (1) Any power of the Minister to make regulations or orders under the foregoing provisions of this Act shall be exercisable by statutory instrument.

(2) Any Order in Council made under the foregoing provisions of this Act and any instrument containing regulations made under section one of this Act shall be subject to annulment in pursuance of a resolution of either House of Parliament.

COMMENTS.

For 'Minister' read 'Secretary of State'.

See Comments to section 9.

⚓   ⚓   ⚓   ⚓

12 (1) In this Act the following expressions have the *Interpretation, construction* meanings hereby respectively assigned to them, that is to say— *and citation.*

'crew accommodation' has the meaning assigned to it by section one of this Act;

'Minister' means the Minister of Transport;

'owner', in relation to a ship under construction, means the person to whose order she is constructed;

'principal Act' means the Merchant Shipping Act, 1894.

(2) Except so far as the context otherwise requires, any reference in this Act to any other enactment shall be construed as a reference to that enactment as amended, extended or applied by or under any other enactment, including this Act.

(3) This Act shall be construed as one with the Merchant Shipping Acts, 1894 to 1938, and without prejudice to the generality of this provision, references in those Acts to the Merchant Shipping Acts shall be construed as including references to this Act.

(4) This Act may be cited as the Merchant Shipping Act, 1948, and the Merchant Shipping Acts, 1894 to 1938, and this Act may be cited together as the Merchant Shipping Acts, 1894 to 1948.

COMMENTS.

For 'Minister of Transport' read now 'Secretary of State for Trade'.

Merchant Shipping Acts 1894 to 1948—read now Merchant Shipping Acts 1894 to 1974.

⚓   ⚓   ⚓   ⚓

Merchant Shipping (Safety Convention) Act 1949

Introductory Note.

This Act, which enabled effect to be given to an International Convention for the Safety of Life at Sea, was signed in London on the 10th day of June, 1948, and came into operation on the 19th November, 1952, by virtue of S.I. 1952, No. 1418, made under section 37. It amended the provisions of the Merchant Shipping Acts, 1894–1948, relating to the construction of passenger steamers, to life-saving appliances, wireless and radio navigation aids, and to other matters affected by the said Convention, and amended the provisions of those Acts relating to fees.

When the operative part of the statutes are ambiguous, recourse should be made to the convention.

Construction and Equipment

Construction rules.

1 (1) The Minister may make rules (in this Act called 'construction rules') prescribing the requirements that the hull, equipments and machinery of British passenger steamers registered in the United Kingdom shall comply with; and the rules shall include such requirements as appear to the Minister to implement the provisions of the Safety Convention prescribing the requirements that the hull, equipments and machinery of passenger steamers shall comply with, except so far as those provisions are implemented by the rules for life-saving appliances, the radio rules, the rules for direction-finders or the collision regulations.

(2) The powers conferred on the Minister by this section shall be in addition to the powers conferred by any other enactment enabling him to prescribe the requirements that passenger steamers shall comply with.

COMMENTS.

For 'Minister' read 'Secretary of State'.

Construction Rules.

See now the Merchant Shipping (Construction) Rules 1965, S.I. 1965, No. 1103. Consult also section 8, Merchant Shipping Act 1964 in respect of passenger steamers, and section 2 of the same Act in respect of Cargo ships. The Merchant Shipping (Smooth and Partially-Smooth Waters) Rules 1977, No. 252, as amended by S.I. 1977, No. 632.

Power to Exempt.

The Secretary of State has power to exempt from rules. Consult section 28.

Passenger Steamers.

See section 26 for definition.

Rules for Life-saving Appliances.

See section 2.

The Radio Rules.

See section 3.

The Rules for Direction Finders.

See section 5.

Collision Regulations.

See section 36.

⚓   ⚓   ⚓   ⚓

2 (1) For section four hundred and twenty-seven of the Merchant Shipping Act, 1894 (in this Act referred to as 'the principal Act'), there shall be substituted the following section:— *(Rules for life-saving appliances.)*

> 427—(1) The Minister of Transport may, in relation to any ships to which this section applies, make rules (in this Act called 'rules for life-saving appliances') with respect to all or any of the following matters, namely:—
>
> (*a*) the arranging of ships into classes, having regard to the services in which they are employed, to the nature and duration of the voyage, and to the number of persons carried;
>
> (*b*) the number, description, and mode of construction of the boats, life-rafts, line-throwing appliances, life-jackets, and lifebuoys to be carried by ships, according to the classes in which the ships are arranged;
>
> (*c*) the equipment to be carried by any such boats and rafts and the methods to be provided to get the boats and other life-saving appliances into the water, including oil for use in stormy weather;
>
> (*d*) the provision in ships of a proper supply of lights inextinguishable in water, and fitted for attachment to lifebuoys;

(e) the quantity, quality and description of buoyant apparatus to be carried on board ships carrying passengers, either in addition to or in substitution for boats, life-rafts, life-jackets and lifebuoys;

(f) the position and means of securing the boats, life-rafts, life-jackets, lifebuoys and buoyant apparatus;

(g) the marking of the boats, life-rafts and buoyant apparatus so as to show their dimensions and the number of persons authorised to be carried on them;

(h) the manning of the lifeboats and the qualifications and certificates of lifeboat men;

(j) the provision to be made for mustering the persons on board, and for embarking them in the boats (including provision for the lighting of, and the means of ingress to and egress from, different parts of the ship);

(k) the provision of suitable means situated outside the engine-room whereby any discharge of water into the boats can be prevented;

(l) the assignment of specific duties to each member of the crew in the event of emergency;

(m) the methods to be adopted and the appliances to be carried in ships for the prevention, detection and extinction of fire;

(n) the practice in ships of boat-drills and fire-drills;

(o) the provision in ships of means of making effective distress signals by day and by night;

(p) the provision, in ships engaged on voyages in which pilots are likely to be embarked, of suitable pilot-ladders, and of ropes, lights and other appliances designed to make the use of such ladders safe, and

(q) the examination at intervals to be prescribed by the rules of any appliances or equipment required by the rules to be carried.

(2) This section applies to—

(a) British ships, except ships registered in a Dominion within the meaning of the Statute of Westminster, 1931, or in India, Pakistan or

Ceylon, or in any territory administered by His Majesty's government in any such Dominion;

(*b*) other ships while they are within any port in the United Kingdom:

Provided that this section shall not apply to a ship by reason of her being within a port in the United Kingdom if she would not have been in any such port but for stress of weather or any other circumstance that neither the master nor the owner nor the charterer (if any) of the ship could have prevented or forestalled'.

(2) The rules for life-saving appliances shall include such requirements as appear to the Minister to implement the provisions of the Safety Convention relating to the matters mentioned in the said section four hundred and twenty-seven.

(3) For subsection (1) of section nine of the Merchant Shipping Act, 1906, there shall be substituted the following subsection:—

'(1) The master of every ship to which section four hundred and twenty-seven of the principal Act applies as being a British ship shall cause to be entered in the official log-book a statement, or if there is no official log-book cause other record to be kept, of every occasion on which boat-drill or fire-drill is practised on board the ship or on which the appliances and equipment required by the rules for life-saving appliances to be carried are examined to see whether they are fit and ready for use and of the result of any such examination; and if—

(*a*) in the case of a passenger steamer, boat-drill or fire-drill is not practised on board the ship in any week;

(*b*) in the case of any other ship, boat-drill or fire-drill is not practised on board the ship in any month;

(*c*) in the case of any ship, the said appliances and equipment are not examined in any such period as is prescribed by the said rules,

the master shall cause a statement to be entered or other

record to be kept as aforesaid of the reasons why the drill
was not practised or the appliances and equipment were
not examined in that week, month or period.'

COMMENTS.

Repeal.

The whole of sub-section 3 underlined, was repealed by the Merchant
Shipping Act 1970, as from the 1st January, 1973, per Merchant Shipping
Act 1970 (Commencement No. 1), Order 1972, S.I. 1972, No. 1977.

For 'Minister' read 'Secretary of State'.

⚓   ⚓   ⚓   ⚓

Section 3

Amendment and Substitution

See section 85, sub-sections 1 and 3, Schedule 1 of the
Merchant Shipping Act 1970, per the Merchant Shipping
Act 1970 (Commencement No. 3) Order 1974, as from
18th November, 1974.

⚓   ⚓   ⚓   ⚓

Radio
surveyors.

4 Wireless-telegraphy surveyors appointed under section
seven hundred and twenty-four of the principal Act as
amended by section eight of the Merchant Shipping (Safety
and Load Line Conventions) Act, 1932, shall be known as
radio surveyors.

⚓   ⚓   ⚓   ⚓

Rules for
direction-
finders.

5 (1) The Minister may make rules (in this Act called
'rules for direction-finders') requiring ships to which this
section applies to be provided with a direction-finder of such a
nature as may be prescribed by the rules.

(2) This section applies to—

    (*a*) British ships registered in the United Kingdom;

    (*b*) other ships while they are within any port in the
        United Kingdom,

being ships of sixteen hundred tons gross tonnage or upwards.

(3) The said rules shall include such requirements as appear
to the Minister to implement the provisions of the Safety
Convention relating to direction-finders.

(4) Without prejudice to the generality of the preceding provisions of this section, rules under this section may provide for the position of the direction-finder in the ship, for the communication between the direction-finder and the bridge, for testing the direction-finder at intervals and as occasion may require and for recording the result of the tests.

(5) If any of the said rules is not complied with in relation to any ship, the owner or master of the ship shall be liable to a fine not exceeding one hundred pounds.

COMMENTS.

Repeal.

The words underlined are repealed, Merchant Shipping Act 1970, section 85, sub-section 2, per the Merchant Shipping Act 1970 (Commencement No. 3) Order 1974, as from the 18th November, 1974. This being effected by the appendix to the Schedule of the same Order, S.I. 1974, No. 1908.

⚓   ⚓   ⚓   ⚓

Section 6

Amendment and Substitution

See section 85, sub-section 1 and 3, Schedule of the Merchant Shipping Act 1970, per the Merchant Shipping Act 1970 (Commencement No. 3) Order 1974, as from the 18th November, 1974.

⚓   ⚓   ⚓   ⚓

Certificates

7 (1) If the Minister, on receipt of declarations of survey in respect of a British passenger steamer registered in the United Kingdom, is satisfied that the steamer complies with the construction rules, rules for life-saving appliances, radio rules and rules for direction-finders applicable to the steamer and to such international voyages as she is to be engaged on, and that she is properly provided with the lights, shapes and means of making fog-signals required by the collision regulations, he shall, on the application of the owner, issue in respect of the steamer a certificate showing that the steamer complies with the requirements of the Safety Convention applicable as aforesaid; and any certificate issued under this subsection is hereafter in this Act referred to as a 'general safety certificate': *Issue for passenger steamers of safety certificates and exemption certificates.*

Provided that if the voyages on which the steamer is to be engaged are short international voyages and she complies only with such of those rules as are applicable to those voyages, the certificate shall show that the steamer complies with the requirements of the Safety Convention applicable to her as a steamer plying on short international voyages; and any such certificate is hereafter in this Act referred to as a 'short-voyage safety certificate'.

(2) If the Minister, on receipt of declarations of survey in respect of any such passenger steamer as aforesaid is satisfied that the steamer is exempt, by virtue of any exercise by him of a power in that behalf conferred on him by this Act or conferred on him by the rules in question, from any of the requirements of the construction rules, rules for life-saving appliances, radio rules or rules for direction-finders applicable to the steamer and to such international voyages as she is to be engaged on, whether short voyages or otherwise, that she complies with the rest of those requirements and that she is properly provided with the lights, shapes and means of making fog-signals required by the collision regulations, he shall, on the application of the owner, issue in respect of the steamer—

(*a*) an exemption certificate stating which of the requirements of the Safety Convention applicable as aforesaid the steamer is exempt from and that the exemption is conditional on the steamer's plying only on the voyages and being engaged only in the trades and complying with the other conditions (if any) specified in the certificate, and

(*b*) a certificate showing that the steamer complies with the rest of those requirements;

and any certificate issued under paragraph (*b*) of this subsection is hereafter in this Act referred to as a 'qualified safety certificate' or a 'qualified short-voyage safety certificate', as the case may be.

COMMENTS.

For 'Minister' read 'Secretary of State for Trade'.

Declaration of Survey; International Voyage.
Short International Voyage; Collision Regulations.

These terms are defined in section 36 q.v.

Passenger Steamer.

For definition, *see* section 26.

Exemptions.

See sections 28 and 29.

Fees.

See now Merchant Shipping (Fees) Regulations 1977, S.I. 1977, No. 2049.

⚓   ⚓   ⚓   ⚓

8 (1) If the Minister, on receipt of declarations of survey in respect of a British ship registered in the United Kingdom, not being a passenger steamer, is satisfied that the ship complies with the rules for life-saving appliances applicable to the ship and to such international voyages as she is to be engaged on, and that she is properly provided with the lights, shapes and means of making fog-signals required by the collision regulations, he shall, on the application of the owner, issue in respect of the ship a certificate showing that the ship complies with such of the requirements of the Safety Convention relating to those matters as are applicable as aforesaid; and any certificate issued under this subsection is hereafter in this Act referred to as a 'safety-equipment certificate'. *Issue for cargo ships of safety-equipment certificates and exemption certificates.*

(2) If the Minister, on the receipt of declarations of survey in respect of any such ship as aforesaid, is satisfied that the ship is exempt, by virtue of any exercise by him of a power in that behalf conferred on him by this Act or conferred on him by the rules for life-saving appliances, from any of the requirements of those rules applicable to the ship and to such international voyages as she is to be engaged on, and that she complies with the rest of those requirements and is properly provided with the lights, shapes and means of making fog-signals required by the collision regulations, he shall, on the application of the owner, issue in respect of the ship—

(*a*) an exemption certificate stating which of the requirements of the Safety Convention, being requirements the subject of the rules for life-saving appliances and applicable as aforesaid, the ship is exempt from and that the exemption is conditional on the ship's plying only on the voyages and complying with the other conditions (if any) specified in the certificate, and

(*b*) a certificate showing that the ship complies with the rest of those requirements;

and any certificate issued under paragraph (*b*) of this subsection is hereafter in this Act referred to as a 'qualified safety-equipment certificate'.

COMMENTS.

For 'Minister' read 'Secretary of State for Trade'.

Declaration of Survey; International Voyage.
Short International Voyage; Collision Regulations.

These terms defined in section 36 q.v.

Passenger Steamer.

For definition *see* section 26.

Exemption(s).

See sections 28 and 29.

Fees.

See now Merchant Shipping (Fees) Regulations 1977, S.I. 1977, No. 2049.

⚓   ⚓   ⚓   ⚓

Issue for cargo ships of radio certificates and exemption certificates.

9 (1) If the Minister, on receipt of declarations of survey in respect of a British ship registered in the United Kingdom not being a passenger steamer, is satisfied that the ship complies with the radio rules and rules for direction-finders applicable to the ship and to such international voyages as she is to be engaged on, he shall, on the application of the owner, issue in respect of the ship a certificate showing that the ship complies with such of the requirements of the Safety Convention relating to radiotelegraphy, radiotelephony and direction-finders as are applicable as aforesaid; and any certificate issued under this subsection is hereafter in this Act referred to as a 'radio certificate'.

(2) If the Minister, on receipt of declarations of survey in respect of any such ship as aforesaid, is satisfied that the ship is exempt, by virtue of any exercise by him of a power in that behalf conferred on him by this Act or conferred on him by the rules in question, from any of the requirements of the radio rules or rules for direction-finders applicable to the ship and to such international voyages as she is to be engaged on, and that she complies with the rest of the requirements of the radio rules and rules for direction-finders, he shall, on the application of the owner, issue in respect of the ship—

(*a*) an exemption certificate stating which of the requirements of the Safety Convention relating to radiotelegraphy, radiotelephony and direction-finders, being requirements applicable as aforesaid, the ship is exempt from and

that the exemption is conditional on the ship's plying only
on the voyages and complying with the other conditions
(if any) specified in the certificate, and

(b) a certificate showing that the ship complies with the rest
of those requirements;

and any certificate issued under paragraph (b) of this sub
section is hereafter in this Act referred to as a 'qualified radio
certificate'.

(3) Where any British ship registered in the United
Kingdom is wholly exempt from the requirements of the radio
rules and the rules for direction-finders, the Minister shall on
the application of the owner issue an exemption certificate
stating that the ship is wholly exempt from the requirements of
the Safety Convention relating to radiotelegraphy, radiotelephony and direction-finders and specifying the voyages on
which, and conditions (if any) on which, the ship is so exempt.

COMMENTS.
For 'Minister' read 'Secretary of State for Trade'.

Declaration of Survey; International Voyages.
These terms defined in section 36 q.v.

Passenger Steamer.
For definition, *see* section 26.

Exemption from Safety Requirements.
See section 28.

Fees.
See now Merchant Shipping (Fees) Regulations 1977, S.I. 1977,
No. 2049.

⚓   ⚓   ⚓   ⚓

10 Where a ship complies with all the requirements of Issue of general safety
the construction rules, rules for life-saving appliances, radio certificates, etc.,
rules or rules for direction-finders applicable to the ship and on partial compliance
to the voyages on which she is to be engaged so far as those with rules.
requirements are requirements of the Safety Convention
applicable as aforesaid, the Minister may issue in respect of
the ship a general safety certificate, short-voyage safety
certificate, safety-equipment certificate or radio certificate, as
the case may be, notwithstanding that she is exempt from, or
for some other reason does not comply with, any require-

H

ments of those rules that are not applicable requirements of the Safety Convention.

COMMENTS.

Definitions of Terms in this Section.

Consult generally, sections 1, 2, 3, 5, 7, 8 and 9.

For 'Minister' read 'Secretary of State for Trade'.

⚓ ⚓ ⚓ ⚓

Notice of
alterations and
additional
surveys.

11 (1) The owner or master of a passenger steamer in respect of which any passenger steamer's certificate issued under the principal Act, or any certificate issued under this Act, is in force shall, as soon as possible after any alteration is made in the steamer's hull, equipments or machinery affecting the efficiency thereof or the seaworthiness of the steamer, give written notice to the Minister containing full particulars of the alteration.

(2) The owner or master of a ship in respect of which any certificate issued under this Act is in force, other than a passenger steamer, shall, as soon as possible after any alteration is made in the appliances or equipments required by the rules for life-saving appliances, the radio rules, the rules for direction-finders or the collision regulations to be carried by the ship, being an alteration affecting the efficiency or completeness of those appliances or equipments, give written notice to the Minister containing full particulars of the alteration.

(3) If notice of any alteration is not given as required by this section, the owner or master of the ship shall be liable to a fine not exceeding fifty pounds.

(4) If the Minister has reason to believe that since the making of the last declaration of survey in respect of any such ship as aforesaid—

(a) any such alteration has been made as is mentioned in subsection (1) or, as the case may be, in subsection (2) of this section; or

(b) the hull, equipments or machinery of the ship (being a passenger steamer) have sustained any injury or are otherwise insufficient; or

(c) the appliances or equipments of the ship (not being a passenger steamer) mentioned in subsection (2) of this

section have sustained any injury or are otherwise insufficient;

the Minister may, without prejudice to his powers under
section two hundred and seventy-nine of the principal Act
(which relates to the cancellation of certificates and additional
surveys), require the ship to be again surveyed to such extent
as he thinks fit, and, if such requirement is not complied with,
may cancel any passenger steamer's certificate issued in respect
of the ship under the principal Act or any certificate issued in
respect of the ship under this Act.

(5) For the purpose of this section the expression 'alteration' in relation to anything includes the renewal of any part
of it.

COMMENTS.

For 'Minister' read 'Secretary of State for Trade'.

Passenger Steamer.

For definition, *see* section 26.

Issue of Safety Certificates and Exemption Certificates.

For passenger steamers, *see* section 7.

For ships other than passenger steamers, *see* sections 8 and 9.

General.

Consult Merchant Shipping Act 1964, section 4, sub-sections 1 and 2,
for modification and/or extension of sub-sections 1, 2 and 4 of this
section.

⚓   ⚓   ⚓   ⚓

12 (1) No British ship registered in the United Kingdom
shall proceed to sea on an international voyage from a port in
the United Kingdom unless there is in force in respect of the
ship—

Prohibition on proceedings to sea without appropriate certificates.

(*a*) if she is a passenger steamer, a general safety certificate,
a short-voyage safety certificate, a qualified safety certificate or a qualified short-voyage safety certificate which
(subject to the provisions of this section relating to short-
voyage safety certificates) is applicable to the voyage on
which the ship is about to proceed and to the trade in
which she is for the time being engaged;

(*b*) if she is not a passenger steamer, both—

(i) a safety-equipment certificate or a qualified safety-
equipment certificate, and

(ii) a radio certificate or a qualified radio certificate, or an exemption certificate stating that she is wholly exempt from the requirements of the Safety Convention relating to radiotelegraphy, radiotelephony and direction-finders:

Provided that this subsection shall not prohibit a ship, not being a passenger steamer, from proceeding to sea as aforesaid if there is in force in respect of the ship such certificate or certificates as would be required if she were a passenger steamer.

(2) For the purposes of this section, a qualified certificate shall not be deemed to be in force in respect of a ship unless there is also in force in respect of the ship the corresponding exemption certificate; and an exemption certificate shall be of no effect unless it is by its terms applicable to the voyage on which the ship is about to proceed.

(3) If any ship proceeds, or attempts to proceed, to sea in contravention of this section—

(a) in the case of a passenger steamer, the owner or master of the steamer shall, without prejudice to any other, remedy or penalty under the Merchant Shipping Acts, be liable on summary conviction to a fine not exceeding ten pounds for every passenger carried on board the steamer, and the owner or master of any tender by means of which passengers have been taken on board the steamer shall be liable on summary conviction to a like fine for every passenger so taken on board; and

(b) in the case of a ship not being a passenger steamer, the owner or master of the ship shall be liable to a fine not exceeding one hundred pounds.

(4) The master of every British ship registered in the United Kingdom shall produce to the officer of customs from whom a clearance for the ship is demanded for an international voyage the certificate or certificates required by the foregoing provisions of this section to be in force when the ship proceeds to sea; and a clearance shall not be granted, and the ship may be detained, until the said certificate or certificates are so produced.

(5) Where the Minister permits any passenger steamer in respect of which there is in force a short-voyage safety certificate, whether qualified or not, to proceed to sea on an inter-

national voyage from a port in the United Kingdom not exceeding twelve hundred nautical miles in length between the last port of call in the United Kingdom and the final port of destination, the certificate shall for the purposes of this section be deemed to be applicable to the voyage on which the steamer is about to proceed notwithstanding that the voyage exceeds six hundred nautical miles between the said ports.

(6) Where an exemption certificate issued in respect of any British ship registered in the United Kingdom specifies any conditions on which the certificate is issued and any of those conditions is not complied with, the owner or master of the ship shall be liable to a fine not exceeding one hundred pounds.

COMMENTS.

Prohibition on Proceeding to Sea without Appropriate Certificate.

Consult section 39, which lists ships exempted from this prohibition.

Exemption of H.M. Ships.

Consult section 741 of Merchant Shipping Act 1894.

Other Penalty.

See Merchant Shipping Act 1894, section 430.

Fine.

See Merchant Shipping (Load Lines) Act 1967, section 25, Schedule 1, where the old penalty of a fine not exceeding £10 for each passenger carried, has been increased, irrespective of the number of passengers on summary conviction to a fine not exceeding £400 and, on indictment, a fine.

A Ship may be Detained.

Consult Merchant Shipping Act 1894, section 459 *et seq.*, and section 892. Also section 35, sub-section 2 of this Act, and section 9, Merchant Shipping (Load Lines) Act 1967.

For 'Minister' read 'Secretary of State for Trade'.

⚓   ⚓   ⚓   ⚓

13 (1) Subsections (3) to (5) of section two hundred and seventy-two of the principal Act (which prescribe the contents of declarations of survey) shall cease to have effect.

Miscellaneous provisions as to surveys and certificates.

(2) Subsection (2) of section two hundred and seventy-two of the principal Act (which requires a surveyor to deliver declarations of survey to the owner of a ship), section two

hundred and seventy-three of that Act (which requires the owner to deliver the declaration to the Minister) and section two hundred and seventy-five of that Act (which relates to appeals to the court of survey) shall apply to surveys for the purpose of the issue of any certificate in respect of a ship under this Act as they apply to surveys for the purpose of the issue of passenger steamers' certificates.

(3) A safety certificate or radio certificate or an exemption certificate stating that a ship is wholly exempt from the provisions of the Safety Convention relating to radiotelegraphy, radiotelephony and direction-finders shall be in force for one year, and a safety-equipment certificate shall be in force for twenty-four months, from the date of its issue, or for such shorter period as may be specified in the certificate:

Provided that no such certificate shall remain in force after notice is given by the Minister to the owner or master of the ship in respect of which it has been issued that the Minister has cancelled the certificate.

(4) An exemption certificate, other than a certificate stating that a ship is wholly exempt from the provisions of the Safety Convention relating to radiotelegraphy, radiotelephony and direction-finders, shall be in force for the same period as the corresponding qualified certificate.

(5) The Minister or any person authorised by him for the purpose may grant an extension of any certificate issued under this Act in respect of a British ship registered in the United Kingdom for a period not exceeding one month from the date when the certificate would, but for the extension, have expired, or, if the ship is absent from the United Kingdom on that date, for a period not exceeding five months from that date.

(6) Any general safety certificate or short-voyage safety certificate, whether qualified or not, may be combined in one document with a passenger steamer's certificate.

(7) Any certificate issued by the Minister under this Act, and any passenger steamer's certificate, whether or not combined in one document with a safety certificate under the last preceding subsection, shall be admissible in evidence.

(8) The following provisions of the principal Act shall apply to and in relation to certificates issued by the Minister, and ships certified, under this Act in the same manner as they apply to and in relation to passenger steamers' certificates and

passenger steamers, namely, section two hundred and seventy-six (which relates to the transmission of a certificate to the owner of the steamer), section two hundred and seventy-nine (which relates to the cancellation of certificates), section two hundred and eighty (which relates to the surrender of certif-icates no longer in force), section two hundred and eight-one (which relates to the posting up of a certificate on board) and section two hundred and eighty-two (which relates to the forging and falsification of certificates).

(9) The Minister may request the government of a country to which the Safety Convention applies to issue in respect of a British ship registered in the United Kingdom any certificate the issue of which is authorised under this Act; and a certif-icate issued in pursuance of such a request and containing a statement that it has been so issued shall have effect for the purposes of this Act as if it had been issued by the Minister and not by the government of that country.

COMMENTS.

Repeal.

Sub-section 1 repealed as spent, Statute Law Revision Act 1953. For 'Minister' read 'Secretary of State for Trade'.

Renewal of Radio Certificates.

Consult Merchant Shipping Act 1964, section 12.

Extension of Certificate.

See also Merchant Shipping Act 1964, section 3, sub-section 5.

Issue of Exemption Certificates by Convention Country.

See Merchant Shipping Act 1964, section 13.

Safety Equipment Certificate.

See section 8 of this Act.

Provisions of the Principal Act.

With the exception of section 276, the provisions of this sub-section are applied by Merchant Shipping Act 1964, section 3, sub-section 6.

⚓   ⚓   ⚓   ⚓

Safety Convention Ships not registered in the United Kingdom

14 (1) The Minister may, at the request of the govern-ment of a country to which the Safety Convention applies, issue in respect of a ship registered in that country any certificate the issue of which in respect of British ships regis-tered in the United Kingdom is authorised under the preceding provisions of this Act if he is satisfied that it is proper for him

Certificates of Convention ships not registered in United Kingdom.

to do so; and a certificate issued in pursuance of such a request and containing a statement that it has been so issued shall have effect for the purposes of this Act as if it had been issued by the said government and not by the Minister.

(2) The Minister shall make such regulations as appear to him to be necessary for the purpose of securing that certificates issued in accordance with the Safety Convention by the government of any country other than the United Kingdom in respect of Safety Convention ships not registered in the United Kingdom or having effect under the preceding subsection as is so issued, shall be accepted as having the same force as corresponding certificates issued by the Minister under this Act; and any certificate required by those regulations to be so treated is in this Act referred to as an 'accepted Safety Convention certificate.'

(3) A surveyor of ships, for the purpose of verifying—

(a) that there is in force in respect of a Safety Convention ship not registered in the United Kingdom an accepted Safety Convention certificate; or

(b) that the condition of the hull, equipments and machinery of any such Safety Convention ship corresponds substantially with the particulars shown in such a certificate; or,

(c) except where such a certificate states that the ship is wholly exempt from the provisions of the Safety Convention relating to radiotelegraphy and radiotelephony, that the number, grades and qualifications of radio officers or operators on board correspond with those shown in the certificate; or

(d) that any conditions on which such a certificate, being the equivalent of an exemption certificate, is issued are complied with,

shall have all the powers of a Ministry of Transport inspector under the Merchant Shipping Acts.

(4) Where there is attached to an accepted Safety Convention certificate in respect of a Safety Convention passenger steamer not registered in the United Kingdom a memorandum which—

(a) has been issued by or under the authority of the government of the country in which the steamer is registered; and

(b) modifies for the purpose of any particular voyage in view of the number of persons carried on that voyage, the particulars stated in the certificate with respect to life-saving appliances,

the certificate shall have effect for the purpose of that voyage as if it were modified in accordance with the memorandum.

COMMENTS.

Repeal.

The words underlined in sub-section 1 repealed by Merchant Shipping Act 1964, section 18, sub-section 4.

For 'Minister' read 'Secretary of State for Trade'.

For 'Ministry of Transport Inspector' read 'Department of Trade Inspector'.

Countries to which the Safety Convention Applies.

See section 31, and comments thereto.

Exemption Certificates (issue of).
British Ships and Passenger Steamers Registered in the U.K.

Consult sections 7, sub-section 2, and Section 8, sub-section 2, section 9, sub-section 2 and 3.

⚓   ⚓   ⚓   ⚓

15 (1) Where an accepted Safety Convention certificate is produced in respect of a Safety Convention passenger steamer not registered in the United Kingdom— *Modified survey of passenger steamers holding Convention certificates.*

(a) the steamer shall not be required to be surveyed under the Merchant Shipping Acts by a surveyor of ships except for the purpose of determining the number of passengers that she is fit to carry;

(b) on receipt of any declaration of survey for the purpose aforesaid, the Minister shall issue a certificate under section two hundred and seventy-four of the principal Act containing only a statement of the particulars set out in paragraph (b) of that section (which relates to the said number of passengers); and a certificate so issued shall have effect as a passenger steamer's certificate.

(2) Where there is produced in respect of any such passenger steamer as aforesaid an accepted Safety Convention certificate, and also a certificate issued by or under the authority of the government of the country in which the

steamer is registered showing the number of passengers that the steamer is fit to carry, and the Minister is satisfied that that number has been determined substantially in the same manner as in the case of a British passenger steamer registered in the United Kingdom, he may if he thinks fit dispense with any survey of the steamer for the purpose of determining the number of passengers that she is fit to carry and direct that the last-mentioned certificate shall have effect as a passenger steamer's certificate.

COMMENTS.

Accepted Safety Convention Certificate.

See sections 14 and 36.

For 'Minister' read 'Secretary of State for Trade'.

Appointment of Surveyors.

See section 724 of Merchant Shipping Act 1894.

Declaration of Surveys.

See Merchant Shipping Act 1894, section 272 and section 36 of this Act.

⚓   ⚓   ⚓   ⚓

Miscellaneous privileges of ships holding Convention certificates.

16 (1) Where an accepted Safety Convention certificate is produced in respect of a Safety Convention passenger steamer not registered in the United Kingdom, the steamer shall be exempt from paragraphs (*d*) and (*f*) of subsection(1) of section two hundred and ninety of the principal Act (which relate to the equipments of emigrant ships) and section four hundred and twenty of that Act (which relates to lights and fog-signals) and from the rules for life-saving appliances.

(2) Where an accepted Safety Convention certificate, being the equivalent of a safety-equipment certificate, is produced in respect of a Safety Convention ship (other than a passenger steamer) not registered in the United Kingdom, the ship shall be exempt from section four hundred and twenty of the principal Act (which relates to lights and fog-signals) and from the rules for life-saving appliances.

(3) Where an accepted Safety Convention certificate is produced in respect of a Safety Convention ship not registered in the United Kingdom, and the certificate shows that the ship complies with the requirements of the Safety Convention relating to radiotelegraphy, radiotelephony and direction-finders, or that she is exempt from some of those requirements

and complies with the rest, or that she is wholly exempt from those requirements, the ship shall be exempt from the provisions of the radio rules and the rules for direction-finders.

COMMENTS.

Section 290 of the Merchant Shipping Act 1894.

Repealed Merchant Shipping Act 1970, section 100, sub-section 3, Schedule 5, per the Merchant Shipping Act 1970 (Commencement No. 1) Order 1972 as from 1st January, 1973, S.I. 1972, No. 1977.

Accepted Safety Convention Certificate.

See sections 14 and 36 of this Act.

Rules for Life-saving Appliances.

See section 2.

Radio Rules.

See section 3.

Rules for Direction Finders.

See section 5.

⚓   ⚓   ⚓   ⚓

17 (1) The master of every Safety Convention ship not registered in the United Kingdom shall produce to the officer of customs from whom a clearance for the ship is demanded in respect of an international voyage from a port in the United Kingdom accepted Safety Convention certificates that are the equivalent of the certificates issued by the Minister under this Act that would be required to be in force in respect of the ship if she were a British ship so registered; and a clearance shall not be granted, and the ship may be detained, until such certificates are so produced. *Further provisions as to the production of Convention certificates.*

(2) The production of an accepted Safety Convention certificate being the equivalent of—

(*a*) a qualified certificate, or

(*b*) an exemption certificate, other than a certificate stating that a ship is wholly exempt from the provisions of the Safety Convention relating to radiotelegraphy, radiotelephony and direction-finders,

shall not avail for the purposes of either of the last two preceding sections unless there is also produced the corresponding exemption certificate or qualified certificate as the case may be.

COMMENTS.

For 'Minister' read 'Secretary of State for Trade'.

Qualified and Exemption Certificates.

See sections 7, sub-section 2, section 8, sub-section 2, section 8, sub-sections 2 and 3.

⚓   ⚓   ⚓   ⚓

Section 18

Repealed

Merchant Shipping (Load Lines) Act 1967, section 33, sub-section 1, and Schedule 2. Sub-section 5 also repealed per the Merchant Shipping Act 1970 (Commencement No. 1) Order 1972, S.I. 1972, No. 1977.

⚓   ⚓   ⚓   ⚓

Openings in passenger steamers' hulls and watertight bulkheads.

19 (1) The Minister may in relation to British passenger steamers registered in the United Kingdom make rules for any of the following matters—

(*a*) for closing and keeping closed the openings in steamers' hulls and in watertight bulkheads;

(*b*) for securing, keeping in place and inspecting contrivances for closing any such openings as aforesaid;

(*c*) for operating the mechanisms of contrivances for closing any such openings as aforesaid and for drills in connection with the operation thereof;

(*d*) for requiring entry to be made in the official log-book or other record to be kept of any of the matters aforesaid.

(2) If any of the said rules is not complied with in relation to any such steamer as aforesaid, the master of the steamer shall be liable to a fine not exceeding one hundred pounds.

COMMENTS.

Repeal.

The words underlined—sub-section 1(*d*) repealed Merchant Shipping Act 1970, section 100, sub-section 3, Schedule 5, per the Merchant Shipping Act 1970 (Commencement No. 1) Order 1972, S.I. 1972, No. 1977, as from 1st January, 1973.

General.

See section 29 for certain classes of vessels which are exempt from any provision invoking a penalty for the contravention of any rules relating to openings in steamers' hulls and watertight bulkheads.

For 'Minister' read 'Secretary of State for Trade'.

⚓   ⚓   ⚓   ⚓

Section 20

Repealed

Merchant Shipping (Load Lines) Act 1967, section 33 sub-section 1, Schedule 2

⚓   ⚓   ⚓   ⚓

21 (1) His Majesty in Council may prescribe what Signals of distress. signals shall be used by ships as signals of distress.

(2) Rules may be made by the Minister prescribing the circumstances in which, and the purposes for which, any signal prescribed by Order in Council under the last preceding subsection is to be used and the circumstances in which it is to be revoked.

(3) If the master of a ship uses or displays or causes or permits any person under his authority to use or display—

(*a*) any signal prescribed by Order in Council under this section except in the circumstances and for the purposes prescribed by the rules made under this section; or

(*b*) any private signal, whether registered or not, that is liable to be mistaken for any signal so prescribed by Order in Council.

he shall be liable to a fine not exceeding fifty pounds and shall further be liable to pay compensation for any labour undertaken, risk incurred or loss sustained in consequence of the signal's having been supposed to be a signal of distress; and that compensation may, without prejudice to any other remedy, be recovered in the same manner as salvage.

(4) Nothing in subsection (4) of section twenty-four of the Merchant Shipping (Safety and Load Line Conventions) Act, 1932 (which requires persons in charge of wireless stations to give facilities for the reception of reports relating to dangers to navigation), shall interfere with the transmission of signals prescribed under this section.

COMMENTS.

General—Signals of Distress.

This section substituted the relevant section of the Merchant Shipping (Safety and Load Lines Convention) Act of 1932, which was repealed. Section 37, sub-section 5 and Third Schedule of this Act, now repealed as spent by the Statute Law Revision Act 1953. Signals of Distress are prescribed under this section by the Merchant Shipping Collision Regulations and Distress Signals Order 1977, S.I. 1977, No. 982 and in respect of Hovercraft by the Hovercraft (Application of Enactments) (Amendment) Order 1977. The circumstances in which the signals of distress prescribed in S.I. 1977, No. 982, are to be used are contained in The Merchant Shipping (Signals of Distress) Rules 1977, S.I. 1977, No. 1010. S.I. 1977, No. 982 has been subsequently amended by the Collision Regulations and Distress Signals (Amendment) Order 1977, No. 1301.

For 'Minister' now read 'Secretary of State for Trade'.

Registration of Private Signals.

Consult Merchant Shipping Act 1894, section 733.

Misuse of Distress Signals.

Section 434 of the principal Act, which dealt with signals of distress was repealed, modified, and extended by section 25 of the Merchant Shipping (Safety and Load Lines Convention) Act 1932, which in turn was repealed by the Merchant Shipping (Safety Convention) Act 1949 and re-enacted by section 21 of that Act.

It was held that the sub-section of the principal Act did not by implication give any right to compensation for labour undertaken, risk incurred or loss sustained in going out in response to signals properly displayed, although on arrival, the proferred services were not required, *The Elswick Park*, 1904. It is submitted that this decision is applicable to this present section.

⚓   ⚓   ⚓   ⚓

Obligation to assist vessels, etc., in distress.
22 (1) The master of a British ship registered in the United Kingdom, on receiving at sea a signal of distress or information from any source that a vessel or aircraft is in distress, shall proceed with all speed to the assistance of the persons in distress (informing them if possible that he is doing so) unless he is unable, or in the special circumstances of the case considers it unreasonable or unnecessary, to do so, or unless he is released under the provisions of subsection (3) or subsection (4) of this section.

(2) Where the master of any ship in distress has re-

quisitioned any British ship registered in the United Kingdom that has answered his call, it shall be the duty of the master of the requisitioned ship to comply with the requisition by continuing to proceed with all speed to the assistance of the persons in distress.

(3) A master shall be released from the obligation imposed by subsection (1) of this section as soon as he is informed of the requisition of one or more ships other than his own and that the requisition is being complied with by the ship or ships requisitioned.

(4) A master shall be released from the obligation imposed by subsection (1) of this section, and, if his ship has been requisitioned, from the obligation imposed by subsection (2) of this section, if he is informed by the persons in distress, or by the master of any ship that has reached the persons in distress, that assistance is no longer required.

(5) If a master fails to comply with the preceding provisions of this section, he shall be guilty of a misdemeanour.

(6) If the master of a British ship registered in the United Kingdom, on receiving at sea a signal of distress or information from any source that a vessel or aircraft is in distress, is unable, or in the special circumstances of the case considers it unreasonable or unnecessary, to go to the assistance of the persons in distress, he shall forthwith cause a statement to be entered in the official log-book, or if there is no official log-book cause other record to be kept, of his reasons for not going to the assistance of those persons, and if he fails to do so he shall be liable to a fine not exceeding one hundred pounds.

(7) The master of every British ship registered in the United Kingdom for which an official log is required shall enter ro cause to be entered in the official log-book every signal of distress or message that a vessel, aircraft or person is in distress at sea.

(8) Nothing in this section shall affect the provisions of section six of the Maritime Conventions Act, 1911; and compliance by the master of a ship with the provisions of this section shall not affect his right, or the right of any other person, to salvage.

COMMENTS.

Repeal.

The words underlined, i.e. sub-sections 5 and 6, repealed. Merchant Shipping Act 1970, section 100, sub-section 3 and Schedule 5, per the Merchant Shipping Act 1970 (Commencement No. 1) Order 1972, S.I. 1972, No. 1977.

⚓   ⚓   ⚓   ⚓

Carriage of
dangerous
goods.

23 (1) The Minister may make rules for regulating in the interests of safety the carriage of dangerous goods in ships to which this section applies.

(2) This section applies to—

(*a*) British ships registered in the United Kingdom;

(*b*) other ships while they are within any port in the United Kingdom, or are embarking or disembarking passengers within the territorial waters of the United Kingdom, or are loading or discharging cargo or fuel within those waters.

(3) If any of the rules made in pursuance of this section is not complied with in relation to any ship, the owner or master of the ship shall be liable on conviction on indictment to a fine not exceeding three hundred pounds, or on summary conviction to a fine not exceeding one hundred pounds, and the ship shall be deemed for the purposes of Part V of the principal Act to be unsafe by reason of improper loading.

(4) Any goods declared by the rules made under this section to be dangerous in their nature shall be deemed to be dangerous goods for the purposes of Part V of the principal Act.

COMMENTS.

For 'Minister' read 'Secretary of State for Trade'.

Rules Under this Section.

Consult Merchant Shipping (Dangerous Goods) Rules 1965, S.I. 1965, No. 1067, as amended by Merchant Shipping (Dangerous Goods) Rules 1968, S.I. 1968, No. 332 and Merchant Shipping (Dangerous Goods) Rules 1972, S.I. 1972, No. 666.

Part V of the Principal Act.

I.e. sections 446 to 450 (inc.) of the Principal Act.

⚓   ⚓   ⚓   ⚓

24 (1) Where grain is loaded on board any British ship registered in the United Kingdom, or is loaded within any port in the United Kingdom on board any ship, all necessary and reasonable precautions shall be taken to prevent the grain from shifting; and if such precautions as aforesaid are not taken, the owner or the master of the ship, or any agent of the owner who was charged with the loading or with sending the ship to sea laden with the grain, shall be guilty of an offence under this subsection, and the ship shall be deemed for the purposes of Part V of the principal Act to be unsafe by reason of improper loading.

(2) Where any ship, having been loaded with grain outside the United Kingdom without the taking of all necessary and reasonable precautions to prevent the grain from shifting, enters any port in the United Kingdom so laden, the owner or master of the ship shall be guilty of an offence under this subsection, and the ship shall be deemed for the purposes of Part V of the principal Act to be unsafe by reason of improper loading:

Provided that this subsection shall not have effect if the ship would not have entered any such port but for stress of weather or any other circumstance that neither the master nor the owner nor the charterer (if any) could have prevented or forestalled.

(3) Without prejudice to the generality of the two preceding subsections, any particular precaution prescribed by rules made by the Minister under this subsection, in relation to the loading of ships generally or of ships of any class, as being a precaution to be treated for the purposes of those subsections as a necessary or reasonable precaution to prevent grain from shifting, shall be so treated in the case of ships generally, or of ships of that class, as the case may be:

Provided that this subsection shall not apply where a ship is loaded in accordance in all respects with any provisions approved by the Minister as respects the loading in question other than rules made under this subsection.

(4) If any person commits an offence under subsection (1) or subsection (2) of this section he shall be liable on conviction on indictment to a fine not exceeding three hundred pounds, or on summary conviction to a fine not exceeding one hundred pounds.

(5) On the arrival at a port in the United Kingdom from a port outside the United Kingdom of any ship carrying a cargo of grain, the master shall cause to be delivered to the proper officer of Customs in the United Kingdom, together with the report required by the Customs Consolidation Act, 1876, a notice stating—

(*a*) the draught of water and freeboard, as defined by Part V of the principal Act, of the said ship after the loading of her cargo was completed at the final port of loading; and

(*b*) the following particulars of the grain carried, namely,

    (i) the kind of grain and the quantity thereof, stated in cubic feet, quarters, bushels, or tons weight;

    (ii) the mode in which the grain is stowed, and

    (iii) the precautions taken to prevent the grain from shifting;

and if the master fails to deliver any notice required by this subsection, or if in any such notice he makes any statement that he knows to be false in a material particular or recklessly makes any statement that is false in a material particular, he shall be liable to a fine not exceeding one hundred pounds.

(6) Any person having a general or special authority in that behalf from the Minister may, for securing the observance of the provisions of this section, inspect any grain, and the mode in which it is stowed, and for that purpose shall have all the powers of a Ministry of Transport inspector under the principal Act.

(7) In this section the expression 'grain' includes wheat, maize, oats, rye, barley, rice, pulses and seeds, and the expression 'ship carrying a cargo of grain' means a ship carrying a quantity of grain exceeding one-third of the ship's registered tonnage, reckoning one hundred cubic feet, or two tons weight, of grain as equivalent to one ton of registered tonnage.

COMMENTS.

For 'Minister' now read 'Secretary of State for Trade'.

Necessary or Reasonable Precautions.

See The Standale 1938, where Langton, J. regarded the regulations as laid down in the Merchant Shipping Act 1894, Schedule 18, (since repealed) as showing the standard which 'reasonable people have considered to be the proper precautions'.

Rules Relating to the Carrying of Grain.

Consult Merchant Shipping (Grain) Rules 1965, S.I. 1965, No. 1062.

⚓   ⚓   ⚓   ⚓

25 Any sums required for the contribution from the United Kingdom towards maintaining, in accordance with the Safety Convention, a service in the North Atlantic for the study and observation of ice, and for ice patrol, shall be paid by the Minister out of moneys provided by Parliament.

COMMENTS.

For 'Minister' now read 'Secretary of State for Trade'.

⚓   ⚓   ⚓   ⚓

Supplemental

26 (1) In Part III of the principal Act, in the Merchant Shipping (Safety and Load Line Conventions) Act, 1932, and in this Act the expression 'passenger' means any person carried in a ship, except— Definition of 'passenger' and 'passenger steamer'.

(*a*) a person employed or engaged in any capacity on board the ship on the business of the ship,

(*b*) a person on board the ship either in pursuance of the obligation laid upon the master to carry shipwrecked, distressed or other persons, or by reason of any circumstance that neither the master nor the owner nor the charterer (if any) could have prevented or forestalled, and

(*c*) a child under one year of age.

(2) In the Merchant Shipping (Safety and Load Line Conventions) Act, 1932, and in this Act, the expression 'passenger steamer' means a steamer carrying more than twelve passengers.

COMMENTS.

Passenger; Passenger Steamer.

This section extends the definition of 'Passenger' to the Merchant Shipping Act 1894 and that of 'passenger steamer' to the Merchant Shipping (Safety and Load Lines Conventions) Act 1932. It does not affect the definition of 'passenger steamer' in Part 3 of the Merchant Shipping Act 1894 as amended by the Merchant Shipping Act 1906. As a result of this section, passengers as defined in section 267 of the principal Act, section 33 of the Merchant Shipping (Safety and Load Line Conventions) Act 1932, which amended section 267 of the principal Act, as well as the definitions of 'passenger' and 'passenger steamer' as contained in section 73, sub-section 1 of the Merchant Shipping (Safety and Load Line Conventions) Act 1932, were repealed by section 37, sub-section 5 and Third Schedule of this Act.

Sub-section 2, above, defines 'passenger steamer' as a steamer carrying more than twelve passengers. This is in contrast to the definition in section 267 of the Merchant Shipping Act 1894, viz.: 'a steamer carrying passengers in less number than twelve, brings the steamer within the definition of a 'passenger steamer'.

⚓   ⚓   ⚓   ⚓

Removing persons in case of danger.

27 Where the Minister for the purpose of enabling persons to be moved from any place in consequence of a threat to their lives has permitted more persons to be carried on board a ship than are permitted under the Merchant Shipping Acts apart from this section, the carriage of that excess of persons shall not be an offence under those Acts.

⚓   ⚓   ⚓   ⚓

COMMENTS.

For 'Minister' now read 'Secretary of State for Trade'.

⚓   ⚓   ⚓   ⚓

Power of Minister to exempt from safety requirements.

28 (1) The Minister may exempt any ships or classes of ships from any requirements of the rules for life-saving appliances or any rules or regulations made under this Act, either absolutely or subject to such conditions as he thinks fit.

(2) Without prejudice to the preceding provisions of this section, where a ship not normally engaged on international voyages is required to undertake a single international voyage, the Minister may, if he is of opinion that the ship complies with safety requirements that are adequate for that voyage, exempt the ship from any of the safety requirements imposed by or under the Merchant Shipping Acts.

COMMENTS.

For 'Minister' read 'Secretary of State for Trade'.

International Voyage.

Defined in section 36.

⚓   ⚓   ⚓   ⚓

29   (1) Nothing in this Act—

(*a*) prohibiting or preventing a ship from proceeding to sea
unless there are in force in relation to the ship, or are
produced, the appropriate certificates issued by the
Minister under this Act or the appropriate accepted
Safety Convention certificates;

(*b*) conferring powers on a surveyor of ships for the purpose
of verifying the existence, validity or correctness of any
Safety Convention certificate or that the conditions on
which any such certificate was issued are complied with;

(*c*) requiring information about a ship's stability to be
carried on board;

(*d*) imposing a penalty for the contravention of any rules
relating to openings in ships' hulls and watertight bulkheads,

shall, unless in the case of information about a ship's stability
the Minister otherwise orders, apply to any troopship, pleasure
yacht or fishing vessel, or to any ship of less than five hundred
tons gross tonnage other than a passenger steamer or to any
ship not propelled by mechanical means.

(2) Nothing in the preceding subsection shall affect the
exemption conferred by section seven hundred and forty-one
of the principal Act on ships belonging to His Majesty.

(3) Notwithstanding that any provision of this Act is
expressed to apply to ships not registered in the United
Kingdom while they are within any port in the United
Kingdom, that provision shall not apply to a ship that would
not be within any such port but for stress of weather or any
other circumstance that neither the master nor the owner, nor
the charterer (if any) of the ship could have prevented or
forestalled.

COMMENTS.

Repeal.

The words underlined, paragraph (*c*) in sub-section 1 and the words
'unless in the case of' to 'Minister otherwise orders' repealed.   Merchant
Shipping (Load Lines) Act 1967, section 33, sub-section 1, and Schedule 2.

For 'Minister' read 'Secretary of State for Trade'.

Troopships.

There is no definition in respect of this term, but it is submitted that whether a ship is a 'Troopship' within the meaning of this section, is a matter of fact, and need not be habitually engaged in the carriage of troops.

Passenger Steamer.

See section 26.

⚓   ⚓   ⚓   ⚓

Application to colonies etc.

30 Section thirty-six of the Merchant Shipping (Safety and Load Line Conventions) Act 1932 (which enables Orders in Council to be made applying Part I of that Act to territories outside the United Kingdom), shall have effect as if references therein to Part I of that Act included references to this Act.

⚓   ⚓   ⚓   ⚓

Countries to which Safety Convention applies.

31 His Majesty, if satisfied—

(*a*) that the government of any country has accepted, or denounced, the Safety Convention; or

(*b*) that the Safety Convention extends, or has ceased to extend, to any territory,

may by Order in Council make a declaration to that effect.

COMMENTS.

The countries which have accepted the International Convention, for the Safety of Life at Sea signed in London on the 17th June, 1960, are contained in the Merchant Shipping (Safety Convention) (Various Countries) Order 1977, S.I. 1977, No. 1876.

This section should be read as if for the reference to the Safety Convention there is substituted a reference to the 1960 Convention.

⚓   ⚓   ⚓   ⚓

Transitional provisions.

32 Without prejudice to the effect of section thirty-eight of the Interpretation Act, 1889, the provisions of the First Schedule to this Act shall have effect for the purpose of the transition from the law in force before the commencement of this Act to the provisions of this Act.

COMMENTS.

This Act came into force on the 19th November, 1952, per Merchant Shipping (Safety Convention) Act 1949 (Commencement) Order 1952, S.I. 1952, No. 1418.

⚓   ⚓   ⚓   ⚓

33 (1) There shall be paid in respect of any certificate Provision as to certain fees and fines under the Merchant Shipping Acts. issued by the Minister under this Act, including a certificate issued by him under subsection (1) of section fourteen of this Act, and in respect of any inspection of a ship under this Act for the purpose of seeing that she is properly provided with a radio installation and radio officers or operators in conformity with the radio rules, such fees as may be prescribed by regulations made by the Minister with the approval of the Treasury.

(2) The Minister with the approval of the Treasury may make regulations prescribing the amount or the maximum amount of the fees payable under the enactments specified in the Second Schedule to this Act; and so much of those enactments as fixes the amount or the maximum amount of any such fees shall cease to have effect.

(3) Any fees payable under subsection (1) of this section shall be paid into the Exchequer.

(4) Subsection (2) of section seven hundred and sixteen of the principal Act (which provides for the application of fines) shall apply to fines under this Act as it applies to fines under that Act.

COMMENTS.
For 'Minister' read 'Secretary of State for Trade'.

Fees—Regulations.
See the Merchant Shipping (Fees) Regulations 1977, S.I. 1977, No. 2049.

Certificates Issued Under this Act.
Consult sections 7–13 of this Act.

⚓   ⚓   ⚓   ⚓

34 (1) The power to make rules and regulations under Rules and regulations. the preceding provisions of this Act or the First Schedule to this Act, or to make rules for lifesaving appliances, shall be exercisable by statutory instrument.

(2) Any statutory instrument by which any such power as aforesaid is exercised shall be subject to annulment in pursuance of a resolution of either House of Parliament.

COMMENTS.

Repeal.

The words underlined in this section repealed by the Merchant Shipping Act 1964, section 18, sub-section 4.

Rules for Life-saving Appliances.

See section 2 of this Act.

⚓   ⚓   ⚓   ⚓

Consequential
amendments
of Merchant
Shipping Acts.
    35 (1) In subsection (3) of section seven hundred and twenty-four of the principal Act, for the words 'passenger steamers' there shall be substituted the word 'ships'.

(2) Where a ship is detained under any provision of this Act authorising the detention of a ship until the production of a certificate, subsection (2) of section four hundred and sixty of the principal Act (which makes the owner of a ship liable to pay to the Minister his costs in connection with her detention and survey) shall apply as if she had been finally detained under that Act.

(3) So far as Part I of the Merchant Shipping (Safety and Load Line Conventions) Act, 1932, requires that any rules or regulations shall implement the International Convention for the Safety of Life at Sea, 1929, it shall cease to have effect.

(4) Section sixty-nine of the said Act of 1932 (which requires notice to be given to a consular officer of the detention of a foreign ship, or of proceedings against her master or owner, under that Act), and subsection (3) of section seventy-three of that Act (which requires ships registered in the Channel Islands or the Isle of Man to be treated for the purpose of any provisions of that Act relating to Safety Convention ships not registered in the United Kingdom as if they were registered in the United Kingdom), shall have effect as if any reference therein to that Act included a reference to this Act.

(5) In subsection (1) of section two hundred and seventy-two of the principal Act and in subsection (1) of section nine of the said Act of 1932, for any reference to a wireless telegraph installation there shall be substituted a reference to a radio installation.

(6) In subsection (1) of section nine of the said Act of 1932 (which relates to the survey of passenger steamers by radio

surveyors), for any reference to an exemption under the
Merchant Shipping (Wireless Telegraphy) Act, 1919, from the
obligations imposed by that Act, there shall be substituted a
reference to an exemption from the obligations imposed by
the radio rules.

COMMENTS.

Repeal.

Sub-section 3 above underlined, repealed as spent by the Statute Law
Revision Act 1953, section 1.

Merchant Shipping (Wireless Telegraphy) Act 1919.

Repealed—Section 37, sub-section 5 and Third Schedule of this Act,
since repealed by the Statute Law Revision Act 1953.

For 'Minister' now read 'Secretary of State for Trade'.

36 (1) In this Act the following expressions have the ^{Interpretation.}
meanings hereby respectively assigned to them, that is to
say:—

 'Accepted Safety Convention certificate' has the meaning
  assigned to it by section fourteen of this Act;

 'Collision regulations' means regulations made under
  section four hundred and eighteen of the principal
  Act;

 'Construction rules' means rules made under section one
  of this Act;

 'Country to which the Safety Convention applies' means—

  (*a*) a country the government of which has been
  declared under section thirty-one of this Act to have
  accepted the Safety Convention, and has not been
  so declared to have denounced that Convention;

  (*b*) a territory to which it has been so declared
  that the Safety Convention extends, not being a
  territory to which it has been so declared that that
  Convention has ceased to extend;

 'Declaration of survey' means a declaration made under
  section two hundred and seventy-two of the principal
  Act;

 'International voyage' means a voyage from a port in one
  country to a port in another country, either of those

countries being a country to which the Safety Convention applies, and 'short international voyage' means an international voyage—

(*a*) in the course of which a ship is not more than two hundred nautical miles from a port or place in which the passengers and crew could be placed in safety and

(*b*) which does not exceed six hundred nautical miles in length between the last port of call in the country in which the voyage begins and the final port of destination;

so however that for the purpose of the definitions contained in this paragraph—

(i) no account shall be taken of any deviation by a ship from her intended voyage due solely to stress of weather or any other circumstance that neither the master nor the owner nor the charterer (if any) of the ship could have prevented or forestalled; and

(ii) every colony, overseas territory, protectorate or other territory for whose international relations a government that has accepted the Safety Convention is responsible, or for which the United Nations are the administering authority, shall be deemed to be a separate country;

'The Merchant Shipping Acts' means the Merchant Shipping Acts, 1894 to 1948, and this Act;

'The Minister' means the Minister of Transport;

'The principal Act' means the Merchant Shipping Act, 1894;

'Radio navigational aid' means radio apparatus on board a ship being apparatus designed for the purpose of determining the position or direction of ships or other objects;

'Radio rules' means rules made under section three of this Act;

Rules for direction-finders' means rules made under section five of this Act;

'Rules for life-saving appliances' means rules made under section four hundred and twenty-seven of the principal Act as amended by section two of this Act;

'Safety Convention ship' means a ship registered in a country to which the Safety Convention applies; and the expression 'Safety Convention passenger steamer' shall be construed accordingly.

(2) If any amendment of the Safety Convention comes into force, references in this Act to the Safety Convention shall, unless the context otherwise requires, be construed as references to the Safety Convention as amended.

COMMENTS.

Repeal.

The words underlined repealed by section 18, sub-section 4 of the Merchant Shipping Act 1964. *See* now section 19, sub-section 2 of that Act.

For 'Minister' *now read* 'Secretary of State for Trade'.

Passenger Steamer.

Defined in section 26.

⚓   ⚓   ⚓   ⚓

37 (1) This Act shall come into force on such day as His Majesty may by Order in Council appoint.

(2) Except so far as the context otherwise requires, any reference in this Act to any other enactment shall be construed as a reference to that enactment as amended, extended or applied by or under any other enactment including this Act.

(3) Except so far as the context otherwise requires, this Act shall be construed as one with the Merchant Shipping Acts, 1894 to 1948, and, without prejudice to the generality of this provision, references in those Acts to the Merchant Shipping Acts shall be construed as including references to this Act.

(4) This Act may be cited as the Merchant Shipping (Safety Convention) Act, 1949, and the Merchant Shipping Acts, 1894 to 1948, and this Act may be cited together as the Merchant Shipping Acts, 1894 to 1949.

(5) The enactments mentioned in the Third Schedule to this Act are hereby repealed to the extent specified in the third column of that Schedule.

Commencement, construction, citation and appeal.

COMMENTS.

Repeal.

Sub-section 5 above underlined, repealed as spent by the Statute Law Revision Act 1953, section 1, Schedule 1.

⚓ ⚓ ⚓ ⚓

Section 32

FIRST SCHEDULE

Transitional Provision

Sub-section 1

Any rules or regulations made or having effect as if made under any enactment repealed by this Act shall, until revoked have effect as if they had been made under the corresponding provision of this Act.

Repeal

The remainder of this Schedule repealed by the Merchant Shipping Act 1964, section 18, sub-section 4.

⚓ ⚓ ⚓ ⚓

SECOND SCHEDULE

ENACTMENTS FIXING THE AMOUNT OF FEES

The Merchant Shipping Act, 1894, sections 64 (1), 77 (2), 83, 97, 125 (3), 126 (2), 210 (3), 277, 306 (2), 360 (2), 420 (8), 567 (1), 695 (2).
The Merchant Shipping (Mercantile Marine Fund) Act, 1898, section 3.
The Fees (Increase) Act, 1923, section 2 (1) to (4).

Repeal

Section 77, sub-section 2, repealed by Merchant Shipping Act 1965, section 1, section 7 sub-section 2, and Schedule 2.

⚓ ⚓ ⚓ ⚓

Section 37

THIRD SCHEDULE

Repealed as spent—Statute Law Revision Act 1953

Section 1, Schedule 1

⚓ ⚓ ⚓ ⚓

Merchant Shipping Act 1950

An Act to provide for regulating crew accommodation in fishing boats and for amending the Merchant Shipping Acts, 1894 to 1949, with respect to the engagement and discharge of crews, the review of punishments imposed by naval courts, fishing boats engaged in the Newfoundland cod fisheries, and proceedings in summary courts in Northern Ireland; and for purposes connected with the matters aforesaid.

[12th July, 1950.]

General Note

It is anticipated that this Act will be largely repealed, as from a day to be appointed by the Merchant Shipping Act 1970, section 100, sub-section 3, Fifth Schedule.

Attention will be drawn to the sections prospectively repealed by underlining the particular sections with suitable notations in the Comments. The Comments themselves will be kept to an absolute minimum.

1 (1) The Minister may, after consultation with such organisation or organisations as appear to him to be representative of owners of British fishing boats and with such organisation or organisations as appear to him to be representative of seamen employed in British fishing boats, make regulations with respect to the crew accommodation to be provided in fishing boats of any class specified in the regulations, being— *Regulations with respect to crew accommodation in fishing boats.*

(*a*) British fishing boats registered in the United Kingdom, whether under Part I or Part IV of the principal Act and and whether so registered before or after the date on which the regulations come into force; or

(*b*) boats which at any time after the said date are being constructed for use as fishing boats, and are being so constructed to the order of any person qualified under the principal Act to be the owner of a British ship, and have not been registered in the United Kingdom or elsewhere;

Provided that, subject to the provisions of any Order in Council made under the First Schedule to this Act, such regulations shall not apply to any fishing boat under construction which is being constructed at any place in His Majesty's dominions outside the United Kingdom, in India, in the Republic of Ireland or in any protectorate, protected state, trust territory or mandated territory within the meaning of the British Nationality Act, 1948, or is intended on her first registration to be registered at any such place.

(2) Without prejudice to the generality of the preceding sub-section, regulations made thereunder may, in particular—

(a) prescribe the minimum space per man which must be provided in any fishing boat to which the regulations apply by way of sleeping accommodation for seamen and apprentices, and the maximum number of persons by whom any specified part of such accommodation may be used)

(b) regulate the position in any such fishing boat in which the crew accommodation or any part thereof may be located, and the standards to be observed in the construction, equipment and furnishing of any such accommodation;

(c) require the submission to a surveyor of ships of plans and specifications of any works proposed to be carried out for the purpose of the provision or alteration of any such accommodation, and authorise the surveyor to inspect any such works;

(d) provide for the maintenance and repair of any such accommodation, and prohibit or restrict the use of any such accommodation for purposes other than those for which it is designed;

and may make different provision in respect of different

classes of fishing boats and in respect of crew accommodation provided for different classes of persons.

(3) If the provisions of any regulations made under this section are contravened in the case of any fishing boat, the owner or skipper of the fishing boat shall be liable to a fine not exceeding one hundred pounds.

(5) The provisions of the First Schedule to this Act (being provisions contained in sections two, three, four, nine and eleven of the Merchant Shipping Act, 1948, set out with modifications) shall have effect in relation to fishing boats to which regulations made under this section apply.

(6) The power of the Minister to make regulations under this section shall be exercisable by statutory instrument, and any such statutory instrument shall be subject to annulment in pursuance of a resolution of either House of Parliament.

COMMENTS:

The words underlined in this section will be repealed as from a day to be appointed by the Merchant Shipping Act 1970, section 100, sub-section 3, Fifth Schedule.

An additional sub-section, viz.: (2a):

'The Minister may exempt any fishing vessel or classes of fishing boats from any requirements or regulations made under this section, either absolutely, or subject to such conditions as he thinks fit.'

Has been added to this section by the Merchant Shipping Act 1952, section 1, sub-section 2.

Sub-section 4—omitted from the text, was repealed by the Merchant Shipping Act 1965, section 7, sub-section 2 and Schedule 2.

For 'Minister' read 'Secretary of State for Trade'.

⚓   ⚓   ⚓   ⚓

Section 2

Repealed

Merchant Shipping Act 1970, section 100, sub-section 3, Fifth Schedule per The Merchant Shipping Act 1970 (Commencement No. 1) Order 1972, S.I. 1972, No. 1977

⚓   ⚓   ⚓   ⚓

3 (1) Where a naval court summoned under Part VI of the principal Act imposes on any person any one or more of the following punishments, that is to say:—

(*a*) sentences him to imprisonment;

(*b*) imposes on him any fine or forfeiture of wages;

(*c*) removes or discharges him from his ship; or

(*d*) in the case of a certificated officer, cancels or suspends his certificate;

the order of the court, so far as it imposes any such punishment, shall be subject to review by the senior naval or consular officer (hereafter in this section referred to as 'the reviewing officer') present at the place where the court is held:

Provided that, if the senior naval or consular officer present at the said place is a member of the naval court, the functions of the reviewing officer under this section shall be exercised in relation to that court by the naval commander-in-chief or the naval officer within whose command the said place is situated.

(2) The reviewing officer may, in reviewing any such order, confirm or refuse to confirm the order so far as it imposes on any person any such punishment, or vary the order, as respects any such punishment imposed thereby, as follows:—

(*a*) in the case of imprisonment, reduce the term thereof or substitute a fine, forfeiture of wages or removal or discharge from his ship;

(*b*) in the case of a fine or forfeiture of wages, reduce the amount thereof or substitute removal or discharge from his ship;

(*c*) in the case of any other punishment, being a punishment imposed on a certificated officer, substitute any punishment which is lower in the following scale:—
  cancellation of certificate,
  suspension of certificate,

removal or discharge from his ship; or

(*d*) in the case of suspension of certificate, reduce the period thereof:

Provided that the reviewing officer shall not substitute under this subsection any punishment which the naval court could not have imposed.

(3) Where any such order imposes two or more such punishments as are referred to in subsection (1) of this section, whether of the same kind or different kinds, the reviewing officer may, in exercising his powers under the last foregoing subsection, deal separately with each such punishment.

(4) Where any such naval court imposes a sentence of imprisonment and directs the offender to be sent to the United Kingdom or any other place under section sixty-seven of the Merchant Shipping Act, 1906, the reviewing officer may revoke that direction.

(5) The place of imprisonment, whether on land or on board ship, of any person sentenced by any such naval court shall, unless he is sent to the United Kingdom or any other place under the said section sixty-seven, be a place approved in writing by the reviewing officer as a proper place for the purpose.

(6) Where any order reviewed under this section requires the offender to pay the costs of the proceedings or any part thereof, the reviewing officer may also revoke that requirement or may vary it, but not so as to increase the amount payable by the offender in respect of those costs.

(7) The reviewing officer shall, on reviewing an order under this section, record his decision in writing, and if he refuses to confirm the order (so far as it imposes any such punishment as aforesaid), the order shall to that extent cease to have effect and if he varies the order, it shall thereafter have effect as if it had been made by the court as so varied.

COMMENTS.

Repeal.

Sub-section 8 of this section omitted from the text, repealed as spent by the Statute Law Revision Act 1953. It is anticipated that as from a day to be appointed, the remainder of this section will be repealed. Merchant Shipping Act 1970, section 100, sub-section 3, Fifth Schedule.

Naval Courts.

Generally, *see* sections 480 to 486 of the principal Act.

⚓   ⚓   ⚓   ⚓

Amendment of s. 744 of the Merchant Shipping Act, 1894.

4 A ship shall not be deemed to be a foreign-going ship for the purposes of the principal Act by reason only that she is engaged in the Newfoundland cod fisheries, and accordingly section seven hundred and forty-four of that Act shall have effect with the substitution for the words 'whale, seal, walrus or Newfoundland cod fisheries' of the words 'whale, seal or walrus fisheries' and with the omission of the words 'of ships engaged in the Newfoundland cod fisheries which belong to ports in Canada or Newfoundland and'.

COMMENTS.

Prior to the amendment provided in this section, per section 744 of the principal Act, ships engaged in the Newfoundland cod fisheries were deemed to be foreign-going ships, and therefore subject to the provisions of the Merchant Shipping Act, applicable to such vessels.

⚓   ⚓   ⚓   ⚓

Section 5

Repealed

Northern Ireland Act 1962

Section 30, sub-section 2, Schedule 4, Part IV

See now: section 27 of that Act

⚓   ⚓   ⚓   ⚓

Payment of fees into the Exchequer.

6 Any fees received by the Minister under or by virtue of this Act or regulations made thereunder shall be paid into the Exchequer.

COMMENTS.

For 'Minister' read 'Secretary of State for Trade'.

This section will be repealed as from a day to be appointed by the Merchant Shipping Act 1970, section 100, sub-section 3, Fifth Schedule.

⚓   ⚓   ⚓   ⚓

7 (1) In this Act, the following expressions have the meanings hereby respectively assigned to them, that is to say:— *Interpretation.*

'crew accommodation' includes sleeping rooms, mess rooms, sanitary accommodation, hospital accommodation, recreation accommodation, store rooms and catering accommodation provided for the use of seamen and apprentices;

'fishing boat' has the same meaning as in Part IV of the principal Act, except that it includes a vessel which is being constructed for the purpose of being employed in sea fishing or in the sea-fishing service;

'local authority' means the Common Council of the City of London, the council of a metropolitan borough, the council of any county, county borough or county district in England and Wales or Northern Ireland, and, in Scotland, any county, town or district council;

'the Minister' means the Minister of Transport;

'owner', in relation to a fishing boat under construction, means the person to whose order she is being constructed;

'pilotage authority' has the same meaning as in the Pilotage Act, 1913;

'the principal Act' means the Merchant Shipping Act, 1894;

and any reference in this Act to the re-registration of a fishing boat shall not include a reference to a re-registration which is only required in consequence of a change in the ownership of the boat.

(2) Except so far as the context otherwise requires, any reference in this Act to any other enactment shall be construed as a reference to that enactment as amended, extended, or applied by or under any other enactment, including this Act.

COMMENTS.

For 'Minister of Transport' *read* 'Secretary of State for Trade'.

⚓   ⚓   ⚓   ⚓

Short title,
construction,
citation and
commence-
ment.

8 (1) This Act may be cited as the Merchant Shipping Act, 1950.

(2) This Act shall be construed as one with the Merchant Shipping Acts, 1894 to 1949, and, without prejudice to the generality of this provision, references in those Acts to the Merchant Shipping Acts shall be construed as including references to this Act; and the said Acts and this Act may be cited together as the Merchant Shipping Acts, 1894 to 1950.

(3) This Act shall come into operation on such date as the Minister may by order appoint, and different dates may be appointed for the purpose of different provisions of this Act, and the power of the Minister to make orders under this subsection shall be exercisable by statutory instrument.

COMMENTS.

This Act came into force on the 10th December, 1950 per Merchant Shipping Act 1950 (Commencement) Order 1950, S.I. 1950, No. 1845(*c*).

For 'Minister' *read* 'Secretary of State for Trade'.

⚓   ⚓   ⚓   ⚓

N.B.—See Comments at end of this Schedule regarding prospective Repeal.

SCHEDULES

FIRST SCHEDULE

PROVISIONS OF MERCHANT SHIPPING ACT, 1948, APPLIED WITH MODIFICATIONS FOR THE PURPOSES OF SECTION ONE OF THIS ACT.

Application of regulations to fishing boats already registered, under construction &c. (s. 2 (2) to (5) of 1948 Act)

1. Where any fishing boat to which regulations made under section one of this Act apply was registered in the United Kingdom under Part I or Part IV of the principal Act immediately before the date on which those regulations came into force, then, unless and until, after that date, the fishing boat is re-registered in the United Kingdom or undergoes substantial structural alterations or repairs (not being repairs carried out in consequence of damage or in an emergency)—

(*a*) any requirements of the regulations (including any subsequent regulations amending or substituted for those regulations) relating to matters specified in paragraph (*a*) or paragraph (*b*) of subsection (2) of section one of this Act (in this Schedule referred to as 'the construction requirements') shall—

    (i) in the case of a fishing boat to which corresponding requirements under the law in force immediately before that date were applicable, be deemed to be complied with if those requirements are complied with;

    (ii) in any other case, not apply; and

(*b*) any requirements of any such regulations relating to matters specified in paragraph (*c*) of the said subsection (2) (in this Schedule referred to as 'the survey requirements') shall not apply to any works other than works proposed to be carried out for the purpose of any such alterations or repairs as aforesaid.

2. Where regulations made under section one of this Act become applicable—

(a) to a fishing boat under construction of which the keel was laid before the date on which those regulations came into force;

(b) to a fishing boat registered in the United Kingdom under Part I or Part IV of the principal Act after that date, not being a fishing boat to which such regulations applied while she was under construction.

or where any such fishing boat as is mentioned in the preceding paragraph is re-registered, altered or repaired as mentioned in that paragraph, then, if, upon application made to him by the owner of the fishing boat, the Minister is satisfied, after consultation with the owner of the fishing boat or an organisation or organisations appearing to the Minister to be representative of owners of British fishing boats, and with an organisation or organisations appearing to the Minister to be representative of seamen employed in British fishing boats, that such steps, if any, as are reasonable and practicable have been taken for securing compliance with the construction requirements of the regulations in the case of the fishing boat, he shall certify accordingly.

3. In determining for the purposes of the last preceding paragraph what steps for securing compliance with the construction requirements of any regulations are reasonable and practicable, the Minister shall have regard to the age of the fishing boat, to the purpose for which she is or is intended to be used and to the nature of any alterations or repairs which are carried out, or to the extent to which the construction of the fishing boat had been completed before the date on which the regulations came into force, as the case may be.

4. Where any such certificate is issued by the Minister as

aforesaid, then, subject to compliance with such conditions, if any, as may be specified in the certificate—

(*a*) the construction requirements of the regulations (including any subsequent regulations amending or substituted for those regulations) shall be deemed to be complied with in the case of the fishing boat; and

(*b*) the survey requirements of any such regulations shall not apply to any works other than works proposed to be carried out for the purpose of any such alteration or repairs as are mentioned in paragraph 1 of this Schedule:

Provided that on the occurrence of any such event as is mentioned in the said paragraph 1, the provisions of this paragraph shall cease to have effect in relation to the fishing boat, but without prejudice to the issue of a further certificate under paragraph 2 of this Schedule.

Inspection of crew accommodation (s. 3 of 1948 Act)

5. Whenever a fishing boat to which regulations made under section one of this Act apply is registered or re-registered in the United Kingdom under Part I or Part IV of the principal Act and whenever a complaint in respect of crew accommodation in any such fishing boat is duly made in accordance with the regulations, and on such other occasions as may be prescribed by the regulations, a surveyor of ships shall inspect the crew accommodation.

6. If, upon any such inspection the surveyor is satisfied that the crew accommodation complies with the regulations, he shall (except where the inspection is made in consequence of a complaint) give to the registrar of British ships a certificate specifying as space deductible under section seventy-nine of the principal Act the whole of the space comprised in that accommodation, except any part thereof required by the regulations to be disregarded in estimating the space so to be deducted.

7. If, upon any such inspection, it appears to the surveyor that the accommodation does not comply in all respects with

the regulations, he may give to the registrar a certificate specifying as space deductible as aforesaid such part of the space comprised in the accommodation as he considers appropriate having regard to the extent to which it complies with the regulations, but if he does not give such a certificate he shall report to the registrar that no space is deductible as aforesaid:

Provided that the surveyor shall not be required to make such a report as aforesaid—

(*a*) if the inspection is made on the occasion of the registration or re-registration of the fishing boat; or

(*b*) if it appears to him that the failure to comply with the regulations is not substantial and will be remedied within a reasonable time.

8. Where any certificate is given or report made under either of the two last preceding paragraphs in respect of a fishing boat already registered, any certificate previously given thereunder in respect of that fishing boat shall cease to have effect, and the register tonnage of the fishing boat shall be altered accordingly.

9. In respect of any inspection of a fishing boat carried out by a surveyor for the purposes of this Schedule, there shall be paid such fees as may be prescribed by regulations made under section one of this Act.

10. Regulations made under section one of this Act may require the skipper of any fishing boat to which the regulations apply, or any officer authorised by him for the purpose, to carry out such inspections of the crew accommodation as may be prescribed by the regulations, and to record, in such manner as may be so prescribed, such particulars of any such inspection as may be so prescribed.

Consequential amendments of principal Act (Section 4 of 1948 Act)

11. In relation to fishing boats to which regulations made under section one of this Act apply, section seventy-nine of

the principal Act (which authorises certain deductions in ascertaining the register tonnage of ships) shall have effect as if in sub-paragraph (*a*) (i) of subsection (1) for the words 'any space occupied by seamen or apprentices and appropriated to their use, which is certified under the regulations scheduled to this Act with regard thereto' there were substituted the words 'any space provided by way of crew accommodation which is certified under the Merchant Shipping Act, 1950, to be space deductible under this section'.

13. Section two hundred and ten of the principal Act and the Sixth Schedule to that Act shall not apply to any fishing boat to which regulations made under section one of this Act apply (but without prejudice to the provisions of paragraph 1 of this Schedule):

Provided that any certificate given in relation to any such fishing boat as aforesaid, under paragraph (3) of the said Sixth Schedule before the date on which the regulations apply thereto shall have effect for the purposes of this Act and of the principal Act as if it had been given under paragraph 6 of this Schedule.

Application to certain countries and territories (*Sections* 9 *and* 11 (2) *of* 1948 *Act*)

14. His Majesty may by Order in Council direct that any of the provisions of section one of this Act or of this Schedule (including any enactments for the time being in force amending or substituted for the said provisions) shall extend, with such exceptions, adaptations and modifications, if any, as may be specified in the Order, to the Isle of Man, any of the Channel Islands or any colony.

15. The Foreign Jurisdiction Act, 1890, shall have effect as if the provisions of section one of this Act and of this Schedule were included among the enactments which, by virtue of section five of that Act, may be extended by Order in Council to countries in which for the time being His Majesty has jurisdiction.

16. His Majesty may by Order in Council direct that any of the provisions of section one of this Act or of this Schedule shall apply, subject to such exceptions, adaptations and modifications, if any, as may be specified in the Order, to fishing boats registered in any country or territory to which the said provisions can be extended by virtue of either of the two last preceding paragraphs, or under construction in any such country or territory, or to be registered on first registration in any such country or territory, as it applies to fishing boats registered in the United Kingdom under Part I or Part IV of the principal Act, under construction in the United Kingdom or to be so registered on first registration, as the case may be.

17. Any Order in Council made under the preceding provisions of this Schedule shall be subject to annulment in pursuance of a resolution of either House of Parliament.

COMMENTS.

Fishing Boat.

For meaning, *see* section 7 of this Act.

Paragraph 12 (Repeal).

This paragraph was repealed by the Merchant Shipping Act 1965, section 7, sub-section 2, Schedule 2.

Prospective Repeal.

It is anticipated that with the exception of paragraph 12 above (now repealed q.v.) the whole of this Schedule will as from a day to be appointed, be repealed by the Merchant Shipping Act 1970, section 100, sub-section 3, Fifth Schedule.

For 'Minister' read 'Secretary of State for Trade'.

⚓   ⚓   ⚓   ⚓

SECOND SCHEDULE

Repealed

Merchant Shipping Act 1970, section 100, sub-section 3
Fifth Schedule, as from the 1st January, 1973, per S.I.
The Merchant Shipping Act 1970 (Commencement No. 1)
Order 1972

Merchant Shipping Act 1952

Prospective Repeal

It is anticipated that as from a day to be appointed, this Act will be repealed by the Merchant Shipping Act 1970 section 100, sub-section 3, Fifth Schedule.

An Act to enable the Minister of Transport to grant exemptions from requirements as to crew accommodation imposed under the Merchant Shipping Act, 1948, and the Merchant Shipping Act, 1950.

1 (1) Section one of the Merchant Shipping Act, 1948 (which section enables the Minister of Transport to make regulations with respect to crew accommodation in ships other than fishing boats), shall have effect as if, after subsection (2) thereof, there were inserted the following subsection:— *Power of Minister of Transport to exempt from requirements as to crew accommodation.*

'(2A) The Minister may exempt any ships or classes of ships from any requirements of regulations made under this section, either absolutely or subject to such conditions as he thinks fit.'

(2) Section one of the Merchant Shipping Act, 1950 (which section enables the Minister of Transport to make regulations with respect to crew accommodation in fishing boats), shall have effect as if, after subsection (2) thereof, there were inserted the following subsection:—

'(2A) The Minister may exempt any fishing boats or classes of fishing boats from any requirements of regulations made under this section, either absolutely or subject to such conditions as he thinks fit.'

COMMENTS.

For 'Minister of Transport' read 'Secretary of State for Trade'.

⚓   ⚓   ⚓   ⚓

Short title
and citation.   **2**   This Act may be cited as the Merchant Shipping Act
1952, and this Act and the Merchant Shipping Acts, 1894 to
1950, may be cited together as the Merchant Shipping Acts,
1894 to 1952.

COMMENTS.

Now read 1894 to 1974.

⚓   ⚓   ⚓   ⚓

Merchant Shipping Act 1954

Repealed

Merchant Shipping Act 1965, section 7, sub-section 2, Schedule 2

⚓   ⚓   ⚓   ⚓

Merchant Shipping (Liability of Shipowners and Others) Act 1958

This Act has been taken out of its chronological order and for the sake of convenience and clarity, grouped together with the other Limitation Acts 1894, etc., in Volume I of this work.

⚓   ⚓   ⚓   ⚓

Merchant Shipping (Minicoy Lighthouse) Act 1960

An Act to enable the lighthouse on Minicoy Island and sums held in the General Lighthouse Fund in connection therewith to be transferred to the Government of India, and for purposes connected with the matter aforesaid.

[2nd June, 1960]

Whereas the lighthouse on Minicoy Island (in this Act referred to as 'the lighthouse') between the Laccadive and Maldive Islands, is a colonial light within the meaning of the Merchant Shipping (Mercantile Marine Fund) Act, 1898, but has, since the second day of April, nineteen hundred and fifty-six, been administered by the Government of India:

And whereas it is expedient that the lighthouse and the sums held in the General Lighthouse Fund in connection therewith should be transferred to the Government of India;

1 (1) The Minister of Transport (in this Act referred to as 'the Minister') shall have power to transfer to the Government of India on such date as may be agreed between him and that Government all the interest held by him in the lighthouse and in the appurtenances thereto.

Power to transfer to India Minicoy Lighthouse and assets attributable thereto.

(2) On the date referred to in the foregoing subsection the lighthouse shall cease to be a colonial light within the meaning of the Act of 1898, and accordingly section six hundred and seventy of the Merchant Shipping Act, 1894 (which empowers Her Majesty to fix colonial light dues) shall cease to have effect in relation to the lighthouse, and in the Third Schedule to the Act of 1898, the words 'Minicoy Island, between the Laccadive and Maldive Islands' shall be repealed.

(3) There shall be paid to the Government of India out of the General Lighthouse Fund (in this section referred to as 'the Fund') the following sums, that is to say—

(a) such sum as the Minister, with the consent of the Treasury, may determine to be equivalent to the excess of the proportion of the Fund attributable to light dues in respect of the lighthouse for the period ending with the second day of April, nineteen hundred and fifty-six, over the aggregate of the expenses in connection with the lighthouse relating to that period and falling to be paid out of the Fund;

(*b*) a sum equal to interest at the rate of four per cent. per annum on the sum payable by virtue of the foregoing paragraph for the period beginning with the third day of April, nineteen hundred and fifty-six, and ending with the day on which the last mentioned sum is paid;

(*c*) all the sums carried to the Fund and attributable to light dues due in respect of the lighthouse after the second day of April, nineteen hundred and fifty-six;

(*d*) in respect of each of the sums referred to in the last foregoing paragraph, a sum equal to interest at the rate of four per cent. per annum thereon for the period beginning with the relevant day and ending with the day on which the sum so referred to is paid.

(4) In the last foregoing subsection,—

(*a*) in paragraph (*a*), the reference to expenses falling to be paid out of the Fund includes a reference to expenses which fell to be paid out of the Basses Lights Fund (the balance of which was transferred to the Fund by the Act of 1898), and

(*b*) in paragraph (*d*), 'relevant day' means, in relation to a sum referred to in paragraph (*c*) of that subsection, the thirtieth day of September falling in the year in which that sum was carried to the Fund, and for the purposes of this paragraph a year shall be treated as a period of twelve months ending with the thirty-first day of March.

COMMENTS.

For 'Minister of Transport' read 'Secretary of State for Trade'.

Agreed Date.

2nd April, 1956.

⚓   ⚓   ⚓   ⚓

Interpretation and citation.

2 (1) In this Act—

'the Act of 1898' means the Merchant Shipping (Mercantile Marine Fund) Act, 1898, and

'the General Lighthouse Fund' means the fund of that name established under the Act of 1898.

(2) This Act may be cited as the Merchant Shipping (Minicoy Lighthouse) Act, 1960, and this Act and the Merchant Shipping Acts, 1894 to 1958, may be cited together as the Merchant Shipping Acts, 1894 to 1960.

⚓   ⚓   ⚓   ⚓

Merchant Shipping Act 1964

Application of Act of 1949 to new Convention

Application of
Act of 1949 to
Convention of
1960.

1   For the purpose of enabling effect to be given to the International Convention for the Safety of Life at Sea signed in London on 17th June 1960 (in this Act referred to as 'the Convention') which replaces the International Convention for the Safety of Life at Sea signed in London on 10th June 1948 (in this Act referred to as 'the Safety Convention') the Merchant Shipping (Safety Convention) Act 1949 (in this Act referred to as 'the Act of 1949') shall have effect as if—

(*a*) for references therein, except in the preamble, to the Safety Convention there were substituted references to the Convention; and

(*b*) references therein to that Act, except in subsections (1) and (4) of section 37 (commencement and citation), included references to this Act.

COMMENTS.

The countries which have declared to have accepted the 1960 Convention, signed in London on the 17th June, 1960, are contained in the Merchant Shipping (Safety Convention) (Various Countries) Order 1977, S.I. 1977, No. 1876.

⚓   ⚓   ⚓   ⚓

New requirements for cargo ships

Cargo ship
construction
and survey
rules.

2   (1) The Minister may make rules (in this Act referred to as 'cargo ship construction and survey rules') prescribing requirements for the hull, equipment and machinery of ships to which this section applies and requiring any such ships which are registered in the United Kingdom to be surveyed to such extent, in such manner and at such intervals as may be prescribed by the rules.

(2) The said rules shall include such requirements as appear to the Minister to implement the provisions of the Convention relating to the hull, equipment and machinery of such ships, except so far as those provisions are implemented by any other rules or regulations made under the Merchant Shipping Acts.

(3) This section applies to—

(*a*) sea-going ships of not less than five hundred tons gross tonnage; and

(*b*) sea-going ships of not less than such lower tonnage and of such description as the Minister may by order made by statutory instrument specify;

other than passenger steamers, troopships, pleasure yachts, fishing vessels and ships not propelled by mechanical means; except that it applies to ships not registered in the United Kingdom only while they are within a port in the United Kingdom and are not exempted from the cargo ship construction and survey rules under the following provisions of this Act.

(4) The matters with regard to which fees may be prescribed by regulations under section 33 of the Act of 1949 shall include surveys required by the cargo ship construction and survey rules, and the provisions applied by section 13(2) of that Act (which relate to the delivery of declarations of survey and appeals to the court of survey) shall apply to such surveys whether or not they are made for the purpose of the issue of any certificate.

(5) In relation to surveys required by the cargo ship construction and survey rules which are carried out otherwise than by a surveyor of ships appointed under the Merchant Shipping Acts—

(*a*) so much of the said section 33 as requires fees to be paid into the Exchequer shall not apply; and

(*b*) the provision applied by the said section 13(2) shall apply with such modifications as may be prescribed by the cargo ship construction and survey rules; and

(*c*) the definition of 'declaration of survey' in section 36(1) of the Act of 1949 shall not apply.

(6) An order under subsection (3)(*b*) of this section may be varied or revoked by a subsequent order.

COMMENTS.

For 'Minister' read 'Secretary of State'.

Cargo Ship Construction and Survey Rules.

Consult the Merchant Shipping (Cargo Ship Construction and Survey) Rules 1965, S.I. 1965, No. 1104. The Merchant Shipping (Cargo Ship Construction and Survey) (Tankers and Combination Carriers) Rules, 1975, S.I. 1975, No. 750.

Any Other Rules.

Consult the Merchant Shipping (Safety Convention) Act 1949, sections 2; 3; and 5. The Merchant Shipping Act 1894, section 418 and 427.

Passenger Steamers.

See the Merchant Shipping (Safety Convention) Act 1949, section 26, sub-section 2.

Fees.

See the Merchant Shipping (Fees) Regulations 1977, S.I. 1977, No. 2049.

Surveyor of Ships.

See sections 724 to 727 of the principal Act, and the Merchant Shipping Act 1970, section 76.

⚓   ⚓   ⚓   ⚓

Cargo ship safety construction certificates and exemption certificates.

3 (1) If the Minister or such person as he may authorise for the purpose is satisfied, on receipt of declarations of survey in respect of a ship to which section 2 of this Act applies and which is registered in the United Kingdom, that the ship complies with the cargo ship construction and survey rules applicable to the ship and such voyages as she is to be engaged on he shall, on the application of the owner, issue in respect of the ship—

(*a*) if the ship is of not less than five hundred tons gross tonnage and is to be engaged on international voyages, a certificate in the form prescribed by the Convention;

(*b*) in any other case, a certificate showing that she complies with the said rules;

and any such certificate is in this Act referred to as a cargo ship safety construction certificate.

(2) If the Minister, on receipt of declarations of survey in respect of such a ship, is satisfied that the ship is exempt, by virtue of any exercise by him of a power conferred on him by section 28 of the Act of 1949 or the cargo ship construction and survey rules, from any of the requirements of those rules applicable to the ship and to such voyages as she is to be engaged on, and that she complies with the rest of those requirements, he shall, on the application of the owner, issue in respect of the ship—

(a) if she is of not less than five hundred tons gross tonnage and is to be engaged on international voyages—

   (i) an exemption certificate stating which of the requirements of the Convention, being requirements implemented by the rules and applicable as aforesaid, the ship is exempt from and that the exemption is conditional on the ship's plying on the voyages and complying with the other conditions (if any) specified in the certificate; and

   (ii) a certificate showing that the ship complies with the rest of those requirements;

(b) in any other case, a certificate showing that the ship complies with such of the requirements of the cargo ship construction and survey rules applicable to the ship and to the voyages she is to be engaged on as she is not exempt from;

and any certificate issued under paragraph (a)(ii) or paragraph

(b) of this subsection is in this Act referred to as a qualified cargo ship safety construction certificate.

(3) A certificate issued under this section, other than an exemption certificate, shall remain in force for five years or such shorter period as may be specified in it, but without prejudice to the Minister's power to cancel it; and an exemption certificate issued under this section shall remain in force for the same period as the corresponding qualified certificate.

(4) The Minister may by order made by statutory instrument extend the period for which a certificate under this section may be issued to a period not exceeding six years.

(5) Without prejudice to the power of extension conferred by section 13(5) of the Act of 1949, where a certificate under this section is in force in respect of a ship and the certificate was issued for a shorter period than is allowed under the foregoing provisions of this section, the Minister or any person authorised by him for the purpose may, if satisfied on receipt of declarations of survey in respect of the ship that it is proper to do so, grant an extension of the certificate for a period not exceeding one year, and not exceeding, together with the period for which it was issued and any period by which it has been previously extended under this subsection, the longest period for which it could have been issued under this section.

(6) In relation to a certificate issued or extended under this section by a person authorised by the Minister—

(*a*) the provisions applied by section 13(8) of the Act of 1949 (which relate to the transmission, cancellation, surrender, posting-up and falsification of certificates issued by the Minister) except section 276 of the principal Act (transmission of certificates); and

(*b*) section 33 of the Act of 1949 (fees);
shall apply as they apply in relation to certificates issued by the Minister, except that so much of the said section 33 as requires fees to be paid into the Exchequer shall not apply.

(7) An order under subsection (4) of this section may be varied or revoked by a subsequent order.

COMMENTS.

For 'Minister' read 'Secretary of State'.

Declaration of Survey.

Consult Merchant Shipping Act 1894. section 272 and section 36, sub-section 1 of the Merchant Shipping (Safety Convention) Act 1949.

International Voyage.

See definition in the Merchant Shipping (Safety Convention) Act 1949, section 36, sub-section 1.

⚓   ⚓   ⚓   ⚓

Notice of alterations and additional surveys.

4 (1) The duty of the owner or master of a ship under subsection (2) of section 11 of the Act of 1949 to notify alterations and renewals shall extend, in relation to any ship in respect of which a certificate under section 3 of this Act is in force, to the hull, machinery and any equipment other than that mentioned in that subsection, but may, if the certificate was issued by a person authorised under the said section 3, be discharged by notifying him instead of the Minister.

(2) Subsection (4) of the said section 11 (additional survey and cancellation of certificates) shall have effect, in relation to any such ship, as if—

(*a*) paragraph (*a*) thereof extended to any alteration or renewal which is notifiable by virtue of this section; and

(*b*) paragraph (*b*) and not paragraph (*c*) thereof were applic-

able, notwithstanding that the ship is not a passenger
steamer;

and the power of the Minister under that subsection to cancel
such a certificate shall be exercisable also where the ship has
not been submitted for survey as required by the cargo ship
construction and survey rules.

COMMENTS.

For 'Minister' read 'Secretary of State'.

Passenger Steamer.

See definition under section 26 of the Merchant Shipping (Safety
Convention) Act 1949.

5 (1) No ship to which section 2 of this Act applies and Prohibition on
which is registered in the United Kingdom shall proceed to sea proceeding to sea without
unless there is in force in respect of the ship either— appropriate certificates.

(*a*) a cargo ship safety construction certificate; or

(*b*) a qualified cargo ship safety construction certificate and,
    if the ship is about to proceed on an international voyage,
    a corresponding exemption certificate; or

(*c*) such certificate or certificates as would be required if she
    were a passenger steamer,

applicable to the ship and to the voyage on which she is about
to proceed.

(2) If any ship proceeds, or attempts to proceed, to sea in
contravention of this section the owner or master of the ship
shall be liable to a fine not exceeding one hundred pounds.

(3) The master of every ship to which section 2 of this Act
applies and which is registered in the United Kingdom shall
produce to the officer of cusoms from whom a clearance for
the ship is demanded the certificate or certificates required by
the foregoing provisions of this section; and the clearance
shall not be granted, and the ship may be detained, until the
said certificate or certificates are so produced.

COMMENTS.

International Voyage.

See Merchant Shipping (Safety Convention) Act 1949, section 36,
sub-section 1.

Passenger Steamer.

See definition under section 26, sub-section 2 of the Merchant Shipping (Safety Convention) Act 1949.

⚓   ⚓   ⚓   ⚓

Exemption of
ships holding
appropriate
certificates.

6 Where there is produced in respect of a ship not registered in the United Kingdom—

(*a*) an accepted Safety Convention certificate equivalent to a cargo ship safety construction certificate; or

(*b*) accepted Safety Convention certificates equivalent respectively to a qualified cargo ship safety construction certificate and to a corresponding exemption certificate;

the ship shall be exempt from the cargo ship construction and survey rules.

COMMENTS.

Safety Convention Certificate.

See Merchant Shipping (Safety Convention) Act 1949, section 14, section 36, sub-section 1.

⚓   ⚓   ⚓   ⚓

Penalty for
non-compli-
ance with rules
and power to
detain.

7 (1) If the cargo ship construction and survey rules are contravened in any respect in relation to a ship, the owner or master of the ship shall be liable on conviction on indictment to a fine not exceeding five hundred pounds, or on summary conviction to a fine not exceeding one hundred pounds.

(2) A surveyor of ships may inspect any ship for the purpose of seeing that she complies with the provisions of the cargo ship construction and survey rules (other than those relating to survey) and for that purpose shall have all the powers of a Ministry of Transport inspector under the Merchant Shipping Acts; and if he finds that the ship fails to comply with those provisions he shall give to the owner or master notice in writing stating in what respect she fails to comply with them and what in his opinion is requisite to remedy the failure

(3) Every notice under subsection (2) of this section shall be communicated in manner directed by the Minister to the chief officer of customs of any port at which the ship may seek to obtain a clearance or transire; and the ship shall be detained

until a certificate under the hand of a surveyor of ships is produced to the effect that the failure has been remedied.

COMMENTS.

For 'Ministry of Transport' read 'Department of Trade'.
For 'Minister' read 'Secretary of State'.

Appointment of Surveyor of Ships.

See section 724 of the Principal Act.

⚓   ⚓   ⚓   ⚓

Damage control and life-saving appliances

8 Construction rules (that is to say, rules made under section 1 of the Act of 1949 relating to the hull, equipment and machinery of British passenger steamers registered in the United Kingdom) may require the provision in such ships,— *Damage control plans and stability information for passenger steamers.*

(*a*) of plans exhibited as provided by or under the rules, and of other information, relating to the boundaries of water-tight compartments, the openings therein, the means of closing such openings and the arrangements for correcting any list due to flooding; and

(*b*) of information necessary for the guidance of the master in maintaining sufficient stability to enable the ship to withstand damage.

COMMENTS.

Construction Rules.

Consult the Merchant Shipping (Passenger Ship Construction) Rules 1965, S.I. 1965, No. 1104.

⚓   ⚓   ⚓   ⚓

9 Subsection (1) of section 427 of the principal Act (which empowers the Minister of Transport to make rules for life-saving appliances) shall be amended as follows:— *Extension of power to make rules for life-saving appliances.*

(*a*) in paragraph (*e*) (buoyant apparatus required to be carried on board ships carrying passengers) the words 'carrying passengers' shall be omitted;

(*b*) after paragraph (*m*) there shall be inserted the following paragraph:—

'(*mm*) the provision in ships of plans or other information relating to the means of preventing, detecting, controlling and extinguishing outbreaks of fire';

(c) in paragraph (q) (examination of appliances and equipment required by the rules to be carried) after the word 'examination' there shall be inserted the words 'and maintenance'.

COMMENTS.

For 'Minister of Transport' read 'Secretary of State'.

⚓   ⚓   ⚓   ⚓

Radio installations and certificates

Requirements for portable radio apparatus carried in survival craft.   **10** (1) Radio rules may prescribe requirements for such portable radio apparatus as boats or life rafts may be required to carry by the rules for life-saving appliances.

(2) Subsections (7) and (8) of section 3 of the Act of 1949 (which relate to the inspection and detention of ships to ensure conformity with the radio rules) shall apply in relation to the portable radio apparatus so required to be carried by the boats or life rafts on any ship as they apply in relation to the radio installation of the ship.

COMMENTS.

Substitution.

In lieu of sub-section 2, underlined above, the following has been substituted:—

'Sub-section (6) of section 3 of the Act of 1949 (detention of ships not conforming with radio rules) shall apply in relation to the portable radio apparatus so required to be carried by the boats or life rafts on any ship as it applies in relation to the radio equipment of the ship.'

The Merchant Shipping Act 1970, section 100, sub-section 1, Schedule 3, paragraph 10, as from the 1st November, 1974.

Radio Rules.

Consult the Merchant Shipping (Radio Rules) 1965, S.I. 1965, No. 1107 as amended by S.I. 1969, No. 1315, and the Merchant Shipping (Radio) (Fishing Vessels) Rules 1974, S.I. 1974, No. 1919.

⚓   ⚓   ⚓   ⚓

11   For subsection (4) of section 3 of the Act of 1949 Radio installations. (which specifies the radio installations to be required under the radio rules) there shall be substituted the following subsection:—

'(4) The radio installation required under the said rules to be provided—

(*a*) for a passenger steamer of whatever tonnage, or for any ship of sixteen hundred tons gross tonnage or upwards which is neither a passenger steamer nor a fishing vessel, shall be a radiotelegraph installation; and

(*b*) for any other ship shall be either a radiotelephone installation or a radiotelegraph installation, at the option of the owner.'

COMMENTS.

It is anticipated that this section (underlined) will be repealed as from a day to be appointed. *See* the Merchant Shipping Act 1970, section 100, sub-section 3, and Schedule 5.

⚓   ⚓   ⚓   ⚓

12   Where a radio certificate or qualified radio certificate Renewal of radio certificates for small cargo ships. is in force in respect of a ship of less than five hundred tons gross tonnage, other than a passenger steamer, and the ship is surveyed by a radio surveyor at a time not earlier than two months before the end of the period for which the certificate is in force, then, if on receipt of the declaration of survey a new certificate is issued before the end of that period,—

(*a*) the current certificate may be cancelled; and

(*b*) the new certificate may, notwithstanding anything in section 13(3) of the Act of 1949, be issued for a period ending not later than twelve months after the end of the first-mentioned period.

COMMENTS.

Radio Certificate.   Qualified Radio Certificate.

See section 9, the Merchant Shipping (Safety Convention) Act 1949.

⚓   ⚓   ⚓   ⚓

Miscellaneous

Issue of
exemption
certificates
where
Convention
country issues
corresponding
qualified
certificates.

13   Where the Minister, under section 13(9) of the Act of 1949, requests the government of a country to which the Convention applies to issue in respect of a ship such certificates as he is authorised to issue under subsection (2) of section 7, 8 or 9 of that Act or under paragraph (a) of section 3(2) of this Act, and that government is willing to issue, in pursuance of that request, a qualified certificate thereunder but is not willing to issue the corresponding exemption certificate, the Minister may issue that exemption certificate in respect of the ship.

COMMENTS.

For 'Minister' read 'Secretary of State'.

⚓   ⚓   ⚓   ⚓

Merchant Shipping Act 1964

Section 14

Repealed

Merchant Shipping (Load Lines) Act 1967
Section 33 and Schedule 2

⚓   ⚓   ⚓   ⚓

Modification
of s. 29 of
Act of 1949.

15   Subsection (1) of section 29 of the Act of 1949 (which exempts certain ships from certain provisions) shall not prevent the application—

(a) to any ship of three hundred tons gross tonnage or upwards, of so much of the provisions mentioned in paragraphs (a) and (b) of that subsection as relates to certificates issued under section 9 of that Act or equivalent accepted Safety Convention certificates;

(b) to any ship to which section 2 of this Act applies and which is registered in the United Kingdom, of so much of the provisions mentioned in paragraph (a) of that subsection as relates to certificates issued under section 3 of this Act;

by reason only that she is of less than five hundred tons gross tonnage.

COMMENTS.

Safety Convention Certificates.

See section 14 of the Merchant Shipping (Safety Convention) Act 1949.

⚓   ⚓   ⚓   ⚓

16   The matters of which information is to be sent by the master of a ship in accordance with rules under section 24 of the Merchant Shipping (Safety and Load Line Conventions) Act 1932 shall include— *Extension of duty to report dangers to navigation.*

(*a*) air temperatures below freezing point associated with gale-force winds causing severe ice accretion on the super-structure of ships; and

(*b*) winds of force 10 or above on the Beaufort Scale for which no storm warning has been received.

⚓   ⚓   ⚓   ⚓

Ships carrying passengers

17   (1) For subsection (1) of section 271 of the principal Act (which prohibits passenger steamers carrying more than twelve passengers from sailing without a certificate of survey) there shall be substituted the following subsection:— *Amendment of Merchant Shipping Act 1894, s. 271.*

'(1) Every passenger steamer which carries more than twelve passengers shall be surveyed once at least in each year in the manner provided in this Part of this Act and no ship (other than a steam ferry boat working in chains) shall proceed to sea or on any voyage or excursion with more than twelve passengers on board, unless there is in force in respect of the ship a certificate as to survey under this Part of this Act, applicable to the voyage or excursion on which the ship is about to proceed, or that voyage or excursion is one in respect of which the Minister of Transport has exempted the ship from the requirements of this subsection.'

and at the end of subsection (2) of that section (which enables a passenger ship to be detained until such a certificate is produced) there shall be inserted the words 'unless the voyage or excursion on which she is about to proceed is one in respect of which she has been exempted as aforesaid'.

(2) References in the Merchant Shipping Acts to a passenger steamer shall be construed as including any ship while

on or about to proceed on a voyage or excursion in any case where a passenger steamer's certificate is required to be in force in respect of her.

COMMENTS.

For 'Minister of Transport' read 'Secretary of State'.

Passenger Steamers.

See section 267 of the Principal Act, and the Merchant Shipping (Safety Convention) Act 1949, section 26, sub-section 2.

⚓ ⚓ ⚓ ⚓

Merchant Shipping Act 1964

Section 18

Repealed

Statute Law (Reform) Act 1974

⚓ ⚓ ⚓ ⚓

Commencement, construction, citation and extent.

19 (1) This Act shall come into force on such day as Her Majesty may by Order in Council appoint.

(2) In the Act of 1949 'the Merchant Shipping Acts' shall mean the Merchant Shipping Acts 1894 to 1958 and this Act; and this Act shall be construed as one with those Acts.

(3) This Act may be cited as the Merchant Shipping Act 1964, and the Merchant Shipping Acts 1894 to 1958 and this Act may be cited together as the Merchant Shipping Acts 1894 to 1964.

(4) This Act extends to Northern Ireland.

COMMENTS.

Appointed Day.

This was the 26th May, 1965. The Merchant Shipping Act 1964 (Commencement) Order 1965, S.I. 1965, No. 317.

⚓ ⚓ ⚓ ⚓

Merchant Shipping Act 1965

An Act to amend the law relating to the measurement of the tonnage of merchant ships and the marking of load lines. The Act came into force on the 1st March, 1967. The Merchant Shipping Act 1965 (Commencement) Order 1967 S.I. 1967, No. 157 (c)

1 (1) The tonnage of any ship to be registered under the Tonnage regulations. principal Act (whether under Part I or Part IV thereof) shall be ascertained in accordance with regulations made by the Board of Trade by statutory instrument; and those regulations shall, as respects anything done after the commencement of this Act, be taken to be the provisions referred to in the principal Act as the tonnage regulations of that Act.

(2) Regulations under this section—

(a) may make different provision for different descriptions of ships or for the same description of ships in different circumstances;

(b) may make any provision thereof dependent on compliance with such conditions, to be evidenced in such manner, as may be specified in the regulations;

(c) may provide for the ascertainment of any space to be taken into account for the purposes of section 85 of the principal Act (payment of dues where goods carried in spaces not forming part of registered tonnage) and may exempt any space from being taken into account for those purposes; and

(d) may prohibit or restrict the carriage of goods or stores in spaces not included in the registered tonnage of a ship and may provide for making the master and the owner each liable to a fine not exceeding one hundred pounds where such a prohibition or restriction is contravened.

(3) Regulations under this section may make provision for assigning to a ship, either instead of or as an alternative to the tonnage ascertained in accordance with the other provisions of the regulations, a lower tonnage applicable where the ship is not loaded to the full depth to which it can be safely loaded,

and for indicating on the ship, by such mark as may be specified in the regulations, that such a lower tonnage has been assigned to it and, where it has been assigned to it as an alternative, the depth to which the ship may be loaded for the lower tonnage to be applicable.

(4) Regulations under this section may provide for the measurement and survey of ships to be undertaken, in such circumstances as may be specified in the regulations and notwithstanding sections 6 and 86 of the principal Act, by persons appointed by such organisations as may be authorised in that behalf by the Board of Trade; and so much of section 83 of the principal Act and section 1 of the Merchant Shipping (Mercantile Marine Fund) Act 1898 as requires the payment of fees into the Exchequer shall not apply to fees payable under the said section 83 to persons appointed in pursuance of this subsection.

(5) Regulations under this section may make provision for the alteration (notwithstanding section 82 of the principal Act) of the particulars relating to the registered tonnage of any ship registered before the coming into operation of the regulations.

(6) Regulations under this section may provide for the issue of documents certifying the registered tonnage of any ship or the tonnage which is to be taken for any purpose specified in the regulations as the tonnage of a ship not registered in the United Kingdom.

(7) Any statutory instrument made under this section shall be subject to annulment in pursuance of a resolution of either House of Parliament.

COMMENTS.

Prospective Substitution.

As from a day to be appointed, sub-sections 5 and 6, underlined, are to be substituted by:—

'(5) Regulations under this section may make provision for the alteration (notwithstanding section 82 of the principal Act) of the particulars relating to the registered tonnage of a ship.'

(6) Regulations under this section may provide for the issue by the Department of Trade or by persons appointed by such organisations as

may be authorised in that behalf by the Department of Trade of certificates of the registered tonnage of any ship or of the tonnage which is to be taken for any purpose specified in the regulations as the tonnage of a ship not registered in the United Kingdom, and for the cancellation and delivery up of such certificates in such circumstances as may be prescribed by the regulations.

(6*a*) Regulations under this section requiring the delivery up of any certificate may make a failure to comply with the requirement an offence punishable on summary conviction, with a fine not exceeding £100.

Regulations.

For these regulations *see*:—

The Merchant Shipping (Tonnage) Regulations 1967

        S.I. No. 172 as amended by:—
        S.I. 1967, No. 1093
        S.I. 1972, No. 656
        S.I. 1975, No. 594.

⚓   ⚓   ⚓   ⚓

Section 2

Repealed

Merchant Shipping (Load Lines) Act 1967

Section 33, Schedule 2

⚓   ⚓   ⚓   ⚓

3   The provisions made with respect to the ascertainment of tonnage by the Merchant Shipping (Fishing Boats Registry, Order 1927) shall have effect as if contained in, and accordingly may be amended or revoked by, regulations under this Act. *Transitional provision. 1927, No. 642.*

⚓   ⚓   ⚓   ⚓

Section 4

Repealed

Industrial Expansion Act 1968

Section 17, section 18, sub-section 2, Schedule 4

⚓   ⚓   ⚓   ⚓

K

Provisions as to Northern Ireland.

5 (1) This Act extends to Northern Ireland.

(2) In the application of this Act to Northern Ireland the amendment made by this Act in the Crown Proceedings Act 1947 is an amendment to that Act as it applied in Northern Ireland.

⚓   ⚓   ⚓   ⚓

Application to British possessions, etc.

6 Her Majesty may by Order in Council direct that the provisions of this Act shall extend, with such exceptions, adaptations and modifications as may be specified in the Order, to—

(*a*) the Isle of Man;

(*b*) any of the Channel Islands;

(*c*) any colony, or any country or place outside Her Majesty's dominions in which for the time being Her Majesty has jurisdiction, or any territory consisting partly of one or more colonies and partly of one or more such countries or places.

⚓   ⚓   ⚓   ⚓

Amendments and repeals.

7 (1) The enactments mentioned in Schedule 1 to this Act shall have effect subject to the amendments specified in relation thereto in the second column of that Schedule, being minor amendments and amendments consequential on the foregoing provisions of this Act.

(2) The enactments mentioned in Schedule 2 to this Act are hereby repealed to the extent specified in the third column of that Schedule.

Sub-section 2, underlined above

Repealed

Statute Law Reform Act 1974

COMMENTS.

Appointed Day.

Consult Merchant Shipping Act 1965 (Commencement) Order 1967, S.I. 1967, No. 157.

⚓   ⚓   ⚓   ⚓

Schedules 1 and 2

Section 7, sub-sections 1 and 2

Minor and Consequential Amendments

All these have been entered in the appropriate places in the body of the text

⚓   ⚓   ⚓   ⚓

Merchant Shipping Act 1967

Introduction:

An Act to amend section 92 of the
Merchant Shipping Act 1894

NOTE:

Prospective Repeal

As from a day to be appointed, it is anticipated that this Act
will be repealed. Merchant Shipping Act 1970, section 100
sub-section 3, Schedule 5.

Extension of, and new penal provision for, section 92 of Merchant Shipping Act 1894.

1 (1) Section 92 of the Merchant Shipping Act 1894
shall be amended in accordance with the following provisions
of this section.

(2) In subsection (1) (which requires every British foreign-
going ship and every British home trade passenger ship, when
going to sea from any place in the United Kingdom, and, in
certain circumstances, other ships, to be provided with officers
duly certificated under that Act according to the scale set out in
that subsection) after the words 'from any place in the United
Kingdom' there shall be inserted the words 'every ship registered in the United Kingdom, being a foreign-going ship or a
home trade passenger ship, when going to sea from a place
outside the United Kingdom'.

(3) After subsection (1), there shall be inserted the following subsection:—

'(1A) If, on an occasion on which a ship of a particular
description registered in the United Kingdom, being a
foreign-going ship or a home trade passenger ship, goes to
sea from a place outside the United Kingdom, one, but
only one, of the duly certificated officers with which a
ship of that description is required to be provided by the
foregoing provisions of this section is not provided, but
all reasonable steps were taken to secure the provision on
that occasion of a duly certificated person as that officer,
so much of the foregoing subsection as requires a ship of
that description to be provided with that officer when

going to sea from a place outside the United Kingdom shall not apply to the ship during whichever is the shorter of the following periods beginning with the day on which the ship goes to sea from that place on that occasion, that is to say—

(*a*) the period of twenty-eight days; and

(*b*) the period ending with the day on which the ship is provided with a duly certificated person as that officer.'

(4) For subsection (2) (which penalises a person engaged as such an officer as is mentioned in the said subsection (1) who goes to sea without being duly certificated and any person who employs another as an officer in contravention of the said subsection (1) without ascertaining that that other is duly certificated) there shall be substituted the following subsection:—

'(2) If the requirements of subsection (1) of this section are not complied with in a case in which they apply to a ship, the master or owner of the ship shall be liable to a fine not exceeding one hundred pounds.'

See note after the introduction to this Act.

⚓   ⚓   ⚓   ⚓

2   (1) This Act may be cited as the Merchant Shipping Act 1967, and this Act and the Merchant Shipping Acts 1894 to 1965 may be cited together as the Merchant Shipping Acts 1894 to 1967. Interpretation and construction.

(2) Any reference in an Act passed before the passing of this Act to section 92 of the Merchant Shipping Act 1894 shall, unless the contrary intention appears, be construed as referring to that section as amended by this Act.

See Note after the introduction to this Act.

⚓   ⚓   ⚓   ⚓

Merchant Shipping (Load Lines) Act 1967

This Act came into force per the Merchant Shipping (Load Lines) 1967 (Commencement) Order 1968, S.I. 1968, No. 1108 as from the 21st July, 1968, section 25 and Schedule 1 of the Act as from 10th May, 1967.

Prospective Repeal

As from a day to be appointed, the whole Act is due to be repealed. Merchant Shipping Act 1970, section 100, subsection 3, Schedule 5.

⚓   ⚓   ⚓   ⚓

Merchant Shipping (Load Lines) Act 1967

An Act to make further provision as to load lines and related matters; to increase penalties under certain provisions of the Merchant Shipping Acts 1894 to 1965 relating to passenger steamers; and for purposes connected with the matters aforesaid.

Whereas a Convention entitled 'the International Convention on Load Lines' (in this Act referred to as 'the Convention of 1966') was signed in London on 5th April, 1966:

And whereas it is intended that the Convention of 1966 shall replace the Convention set out in Schedule 2 to the Merchant Shipping (Safety and Load Line Conventions) Act 1932:

And whereas it is expedient to enable effect to be given to the Convention of 1966:

Be it therefore enacted by the Queen's most Excellent Majesty, by and with the advice and consent of the Lords Spiritual and Temporal, and Commons, in this present Parliament assembled, and by the authority of the same, as follows:—

⚓   ⚓   ⚓   ⚓

General provisions

1 This applies to all ships except—   Ships to which
                                                   Act applies.

(*a*) ships of war;

(*b*) ships solely engaged in fishing; and

(*c*) pleasure yachts.

COMMENTS.

For definition of 'ship' *see* Merchant Shipping Act 1894, section 742.

⚓   ⚓   ⚓   ⚓

2 (1) The Board of Trade shall make rules in accordance Load line
with the following provisions of this Act (in this Act referred rules.
to as 'the load line rules'); and in making those rules the
Board shall have regard in particular to the Convention of
1966.

(2) The load line rules shall make provision—

(*a*) for the surveying and periodical inspection of ships to
which this Act applies;

(*b*) for determining freeboards to be assigned from time to
time to such ships;

(*c*) for determining, in relation to any such ship, the deck
which is to be taken to be the freeboard deck of the ship,
and for requiring the position of that deck to be indicated
on each side of the ship by a mark of a description prescribed by the rules; and

(*d*) for determining, by reference to that mark and the freeboards for the time being assigned to any such ship, the
positions in which each side of the ship is to be marked
with lines of a description prescribed by the rules, indicating the various maximum depths to which the ship may
be loaded in circumstances prescribed by the rules.

(3) The load line rules shall include the following provisions, that is to say—

(*a*) provisions specifying such requirements in respect of the
hulls, superstructures, fittings and appliances of ships to
which this Act applies as appear to the Board of Trade to
be relevant to the assignment of freeboards to such ships;

(*b*) provisions whereby, at the time when freeboards are
assigned to a ship in accordance with the load line rules,

such particulars relating to those requirements as may be determined in accordance with the rules are to be recorded in such manner as may be so determined; and

(*c*) provisions for determining by reference to those requirements and that record whether, at any time after freeboards have been so assigned to a ship and while they continue to be so assigned, the ship is for the purposes of this Act to be taken to comply, or not to comply, with the conditions of assignment;

and those provisions shall be set out separately in the load line rules under the title of 'rules as to conditions of assignment'.

(4) The load line rules shall also include provisions requiring such information relating to the stability of any ship to which freeboards are assigned thereunder, and such information relating to the loading and ballasting of any such ship, as may be determined in accordance with the rules to be provided for the guidance of the master of the ship in such manner as may be so determined.

(5) In relation to any matter authorised or required by this Act to be prescribed by the load line rules, those rules may make different provision by reference to (or to any combination of) any of the following, that is to say, different descriptions of ships, different areas, different seasons of the year and any other different circumstances.

(6) Except in so far as the context otherwise requires, in this Act 'deck-line' means such a mark as is referred to in paragraph (*c*) of subsection (2) of this section and 'load lines' means such lines as are referred to in paragraph (*d*) of that subsection.

COMMENTS.

For 'Board of Trade' read 'Department of Trade' and for 'Board' read 'Department'.

Rules.

Consult the Merchant Shipping (Load Lines) Rules 1968, S.I. 1968, No. 1053 as amended by the Merchant Shipping (Load Lines) Rules 1970, S.I. 1970, No. 1003 and the Merchant Shipping (Load Line) (Amendment) Rules 1975, S.I. 1975, No. 595.

⚓   ⚓   ⚓   ⚓

Ships registered in United Kingdom

3 (1) Subject to any exemption conferred by or under this Act, no ship to which this Act applies, being a ship registered in the United Kingdom, shall proceed or attempt to proceed to sea unless— Compliance with load line rules.

(*a*) the ship has been surveyed in accordance with the load line rules;

(*b*) the ship is marked with a deck-line and with load lines in accordance with those rules;

(*c*) the ship complies with the conditions of assignment; and

(*d*) the information required by those rules to be provided as mentioned in section 2(4) of this Act is provided for the guidance of the master of the ship in the manner determined in accordance with the rules.

(2) If any ship proceeds or attempts to proceed to sea in contravention of the preceding subsection, the owner or master of the ship shall be guilty of an offence and liable on summary conviction to a fine not exceeding £200.

(3) Any ship which in contravention of subsection (1) of this section attempts to proceed to sea without being surveyed and marked as mentioned in paragraphs (*a*) and (*b*) of that subsection may be detained until she has been so surveyed and marked.

(4) Any such ship as is mentioned in subsection (1) of this section which does not comply with the conditions of assignment shall be deemed to be unsafe for the purposes of section 459 of the Merchant Shipping Act 1894 (power to detain unsafe ships, and procedure for detention).

COMMENTS.

Exemptions.

Consult sections 18 to 22 of this Act.

Registered in the United Kingdom.

See section 2 of the principal Act.

May be Detained.

See section 459 of the Principal Act.

Enforcement.

See section 692 of the Principal Act.

Cost of Detention.

See section 460, sub-section 2 of the Principal Act.

⚓   ⚓   ⚓   ⚓

Submersion of
load lines.

4 (1) Where a ship to which this Act applies, being a ship registered in the United Kingdom, is marked with load lines, the ship shall not be so loaded that—

(*a*) if the ship is in salt water and has no list, the appropriate load line on each side of the ship is submerged, or

(*b*) in any other case, the appropriate load line on each side of the ship would be submerged if the ship were in salt water and had no list.

(2) If any ship is loaded in contravention of the preceding subsection, the owner or master of the ship shall (subject to subsection (5) of this section) be guilty of an offence and liable on summary conviction—

(*a*) to a fine not exceeding £400, and

(*b*) to such additional fine, not exceeding an amount calculated in accordance with the next following subsection, as the court thinks fit to impose, having regard to the extent to which the earning capacity of the ship was increased by reason of the contravention.

(3) Any additional fine imposed under subsection (2)(*b*) of this section shall not exceed £400 for every complete inch, and for any fraction of an inch over and above one or more complete inches, by which—

(*a*) in a case falling within paragraph (*a*) of subsection (1) of this section, the appropriate load line on each side of the ship was submerged, or

(*b*) in a case falling within paragraph (*b*) of that subsection, the appropriate load line on each side of the ship would have been submerged as therein mentioned;

and, if the amount by which that load line was or would have been submerged was less than a complete inch, any such additional fine shall not exceed £400.

(4) If the master of a ship takes the ship to sea when she is loaded in contravention of subsection (1) of this section, or if any other person, having reason to believe that the ship is so loaded, sends or is party to sending her to sea when she is

loaded in contravention of that subsection, then (without prejudice to any fine to which he may be liable in respect of an offence under subsection (2) of this section) he shall be guilty of an offence under this subsection and liable—

(a) on conviction on indictment, to a fine;

(b) on summary conviction, to a fine not exceeding £400.

(5) Where a person is charged with an offence under subsection (2) of this section, it shall be a defence to prove that the contravention was due solely to deviation or delay and that the deviation or delay was caused solely by stress of weather or other circumstances which neither the master nor the owner nor the charterer (if any) could have prevented or forestalled.

(6) Without prejudice to any proceedings under the preceding provisions of this section, any ship which is loaded in contravention of subsection (1) of this section may be detained until she ceases to be so loaded.

(7) For the purposes of the application of this section to a ship in any circumstances prescribed by the load line rules in accordance with section 2(2)(d) of this Act, 'the appropriate load line' means the load line which, in accordance with those rules, indicates the maximum depth to which the ship may be loaded in salt water in those circumstances.

COMMENTS.

Shall Not be Loaded.

It is not clear whether this condition refers to the time of sailing, or at at any time during the voyage, which would indeed be difficult to prove. It is considered by many authorities to be at any time during the voyage. Compare Radcliffe v. Buckwell 1927.

Loaded in Contravention.

In St. John Shipping Corporation v. Joseph Rank 1957, it was held that the fact that the ship was overloaded during the performance of a contract of carriage, with the master being prosecuted for an offence under this section, does not entitle the shipowner for the balance of freight under the contract of carriage.

Additional Fine Due to Increased Earning Capacity.

In Rutberg v. Williams 1961, it was held that there must be evidence of increased earning capacity.

⚓   ⚓   ⚓   ⚓

5 Where a ship to which this Act applies, being a ship registered in the United Kingdom, is marked in accordance with any requirements as to marking imposed by or under this Act, then if—

(a) the owner or master of the ship fails without reasonable cause to keep the ship so marked, or

(b) any person conceals, removes, alters, defaces or obliterates, or causes or permits any person under his control to conceal, remove, alter, deface or obliterate, any mark with which the ship is so marked, except where he does so under the authority of a person empowered under the load line rules to authorise him in that behalf.

he shall be guilty of an offence and liable on summary conviction to a fine not exceeding £200.

6 (1) Where a ship to which this Act applies, being a ship registered in the United Kingdom, has been surveyed and marked in accordance with the load line rules, the appropriate certificate shall be issued to the owner of the ship on his application.

(2) For the purposes of this section the appropriate certificate—

(a) in the case of an existing ship of not less than 150 tons gross tonnage, and in the case of a new ship of not less than 24 metres in length, is a certificate to be called an 'International Load Line Certificate (1966)', and

(b) in the case of any other ship, is a certificate to be called a 'United Kingdom load line certificate'.

(3) Subject to the next following subsection, any certificate required by subsection (1) of this section to be issued—

(a) shall be issued by the Board of Trade or by a person authorised in that behalf by the Board, and

(b) shall be in such form, and shall be issued in such manner, as may be prescribed by the load line rules.

(4) The Board of Trade may request a Contracting Government, other than Her Majesty's Government in the United Kingdom, to issue an International Load Line Certificate (1966) in respect of any ship to which this Act applies which is a ship registered in the United Kingdom and

falling within subsection (2)(*a*) of this section; and the following provisions of this Act shall have effect in relation to such a certificate so issued, which contains a statement that it has been issued at the request of Her Majesty's Government in the United Kingdom, as they have effect in relation to an International Load Line Certificate (1966) issued by the Board of Trade.

COMMENTS.

For 'Board of Trade' read 'Department of Trade', for 'Board' read 'Department'.

A Person Authorised.

This means an authorised Classification Society.

⚓   ⚓   ⚓   ⚓

7 Where a certificate, issued in pursuance of the last preceding section and for the time being in force, is produced in respect of the ship to which the certificate relates,— *Effect of load line certificate.*

(*a*) the ship shall be deemed to have been surveyed in accordance with the load line rules, and

(*b*) if lines are marked on the ship corresponding in number and description to the deck-line and load lines as required by the load line rules, and the positions of those lines so marked correspond to the positions of the deck-line and load lines as specified in the certificate, the ship shall be deemed to be marked as required by those rules.

⚓   ⚓   ⚓   ⚓

8 (1) The load line rules shall make provision for determining the period during which any certificate issued under section 6 of this Act is to remain in force, including— *Duration endorsement and cancellation of load line certificates.*

(*a*) provision enabling the period for which any such certificate is originally issued to be extended within such limits and in such circumstances as may be prescribed by the rules, and

(*b*) provision for cancelling any such certificate in such circumstances as may be so prescribed.

(2) While any such certificate is in force in respect of a ship, there shall be endorsed on the certificate such information relating to—

(*a*) periodical inspections of the ship in accordance with the load line rules, and

(*b*) any extension of the period for which the certificate was issued,

as may be prescribed by the rules.

⚓   ⚓   ⚓   ⚓

Ships not to proceed to sea without load line certificate.

9 (1) Subject to any exemption conferred by or under this Act, no ship to which this Act applies, being a ship registered in the United Kingdom, shall proceed or attempt to proceed to sea unless the appropriate certificate is in force in respect of the ship.

(2) Before any such ship proceeds to sea, the master of the ship shall produce the appropriate certificate to the officer of customs from whom a clearance for the ship is demanded; and a clearance shall not be granted, and the ship may be detained, until the appropriate certificate is so produced.

(3) If any ship proceeds or attempts to proceed to sea in contravention of this section, the master of the ship shall be guilty of an offence and liable on summary conviction to a fine not exceeding £200.

(4) In this section 'the appropriate certificate' means the certificate which is the appropriate certificate for the purposes of section 6 of this Act.

⚓   ⚓   ⚓   ⚓

Publication of load line certificate and entry of particulars in official log-book.

10 (1) Where a certificate is issued in respect of a ship under section 6 of this Act—

(*a*) the owner of the ship shall forthwith on receipt of the certificate cause it to be framed and posted up in some conspicuous place on board the ship, and shall cause it to be kept so framed and posted up and legible so long as the certificate remains in force and the ship is in use, and

(*b*) the master of the ship, before making any other entry in any official log-book relating to the ship, shall enter in it the particulars as to the positions of the deck-line and the load lines which are specified in the certificate.

(2) Before any ship to which this Act applies, being a ship

registered in the United Kingdom, leaves any dock, wharf, harbour or other place for the purpose of proceeding to sea, the master of the ship—

(a) shall enter in the official log-book such particulars relating to the depth to which the ship is for the time being loaded as may be prescribed by regulations made by the Board of Trade under this Act, and

(b) subject to the next following subsection, shall cause a notice, [in such form and containing such of those particulars as may be specified in the regulations for the purposes of this paragraph, to be posted up in some conspicuous place on board the ship;]

and, where such a notice has been posted up, the master of the ship shall cause it to be kept so posted up and legible until the ship arrives at some other dock, wharf, harbour or place.

(3) The regulations may exempt home trade ships, or any class of home trade ships specified in the regulations, from the requirements as to notices contained in the last preceding subsection.

(4) If the owner or master of a ship fails to comply with any requirement imposed on him by the preceding provisions of this section, he shall be guilty of an offence and liable on summary conviction to a fine not exceeding £50.

COMMENTS.

For 'Board of Trade' read 'Department of Trade'.

Repeal and Substitution.

Section 10, sub-section 1, paragraph (b) and the word 'and' immediately preceding the paragraph underlined, and section 10, sub-section 2, paragraph (a) underlined, Repealed Merchant Shipping Act 1970, section 100, Schedule 3, paragraph 12, and Fifth Schedule. The Merchant Shipping Act 1970 (Commencement No. 1) Order 1972, S.I. 1972, No. 1977.

Substitution.

In lieu of the words contained in square brackets from 'in such form' to the end of the paragraph, there shall be substituted the words 'to be posted up in some conspicuous place on board the ship, which shall be in such form and containing such particulars relating to the depth to which the ship is for the time being loaded as may be specified in regulations made by the Secretary of State for Trade under this Act'. Merchant Shipping Act 1970, Third Schedule, paragraph 12.

Regulations Made by the Department of Trade.

Consult the Merchant Shipping (Load Lines) (Particulars of Depth of Loading) Regulations 1972, S.I. 1972, No. 1841.

Forthwith—Meaning of.

Consult Re Muscovitch *ex parte* Muscovitch 1939, also Sameen *v.* Abeyenickrema 1963.

⚓ ⚓ ⚓ ⚓

Inspection of ships.

11 (1) A ship surveyor or engineer surveyor may inspect any ship to which this Act applies, being a ship registered in the United Kingdom, for the purpose of seeing that the provisions of this Act have been complied with in respect of the ship.

(2) For the purposes of any such inspection any such surveyor shall have all the powers of a Board of Trade inspector under the Merchant Shipping Act 1894.

⚓ ⚓ ⚓ ⚓

Ships not registered in United Kingdom

Valid Convention certificates.

12 (1) This section applies to any ship which, being a ship to which this Act applies and not being registered in the United Kingdom,—

(*a*) is registered in a Convention country or, not being registered in any such country or elsewhere, flies the flag of a Convention country, and

(*b*) is either an existing ship of not less than 150 tons gross tonnage or a new ship of not less than 24 metres in length.

(2) The Board of Trade may, at the request of the Government of the parent country of a ship to which this section applies, issue in respect of the ship a certificate in such form as may be prescribed by the load line rules, if the Board are satisfied that they could properly issue a certificate in respect of the ship under section 6(1) of this Act if the ship were registered in the United Kingdom.

(3) The load line rules shall make such provision as appears to the Board of Trade to be appropriate for securing that certificates which are issued as International Load Line Certificates (1966) in respect of ships to which this section applies, and are so issued by Governments other than Her Majesty's Government in the United Kingdom, shall be

recognised for the purposes of this Act in such circumstances as may be prescribed by the rules.

(4) Certificates issued as mentioned in subsection (2) or subsection (3) of this section shall be included among the certificates to be called 'International Load Line Certificates (1966)'.

5. In this Act 'valid Convention certificate' means a certificate which either—

(*a*) has been issued under subsection (2) of this section and is for the time being in force, or

(*b*) having been issued as mentioned in subsection (3) of this section, is produced in circumstances in which it is required by the load line rules to be recognised for the purposes of this Act.

⚓   ⚓   ⚓   ⚓

13 (1) Subject to the next following subsection, and to any exemption conferred by or under this Act, no ship to which this Act applies, not being a ship registered in the United Kingdom, shall proceed or attempt to proceed to sea from any port in the United Kingdom unless— *Compliance with load line rules.*

(*a*) the ship has been surveyed in accordance with the load line rules;

(*b*) the ship is marked with a deck-line and with load lines in accordance with those rules;

(*c*) the ship complies with the conditions of assignment; and

(*d*) the information required by those rules to be provided as mentioned in section 2(4) of this Act is provided foɹ the guidance of the master of the ship in the manner determined in accordance with the rules.

(2) The preceding subsection does not apply to a ship in respect of which a valid Convention certificate is produced.

(3) If any ship proceeds or attempts to proceed to sea in contravention of the preceding provisions of this section, the owner or master of the ship shall be guilty of an offence and liable on summary conviction to a fine not exceeding £200.

(4) Any ship which in contravention of this section attempts to proceed to sea without being surveyed and marked as mentioned in paragraphs (*a*) and (*b*) of subsection (1) of

this section may be detained until she has been so surveyed and marked.

(5) If any such ship as is mentioned in subsection (1) of this section, not being a ship in respect of which a valid Convention certificate is produced, does not comply with the conditions of assignment, then—

(a) if the ship is a British ship, she shall be deemed to be unsafe for the purposes of section 459 of the Merchant Shipping Act 1894, or

(b) if the ship is a foreign ship, section 462 of that Act shall have effect in relation to the ship as if she were unsafe by reason of one of the matters specified in that section.

COMMENTS.

Foreign Ship.

In the event of a foreign ship being detained, notice must be to its country's consular officer in accordance with the Merchant Shipping (Safety and Load Lines Conventions) Act 1932, section 69, and section 27, sub-section 1 of this Act.

⚓   ⚓   ⚓   ⚓

Submersion of load lines.

14 (1) Where a ship to which this Act applies, not being a ship registered in the United Kingdom, is within any port in the United Kingdom, and is marked with load lines, the ship shall not be so loaded that—

(a) if the ship is in salt water and has no list, the appropriate load line on each side of the ship is submerged, or

(b) in any other case, the appropriate load line on each side of the ship would be submerged if the ship were in salt water and had no list.

(2) Subsection (2), (3), (5) and (6) of section 4 of this Act shall have effect for the purposes of this section as if any reference in those subsections to subsection (1) of that section, or to paragraph (a) or paragraph (b) of the said subsection (1), were a reference to subsection (1), or (as the case may be) to the corresponding paragraph of subsection (1), of this section:

Provided that, in the case of a ship to which section 12 of this Act applies, the ship shall not be detained, and no proceedings shall be brought by virtue of this subsection, unless the ship has been inspected by a ship surveyor or engineer surveyor in pursuance of section 17 of this Act.

(3) In relation to a ship in respect of which a valid Convention certificate is produced, 'load line' in subsection (1) of this section means a line marked on the ship in the position of a load line specified in that certificate; and for the purposes of the application of the relevant provisions to such a ship in any circumstances for which a particular load line is specified in the certificate, the 'appropriate load line' means the load line which, in accordance with the certificate, indicates the maximum depth to which the ship may be loaded in salt water in those circumstances.

(4) Where a valid Convention certificate is not produced in respect of a ship, then, for the purposes of the application of the relevant provisions to that ship in any circumstances prescribed by the load line rules in accordance with section 2(2)(*d*) of this Act, 'the appropriate load line' means the load line which, in accordance with those rules, indicates the maximum depth to which the ship may be loaded in salt water in those circumstances.

(5) In subsections (3) and (4) of this section 'the relevant provisions' means the provisions of subsection (1) of this section and any provisions of section 4 of this Act as applied by subsection (2) of this section.

⚓   ⚓   ⚓   ⚓

15 (1) Where a ship to which this Act applies, not being *United Kingdom* a ship registered in the United Kingdom, has been surveyed *load line* and marked in accordance with the load line rules, then on the *certificates.* application of the owner of the ship a United Kingdom load line certificate shall be issued to him by the Board of Trade or by a person authorised in that behalf by the Board.

(2) Subject to the next following subsection, the provisions of sections 7 and 8 of this Act shall have effect in relation to a certificate issued under the preceding subsection as they have effect in relation to a certificate issued under section 6 of this Act.

(3) Any certificate issued under subsection (1) of this section in respect of a ship to which section 12 of this Act applies shall be valid only so long as the ship is not plying on international voyages, and shall be cancelled by the Board of Trade if they have reason to believe that the ship is plying on international voyages.

⚓   ⚓   ⚓   ⚓

Production of
certificate
to customs
officer.

16 (1) Subject to any exemption conferred by or under this Act, before a ship to which this Act applies, not being a ship registered in the United Kingdom, proceeds to sea from any port in the United Kingdom, the master of the ship shall produce the appropriate certificate to the officer of customs from whom a clearance for the ship is demanded; and a clearance shall not be granted, and the ship may be detained, until the appropriate certificate is so produced.

(2) For the purposes of this section the appropriate certificate—

(*a*) in the case of a ship to which section 12 of this Act applies, where a clearance for the ship is demanded in respect of an international voyage, is a valid Convention certificate;

(*b*) in the case of any such ship, where a clearance for the ship is demanded in respect of any other voyage, is either a valid Convention certificate or a United Kingdom load line certificate for the time being in force in respect of the ship; and

(*c*) in any other case, is a United Kingdom load line certificate for the time being in force in respect of the ship.

⚓   ⚓   ⚓   ⚓

Provisions as
to inspection.

17 (1) Subject to the following provisions of this section, a ship surveyor or engineer surveyor may inspect any ship to which this Act applies, not being a ship registered in the United Kingdom, while the ship is within any port in the United Kingdom; and for the purposes of any such inspection any such surveyor shall have all the powers of a Board of Trade inspector under the Merchant Shipping Act 1894.

(2) Any such surveyor may go on board any ship to which section 12 of this Act applies, while the ship is within any port in the United Kingdom, for the purpose of demanding production of any International Load Line Certificate (1966) or United Kingdom load line certificate for the time being in force in respect of the ship.

(3) If on any such demand a valid Convention certificate is produced to the surveyor in respect of the ship, the powers of the surveyor under subsection (1) of this section shall be limited to seeing—

(*a*) that the ship is not loaded beyond the limits allowed by the certificate;

(*b*) that lines are marked on the ship in the positions of the load lines specified in the certificate;

(*c*) that no material alterations have taken place in the hull or superstructures of the ship which affect the position in which any of those lines ought to be marked; and

(*d*) that the fittings and appliances for the protection of openings, the guard rails, the freeing ports and the means of access to the crew's quarters have been maintained on the ship in as effective a condition as they were in when the certificate was issued.

(4) If on an inspection of a ship under this section the shid is found to have been so materially altered in respect of the matters referred to in paragraph (*c*) or paragraph (*d*) of the last preceding subsection that the ship is manifestly unfit to proceed to sea without danger to human life, then—

(*a*) if the ship is a British ship, she shall be deemed to be unsafe for the purposes of section 459 of the Merchant Shipping Act 1894, or

(*b*) if the ship is a foreign ship, section 462 of that Act shall have effect in relation to the ship as if she were unsafe by reason of one of the matters specified in that section.

(5) Where a ship is detained under the provisions of that Act as applied by the last preceding subsection, the Board of Trade shall order the ship to be released as soon as they are satisfied that the ship is fit to proceed to sea without danger to human life.

COMMENTS.

For 'Board of Trade' read 'Department of Trade'.

⚓   ⚓   ⚓   ⚓

Exemptions

18 (1) If in the opinion of the Board of Trade the sheltered nature and conditions of international voyages— *Power to make exemption orders.*

(*a*) between near neighbouring ports in the United Kingdom and in another Convention country, or

(*b*) between near neighbouring ports in any two or more countries or territories outside the United Kingdom, make it unreasonable or impracticable to apply the provisions of this Act to ships plying on such voyages, and the Board are satisfied that the Government of the other country or territory (or, as the case may be, of each of the other countries or territories) concurs in that opinion, the Board may by order specifying those ports direct that ships plying on international voyages between those ports, or any class of such ships specified in the order, shall be exempt from the provisions of this Act.

(2) The Board of Trade may by order direct that ships under 80 tons register engaged solely in the coasting trade, or any class of such ships specified in the order, shall be exempt from the provisions of this Act while not carrying cargo, or (if the order so provides) shall be exempt from the provisions of this Act whether carrying cargo or not.

(3) Any order under this section may be made subject to such conditions as the Board of Trade think fit; and where any such order is made subject to conditions, the exemption conferred by the order shall not have effect in relation to a ship unless the ship complies with those conditions.

COMMENTS.

For 'Board of Trade' read 'Department of Trade'; for 'Board' read 'Department'.

Coasting Trade.

There is no definition in the Act of 'Coasting Trade' and 'Home Trade', which terms it is submitted are synonymous. *See* definition of 'home trade' in section 742 of the Principal Act.

'Every ship employed in trading or going within the following limits:—that is to say, the United Kingdom, the Channel Islands, and the Isle of Man, and the continent of Europe between the River Elbe and Brest, inclusive.'

⚓   ⚓   ⚓   ⚓

Further powers to exempt ships.

19 (1) In this section any reference to exempting a ship is a reference to exempting the ship either—

(a) from all the provisions of this Act and of the load line rules, or

(b) from such of those provisions as are specified in the instrument conferring the exemption.

(2) On the application of the owner of a ship to which this Act applies, which is registered in the United Kingdom and is either an existing ship of not less than 150 tons gross tonnage or a new ship of not less than 24 metres in length, the Board

of Trade may exempt the ship if in their opinion the ship embodies features of a novel kind such that, if the ship had to comply with all the requirements of this Act and of the load line rules, the development of those features and their incorporation in ships engaged on international voyages might be seriously impeded.

(3) On the application of the owner of a ship to which this Act applies, which is registered in the United Kingdom and is either—

(a) an existing ship of less than 150 tons gross tonnage or a new ship of less than 24 metres in length, or

(b) a ship (not falling within the preceding paragraph) which does not ply on international voyages,

the Board of Trade may exempt the ship.

(4) Without prejudice to the last preceding subsection, where a ship to which this Act applies, which is registered in the United Kingdom and is either an existing ship of not less than 150 tons gross tonnage or a new ship of not less than 24 metres in length, does not normally ply on international voyages but is, in exceptional circumstances, required to undertake a single international voyage, the Board of Trade, on the application of the owner of the ship, specifying the international voyage in question, may exempt the ship while engaged on that voyage.

(5) Any exemption conferred under this section may be conferred subject to such conditions as the Board of Trade think fit; and, where any such exemption is conferred subject to conditions, the exemption shall not have effect unless those conditions are complied with.

COMMENTS.

For 'Board of Trade' read 'Department of Trade'.

Load Line Rules.

See comments to section 2.

⚓   ⚓   ⚓   ⚓

20 (1) Where the Board of Trade exempt a ship under the last preceding section, the Board shall issue the appropriate certificate to the owner of the ship. Issue of exemption certificates.

(2) For the purposes of this section the appropriate certificate—

(*a*) where the exemption is conferred under subsection (2) or subsection (4) of the last preceding section, is a certificate to be called an 'International Load Line Exemption Certificate', and

(*b*) where the certificate is conferred under subsection (3) of that section, is a certificate to be called a 'United Kingdom load line exemption certificate'.

(3) Any certificate issued under this section shall be in such form, and shall be issued in such manner, as may be prescribed by the load line rules.

COMMENTS.

For 'Board of Trade' read 'Department of Trade'.

Load Line Rules.

See comments to section 2.

⚓   ⚓   ⚓   ⚓

Duration and termination of exemptions, and duration, endorsement and cancellation of exemption certificates.

21 (1) The load line rules shall make provision for determining the period during which any exemption conferred under section 19 of this Act, or any certificate issued under section 20 of this Act, is to remain in force, including—

(*a*) provision enabling the period for which any such exemption or certificate is originally conferred or issued to be extended within such limits and in such circumstances as may be prescribed by the rules, and

(*b*) provision for terminating any such exemption, and for cancelling any such certificate, in such circumstances as may be so prescribed.

(2) While any such certificate is in force in respect of a ship, there shall be endorsed on the certificate such information relating to—

(*a*) periodical inspections of the ship in accordance with the load line rules, and

(*b*) any extension of the period for which the certificate was issued,

as may be prescribed by the rules.

COMMENTS.

Load Line Rules.

See comments to section 2.

⚓   ⚓   ⚓   ⚓

22 (1) The load line rules shall make such provisions as appears to the Board of Trade to be appropriate for securing that exemption certificates which, in accordance with the Convention of 1966, are issued in respect of ships to which section 12 of this Act applies, and are so issued by Governments other than Her Majesty's Government in the United Kingdom, shall in such circumstances as may be prescribed by the rules have the like effect for the purposes of this Act as if they were valid Convention certificates.

(2) Certificates issued as mentioned in the preceding subsection shall be included among the certificates to be called 'International Load Line Exemption Certificates'.

COMMENTS.

For 'Board of Trade' read 'Department of Trade'.

Load Line Rules.

See comments to section 2.

⚓   ⚓   ⚓   ⚓

Subdivision load lines and deck cargo

23 (1) Where in pursuance of any rules for the time Subdivision load lines. being in force under section 1 of the Merchant Shipping (Safety Convention) Act 1949 a passenger steamer to which this Act applies, being a ship registered in the United Kingdom, is marked with subdivision load lines, and the lowest of those lines is lower than the line which, apart from this subsection would be the appropriate load line for the purposes of section 4 of this Act, the said section 4 shall have effect as if that subdivision load line were the appropriate load line for the purposes of that section.

(2) Where in pursuance of any such rules, or in pursuance of the Convention referred to in that Act as the Safety Convention or any law of any country made for the purpose of giving effect to that Convention, a passenger steamer to which this Act applies, not being a ship registered in the United Kingdom, is marked with subdivision load lines, and the lowest of those load lines is lower than the line which, apart from this subsection, would be the appropriate load line for the purposes of section 14 of this Act, that section shall have effect as if that subdivision load line were the appropriate load line for the purposes of that section.

(3) In this section 'passenger steamer' has the meaning assigned to it by section 26 of the Merchant Shipping (Safety Convention) Act 1949.

⚓   ⚓   ⚓   ⚓

Deck cargo.

24 (1) The Board of Trade shall make regulations (in this section referred to as 'the deck cargo regulations') prescribing requirements to be complied with where cargo is carried in any uncovered space on the deck of a ship to which this Act applies; and different requirements may be so prescribed in relation to different descriptions of ships, different descriptions of cargo, different voyages or classes of voyages, different seasons of the year or any other different circumstances.

(2) If the load line rules provide (either generally or in particular cases or classes of cases) for assigning special freeboards to ships which are to have effect only where a cargo of timber is so carried, then (without prejudice to the generality of the preceding subsection) the deck cargo regulations may prescribe special requirements to be complied with in circumstances where any such special freeboard has effect.

(3) In prescribing any such special requirements as are mentioned in the last preceding subsection, the Board of Trade shall have regard in particular to the provisions of Chapter IV of the Convention of 1966.

(4) If any provisions of the deck cargo regulations are contravened—

(a) in the case of a ship registered in the United Kingdom, or
(b) in the case of any other ship while the ship is within any port in the United Kingdom,

the master of the ship shall (subject to the next following subsection) be guilty of an offence and liable on summary conviction to a fine not exceeding £1,000.

(5) Where a person is charged with an offence under the last preceding subsection, it shall be a defence to prove that the contravention was due solely to deviation or delay and that the deviation or delay was caused solely by stress of weather or other circumstances which neither the master nor the owner nor the charterer (if any) could have prevented or forestalled.

(6) For the purpose of securing compliance with the deck cargo regulations, any person authorised in that behalf by the Board of Trade may inspect any ship to which this Act applies which is carrying cargo in any uncovered space on her deck; and for the purposes of any such inspection any such person shall have all the powers of a Board of Trade inspector under the Merchant Shipping Act 1894.

COMMENTS.

For 'Board of Trade' read 'Department of Trade'.

Regulations.

Consult the Merchant Shipping (Load Lines) (Deck Cargo) Regulations 1968, S.I. 1968, No. 1089.

⚓   ⚓   ⚓   ⚓

Miscellaneous and supplementary provisions

25 (1) A person who after the passing of this Act commits an offence under any of the enactments specified in column 1 of Schedule 1 to this Act shall (instead of being liable on summary conviction to the penalty specified in column 2 of that Schedule) be liable, on conviction as mentioned in column 3 of that Schedule, to the penalty specified in the said column 3. *Increase of penalties for offences in connection with passenger steamers.*

(2) Section 1 of this Act shall not have effect for the purposes of this section.

COMMENTS.

This Act was passed on the 10th May, 1967.

⚓   ⚓   ⚓   ⚓

26 (1) In respect of any survey or inspection carried out in pursuance of the load line rules, and in respect of any certificate issued under this Act, there shall be paid such fee as may be prescribed by regulations made by the Board of Trade with the approval of the Treasury. *Provisions as to fees.*

(2) Subject to the next following subsection, any fees payable under the preceding subsection shall be paid into the Exchequer.

(3) The last preceding subsection shall not apply to any fee paid in respect of—

(*a*) a survey or inspection which is carried out otherwise than by a surveyor of ships appointed under the Merchant Shipping Act 1894, or

(*b*) a certificate issued otherwise than by the Board of Trade.

COMMENTS.

Fees Payable.

See now the Merchant Shipping (Fees) Regulations 1977, S.I. 1977, No. 2049, which revokes previous fees regulations.

For 'Board of Trade' read 'Department of Trade'.

Certificate Issued Otherwise.

I.e. by an authorised Classification society.

⚓ ⚓ ⚓ ⚓

Miscellaneous supplementary provisions.

27 (1) Without prejudice to the operation of section 34(2) of this Act, section 69 of the Merchant Shipping (Safety and Load Line Conventions) Act 1932 (notice to be given to consular officer where proceedings taken in respect of foreign ships) shall have effect as if any reference therein to that Act included a reference to this Act.

(2) Where a ship is detained under any provision of this Act which provides for the detention of a ship until an event specified in that provision occurs, section 460(2) of the Merchant Shipping Act 1894 (which relates to the costs of detention) shall apply as if the ship had been finally detained under that Act.

(3) The provisions of section 280 of that Act (delivery up of certificate) and of section 282 of that Act (penalty for forgery of certificate or declaration) shall have effect in relation to any certificate which can be issued under this Act as they have effect in relation to a passenger steamer's certificate.

(4) Section 436(3) of that Act (which provides for recording the draught of water and the freeboard of ships) shall not have effect in relation to ships to which this Act applies, except any such ship which, by virtue of any order made or exemption conferred under this Act, is exempt from all the provisions of this Act.

(5) Any certificate issued under this Act shall be admissible in evidence.

⚓ ⚓ ⚓ ⚓

28 (1) Her Majesty may by Order in Council direct that the provisions of this Act shall extend, with such exceptions, adaptations or modifications as may be specified in the Order, to— *Application of Act in relation to certain territories outside United Kingdom.*

(a) the Isle of Man;

(b) any of the Channel Islands;

(c) any colony;

(d) any territory outside Her Majesty's dominions in which for the time being Her Majesty has jurisdiction.

(2) In respect of any territory falling within any of paragraphs (a) to (d) of the preceding subsection, Her Majesty may by Order in Council, specifying that territory, give either or both of the following directions, that is to say—

(a) that, with such exceptions, adaptations or modifications as may be specified in the Order, the provisions of this Act shall have effect as if references in this Act to a ship registered in the United Kingdom included references to a ship registered in that territory;

(b) that, with such exceptions, adaptations or modifications as may be so specified, the provisions of this Act shall have effect as if references in this Act to a port in the United Kingdom included references to a port in that territory.

(3) If, in the case of any country or territory outside the United Kingdom, it appears to Her Majesty in Council—

(a) that the provisions which, as part of the law of that country or territory, have effect for marking ships with load lines, and for the issue of certificates in respect of ships so marked, are based on the same principles as the corresponding provisions of this Act and are equally effective, and

(b) that provision has been, or in pursuance of any agreement will be, made by the law of that country or territory for recognising United Kingdom load line certificates as having the like effect in ports of that country or territory as certificates issued under the provisions referred to in the preceding paragraph,

Her Majesty may by Order in Council direct (subject to the next following subsection) that certificates issued under those provisions shall have the like effect for the purposes of this Act as if they were United Kingdom load line certificates.

(4) An Order in Council under subsection (3) of this section shall not have effect in relation to any ship which—

(*a*) plies on international voyages, and

(*b*) is a ship of a Convention country, and

(*c*) is either an existing ship of not less than 150 tons gross tonnage or a new ship of not less than 24 metres in length.

(5) In this section any reference to the provisions of this Act shall be construed as including a reference to the provisions of any rules or regulations made under this Act.

COMMENTS.

Order in Council.

Consult in respect of any country or territory outside the United Kingdom, the Merchant Shipping (Load Lines Certificates) (Various Countries) Order 1968, S.I. 1968, No. 1110.

⚓   ⚓   ⚓   ⚓

Application of Act to certain unregistered British ships.

29 (1) This section applies to ships which—

(*a*) are British ships to which this Act applies, but

(*b*) are not registered, whether in the United Kingdom or eslewhere.

(2) The Board of Trade may by order specify a class of ships to which this section applies and direct that, in such circumstances as may be specified in the order, the provisions of this Act relating to ships registered in the United Kingdom shall have effect in relation to ships of that class as if they were registered in the United Kingdom.

COMMENTS.

For 'Board of Trade' read 'Department of Trade'.

Order.

No order has been made under this section.

⚓   ⚓   ⚓   ⚓

30 (1) Any Order in Council, order, rules or regulations made under this Act may contain such transitional or other incidental and supplementary provisions as may appear to Her Majesty in Council, or (as the case may be) to the Board of Trade, to be appropriate.

Provisions as to orders, rules and regulations, and as to functions of Board of Trade.

(2) Any power of the Board of Trade to make an order under this Act shall include power to revoke or vary the order by a subsequent order.

(3) Any power to make orders under section 18 or section 29 of this Act, and any power to make rules or regulations under any provision of this Act, shall be exercisable by statutory instrument; and any statutory instrument containing any such order, rules or regulations shall be subject to annulment in pursuance of a resolution of either House of Parliament.

(4) Without prejudice to the operation of section 34(2) of this Act, section 4 of the Merchant Shipping Act 1965 (exercise of powers of Board of Trade) shall have effect for the purposes of this Act as it has effect for the purposes of that Act.

COMMENTS.

Repeal.

Sub-section 4 above, underlined, repealed Industrial Expansion Act 1968, section 18, sub-section 2, and Schedule 4.

For 'Board of Trade' read 'Department of Trade'.

⚓   ⚓   ⚓   ⚓

31 (1) Her Majesty, if satisfied—

Convention countries.

(*a*) that the Government of a country has accepted or acceded to, or has denounced, the Convention of 1966, or

(*b*) that the Convention of 1966 extends, or has ceased to extend, to a particular territory.

may by Order in Council make a declaration to that effect.

(2) In this Act 'Convention country' means a country or territory which is either—

(*a*) a country the Government of which has been declared

under this section to have accepted or acceded to the Convention of 1966, and has not been so declared to have denounced that Convention, or

(b) a territory to which it has been so declared that the Convention of 1966 extends, not being a territory to which it has been so declared that that Convention has ceased to extend,

and 'Contracting Government' means any such Government as is referred to in paragraph (a) of this subsection.

COMMENTS.

Order in Council.

Consult The Merchant Shipping (Load Lines Convention) (Various Countries) Order 1977, S.I. 1977, No. 1875, for the complete list of the countries which have accepted or acceded to the 1966 Convention.

This Order came into operation on the 14th November, 1977.

⚓   ⚓   ⚓   ⚓

32 (1) In this Act, except in so far as the context otherwise requires, the following expressions have the meanings hereby assigned to them respectively, that is to say:—

'alteration' includes deterioration;

'clearance' includes a transire;

'Convention country' and 'Contracting Government' have the meanings assigned to them by section 31(2) of this Act;

'parent country', in relation to a ship, means the country or territory in which the ship is registered, or, if the ship is not registered anywhere, means the country or territory whose flag the ship flies;

'valid Convention certificate' has the meaning assigned to it by section 12(5) of this Act.

(2) In this Act, subject to the next following subsection, 'international voyage' means a voyage between—

(a) a port in the United Kingdom and a port outside the United Kingdom, or

(b) a port in a Convention country (other than the United Kingdom) and a port in any other country or territory (whether a Convention country or not) which is outside the United Kingdom.

(3) In determining, for the purposes of the last proceeding subsection, what are the ports between which a voyage is made, no account shall be taken of any deviation by a ship from her intended voyage which is due solely to stress of weather or any other circumstance which neither the master nor the owner nor the charterer (if any) of the ship could have prevented or forestalled; and for the purposes of that subsection any colony, protectorate or other dependency, any territory for whose international relations a Government is separately responsible, and any territory for which the United Nations are the administering authority, shall be taken to be a separate territory.

(4) In this Act 'new ship' means a ship whose keel is laid, or which is at a similar stage of construction, on or after the material date, and 'existing ship' means a ship which is not a new ship; and for the purposes of this subsection the material date—

(a) in relation to a ship whose parent country is a convention country other than the United Kingdom, is the date as from which it is declared under section 31 of this Act either that the Government of that country has accepted or acceded to the Convention of 1966 or that it is a territory to which that Convention extends, and

(b) in relation to any other ship, is the date of the commencement of this Act.

(5) Any reference in this Act to the gross tonnage of a ship shall be construed as a reference to the tonnage of the ship as ascertained in accordance with the tonnage regulations of the Merchant Shipping Act 1894; and, where in accordance with those regulations alternative tonnages are assigned to a ship, the gross tonnage of the ship shall, for the purposes of this Act, be taken to be the larger of those tonnages.

(6) For the purposes of this Act the length of a ship shall be ascertained in accordance with regulations made by the Board of Trade under this Act.

(7) Any reference in this Act to any provision of the Convention of 1966 shall, in relation to any time after that provision has been amended in pursuance of Article 29 of that Convention, be construed as a reference to that provision as so amended.

L

(8) Except in so far as the context otherwise requires, any referrence in this Act to an enactment shall be construed as a reference to that enactment as amended or extended by or under any other enactment.

COMMENTS.

Tonnage Regulations, Merchant Shipping Acts 1894.

These are now replaced by the Merchant Shipping Act 1965, section 1, Schedule 1.

See also Merchant Shipping (Tonnage Regulations) 1967, S.I. No. 172 as amended by:

Merchant Shipping (Tonnage Regulations) 1967, S.I. No. 1093.
Merchant Shipping (Tonnage Regulations) 1972, S.I. No. 656.
Merchant Shipping (Tonnage Regulations) 1975, S.I. No. 594.

For 'Board of Trade' read 'Department of Trade'.

Length of Ship.

Consult Merchant Shipping (Load Lines) (Length of Ship) Regulations 1968, S.I. 1968, No. 1072.

⚓   ⚓   ⚓   ⚓

Repeals and transitional provisions.

33 (1) Subject to the following provisions of this section, the enactments specified in Schedule 2 to this Act are hereby repealed to the extent specified in the third column of that Schedule.

(2) The repeal effected by the preceding subsection shall not affect the operation of any enactment as part of the law of any territory outside the United Kingdom, and accordingly shall not affect any Order in Council made under subsection (1) of section 64 of the Merchant Shipping (Safety and Load Line Conventions) Act 1932, or made by virtue of the Foreign Jurisdiction Act 1890 as modified by subsection (2) of that section, or any power to revoke or vary any such Order in Council.

(3) Without prejudice to the last preceding subsection and to the operation of section 38 of the Interpretation Act 1889 (which relates to the effect of repeals), for the purposes of the transition from the law in force immediately before the commencement of this Act to the provisions of this Act the Board of Trade may by regulations provide that those provisions shall have effect subject to such transitional provisions as may be contained in the regulations.

COMMENTS.

For 'Board of Trade' read 'Department of Trade'.

Regulations.

Consult Merchant Shipping (Load Lines) (Transitional Provisions) Regulations 1968, S.I. No. 1052.

⚓   ⚓   ⚓   ⚓

34 (1) This Act may be cited as the Merchant Shipping (Load Lines) Act 1967.

Short title, construction, citation, commencement and extent.

(2) This Act shall be construed as one with the Merchant Shipping Acts 1894 to 1965, and, without prejudice to the generality of this provision, references in those Acts to the Merchant Shipping Acts shall be construed as including references to this Act; and this Act shall be included among the Acts which may be cited together as the Merchant Shipping Acts 1894 to 1967.

(3) Section 25 of, and Schedule 1 to, this Act shall come into operation on the passing of this Act; and all the other provisions of this Act shall come into operation on such day as Her Majesty may by Order in Council appoint.

(4) For the purposes of the operation in relation to this Act of sections 36 and 37 of the Interpretation Act 1889 (which relate respectively to the meaning of 'commencement' with reference to an Act and to the exercise of statutory powers between the passing and the commencement of an Act) the day appointed under the last preceding subsection shall be taken to be the date on which this Act comes into operation; and references in this Act to the commencement of this Act shall be construed accordingly.

(5) This Act extends to Northern Ireland.

COMMENTS.

Passing of this Act.

The Act was passed on the 10th May, 1967.

Appointed Day.

21st July, 1968.

⚓   ⚓   ⚓   ⚓

Schedules 1 and 2

The increases in penalties contained in Schedule 1 and the enactments repealed in Schedule 2 have been entered in the appropriate place in the body of the text.

⚓   ⚓   ⚓   ⚓

Anchors and Chain Cables Act 1967

An Act to make new provision in substitution for the Anchors
and Chain Cables Act 1899.

NOTE:

This Act, which Repeals The Anchors and Chain Cables Act
1899, came into force on the 19th October 1970 per The
Anchors and Chain Cables Act 1967 (Commencement)
Order 1970, S.I. 1970, No. 1443.

1 (1) The Board of Trade shall make rules with respect ^{Rules for testing anchors}
to the testing of anchors and chain cables for use in ships ^{and chain cables.}
registered in the United Kingdom, and such rules may in
particular—

(*a*) prescribe the manner in which tests of anchors and cables
are to be carried out, the tensile strains and breaking
strains to be employed in such tests and the requirements
to be fulfilled by equipment used for the purposes of such
tests;

(*b*) provide for the marking of anchors and cables which have
passed such tests and for the issue of certificates in respect
of such anchors and cables;

(*c*) provide for the supervision of such tests and marking,
and for the inspection of such equipment, by surveyors
of ships appointed under the Merchant Shipping Act 1894
or by such other persons as the Board of Trade may
authorise for the purpose;

(*d*) provide for the payment of fees in respect of such supervision and inspection and in respect of the issue of certificates under the rules; and

(*e*) provide that the rules shall not apply to anchors or cables
of such classes or descriptions as may be specified in the
rules or which are exempted therefrom by the Board of
Trade in accordance with any provision in that behalf
contained in the rules.

(2) No ship registered in the United Kingdom shall have
on board as part of her equipment an anchor or chain

cable, being an anchor or cable which was first taken on board after the commencement of this Act, unless—

(*a*) the anchor or cable has been marked, and a certificate in respect of it has been issued, in accordance with rules under this section; or

(*b*) the anchor or cable is one to which those rules do not apply by virtue of any provision therein made under paragraph (*e*) of subsection (1) of this section;

and if this subsection is contravened in respect of any ship the owner or master of the ship shall be liable on summary conviction to a fine not exceeding four hundred pounds.

(3) If any person applies to any anchor or cable which has not passed the tests prescribed by rules under this section any mark prescribed by those rules for denoting that it has passed those tests, or any other mark calculated to suggest that it has passed those tests, he shall be liable on summary conviction to a fine not exceeding four hundred pounds.

(4) Section 684 of the Merchant Shipping Act 1894 (jurisdiction) shall apply for the purposes of this section as it applies for the purposes of that Act.

(5) Any fees payable by virtue of this section in respect of any functions of a surveyor of ships appointed under the said Act of 1894 shall be paid into the Exchequer.

(6) The power to make rules under this section shall be exercisable by statutory instrument, and any such statutory instrument shall be subject to annulment in pursuance of a resolution of either House of Parliament.

(7) In this section 'anchor' and 'chain cable' include any shackle attached to or intended to be used in connection with the anchor or cable, and 'ship' and 'master' have the same meanings respectively as in the said Act of 1894.

(8) The powers of the Board of Trade under this section or any rules made thereunder may be exercised by the President of the Board, any Minister of State with duties concerning the affairs of the Board, any secretary, under-secretary or assistant secretary of the Board or any person authorised in that behalf by the President.

COMMENTS.

For 'Board of Trade' read 'Department of Trade.'

For 'President of the Board' read 'Secretary of State for Trade'.
For 'Board' read 'Department'.
For 'President' read 'Secretary of State'.

Shall Make Rules.
Consult the Anchors and Chain Cables Rules 1970, S.I. 1970, No. 1453.

⚓   ⚓   ⚓   ⚓

2 (1) This Act may be cited as the Anchors and Chain Cables Act 1967.

(2) The Anchors and Chain Cables Act 1899 is hereby repealed.

(3) Any anchor or cable tested or marked, and any certificate issued, before the commencement of this Act under the said Act of 1899 shall be deemed to have been tested or marked, or, as the case may be, issued, in accordance with rules under section 1 of this Act.

(4) This Act shall come into force on such day as Her Majesty may by Order in Council appoint.

(5) This Act extends to Northern Ireland.

Short title, repeal, saving, commencement and extent.
1899 c. 23.

COMMENTS.

Appointed Day.
See note at beginning of Act.

⚓   ⚓   ⚓   ⚓

Fishing Vessels (Safety Provisions) Act 1970

INTRODUCTORY COMMENTS:

The Fishing Vessels (Safety Provisions) Rules 1975, S.I. 1975, No. 330, referred to within the text of this Act are quite voluminous and far reaching in their extent. They have since been amended by the Fishing Vessels (Safety Provisions) (Amendment) Rules 1975, S.I. 1975, No. 471 and the Fishing Vessels (Safety Provisions) (Amendment) Rules 1976, S.I. 1976, No. 432; and Statutory Instruments 1977, Nos. 252, 498.

They amend the Merchant Shipping (Life Saving Appliances) Rules 1965, S.I. 1965, No. 1105; The Merchant Shipping (Fire Appliances) Rules 1965, S.I. 1965, No. 1106; The Merchant Shipping (Musters) Rules 1965, S.I. 1965, No. 1113 and the Merchant Shipping (Official Log Books) (Fishing Vessels) Regulations 1972, S.I. 1972, No. 1873, as amended S.I. 1975, No. 330, S.I. 1975, No. 2220, S.I. 1977, No. 628.

Parts 1, 3 and 4, came into operation on the 1st May, 1975. The remaining provisions being effective at different specified times in the near future. They institute:

(1) A system of surveys and periodical inspections for fishing vessels registered in the United Kingdom; a United Kingdom fishing vessel certificate will be issued to vessels which meet the specified requirements; and

(2) Construction rules for fishing vessels including specified requirements in respect of the hull and equipment, watertight integrity, freeboard and stability, boilers and machinery, bilge pumping arrangements, electrical equipment and installations, miscellaneous plant and equipment, structural fire protection and fire detection, protection of the crew, nautical equipment, including charts and documentation to be carried.

From the date of coming into operation of these rules:

(*a*) fishing vessels must comply with specified requirements for life-saving appliances and equipment, including fire appliances to be carried and requirements for musters and drills (these provisions reproduce existing requirements); and

(*b*) provision is made for excepting vessels from requirements relating to the constructions of the hull or machinery in a particular manner or to the provision of particular equipment or to the making of particular provisions if another manner of construction or provisions of equipment or other provision is made which is at least as effective as that required by the Rules.

⚓   ⚓   ⚓   ⚓

1 (1) The Board of Trade may make rules (in this Act referred to as 'fishing vessel construction rules') prescribing requirements for the hull, equipment and machinery of fishing vessels of any description registered in the United Kingdom (including any description framed by reference to the areas in which the vessels operate or the dates on which they were first registered in the United Kingdom or on which their construction was begun). *Fishing vessel construction rules.*

(2) The Board of Trade may exempt any fishing vessel or description of fishing vessel from any requirement of the fishing vessel construction rules, either generally or for a specified time or with respect to a specified voyage or to voyages in a specified area, and may do so subject to any specified conditions.

(3) A surveyor of ships may inspect any fishing vessel for the purpose of seeing that it complies with the fishing vessel construction rules, and for that purpose shall have all the powers of a Board of Trade inspector under the Merchant Shipping Act 1894.

(4) If—

(a) the fishing vessel construction rules are contravened with respect to any vessel; or

(b) a vessel is, under subsection (2) of this section, exempted from any requirement subject to a condition and the condition is not complied with;

the owner or master of the vessel shall be liable on summary conviction to a fine not exceeding £400.

COMMENTS.

For 'Board of Trade' read 'Department of Trade'.

Rules.

Consult the introductory comments to this Act.

⚓   ⚓   ⚓   ⚓

2 (1) The Board of Trade may make rules (in this Act referred to as 'fishing vessel survey rules') for the surveying and periodical inspection of fishing vessels registered in the *Fishing vessel survey rules.*

United Kingdom, or any description of such fishing vessels, for the purpose of ensuring their compliance with the requirements of the fishing vessel construction rules, the rules for life-saving appliances, the radio rules, the rules for direction-finders and the rules for radio navigational aids applicable to them.

(2) Section 275 of the Merchant Shipping Act 1894 (appeals to the court of survey) shall apply to surveys carried out under the fishing vessel survey rules with such modifications as may be prescribed by the rules.

COMMENTS.

For 'Board of Trade' read 'Department of Trade'.

Fishing Construction Rules.

Consult the introductory comments to this Act.

Rules for Life-saving Appliances.

See the Merchant Shipping (Life-saving Appliances) Rules 1965, S.I. 1965, No. 1105 as amended by:—

S.I. 1966, No. 744; S.I. 1969, No. 409; S.I. 1975, No. 330; S.I. 1977, No. 229; The Merchant Shipping (Fire Appliances) Rules 1965, S.I. 1965, No. 1106 as amended by S.I. 1975, No. 330; The Merchant Shipping (Musters) Rules 1965, S.I. 1965, No. 1113; S.I. 1977, No. 252, as amended by S.I. 1975, No. 330.

The Radio Rules.

See the Merchant Shipping (Radio) (Fishing Vessels) Rules 1974, S.I. 1974, No. 1919.

Radio Navigational Aids.

No rules have yet been promulgated.

Rules for Direction-finders.

See the Merchant Shipping (Direction Finders) Rules 1965, S.I. 1965, No. 1112.

⚓ ⚓ ⚓ ⚓

Fishing
vessel
certificates.

3 (1) If the Board of Trade or any person authorised by them for the purpose are satisfied, on receipt of a declaration of survey in respect of a fishing vessel surveyed under the fishing vessel survey rules, that the vessel complies with such of the requirements of—

(*a*) the fishing vessel construction rules;

(*b*) the rules for life-saving appliances; or

(*c*) the radio rules, the rules for direction-finders and the rules for radio navigational aids;

as are or will be applicable to the vessel, then, subject to sub-section (2) of this section, the Board or person shall, on the application of the owner, issue a certificate showing that the vessel complies with those requirements; and for this purpose any requirement from which the vessel has been exempted under section 1(2) of this Act or any other provision of the Merchant Shipping Acts shall be deemed not to be applicable to it.

(2) Fishing vessel survey rules may require, in the case of such certificate to be issued under this section as may be specified in the rules, that the Board of Trade or person authorised to issue it shall not issue the certificate unless satisfied that the vessel in respect of which it is to be issued is provided with the lights, shapes and means of making fog signals required by the collision regulations.

(3) A certificate issued under this section shall be in such form as may be prescribed by the fishing vessel survey rules; and those rules may make provision for the duration, extension or cancellation of any such certificate and for the endorsement on it of information relating to the inspection, in accordance with the rules, of the vessel to which it relates and of any extension of the period for which the certificate was issued.

(4) Sections 280 to 282 of the Merchant Shipping Act 1894 (delivery up and posting up of certificates and penalty for forgery) shall apply in relation to any certificate provided for by this section as they apply in relation to a passenger steamer's certificate.

(5) Any certificate issued under this section shall be admissible in evidence.

COMMENTS.

For 'Board of Trade' read 'Department of Trade'.

See generally also, comments to section 2.

⚓   ⚓   ⚓   ⚓

4 (1) No fishing vessel required to be surveyed under the fishing vessel survey rules shall go to sea unless there are in force certificates issued under section 3 of this Act showing that the vessel complies with such of the requirements of the *Prohibition on going to sea without appropriate certificates.*

fishing vessel construction rules, the rules for life-saving appliances, the radio rules, the rules for direction-finders and the rules for radio navigational aids as are applicable to the vessel.

(2) If any fishing vessel goes to sea or attempts to go to sea in contravention of this section, the owner or master of the vessel shall be liable on summary conviction to a fine not exceeding £200.

(3) The master of any fishing vessel registered in the United Kingdom shall on demand produce to any officer of customs or of the Board of Trade any certificate required by this Act; and the fishing vessel may be detained until the certificate is so produced.

(4) Where a fishing vessel is detained under this section, section 460(2) of the Merchant Shipping Act 1894 (which relates to the cost of detention) shall apply as if the vessel had been finally detained under that Act.

COMMENTS.

For 'Board of Trade' read 'Department of Trade'.

See generally, also, comments to section 2.

⚓   ⚓   ⚓   ⚓

Notice of alterations.

5 (1) Where a certificate issued under section 3 of this Act is in force in respect of a fishing vessel and—

(*a*) the certificate shows compliance with requirements of the fishing vessel construction rules and an alteration is made in the vessel's hull, equipment or machinery which affects the efficiency thereof or the seaworthiness of the vessel; or

(*b*) the certificate shows compliance with requirements of the rules for life-saving appliances and an alteration is made affecting the efficiency or completeness of the appliances or equipment which the vessel is required to carry by those rules; or

(*c*) the certificate shows compliance with requirements of the rules mentioned in section 3(1)(*c*) of this Act and an alteration is made affecting the efficiency or completeness of the equipment which the vessel is required to carry by those rules;

the owner or master shall, as soon as possible after the alteration is made, give written notice containing full particulars of it to the Board of Trade or, if the certificate was issued by another person, to that person; and if the notice is not given as required by this section the owner or master shall be liable on summary conviction to a fine not exceeding £50.

(2) In this section 'alteration' in relation to anything includes the renewal of any part of it.

COMMENTS.

For 'Board of Trade' read 'Department of Trade'.

See generally, also, comments to section 2.

⚓   ⚓   ⚓   ⚓

6 The Board of Trade may with the consent of the ^{Fees.} Treasury make regulations prescribing fees to be paid in respect of the doing of any thing in pursuance of this Act, and any such fee shall be paid into the Consolidated Fund except—

(*a*) a fee paid in respect of a survey or inspection carried out otherwise than by a surveyor of ships appointed under the Merchant Shipping Act 1894; and

(*b*) a fee paid in respect of a certificate issued otherwise than by the Board of Trade.

COMMENTS.

For 'Board of Trade' read 'Department of Trade'.

Regulations Prescribing Fees.

To date no regulations have been made.

⚓   ⚓   ⚓   ⚓

7 (1) Any regulations or rules made under this Act shall ^{Regulations and rules.} be made by statutory instrument which shall be subject to annulment in pursuance of a resolution of either House of Parliament.

(2) Before making any rules under this Act the Board of Trade shall consult with organisations in the United Kingdom appearing to them representative of persons who will be affected by the rules.

COMMENTS.

For 'Board of Trade' read 'Department of Trade'.

⚓   ⚓   ⚓   ⚓

Power to
extend Act
to certain
territories
outside the
United
Kingdom, and
to fishing
vessels
registered
therein.

8 Her Majesty may by Order in Council give with respect to any of the following territories, that is to say—

(a) the Isle of Man;

(b) any of the Channel Islands;

(c) any colony;

(d) any territory outside Her Majesty's dominions in which for the time being Her Majesty has jurisdiction;

either or both of the following directions—

(i) that the provisions of this Act and of regulations and rules made thereunder shall apply to fishing vessels registered in that territory, with such exceptions, adaptations or modifications as may be specified in the Order, as they apply to fishing vessels registered in the United Kingdom;

(ii) that the provisions of this Act and of any regulations and rules made thereunder shall extend to that territory, with such exceptions, adaptations or modifications as may be specified in the Order, as part of the law of that territory.

⚓   ⚓   ⚓   ⚓

9 (1) In this Act—

'collision regulations' means regulations made under section 418 of the Merchant Shipping Act 1894;

'fishing vessel' means a vessel which is for the time being used for or in connection with sea fishing but does not include a vessel used for fishing otherwise than for profit;

'fishing vessel construction rules' has the meaning assigned to it by section 1 of this Act;

'fishing vessel survey rules' has the meaning assigned to it by section 2 of this Act;

'radio rules' means rules made under section 3 of the Merchant Shipping (Safety Convention) Act 1949;

'rules for direction-finders' means rules made under section 5 of the Merchant Shipping (Safety Convention) Act 1949;

'rules for life-saving appliances' means rules made under section 427 of the Merchant Shipping Act 1894;

"rules for radio navigational aids' means rules made under section 6 of the Merchant Shipping (Safety Convention) Act 1949; and

"the Merchant Shipping Acts' means the Merchant Shipping Acts 1894 to 1967, the Merchant Shipping Act 1970 and this Act.

(2) References in this Act to any enactment are references thereto as amended by any other enactment.

⚓   ⚓   ⚓   ⚓

10 Any expenses incurred by the Board of Trade under this Act shall be defrayed out of moneys provided by Parliament. Expenses.

COMMENTS.

For 'Board of Trade' read 'Department of Trade'.

⚓   ⚓   ⚓   ⚓

11 (1) This Act may be cited as the Fishing Vessels (Safety Provisions) Act 1970. Citation, construction, commencement and extent.

(2) This Act, the Merchant Shipping Acts 1894 to 1967 and the Merchant Shipping Act 1970 may be cited together as the Merchant Shipping Acts 1894 to 1970.

(3) This Act shall be construed as one with the Merchant Shipping Acts 1894 to 1967 and the Merchant Shipping Act 1970.

(4) This Act shall come into force on such day as the Board of Trade may by order made by statutory instrument appoint, and different days may be so appointed for different provisions and for different descriptions of fishing vessel.

(5) This Act extends to Northern Ireland.

COMMENTS.

For 'Board of Trade' read 'Department of Trade'.

Appointed Day.

See introductory comments to this Act.

⚓   ⚓   ⚓   ⚓

MERCHANT SHIPPING ACT 1970

ARRANGEMENT OF SECTIONS

⚓   ⚓   ⚓   ⚓

Merchant Shipping Act 1970

An Act to make fresh provision in place of certain enactments relating to merchant ships and seamen and to repeal some of those enactments without replacement; to make further provision relating to merchant ships and seamen; and for purposes connected therewith.

Engagement and Discharge of Crews

1 (1) Except as provided under subsection (5) of this section an agreement in writing shall be made between each person employed as a seaman in a ship registered in the United Kingdom and the persons employing him and shall be signed both by him and by or on behalf of them. *Crew agreements.*

(2) The agreements made under this section with the several persons employed in a ship shall be contained in one document (in this Act referred to as a crew agreement) except that in such cases as the Board of Trade may approve—

(*a*) the agreements to be made under this section with the persons employed in a ship may be contained in more than one crew agreement; and

(*b*) one crew agreement may relate to more than one ship.

(3) The provisions and form of a crew agreement must be of a kind approved by the Board of Trade; and different provisions and forms may be so approved for different circumstances.

(4) Subject to the following provisions of this section, a crew agreement shall be carried in the ship to which it relates whenever the ship goes to sea.

(5) The Board of Trade may make regulations providing for exemptions from the requirements of this section—

(*a*) with respect to such descriptions of ship as may be specified in the regulations or with respect to voyages in such areas or such description of voyages as may be so specified; or

(*b*) with respect to such descriptions of seamen as may be specified in the regulations;

and the Board of Trade may grant other exemptions from those requirements (whether with respect to particular seamen or with respect to seamen employed by a specified person or in a specified ship or in the ships of a specified person) in cases where the Board are satisfied that the seamen to be employed otherwise than under a crew agreement will be adequately protected.

(6) Where, but for an exemption granted by the Board of Trade, a crew agreement would be required to be carried in a ship or a crew agreement carried in a ship would be required to contain an agreement with a person employed in the ship, the ship shall carry such document evidencing the exemption as the Board of Trade may direct.

(7) Regulations under this section may enable ships required under this section to carry a crew agreement to comply with the requirement by carrying a copy thereof, certified in such manner as may be provided by the regulations.

(8) If a ship goes to sea or attempts to go to sea in contravention of the requirements of this section the master or the person employing the crew shall be liable on summary conviction to a fine not exceeding £100 and the ship, if in the United Kingdom, may be detained.

COMMENTS.

For 'Board of Trade' read 'Secretary of State for Trade'.

Persons Employing Him.

The agreement is made with the seamen's employer and not with the master, as formerly required by section 113 of the principal Act.

Form of Crew Agreement.

Note that the Contracts of employment Act 1972 does not apply to a master or to seamen in a sea-going British ship of 80 tons or more. *See* Contracts of Employment Act 1972, section 9, sub-section 2.

Different Provisions and Forms.

This brings into being the recommendation of the Pearson Report in regard to flexibility in the forms of agreement.

Regulations.

Consult Merchant Shipping (Crew Agreements, etc.), Regulations 1972, S.I. 1972, No. 918, and Merchant Shipping (Crew Agreements, etc.) (Fishing Vessels) Regulations 1972, S.I. 1972, No. 919, as amended by S.I. 1977, No. 45.

2 (1) The Board of Trade may make regulations—

(a) requiring such notice as may be specified in the regulations to be given to a superintendent or proper officer, except in such circumstances as may be so specified, before a crew agreement is made or an agreement with any person is added to those contained in a crew agreement;

(b) providing for the delivery to a superintendent or proper officer or the Registrar General of Shipping and Seamen of crew agreements and agreements added to those contained in a crew agreement and of copies of crew agreements and of agreements so added;

(c) requiring the posting in ships of copies of or extracts from crew agreements;

(d) requiring copies of or extracts from crew agreements to be supplied to members of the crew demanding them and requiring copies of or extracts from documents referred to in crew agreements to be made available, in such circumstances as may be specified in the regulations, for inspection by members of the crew; and

(e) requiring any document carried in a ship in pursuance of section 1 of this Act to be produced on demand to an officer of customs and excise.

(2) Regulations under this section may make a contravention of any provision thereof an offence punishable on summary conviction with a fine not exceeding £50 or such less amount as may be specified in the regulations.

COMMENTS.

For 'Board of Trade' read 'Secretary of State for Trade'.

Regulations.

See comments regarding regulations, etc., to section 1.

Superintendent.

Defined in section 742 of the principal Act.

Proper Officer.

See section 97, sub-section 1 of this Act.

Registrar General of Shipping and Seamen.

See section 80 of this Act.

⚓   ⚓   ⚓   ⚓

3 (1) The Board of Trade may make regulations pre-scribing the procedure to be followed in connection with the discharge of seamen from ships registered in the United Kingdom.

(2) Without prejudice to the generality of subsection (1) of this section, regulations under this section may make pro-vision—

(*a*) requiring notice of such a discharge to be given at such time as may be specified in the regulations to the superin-tendent or proper officer at a place specified in or deter-mined under the regulations;

(*b*) requiring such a discharge to be recorded, whether by entries in the crew agreement and discharge book or otherwise, and requiring copies of any such entry to be given to a superintendent or proper officer or the Registrar General of Shipping and Seamen.

(3) Regulations under this section may provide that in such cases as may be specified in the regulations, or except in such cases as may be specified in or determined under the regulations, a seaman shall not be discharged outside the United Kingdom from a ship registered in the United Kingdom without the consent of the proper officer.

(4) Regulations under this section may make a contra-vention of any provision thereof an offence punishable on summary conviction with a fine not exceeding £100 or such less amount as may be specified in the regulations.

COMMENTS.
For 'Board of Trade' read 'Secretary of State for Trade'.
Regulations.
See comments to section 1 regarding regulations.
Procedure to be Followed:—
If correct procedure not followed, dismissal is illegal, and the agree-ment remains in force.   Hassan *v.* Trader Navigation Co. 1965.
Superintendent.
Defined in section 742 of the Principal Act.
Proper Officer.
See section 97, sub-section 1 of this Act.
Registrar General of Shipping and Seamen.
See section 80 of this Act.

⚓   ⚓   ⚓   ⚓

4 Regulations made under section 3 of this Act may apply any provision thereof, with such modifications as appear to the Board of Trade to be appropriate, to cases where a seaman employed in a ship registered in the United Kingdom is left behind outside the United Kingdom otherwise than on being discharged from the ship.

COMMENTS.

Regulations.

The regulations made under section 3, The Merchant Shipping (Crew Agreements, etc.) Regulations 1972, S.I. 1972, No. 918, do not as yet apply to the situation as outlined in this section.

⚓   ⚓   ⚓   ⚓

5 Where a ship registered in the United Kingdom ceases to be so registered, any seaman employed in the ship shall be discharged from the ship unless he consents in writing to continue his employment in the ship; and sections 7 to 10 of this Act shall apply in relation to his wages as if the ship had remained registered in the United Kingdom.

⚓   ⚓   ⚓   ⚓

6 (1) A person shall not for reward make arrangements for finding seamen for persons seeking to employ seamen or for finding employment for seamen, unless—

(*a*) he is the holder of a licence under this section authorising him to do so or is in the regular employment of the holder of such a licence; or

(*b*) he is in the regular employment of the persons seeking to employ the seamen or makes the arrangements in the course of acting as ship's agent for those persons or is the master of the ship in which the seamen are to serve or an officer acting under his authority; or

(*c*) the employment is such as is exempted from the provisions of this subsection by regulations made by the Board of Trade.

(2) A person shall not demand or directly or indirectly receive from any person any remuneration for providing him with employment as a seaman.

(3) The Board of Trade may grant licences for the purposes of this section for such periods, on such terms and subject to such conditions, including conditions providing for revocation, as they think fit.

(4) If a person acts in contravention of subsection (1) of this section he shall be liable on summary conviction to a fine not exceeding £50 and if a person acts in contravention of subsection (2) of this section he shall be liable on summary conviction to a fine not exceeding £20.

COMMENTS.

This section is not as yet in force.

Licences granted under section 110 of the Principal Act are saved by section 100 and Schedule 4, paragraph 5 of this Act.

⚓   ⚓   ⚓   ⚓

Wages, etc.

Payment of seamen's wages.

7 (1) Except as provided by or under this Act or any other enactment, the wages due to a seaman under a crew agreement relating to a ship shall be paid to him in full at the time when he leaves the ship on being discharged therefrom (in this section and section 8 of this Act referred to as the time of discharge).

(2) If the amount shown in the account delivered to a seaman under section 8(1) of this Act as being the amount payable to him under subsection (1) of this section is replaced by an increased amount shown in a further account delivered to him under section 8(3) of this Act, the balance shall be paid to him within seven days of the time of discharge; and if the amount so shown in the account delivered to him under section 8(1) of this Act exceeds £50 and it is not practicable to pay the whole of it at the time of discharge, not less than £50 nor less than one-quarter of the amount so shown shall be paid to him at that time and the balance within seven days of that time.

(3) If any amount which, under the preceding provisions of this section, is payable to a seaman is not paid at the time at which it is so payable the seaman shall be entitled to wages at the rate last payable under the crew agreement for every day on which it remains unpaid during the period of fifty-six days following the time of discharge; and if any such amount or

any amount payable by virtue of this subsection remains unpaid after the end of that period it shall carry interest at the rate of 20 per cent per annum.

(4) Subsection (3) of this section does not apply if the failure to pay was due to a mistake, to a reasonable dispute as to liability or to the act or default of the seaman or to any other cause, not being the wrongful act or default of the persons liable to pay his wages or of their servants or agents; and so much of that subsection as relates to interest on the amount due shall not apply if a court in proceedings for its recovery so directs.

(5) Where a seaman is employed under a crew agreement relating to more than one ship the preceding provisions of this section shall have effect, in relation to wages due to him under the agreement, as if for any reference to the time of discharge there were substituted a reference to the termination of his employment under the crew agreement.

(6) Where a seaman, in pursuance of section 5 of this Act, is discharged from a ship outside the United Kingdom but returns to the United Kingdom under arrangements made by the persons who employed him, the preceding provisions of this section shall have effect, in relation to the wages due to him under a crew agreement relating to the ship, as if for the references in subsections (1) to (3) to the time of discharge there were substituted references to the time of his return to the United Kingdom, and subsection (5) were omitted.

COMMENTS.
Section 5 of this Act.
Relates to seamen when ship ceases to be registered in the U.K.

⚓   ⚓   ⚓   ⚓

8 (1) Subject to subsection (4) of this section and to regulations made under section 9 or 62 of this Act, the master of every ship registered in the United Kingdom shall deliver to every seaman employed in the ship under a crew agreement an account of the wages due to him under that crew agreement and of the deductions subject to which the wages are payable. _{Account of seaman's wages.}

(2) The account shall indicate that the amounts stated therein are subject to any later adjustment that may be found necessary and shall be delivered not later than twenty-four

hours before the time of discharge or, if the seaman is discharged without notice or at less than twenty-four hours'
notice, at the time of discharge.

(3) If the amounts stated in the account require adjustment the persons who employed the seaman shall deliver to
him a further account stating the adjusted amounts; and that
account shall be delivered not later than the time at which
the balance of his wages is payable to the seaman.

(4) Where a seaman is employed under a crew agreement
relating to more than one ship any account which under the
preceding provisions of this section would be required to be
delivered to him by the master shall instead be delivered to
him by the persons employing him and shall be so delivered on
or before the termination of his employment under the crew
agreement.

(5) If a person fails without reasonable cause to comply
with the preceding provisions of this section he shall be liable
on summary conviction to a fine not exceeding £20.

COMMENTS.

This section, particularly sub-section 2 and 3, recognises that a master
may not always be able to produce an exact account without adjustment,
due to being engaged in the safe navigation of his ship.

⚓   ⚓   ⚓   ⚓

Regulations
relating to
wages and
accounts.

9   The Board of Trade may make regulations—

(a) authorising deductions to be made from the wages due
to a seaman under a crew agreement (in addition to any
authorised by any provision of this Act or of any other
enactment for the time being in force) in cases where a
breach of his obligations under the agreement is alleged
against him and such conditions, if any, as may be
specified in the regulations are complied with, or in such
other cases as may be specified in the regulations;

(b) regulating the manner in which any amounts deducted
under the regulations are to be dealt with;

(c) prescribing the manner in which wages due to a seaman
under a crew agreement are to be or may be paid;

(d) regulating the manner in which such wages are to be
dealt with and accounted for in circumstances where a

seaman leaves his ship in the United Kingdom otherwise than on being discharged therefrom;

(*e*) prescribing the form and manner in which any account required to be delivered by section 8 of this Act is to be prepared and the particulars to be contained therein (which may include estimated amounts).

COMMENTS.

For 'Board of Trade' read 'Secretary of State for Trade'.

Regulations.

Consult Merchant Shipping (Seamen's Wages and Accounts) Regulations 1972, S.I. 1972, No. 1700, and in the case of fishing vessels, Merchant Shipping (Seamen's Wages and Accounts) (Fishing Vessels) Regulations 1972, S.I. 1972, No. 1701.

Crew Agreement.

See section 97, sub-section 1 of this Act.

⚓   ⚓   ⚓   ⚓

10 (1) Any dispute relating to the amount payable to a seaman employed under a crew agreement may be submitted by the parties to a superintendent or proper officer for decision; but the superintendent or proper officer shall not be bound to accept the submission or, if he has accepted it, to decide the dispute, if he is of opinion that the dispute, whether by reason of the amount involved or for any other reason, ought not to be decided by him.

Power of superintendent or proper officer to decide disputes about wages.

(2) The decision of a superintendent or proper officer on a dispute submitted to him under this section shall be final.

COMMENTS.

Crew Agreement.

See section 97, sub-section 1 of this Act.

⚓   ⚓   ⚓   ⚓

11 (1) Subject to subsections (2) and (3) of this section, the following provisions shall have effect with respect to the wages due or accruing to a seaman employed in a ship registered in the United Kingdom, that is to say,—

Restriction on assignment of and charge upon wages.

(*a*) the wages shall not be subject to attachment or arrestment;

(*b*) an assignment thereof before they have accrued shall not bind the seaman and the payment of the wages to the seaman shall be valid notwithstanding any previous assignment or charge; and

(*c*) a power of attorney or authority for the receipt of the wages shall not be irrevocable.

(2) Nothing in this section shall affect the provisions of this Act with respect to allotment notes.

(3) Nothing in this section applies to any disposition relating to the application of wages—

(*a*) in the payment of contributions to a fund declared by regulations made by the Board of Trade to be a fund to which this section applies; or

(*b*) in the payment of contributions in respect of the membership of a body declared by regulations made by the Board of Trade to be a body to which this section applies;

or to anything done or to be done for giving effect to such a disposition.

COMMENTS.

For 'Board of Trade' read 'Secretary of State for Trade'.

Regulations.

Consult Merchant Shipping (Seamen's Wages) (Contributions) Regulations 1972, S.I. 1972, No. 1699.

⚓   ⚓   ⚓   ⚓

Power of court to award interest on wages due otherwise than under crew agreement.

12 In any proceedings by the master of a ship or a person employed in a ship otherwise than under a crew agreement for the recovery of any sum due to him as wages the court, unless it appears to it that the delay in paying the sum was due to a mistake, to a reasonable dispute as to liability or to the act or default of the person claiming the amount or to any other cause, not being the wrongful act or default of the persons liable to make the payment or their servants or agents, may order them to pay, in addition to the sum due, interest on it at the rate of twenty per cent per annum or such lower rate as the court may specify, for the period beginning seven days after the sum became due and ending when the sum is paid.

⚓   ⚓   ⚓   ⚓

13 (1) Subject to the following provisions of this section, Allotment a seaman may, by means of an allotment note issued in accordance with regulations made by the Board of Trade, allot to any person or persons part of the wages to which he will become entitled in the course of his employment in a ship or ships registered in the United Kingdom.

(2) A seaman's right to make an allotment under this section shall be subject to such limitations as may, by virtue of the following provisions of this section, be imposed by regulations made by the Board of Trade.

(3) Regulations made by the Board of Trade for the purposes of this section may prescribe the form of allotment notes and—

(a) may limit the circumstances in which allotments may be made;

(b) may limit (whether by reference to an amount or by reference to a proportion) the part of the wages that may be allotted and the number of persons to whom it may be allotted and may prescribe the method by which that part is to be calculated;

(c) may limit the persons to whom allotments may be made by a seaman to persons of such descriptions or persons standing to him in such relationships as may be prescribed by the regulations;

(d) may prescribe the times and the intervals at which payments under allotment notes are to be made.

(4) Regulations under this section may make different provision in relation to different descriptions of seamen and different circumstances.

COMMENTS.

For 'Board of Trade' read 'Secretary of State for Trade'.

Regulations.

Consult Merchant Shipping (Seamen's Allotments) Regulations 1972, S.I. 1972, No. 1698.

⚓   ⚓   ⚓   ⚓

14 (1) A person to whom any part of a seaman's wages Right of person named has been allotted by an allotment note issued in accordance in allotment with regulations made under section 13 of this Act shall have note to sue in own name.

the right to recover that part in his own name and for that purpose shall have the same remedies as the seaman has for the recovery of his wages.

(2) In any proceedings brought by a person named in such an allotment note as the person to whom any part of a seaman's wages has been allotted it shall be presumed, unless the contrary is shown, that the seaman is entitled to the wages specified in the note and that the allotment has not been varied or cancelled.

⚓   ⚓   ⚓   ⚓

Right, or loss of right, to wages in certain circumstances.

15 (1) Where a ship registered in the United Kingdom is wrecked or lost a seaman whose employment in the ship is thereby terminated before the date contemplated in the agreement under which he is so employed shall, subject to the following provisions of this section, be entitled to wages at the rate payable under the agreement at the date of the wreck or loss for every day on which he is unemployed in the two months following that date unless it is proved that he did not make reasonable efforts to save the ship and persons and property carried in it.

(2) Where a ship registered in the United Kingdom is sold while outside the United Kingdom or ceases to be so registered and a seaman's employment in the ship is thereby terminated before the date contemplated in the agreement under which he is so employed, then, unless it is otherwise provided in the agreement, he shall, subject to the following provisions of this section, be entitled to wages at the rate payable under the agreement at the date on which his employment is terminated for every day on which he is unemployed in the two months following that date.

(3) A seaman shall not be entitled to wages by virtue of subsection (1) or subsection (2) of this section for a day on which he was unemployed, if it is shown—

(a) that the unemployment was not due to the wreck or loss of the ship or, as the case may be, the termination of his employment on the sale of the ship or its ceasing to be registered in the United Kingdom; or

(*b*) that the seaman was able to obtain suitable employment for that day but unreasonably refused or failed to take it.

COMMENTS.

This section, underlined, is not yet in force.

Termination of Employment.

See 'Comments' to section 158, Merchant Shipping Act 1894, contained in Volume I of this work.

⚓   ⚓   ⚓   ⚓

16 (1) A seaman's lien, his remedies for the recovery of his wages, his right to wages in case of the wreck or loss of his ship, and any right he may have or obtain in the nature of salvage shall not be capable of being renounced by any agreement. Protection of certain rights and remedies.

(2) Subsection (1) of this section does not affect such of the terms of any agreement made with the seamen belonging to a ship which, in accordance with the agreement, is to be employed on salvage service, as provide for the remuneration to be paid to them for salvage services rendered by that ship.

COMMENTS.

Seamen.

It would appear that this section does not apply to masters. *The William Tell*, 1892.

Lien.

This is applicable to both ship and freight. *The Andalina* 1886.

Transference of Maritime Lien.

A person who freely pays off a seaman's lien in respect of wages, without leave of the court, does not acquire a lien on the ship. However, it would appear that in Scotland, a person who pays off a maritime lien even without leave of the court, will obtain a maritime lien on the ship. *See The Petone*, 1917 in the first instance, and Clark *v* Bowring, 1908 in the latter.

Salvage.

The agreement and the apportionment of salvage must be equitable. *See The Enchantress*, 1860; *The Afrika*, 1880.

M

Ship Employed on Salvage Service (sub-section 2).

Neither the agreement for the vessel to be employed in salvage service, nor an agreement for the seaman to waive his claim for salvage need be in writing, but in such circumstances, it behoves those who dispute his right to salvage, to prove that an agreement by precedent or verbal, was in existence.

⚓   ⚓   ⚓   ⚓

Claims against seaman's wages for maintenance, etc. of dependants.

17 (1) Where, during a seaman's employment in a ship, expenses are incurred by a responsible authority for the benefit of any dependant of his and the expenses are of a kind specified in regulations under this section and such further conditions, if any, as may be so specified are satisfied, the authority may by notice in writing complying with the regulations require the persons employing the seaman—

(a) to retain for a period specified in the notice such proportion of his net wages as may be so specified; and

(b) to give to the responsible authority as soon as may be notice in writing of the seaman's discharge from the ship;

and the persons employing the seaman shall comply with the notice (subject to subsection (3) of this section) and give notice in writing of its contents to the seaman.

(2) For the purposes of this section—

(a) the following persons, and no others, shall be taken to be a seaman's dependants, that is to say, his spouse and any person under the age of sixteen whom he is liable, for the purposes of any enactment in force in any part of the United Kingdom, to maintain or in respect of whom he is liable under any such enactment to make contributions to a local authority; and

(b) expenses incurred for the benefit of any person include (in addition to any payments made to him or on his behalf) expenses incurred for providing him with accommodation or care or for exercising supervision over him;

but no expenses shall be specified in regulations under this section unless they are such that a magistrates' court has power under any enactment in force in any part of the United Kingdom to order the making of payments in respect thereof.

(3) Not more than the following proportion of a seaman's net wages shall be retained under subsection (1) of this section (whether in pursuance of one or more notices) that is to say,—

(a) one-half if the notice or notices relate to one dependant only;

(b) two-thirds if the notice or notices relate to two or more dependants.

(4) Where a responsible authority have served a notice under this section on the persons employing a seaman, a magistrates' court may, on the application of the authority, make an order for the payment to the authority of such sum, not exceeding the proportion of the seaman's wages which those persons were required by virtue of this section to retain, as the court, having regard to the expenses incurred by the authority and the seaman's means, thinks fit.

(5) Any sums paid out of a seaman's wages in pursuance of an order under this section shall be deemed to be paid to him in respect of his wages; and the service, on the persons who employed the seaman, of such an order or of an order dismissing an application for such an order shall terminate the period for which they were required to retain the wages.

(6) An application for an order under this section for the payment of any sum by the persons who employed a seaman shall be deemed, for the purposes of any proceedings, to be an application for an order against the seaman; but the order, when served on those persons, shall have effect as an order against them and may be enforced accordingly.

(7) Parts I and III of the Maintenance Orders Act 1950 shall have effect as if an order under this section were included among those referred to in subsections (1) and (2) of section 4, subsections (1) and (2) of section 9 and subsections (1) and (2) of section 12 of that Act; and any sum payable by any persons under an order made under this section in any part of the United Kingdom may, in any other part of the United Kingdom, be recovered from them as a debt due to the authority on whose application the order was made.

(8) Any notice on order under this section may be served by registered post or recorded delivery service.

(9) The Board of Trade may make regulations specifying—

(a) the expenses in respect of which a notice may be served by a responsible authority under subsection (1) of this section;

(b) any conditions that must be satisfied if such a notice is to be served;

(c) the period that may be specified in such a notice (being a period beginning with the service of the notice and ending a specified number of days after the seaman's discharge from his ship);

(d) the form of such a notice and the information to be contained therein; and

(e) the amounts to be deducted from a seaman's wages in computing his net wages for the purposes of this section; and the amounts specified under paragraph (e) of this subsection may include amounts allotted by allotment notes issued under section 13 of this Act.

(10) In this section 'responsible authority' means the Secretary of State, the Ministry of Health and Social Services for Northern Ireland or any local authority; but any application to be made or notice to be given under this section by or to a responsible authority may, if the authority is the Secretary of State or the Ministry of Health and Social Services for Northern Ireland, be made or given on behalf of the Secretary of State or Ministry by or to the Supplementary Benefits Commission or, as the case may be, the Supplementary Benefits Commission for Northern Ireland.

(11) In this section 'local authority' includes a welfare authority constituted under the Public Health and Local Government (Administrative Provisions) Act (Northern Ireland) 1946 and 'magistrates' court'—

(a) in relation to Scotland, means the sheriff, and

(b) in relation to Northern Ireland, means a court of summary jurisdiction.

COMMENTS.

Regulations.

Consult the Merchant Shipping (Maintenance of Seamen's Dependants) Regulations 1972, S.I. 1972, No. 1635 as amended by the Merchant Shipping (Maintenance of Seamen's Dependants) Regulations 1972, S.I. 1972, No. 1875.

⚓   ⚓   ⚓   ⚓

Remedies of master for remuneration, disbursements, etc.

18 The master of a ship shall have the same lien for his remuneration, and all disbursements or liabilities properly made or incurred by him on account of the ship, as a seaman has for his wages.

COMMENTS.

Remuneration.

This term is not defined. It is submitted that this is the equivalent of seamen's wages.

Payment of Salary, wages, bonuses, etc., under a special contract does not preclude a master from sueing *in rem*.

Pearson *v. Seapro* (Owners) 1931, but compare *The British Trade* 1924, where it was held that if he sues on a special contract, which is distinct from a mariner's contract, no such lien arises.

See the *Gee Whiz* 1951, where it was held that agreement by the owner that he would pay the master's National Insurance contributions allows a claim that this sum be included in the emoluments. Also, claims for social benefits included in the contract of service. *The Arosa Kulm* (No. 2) 1960; *The Arosa Star* 1959. In *The Fairport* 1965 it was held that deductions from a seaman's gross wages for social services or trade union contributions are within this section. *See* also *The Westport* 1968.

Master's Lien.

The master's lien takes precedence over all others except (*a*) subsequent salvage, *The Panthea* 1871; (*b*) damage (whether subsequent or not), *The Elin* 1883; (*c*) **Seamen's Wages:** The master is no longer by law, liable to pay seamen their wages. It is, therefore, submitted that their lien no longer takes precedence over the master's for wages or disbursement; (*d*) **Bottomry Bond-holder:** A master, having given a bottomry bond bonding himself, ship and freight, does not take precedence over the bondholder. This, however, is for the bondholder's protection and will not be acted upon in the event that the bondholder would not be prejudiced by the master being paid before payment of the bond. In the event that the master has not personally bound himself to pay the bond then his claim for wages takes precedence over the bond. This applies to wages occurring during the voyage in which the bond was given and of a subsequent voyage prior to the issue of the bond, stands back; (*e*) **Mortgagee:** The master's lien takes precedence of a claim of a mortgagee of the ship or shares; (*f*) **Purchaser:** The master can enforce his lien although the ship is in the hands of purchasers; (*g*) **Shipwright—Material, Men:** A shipwright's or material men's possessory lien takes precedence over the master's lien for claims after the shipwright's work was completed or the supply of materials, but stands back in respect of the master's lien for wages previously earned; (*h*) **Bill on Owners:** A master's lien is lost if he elects to take a bill on his owner's for his wages in lieu of cash. It is not lost if he takes a mortgage for the amount due to him.

Disbursements.

A master has no lien for disbursements for which he had no authority to pledge his owner's credit, *The Castlegate* 1893. He has a lien on only those disbursements for which he could have pledged his owner's credit without authority, *The Orienta* 1895. He has also a lien and recover disbursements made to privileged claimants and in such circumstance, he has the benefit of any right they may have, e.g. in the event of him having paid the wages of the crew, he has a lien for that amount in the same priority as they would have had. *The Tagus* 1903. In the event of a master binding himself and the ship for the supply of necessaries and his successor as master, binds himself and ship for further necessaries, the claims rank equally.

It is submitted that this sub-section enables the master to sue for his wages within the statutory period of six years from the date of the cause of the action. Consult the Limitation Act 1939, section 2, sub-section 1, paragraph (*b*).

Master's Right to Wages.

For a Master's right to wages while unemployed, due to loss of his ship, *see* Merchant Shipping (International Labour Conventions) Act 1925, section 1.

Transferability of Maritime Lien.

See comments to section 16 and in particular, *The Petone* 1917. The decision in *The Petone* 1917 was approved, and followed in *The Leoborg* (No. 2) 1964 q.v.

Safety, Health and Welfare

Safety
Regulations.   **19** (1) The Board of Trade may make regulations for securing as far as practicable, safe working conditions and safe means of access for masters and seamen employed in ships registered in the United Kingdom and for requiring the reporting of injuries sustained by them.

(2) Without prejudice to the generality of the preceding subsection, regulations under this section may—

(*a*) require the maintenance, inspection and testing of any equipment and impose conditions on its use;

(*b*) require, prohibit, or regulate the use of any material or process;

(c) require the provision and use of any protective clothing or equipment;

(d) limit the hours of employment of seamen in any specified operation or in any specified circumstances;

(e) make provision for the discharge, by persons appointed from among the persons employed in a ship, of functions in connection with the arrangements to be made under the regulations.

(3) Regulations under this section may make different provisions for different descriptions of ship and for ships of the same description in different circumstances.

(4) The Board of Trade may grant exemptions from any requirement of regulations under this section in respect of any ship or description of ship.

(5) Regulations under this section may make a contravention of any provision thereof an offence punishable on summary conviction with a fine not exceeding, if the offence is committed by the master or owner, £200, and, if it is committed by any other person, £20.

COMMENTS.

This section, underlined, has not yet come into force.

⚓   ⚓   ⚓   ⚓

20 (1) The Board of Trade may make regulations with respect to the crew accommodation to be provided in ships registered in the United Kingdom. *Crew accommodation.*

(2) Without prejudice to the generality of the preceding subsection, regulations made under this section may, in particular—

(a) prescribe the minimum space per man which must be provided by way of sleeping accommodation for seamen and the maximum number of persons by whom a specified part of such sleeping accommodation may be used;

(b) regulate the position in the ship in which the crew accommodation or any part thereof may be located and the standards to be observed in the construction, equipment and furnishing of any such accommodation;

(c) require the submission to a surveyor of ships of plans and specifications of any works proposed to be carried out for the purpose of the provision or alteration of any such accommodation and authorise the surveyor to inspect any such works; and

(d) provide for the maintenance and repair of any such accommodation and prohibit or restrict the use of any such accommodation for purposes other than those for which it is designed.

(3) Regulations under this section may make different provisions with respect to different descriptions of ships or with respect to ships which were registered in the United Kingdom at different dates or the construction of which was begun at different dates and with respect to crew accommodation provided for seamen of different descriptions.

(4) Regulations under this section may exempt ships of any description from any requirements of the regulations and the Board of Trade may grant other exemptions from any such requirement with respect to any ship.

(5) Regulations made under this section may require the master of a ship or any officer authorised by him for the purpose to carry out such inspections of the crew accommodation as may be prescribed by the regulations.

(6) If the provisions of any regulations made under this section are contravened in the case of a ship the owner or master shall be liable on summary conviction to a fine not exceeding £200, and the ship, if in the United Kingdom, may be detained.

(7) In this section 'crew accommodation' includes sleeping rooms, mess rooms, sanitary accommodation, hospital accommodation, recreation accommodation, store rooms and catering accommodation provided for the use of seamen but does not include any accommodation which is also used by or provided for the use of passengers.

COMMENTS.

This section came into operation on the 19th December, 1975. *See* the Merchant Shipping Act 1970 (Commencement No. 4) Order 1975, S.I. 1975, No. 2156.

For 'Board of Trade' read 'Secretary of State for Trade'.

Regulations.

The following regulations made under section 1 of the Merchant Shipping Act 1948 will have effect as made under this section by section 100, sub-section 2, and Schedule 4, paragraph 6 of this Act.

(1) Merchant Shipping (Crew Accommodation) Regulations 1953, S.I. 1953, No. 1036, as amended by S.I. 1954, No. 1660, S.I. 1961, No. 393, S.I. 1965, No. 1047, S.I. 1975, No. 341.

and as affected by the repeal of the proviso to sub-section 3 of that section by the Merchant Shipping Act 1965, section 7, sub-section 2 and Schedule 2.

(2) Merchant Shipping (Crew Accommodation) (Isle of Man) Regulations 1960, S.I. 1960, No. 1967.

(3) For Regulations in relation to Crew Accommodation in Fishing Vessels, *see* Merchant Shipping (Fishing Vessels) Regulations 1975, S.I. 1975, No. 2220.

21 (1) The Board of Trade may make regulations requiring such provisions and water to be provided for seamen employed in ships registered in the United Kingdom or any description of such ships as may be specified in the regulations; and regulations under this section may make different provision for different circumstances and different descriptions of seamen.   *Provisions and water.*

(2) Regulations under this section may require a ship to carry such weighing and measuring equipment as may be necessary to ensure that the quantities of provisions and water supplied to seamen employed in the ship are in accordance with the regulations.

(3) The Board of Trade may exempt any ship from any requirement of regulations made under this section, either generally or in respect of a particular voyage.

(4) If the provisions of any regulations made under this section are not complied with in the case of a ship the master or owner shall be liable on summary conviction to a fine not exceeding £100 unless he proves that the failure to comply was not due to his neglect or default.

(5) If a person empowered under this Act to inspect the provisions and water to be supplied to the seamen employed in a ship is not satisfied that they are in accordance with

regulations made under this section the ship, if in the United Kingdom, may be detained.

COMMENTS.

For 'Board of Trade' read 'Secretary of State for Trade'.

Regulations.

Consult the Merchant Shipping (Provisions and Water) Regulations 1972, S.I. No. 1871 and the Merchant Shipping (Provisions and Water) (Fishing Vessels) Regulations 1972, S.I. 1972, No. 1872, both as amended by the Merchant Shipping (Provisions and Water) (Fishing and other Vessels) (Amendment) Regulations 1975, S.I. 1975, No. 733, and in the case of seamen ordinarily resident in Bangladesh, as further amended by S.I. 1978, No. 36.

Complaints about provisions or water.

22 (1) If three or more seamen employed in a ship registered in the United Kingdom consider that the provisions or water provided for the seamen employed in that ship are not in accordance with regulations made under section 21 of this Act (whether because of bad quality, unfitness for use or deficiency in quantity) they may complain to the master, who shall investigate the complaint.

(2) If the seamen are dissatisfied with the action taken by the master as a result of his investigation or by his failure to take any action they may state their dissatisfaction to him and may claim to complain to a superintendent or proper officer: and thereupon the master shall make adequate arrangements to enable the seamen to do so as soon as the service of the ship permits.

(3) The superintendent or proper officer to whom a complaint has been made under this section shall investigate the complaint and may examine the provisions or water or cause them to be examined.

(4) If the master fails without reasonable cause to comply with the provisions of subsection (2) of this section he shall be liable on summary conviction to a fine not exceeding £20, and if he has been notified in writing by the person making an examination under subsection (3) of this section that any provisions or water are found to be unfit for use or not of the quality required by the regulations, then,—

(*a*) if they are not replaced within a reasonable time the master or owner shall be liable on summary conviction to a fine not exceeding £100 unless he proves that the failure to replace them was not due to his neglect or default; and

(*b*) if the master, without reasonable cause, permits them to be used he shall be liable on summary conviction to a fine not exceeding £100.

⚓   ⚓   ⚓   ⚓

23 (1) If a seaman employed in a ship registered in the United Kingdom considers that he has cause to complain about the master or any other seaman employed in the ship or about the conditions on board the ship he may complain to the master. Other complaints.

(2) If the seaman is dissatisfied with the action taken by the master on the complaint or by his failure to take any action he may state his dissatisfaction to him and, if the ship is outside the United Kingdom, claim to complain to a proper officer; and thereupon the master shall make adequate arrangements to enable the seaman to do so as soon as the service of the ship permits.

(3) If the master of a ship fails without reasonable cause to comply with the provisions of this section he shall be liable on summary conviction to a fine not exceeding £20.

⚓   ⚓   ⚓   ⚓

24 (1) The Board of Trade may make regulations requiring ships registered in the United Kingdom, or such descriptions of ships registered in the United Kingdom as may be specified in the regulations, to carry such medicines and other medical stores (including books containing instructions and advice) as may be specified in the regulations; and the regulations may make different provision for different circumstances. Medical stores.

(2) If a ship goes to sea or attempts to go to sea without carrying the medical stores which it is required to carry by regulations under this section, the master or owner shall be liable on summary conviction to a fine not exceeding £100 unless he proves that the failure to carry the stores was not due to his neglect or default.

(3) If a person empowered under this Act to inspect the medical stores carried in a ship is not satisfied that the ship carries the stores which it is required to carry by regulations under this section, the ship, if in the United Kingdom, may be detained.

COMMENTS.

For 'Board of Trade' read 'Department of Trade'.

This section came into force on the 1st October, 1974, by the Merchant Shipping Act 1970 (Commencement No. 2) Order 1974, S.I. 1974, No. 1194.

Regulations.

See the Merchant Shipping (Medical Scales) (Fishing Vessels) Regulations 1974, S.I. 1974, No. 1192, and the Merchant Shipping (Medical Scales) Regulations 1974, S.I. 1974, No. 1193, both as amended by the Merchant Shipping (Medical Scales) (Merchant Ships and Other Vessels) (Amendment) Regulations 1975, S.I. 1975, No. 1581, in force as from the 28th October, 1975.

⚓   ⚓   ⚓   ⚓

Medical treatment on board ship. **25** Where a ship registered in the United Kingdom does not carry a doctor among the seamen employed in it the master shall make arrangements for securing that any medical attention on board the ship is given either by him or under his supervision by a person appointed by him for the purpose.

⚓   ⚓   ⚓   ⚓

Expenses of medical treatment, etc., during voyage. **26** If a person, while employed in a ship registered in the United Kingdom, receives outside the United Kingdom any surgical or medical treatment or such dental or optical treatment (including the repair or replacement of any appliance) as cannot be postponed without impairing efficiency, the reasonable expenses thereof shall be borne by the persons employing him; and if he dies while so employed and is buried or cremated outside the United Kingdom, the expenses of his burial or cremation shall also be borne by those persons.

COMMENTS.

While Employed.

In Anchor Line (Henderson Bros.) Ltd. *v.* Mohad 1922, it was held that the employer would not be liable after the date of desertion.

The employer's liability ceases after the return of the seaman to the U.K., Anderson *v.* Rayner 1903.

⚓   ⚓   ⚓   ⚓

Offences by Seamen, etc.

27 (1) If the master or any member of the crew of a Misconduct endangering ship registered in the United Kingdom— ship or persons on

(*a*) does any act which causes or is likely to cause the loss board ship. or destruction of or serious damage to the ship or the death of or serious injury to a person on board the ship; or;

(*b*) omits to do anything required to preserve the ship from loss, destruction or serious damage or to preserve any person on board the ship from death or serious injury; and the act or omission is deliberate, or amounts to a breach or neglect of duty, or he is under the influence of drink or a drug at the time of the act or omission, he shall be liable on conviction on indictment, to imprisonment for a term not exceeding two years or to a fine, and, on summary conviction, to a fine not exceeding £200.

(2) In this section 'breach or neglect of duty', except in relation to a master, includes any disobedience to a lawful command.

COMMENTS.

Fine.

The sum £200 underlined is now £400. *See* the Merchant Shipping Acts 1974, section 19.

Neglect of Duty.

This does not include want of proper care in the performance of duty. Deacon *v.* Evans 1911.

⚓   ⚓   ⚓   ⚓

28 If a seaman employed in a ship registered in the Drunkenness, United Kingdom is, while on duty, under the influence of etc., on duty. drink or a drug to such an extent that his capacity to carry out his duties is impaired, he shall be liable on summary conviction to a fine not exceeding £50.

COMMENTS.

Drug.

This is a new offence. *See* recommendation contained in the Pearson Report, paragraph 311.

⚓   ⚓   ⚓   ⚓

Section 29

Repealed Merchant Shipping Act 1974, Section 19

⚓   ⚓   ⚓   ⚓

Continued
or concerted
disobedience,
neglect of
duty, etc.

30 If a seaman employed in a ship registered in the United Kingdom—

(a) persistently and wilfully neglects his duty; or

(b) persistently and wilfully disobeys lawful commands; or

(c) combines with other seamen employed in that ship to disobey lawful commands or to neglect duty or to impede the navigation of the ship or the progress of a voyage;

he shall be liable on summary conviction to a fine not exceeding £100.

COMMENTS.

Ship.

This section does not apply to fishing vessels. Consult section 95, sub-section 1 of this Act.

To Impede the Progress of a Voyage.

During the Spanish Civil War, the crew refused to proceed to a port to load a cargo of nitrate, for passage to Spain, on the grounds that it could be used for the manufacture of munitions. It was held that they were not guilty of an offence under this section as the proposed voyage was 'something outside the scope of the bargain into which they had entered', Robson v. Sykes 1938. This follows the decision reached in Palace Shipping Co. Ltd. v. Caine 1907.

Substitution.

The words underlined in paragraph (c) have been substituted by:

'(c) combines with other seamen employed in that ship—

(i) to disobey lawful commands which are required to be obeyed at a time while the ship is at sea;

(ii) to neglect any duty which is required to be discharged at such a time, or

(iii) to impede, at such a time, the progress of a voyage or the navigation of the ship, he shall be liable, on summary conviction, to a fine not exceeding £100.'

For the purposes of this section, a ship shall be treated as being at sea at any time when it is not securely moored in a safe berth, per Merchant Shipping Act 1974, section 19.

⚓   ⚓   ⚓   ⚓

Section 31

Repealed

Merchant Shipping Act 1974, Section 19

⚓   ⚓   ⚓   ⚓

32 Where a person goes to sea in a ship without the consent of the master or of any other person authorised to give it or is conveyed in a ship in pursuance of section 62(5)(*b*) of this Act, sections 27, 29 30(*b*) and 30(*c*) of this Act shall apply as if he were a seaman employed in the ship. *Offences committed by certain other persons.*

COMMENTS.

This section does not apply to fishing vessels.

⚓   ⚓   ⚓   ⚓

Defence of drug taken for medical purposes

33 In proceedings for an offence under section 27 or section 28 of this Act it shall be a defence to prove that at the time of the act or omission alleged against the defendant he was under the influence of a drug taken by him for medical purposes and either that he took it on medical advice and complied with any directions given as part of that advice or that he had no reason to believe that the drug might have the influence it had. *Defence of drug taken for medical purposes.*

⚓   ⚓   ⚓   ⚓

Disciplinary offences

34 (1) For the purpose of maintaining discipline on board ships registered in the United Kingdom the Board of Trade may make regulations specifying any misconduct on board as a disciplinary offence and enabling the master, or such officer as may under the regulations be required or *Disciplinary offences.*

authorised to exercise the powers of the master, to impose fines on seamen committing disciplinary offences.

(2) The fine that may be so imposed on a seaman for a disciplinary offence shall be such as may be provided in the regulations either by reference to his pay for such period as may be specified in the regulations, calculated in such manner as may be so specified, or by reference to an amount so specified; but the period so specified shall not exceed five days and the amount so specified shall not exceed £10.

(3) Regulations under this section shall prescribe the procedure to be followed in dealing with disciplinary offences.

(4) Regulations under this section shall enable the master to remit, in such circumstances as may be specified in the regulations, the whole or part of any fine imposed thereunder.

(5) Regulations under this section may make different provision for different descriptions of ship and for seamen employed in different capacities.

COMMENTS.

For 'Board of Trade' read 'Secretary of State for Trade'.

This section does not apply to fishing vessels.

Regulations.

Consult the Merchant Shipping (Disciplinary Offences) Regulations 1972, S.I. 1972, No. 1294, as amended by the Merchant Shipping (Disciplinary Offences) (Amendment) Regulations 1974, S.I. 1974, No. 2047.

Substitution.

The figure of £10 underlined in sub-section 2 is now £20. Merchant Shipping Act 1974, section 19.

Appeal against fine for disciplinary offence.   **35** (1) A seaman on whom a fine has been imposed for a disciplinary offence may, in accordance with regulations made by the Board of Trade, appeal against the decision to a superintendent or proper officer and on such an appeal the superintendent or proper officer may confirm or quash the decision and may remit the whole or part of the fine.

(2) Regulations under this section shall provide for the procedure to be followed on any such appeal, including the

time within which notice of an intended appeal is to be given by the appellant to the master and by the master to the superintendent or proper officer and the place at which the appeal is to be heard.

COMMENTS.

For 'Board of Trade' read 'Secretary of State for Trade'.

Regulations.

Consult the Merchant Shipping (Disciplinary Offences) Regulations 1972, S.I. 1972, No. 1294, as amended by the Merchant Shipping (Disciplinary Offences) (Amendment) Regulations 1974, S.I. 1974, No. 2047.

⚓   ⚓   ⚓   ⚓

36 (1) The Board of Trade may make regulations providing for the setting up in ships to which the regulations apply of committees of persons employed in the ships, to be known as ship's disciplinary committees, and for the exercise by members of those committees of all or any of the powers of the master in dealing with disciplinary offences.

Power to provide for ship's disciplinary committees.

(2) Regulations under this section may contain such provisions excluding, modifying or adding to the provisions of regulations under section 34 of this Act as appear to the Board of Trade necessary or expedient for the proper and effective discharge by members of a ship's disciplinary committee of functions otherwise exercisable by the master.

(3) Regulations under this section may be so made as to apply to ships generally or to any description of ship specified in the regulations and either in all circumstances or in such circumstances as may be so specified, or to apply to such ships or to ships of such descriptions as may for the time being be specified in a direction of the Board of Trade.

(4) No regulations shall be made under this section unless a draft thereof has been laid before Parliament and approved by resolution of each House of Parliament.

COMMENTS.

This section underlined, is not yet in force.

⚓   ⚓   ⚓   ⚓

Prohibition
of double
prosecutions.

37 Where any conduct is both a disciplinary offence and an offence against any provision of the Merchant Shipping Acts, then if it has been dealt with as a disciplinary offence it shall not be dealt with as an offence against that provision.

COMMENTS.

This section is only applicable to disciplinary offences under the Merchant Shipping Acts, and does not apply to prosecutions under other enactments.

See Lewis *v.* Morgan 1943 (Prosecution under the Defence Regulations).

⚓   ⚓   ⚓   ⚓

Payment
of fines for
disciplinary
offences.

38 (1) Subject to subsection (3) of this section, the amount of a fine imposed on a seaman for a disciplinary offence, so far as not remitted by the master or on appeal, may be deducted from his wages or otherwise recovered by the persons employing him and shall be paid by them (whether or not it has been so deducted or otherwise recovered) to a superintendent or proper officer.

(2) Subject to subsection (3) of this section—

(a) if the wages or part of the wages are paid by the master on behalf of the persons employing the seaman, or the master is the person employing the seaman, the said amount shall be paid at the time when the seaman leaves the ship at the end of the voyage or, if earlier, when his employment in the ship is terminated;

(b) in any other case the master shall at that time notify the amount to those persons and they shall pay it when the next payment in respect of the seaman's wages falls to be made by them.

(3) Where an appeal against such a fine is pending at the time mentioned in subsection (2) of this section no amount shall by reason of the fine be deducted, recovered, paid or notified under the preceding provisions of this section until the appeal has been disposed of; but regulations under section 35 of this Act may provide for the amount of the fine to be provisionally deducted from the seaman's wages pending the appeal.

(4) Any amount paid under this section to a superintendent or proper officer shall be transmitted by him to the Board of

Trade and any amount required to be so paid but remaining unpaid shall be recoverable by the Board of Trade.

(5) The Board of Trade shall pay any sums received by them in pursuance of this section into the Consolidated Fund.

COMMENTS.

For 'Board of Trade' read 'Secretary of State for Trade'.
This section does not apply to fishing vessels.

Regulations.

Consult the Merchant Shipping (Disciplinary Offences) Regulations 1972, S.I. 1972, No. 1294, as amended by the Merchant Shipping (Disciplinary Offences) (Amendment) Regulations 1974, S.I. 1974, No. 2047.

⚓   ⚓   ⚓   ⚓

Civil liability for absence without leave, smuggling and fines imposed under immigration laws

39 (1) The following provisions of this section shall Civil liability for absence without leave. apply with respect to the liability of a seaman employed in a ship registered in the United Kingdom to damages for being absent from his ship at a time when he is required under his contract of employment to be on board.

(2) If he proves that his absence was due to an accident or mistake or some other cause beyond his control and that he took all reasonable precautions to avoid being absent his absence shall not be treated as a breach of contract.

(3) Where subsection (2) of this section does not apply, then—
(*a*) if no special damages are claimed his liability shall be £10;
(*b*) if special damages are claimed his liability shall not be more than £100.

(4) In the application of this section to Scotland for the references to special damages there shall be substituted references to damages in respect of specific expense incurred or loss sustained.

⚓   ⚓   ⚓   ⚓

40 If a seaman employed in a ship registered in the Civil liability for smuggling. United Kingdom is found in civil proceedings before a court in the United Kingdom to have committed an act of smuggling, whether within or outside the United Kingdom, he shall be liable to make good any loss or expenses that the act has caused to any other person.

⚓   ⚓   ⚓   ⚓

Civil liability for fines imposed under immigration laws.

41 (1) The following provisions of this section shall apply where, at a time when a ship registered in the United Kingdom is in the national or territorial waters of any country outside the United Kingdom, a seaman employed in the ship is absent without leave and present in that country in contravention of that country's laws.

(2) If, by reason of the contravention, a penalty is incurred under those laws by the persons employing the seaman the penalty shall be treated as being attributable to his absence without leave and may, subject to the provisions of section 39 of this Act, be recovered from him as special damages for breach of contract (or, in Scotland, as damages in respect of specific expense incurred or loss sustained).

(3) If, by reason of the contravention, a penalty is incurred under those laws by any other person the amount thereof, or, if that amount exceeds £100, £100 may be recovered by him from the seaman.

⚓   ⚓   ⚓   ⚓

Trade disputes

Trade disputes involving seamen.

42 (1) The Conspiracy and Protection of Property Act 1875, except section 5, shall apply to seamen as it applies to other persons.

(2) Notwithstanding anything in any agreement, a seaman employed in a ship registered in the United Kingdom may terminate his employment in that ship by leaving the ship in contemplation or furtherance of a trade dispute after giving to the master not less than forty-eight hours' notice of his intention to do so, and shall not be compelled (unless the notice is withdrawn) to go to sea in the forty-eight hours following the giving of such a notice; but such a notice shall be of no effect unless at the time it is given the ship is in the United Kingdom and securely moored in a safe berth.

(3) In this section 'trade dispute' has the same meaning as in section 5(3) of the Trade Disputes Act 1906.

COMMENTS.

Conspiracy and Protection of Property Act 1875.

Section 16 of that Act provided that the Act did not apply to seamen.

Sub-section 3 (Underlined).

Repealed. Trade Union and Labour Relations Act 1974, section 25, Schedule 8.

⚓   ⚓   ⚓   ⚓

Manning and certification

43 (1) Subject to subsection (2) of this section, the Manning. Board of Trade may make regulations—

(a) requiring ships to which this section applies to carry such number of qualified officers of any description, qualified doctors and qualified cooks and such number of other seamen or qualified seamen of any description as may be specified in the regulations; and

(b) prescribing or enabling the Board of Trade to specify standards of competence to be attained and other conditions to be satisfied (subject to any exceptions allowed by or under the regulations) by officers and other seamen of any description in order to be qualified for the purposes of this section.

(2) The Board of Trade shall not exercise their power to make regulations requiring ships to carry seamen other than doctors and cooks except to the extent that it appears to them necessary or expedient in the interests of safety.

(3) Regulations under this section may make different provision for different descriptions of ship or for ships of the same description in different circumstances.

(4) Without prejudice to the generality of paragraph (b) of subsection (1) of this section, the conditions prescribed or specified under that paragraph may include conditions as to nationality, and regulations made for the purposes of that paragraph may make provision, or enable the Board of Trade to make provision, for—

(a) the manner in which the attainment of any standard or the satisfaction of any other condition is to be evidenced;

(b) the conduct of any examinations, the conditions for admission to them and the appointment and remuneration of examiners; and (*c*) the issue, form and recording of certificates and other documents;

and different provisions may be so made or enabled to be made for different circumstances.

(5) If a person makes a statement which he knows to be false or recklessly makes a statement which is false in a material particular for the purpose of obtaining for himself or another person a certificate or other document which may be issued under this section he shall be liable on summary conviction to a fine not exceeding £100.

COMMENTS.

This section came into force as from the 18th December, 1975. The Merchant Shipping Act 1970 (Commencement No. 4) Order 1975, S.I. 1975, No. 2156.

For 'Board of Trade' read 'Secretary of State for Trade'.

Consult The Merchant Shipping (Certification of Deck Officers) Regulations 1977, S.I. 1977, No. 1152, coming into force on the 1st September, 1981.

See also section 93 of the Principal Act.

⚓   ⚓   ⚓   ⚓

Power to exempt from manning requirements.

44 (1) The Board of Trade may exempt any ship or description of ship from any requirements of regulations made under section 43 of this Act.

(2) An exemption given under this section may be confined to a particular period or to one or more particular voyages.

COMMENTS.

This section came into force as from the 18th December, 1975. The Merchant Shipping Act 1970 (Commencement No. 4) Order 1975, S.I. 1975, No. 2156.

For 'Board of Trade' read 'Secretary of State for Trade'.

⚓   ⚓   ⚓   ⚓

Prohibition of going to sea undermanned.

45 Subject to section 44 of this Act, if a ship to which this section applies goes to sea or attempts to go to sea without carrying such officers and other seamen as it is required to carry under section 43 of this Act, the owner or master shall be liable on summary conviction to a fine not exceeding £200 and the ship, if in the United Kingdom, may be detained.

COMMENTS.

This section came into force as from the 18th December, 1975, The Merchant Shipping Act (Commencement No. 4) Order 1975, S.I. 1975, No. 2156.

Substitution.

Consult section 96, sub-section 2, which provides: in lieu of the words underlined from 'goes' to 'sea', the words: 'Plies, or attempts to ply' and the words also underlined 'if in the United Kingdom' were omitted.

Consult the same section for amendment of section 629 of the Merchant Shipping Act 1894.

⚓   ⚓   ⚓   ⚓

46 (1) If a person goes to sea as a qualified officer or seaman of any description without being such a qualified officer or seaman he shall be liable on summary conviction to a fine not exceeding £100. *Unqualified persons going to sea as qualified officers or seamen.*

(2) In this section 'qualified' means qualified for the purposes of section 43 of this Act.

COMMENTS.

This section came into force as from 18th December, 1975. The Merchant Shipping Act 1970 (Commencement No. 4) Order 1975, S.I. 1975, No. 2156.

⚓   ⚓   ⚓   ⚓

47 Any person serving or engaged to serve in any ship to which this section applies and holding any certificate or other document which is evidence that he is qualified for the purposes of section 43 of this Act shall on demand produce it to any superintendent, surveyor or proper officer and (if he is not himself the master) to the master of the ship; and if he fails to do so without reasonable cause he shall be liable on summary conviction to a fine not exceeding £20. *Production of certificates and other documents of qualification.*

COMMENTS.

This section came into force as from the 18th December, 1975. The Merchant Shipping Act 1970 (Commencement No. 4) Order 1975, S.I. 1975, No. 2156.

⚓   ⚓   ⚓   ⚓

Crew's knowledge of English.

48 (1) Where in the opinion of a superintendent or proper officer the crew of a ship to which this section applies consists of or includes persons who may not understand orders given to them in the course of their duty because of their insufficient knowledge of English and the absence of adequate arrangements for transmitting the orders in a language of which they have sufficient knowledge, then—

(*a*) if the superintendent or proper officer has informed the master of that opinion the ship shall not go to sea; and

(*b*) if the ship is in the United Kingdom it may be detained.

(2) If a ship goes to sea or attempts to go to sea in contravention of this section the owner or master shall be liable on summary conviction to a fine not exceeding £200.

⚓ ⚓ ⚓ ⚓

Application of sections 43, 45, 47 and 48.

49 Sections 43, 45, 47 and 48 of this Act apply to every ship registered in the United Kingdom and also to any ship registered elsewhere which carries passengers—

(*a*) between places in the United Kingdom or between the United Kingdom and the Isle of Man or any of the Channel Islands; or

(*b*) on a voyage which begins and ends at the same place in the United Kingdom and on which the ship calls at no place outside the United Kingdom.

COMMENTS.

This section came into force as from the 18th December, 1975. The Merchant Shipping Act 1970 (Commencement No. 4) Order 1975, S.I. 1975, No. 2156.

⚓ ⚓ ⚓ ⚓

Special certificates of competency.

50 (1) The Board of Trade may issue and record documents certifying the attainment of any standard of competence relating to ships or their operation, notwithstanding that the standard is not among those prescribed or specified under section 43(1)(*b*) of this Act; and may, in relation thereto, make regulations for purposes corresponding to those mentioned in section 43(4) of this Act.

(2) If a person makes a statement which he knows to be false or recklessly makes a statement which is false in a material particular for the purpose of obtaining for himself or another person a document which may be issued under this section he shall be liable on summary conviction to a fine not exceeding £100.

COMMENTS.

This section, underlined, is not yet in force.

⚓   ⚓   ⚓   ⚓

51 (1) A person under school-leaving age shall not be employed in any ship registered in the United Kingdom except as permitted by regulations under this section.

Restriction on employment of persons under eighteen on board ship.

(2) The Board of Trade may make regulations—

(*a*) prescribing circumstances in which and conditions subject to which persons under school-leaving age who have attained such age as may be specified in the regulations may be employed in a ship in such capacities as may be so specified;

(*b*) prescribing circumstances and capacities in which persons over school-leaving age but under the age of eighteen or under such lower age as may be specified in the regulations must not be employed in a ship registered in the United Kingdom or may be so employed only subject to such conditions as may be specified in the regulations.

(3) Regulations made for the purposes of this section may make different provision for different employments and different descriptions of ship and any other different circumstances.

(4) If any person is employed in a ship in contravention of this section or if any condition subject to which a person may be employed under regulations made for the purposes of this section is not complied with, the owner or master shall be liable on summary conviction to a fine not exceeding £100.

(5) For the purposes of this section a person employed in a ship shall be deemed to be over school-leaving age if he has, and under school-leaving age if he has not, attained the age which is the upper limit of the compulsory school age (in Scotland school age) under the enactments relating to education in the part of the United Kingdom in which he entered into the agreement under which he is so employed or, if he entered into that agreement outside the United Kingdom or is employed otherwise than under an agreement, under the enactments relating to education in England and Wales; and if he is treated for the purposes of those enactments as not having attained that age he shall be so treated also for the purposes of this section.

COMMENTS.

This section, underlined, is not yet in force.

⚓   ⚓   ⚓   ⚓

Disqualification of seamen, inquiries and investigations

Inquiry into fitness or conduct of officer.

52 (1) If it appears to the Board of Trade that an officer—

(*a*) is unfit to discharge his duties, whether by reason of incompetence or misconduct or for any other reason; or

(*b*) has been seriously negligent in the discharge of his duties; or

(*c*) has failed to comply with the provisions of section 422 of the Merchant Shipping Act 1894 (duty to give assistance and information after collision);

the Board of Trade may cause an inquiry to be held by one or more persons appointed by them and, if they do so, may, if they think fit, suspend, pending the outcome of the inquiry, any certificate issued to the officer in pursuance of section 43 of this Act and require the officer to deliver it to them.

(2) Where a certificate issued to an officer has been suspended under subsection (1) of this section the suspension may,

on the application of the officer, be terminated by the High Court or, if the inquiry is held in Scotland, by the Court of Session, and the decision of the court on such an application shall be final.

(3) An inquiry under this section shall be conducted in accordance with rules made under section 58(1) of this Act and those rules shall require the persons holding the inquiry to hold it with the assistance of one or more assessors.

(4) The persons holding an inquiry under this section into the fitness or conduct of an officer—

(a) may, if satisfied of any of the matters mentioned in paragraphs (a) to (c) of subsection (1) of this section, cancel or suspend any certificate issued to him under section 43 of this Act or censure him:

(b) may make such order with regard to the costs of the inquiry as they think just; and

(c) shall make a report on the case to the Board of Trade; and if the certificate is cancelled or suspended the officer (unless he has delivered it to the Board of Trade in pursuance of subsection (1) of this section) shall deliver it forthwith to the persons holding the inquiry or to the Board of Trade.

(5) Any costs which a person is ordered to pay under subsection (4)(b) of this section may be recovered from him by the Board of Trade.

COMMENTS.
This section, underlined, is not yet in force.

⚓   ⚓   ⚓   ⚓

53 (1) Where it appears to the Board of Trade that a person who is the holder of a certificate to which this section applies is unfit to be the holder of such a certificate, whether by reason of incompetence or misconduct or for any other reason, they may give him notice in writing that they are considering the suspension or cancellation of the certificate.

Disqualification of holder of certificate other than officer's.

(2) The notice must state the reasons why it appears to the Board of Trade that that person is unfit to be the holder of such a certificate and must state that within a period specified in the notice, or such longer period as the Board of Trade may allow, he may make written representations to the Board or claim to make oral representations to the Board.

(3) After considering any representations made in pursuance of the preceding subsection the Board shall decide whether or not to suspend or cancel the certificate and shall give the holder of it written notice of their decision.

(4) Where the decision is to suspend or cancel the certificate the notice shall state the date from which the cancellation is to take effect, or the date from which and the period for which the suspension is to take effect, and shall require the holder to deliver the certificate to the Board not later than the date so specified unless before that date he has required the case to be dealt with by an inquiry under section 54 of this Act.

(5) Where, before the date specified in the notice, he requires the case to be dealt with by such an inquiry, then, unless he withdraws the requirement, the suspension or cancellation shall not take effect except as ordered in pursuance of the inquiry.

(6) The Board of Trade may make regulations prescribing the procedure to be followed with respect to the making and consideration of representations in pursuance of this section, the form of any notice to be given under this section and the period to be specified in any such notice as the period within which any steps are to be taken.

(7) This section applies to every certificate issued under section 50 of this Act and to any certificate issued under section 43 of this Act other than one certifying that a person is qualified as an officer.

COMMENTS.

This section, underlined, is not yet in force.

⚓   ⚓   ⚓   ⚓

54 (1) Where a person has, before the date mentioned in section 53(4) of this Act, required his case to be dealt with by an inquiry under this section the Board of Trade shall cause an inquiry to be held by one or more persons appointed by them.

Inquiry into fitness or conduct of seaman other than officer.

(2) An inquiry under this section shall be conducted in accordance with rules made under section 58(1) of this Act and those rules shall require the persons holding the inquiry to hold it with the assistance of one or more assessors.

(3) The persons holding an inquiry under this section—

(*a*) may confirm the decision of the Board of Trade and cancel or suspend the certificate accordingly;

(*b*) may, where the decision was to cancel the certificate, suspend it instead;

(*c*) may, where the decision was to suspend the certificate, suspend it for a different period;

(*d*) may, instead of confirming the decision of the Board of Trade, censure the holder of the certificate or take no further action;

(*e*) may make such order with regard to the costs of the inquiry as they think just; and

(*f*) shall make a report on the case to the Board of Trade; and if the certificate is cancelled or suspended it shall be delivered forthwith to the persons holding the inquiry or to the Board of Trade.

(4) Any costs which a person is ordered to pay under subsection (3)(*e*) of this section may be recovered from him by the Board of Trade.

COMMENTS.

This section, underlined, is not yet in force.

⚓   ⚓   ⚓   ⚓

Inquiries and investigations into shipping casualties.

55 (1) Where any of the following casualties has occurred, that is to say,—

(*a*) the loss or presumed loss, stranding, grounding, abandonment of or damage to a ship; or

(*b*) a loss of life caused by fire on board or by any accident to a ship or ship's boat, or by any accident occurring on board a ship or ship's boat; or

(*c*) any damage caused by a ship;

and, at the time it occurred, the ship was registered in the United Kingdom or the ship or boat was in the United Kingdom or the territorial waters thereof, the Board of Trade—

(i) may cause a preliminary inquiry into the casualty to be held by a person appointed for the purpose by the Board; and

(ii) may (whether or not a preliminary inquiry into the casualty has been held) cause a formal investigation into the casualty to be held, if in England, Wales or Northern Ireland, by a wreck commissioner and, if in Scotland, by the sheriff.

(2) A person appointed under this section to hold a preliminary inquiry shall for the purpose of the inquiry have the powers conferred on an inspector by section 729 of the Merchant Shipping Act 1894.

COMMENTS.

This section, underlined, is not yet in force.

⚓   ⚓   ⚓   ⚓

56 (1) A wreck commissioner or sheriff holding a formal investigation into a casualty under section 55 of this Act shall conduct it in accordance with rules under section 58(1) of this Act, and those rules shall require the assistance of one or more assessors and, if any question as to the catcellation or suspension of an officer's certificate is likely to arise, the assistance of not less than two assessors.

(2) Subsections (1), (3) and (4) of section 77 of the Magistrates' Courts Act 1952 (which provide for the attendance of witnesses and the production of evidence) shall apply in relation to a formal investigation held by a wreck commissioner as if the wreck commissioner were a magistrates' court and the investigation a complaint; and the wreck commissioner shall have power to administer oaths for the purposes of the investigation.

(3) Where a formal investigation is held in Scotland the sheriff shall, subject to any rules made under section 58(1) of this Act, dispose of it as a summary application, and, subject to section 57 of this Act, his decision on the investigation shall be final.

(4) If as a result of the investigation the wreck commissioner or sheriff is satisfied, with respect to any officer, of any of the matters mentioned in paragraphs (a) to (c) of section 52(1) of this Act and, if it is a matter mentioned in paragraph (a) or (b) of that section, is further satisfied that it caused or contributed to the casualty, he may cancel or suspend any certificate issued to the officer under section 43 of this Act or censure him; and if he cancels or suspends the certificate the officer shall deliver it forthwith to him or to the Board of Trade.

(5) The wreck commissioner or sheriff may make such order with regard to the costs of the investigation as he thinks just and shall make a report on the case to the Board of Trade.

(6) Any costs which a person is ordered to pay under the

preceding subsection may be recovered from him by the Board of Trade.

(7) In its application to Northern Ireland this section shall have effect as if in subsection (2) for the references to sub-sections (1), (3) and (4) of section 77 of the Magistrates' Courts Act 1952 there were substituted references to sub-sections (1) and (3) of section 120 and subsection (1) of section 122 of the Magistrates' Courts Act (Northern Ireland) 1964.

COMMENTS.

This section, underlined, is not yet in force.

⚓   ⚓   ⚓   ⚓

Re-hearing of and appeal from inquiries and investigations.

57 (1) Where an inquiry or formal investigation has been held under the preceding provisions of this Act the Board of Trade may order the whole or part of the case to be re-heard, and shall do so

(a) if new and important evidence which could not be produced at the inquiry or investigation has been discovered; or

(b) if there appear to the Board to be other grounds for suspecting that a miscarriage of justice may have occurred.

(2) An order under subsection (1) of this section may provide for the re-hearing to be as follows.—

(a) if the inquiry or investigation was held in England, Wales or Northern Ireland, by the persons who held it, by a wreck commissioner or by the High Court;

(b) if it was held in Scotland, by the persons who held it, by the sheriff or by the Court of Session.

(3) Any re-hearing under this section which is not held by the High Court or the Court of Session shall be conducted in accordance with rules made under section 58(1) of this Act; and section 56 of this Act shall apply in relation to a re-hearing of an investigation by a wreck commissioner or sheriff as it applies in relation to the holding of an investigation.

(4) Where the persons holding the inquiry or investigation have decided to cancel or suspend the certificate of any person or have found any person at fault, then, if no application for an order under subsection (1) of this section has been made or such an application has been refused, that person or any other person who, having an interest in the inquiry or investigation, has appeared at the hearing and is affected by the decision or finding, may appeal to the High Court or the Court of Session, according as the inquiry or investigation was held in England, Wales or Northern Ireland or in Scotland.

COMMENTS.

This section, underlined, is not yet in force.

⚓   ⚓   ⚓   ⚓

58 (1) The Board of Trade may make rules for the conduct of inquiries under sections 52 and 54 of this Act and of formal investigations under section 55 of this Act and for the conduct of any re-hearing under section 57 of this Act which is not held by the High Court or the Court of Session. *Rules as to enquiries, investigations and appeals.*

(2) Without prejudice to the generality of the preceding subsection, rules under this section may provide for the appointment and summoning of assessors, the manner in which any facts may be proved, the persons allowed to appear, and the notices to be given to persons affected.

(3) Rules of court made for the purpose of rehearings under section 57 of this Act which are held by the High Court, or of appeals to the High Court, may require the court, subject to such exceptions, if any, as may be allowed by the rules, to hold such a rehearing or hear such an appeal with the assistance of one or more assessors.

COMMENTS.

This section, underlined, is not yet in force.

⚓   ⚓   ⚓   ⚓

N

59 If a person fails to deliver a certificate as required under section 52 or 56 of this Act he shall be liable on summary conviction to a fine not exceeding £50; and if a person fails to deliver a certificate as required under section 53 or 54 of this Act he shall be liable on summary conviction to a fine not exceeding £10.

COMMENTS.

This section, underlined, is not yet in force.

⚓   ⚓   ⚓   ⚓

Power to
restore
certificate.

60 Where a certificate has been cancelled or suspended under this Act or under section 478 of the Merchant Shipping Act 1894, the Board of Trade, if of opinion that the justice of the case requires it, may re-issue the certificate or, as the case may be, reduce the period of suspension and return the certificate, or may grant a new certificate of the same or a lower grade in place of the cancelled or suspended certificate.

COMMENTS.

This section, underlined, is not yet in force.

⚓   ⚓   ⚓   ⚓

Inquiries into
deaths of crew
members and
others.

61 (1) Subject to subsection (4) of this section, where—

(*a*) any person dies in a ship registered in the United Kingdom; or

(*b*) the master of or a seaman employed in such a ship dies in a country outside the United Kingdom;

an inquiry into the cause of the death shall be held by a superintendent or proper officer at the next port where the ship calls after the death and where there is a superintendent or proper officer, or at such other place as the Board of Trade may direct.

(2) The superintendent or proper officer holding the inquiry shall for the purpose of the inquiry have the powers conferred on an inspector by section 729 of the Merchant Shipping Act 1894.

(3) The person holding the inquiry shall make a report of

his findings to the Board of Trade and the Board shall make a copy of the report available—

(a) if the deceased person was employed in the ship and a person was named as his next of kin in the crew agreement or list of the crew in which the deceased person's name last appeared, to the person so named;

(b) in any case, to any person requesting it who appears to the Board of Trade to be interested.

(4) No inquiry shall be held under this section in a case where, in England, Wales or Northern Ireland, a coroner's inquest is to be held or, in Scotland, an inquiry is to be held under the Fatal Accidents Inquiry (Scotland) Act 1895 or the Fatal Accidents and Sudden Deaths Inquiry (Scotland) Act 1906.

⚓   ⚓   ⚓   ⚓

Relief and repatriation of seamen left behind

62 (1) Where—

(a) a person employed as a seaman in a ship registered in the United Kingdom is left behind in any country outside the United Kingdom or is taken to such a country on being shipwrecked; or

(b) a person who became so employed under an agreement entered into outside the United Kingdom is left behind in the United Kingdom or is taken to the United Kingdom on being shipwrecked;

Relief and return of seamen left behind, etc.

the persons who last employed him as a seaman shall make such provision for his return and for his relief and maintenance until his return and such other provisions as may be required by regulations made by the Board of Trade.

(2) The provisions to be so made may include the repayment of expenses incurred in bringing a shipwrecked seaman ashore and maintaining him until he is brought ashore and the payment of the expenses of the burial or cremation of a seaman who dies before he can be returned.

(3) The Board of Trade may also make regulations providing for the manner in which any wages due to any person left behind or taken to any country as mentioned in subsection (1) of this section, and any property of his left on board ship, are to be dealt with.

(4) The Board of Trade may make regulations requiring a superintendent or proper officer—

(a) to make such provision as may be prescribed by the regulations with respect to any matter for which provision may be required to be made by regulations under the preceding provisions of this section; and

(b) to make the like provision with respect to citizens of the United Kingdom and Colonies found in distress in any country outside the United Kingdom after being employed in ships registered in, or belonging to the government of, such a country.

(5) Without prejudice to the generality of the preceding provisions, regulations made under this section may make provision—

(a) for determining the place to which a person is to be returned;

(b) for requiring the master of any ship registered in the United Kingdom to convey a person to a place determined in accordance with the regulations and for enabling a superintendent or proper officer to give the master directions for that purpose;

(c) for the making of payments in respect of the conveyance of a person in accordance with the regulations; and

(d) for the keeping of records and the rendering of accounts

(6) Regulations under this section may make a contravention of any provision thereof an offence punishable on summary conviction with a fine not exceeding £100 or such less amount as may be specified in the regulations.

(7) This section applies to a person left behind on being discharged in pursuance of section 5 of this Act, whether or not at the time he is left behind the ship is still registered in the United Kingdom.

COMMENTS.

For 'Board of Trade' read 'Secretary of State for Trade'.

Regulations.

Consult the Merchant Shipping (Repatriation) Regulations 1972, S.I. 1972, No. 1805.

Citizens of the United Kingdom.

Consult the British Nationality Act 1948.

Convey a Person.

Such person, formerly known as a 'distressed British Seaman' is not a passenger for the purpose of Part 3 of the Merchant Shipping Act 1894. A ship conveying such persons is not, on that account alone, liable to compulsory pilotage as carrying passengers.

The Clymene 1897; *The Charles Livingston* 1941.

⚓   ⚓   ⚓   ⚓

63   Where a person left behind in or taken to any country as mentioned in section 62(1) of this Act remains there after the end of a period of three months the persons who last employed him as a seaman shall not be liable under that section to make provision for his return or for any matter arising after the end of that period, unless they have before the end of that period been under an obligation imposed on them by regulations under that section to make provision with respect to him.

Limit of employer's liability under s. 62.

⚓   ⚓   ⚓   ⚓

64   (1) Where any expenses are incurred in respect of any matter for which the employers of a seaman are required to make provision under section 62 of this Act, then—

Recovery of expenses incurred for relief and return, etc.

(a) if the expenses are incurred by the Board of Trade, or are incurred by the government of any country outside the United Kingdom and repaid to them on behalf of the Crown, the Board of Trade may recover them from the employers;

(b) if the expenses are incurred by the seaman he may recover them from the employers unless they prove either that under the terms of his employment they were to be borne by him or that he would not have been left behind but for his own wrongful act or neglect.

(2) Where, in the case of any seaman, expenses are incurred by the Board of Trade or are incurred by the government of any country outside the United Kingdom and repaid to them on behalf of the Crown—

(a) in respect of any matter for which, but for section 63 of this Act, the seaman's last employers would have been required to make provision under section 62 of this Act; or

(b) in respect of any matter for which provision is required to be made under section 62(4)(b) of this Act;

the Board of Trade may recover them from the seaman (or, if he has died, from his personal representatives).

COMMENTS.

For 'Board of Trade' read 'Secretary of State for Trade'.

⚓   ⚓   ⚓   ⚓

Property of deceased seamen

Custody, etc.,
of property of
deceased
seamen.

65 (1) The Board of Trade may make regulations providing for the custody of and dealing with—

(*a*) any property left on board a ship registered in the United Kingdom by a seaman dying while or after being employed in the ship;

(*b*) any property left in a country outside the United Kingdom by a seaman dying while or within six months after being employed in such a ship; and

(*c*) any property left in a country outside the United Kingdom by a citizen of the United Kingdom and colonies dying while or within six months after being employed as a seaman in a ship registered outside the United Kingdom;

until it is disposed of by or under the directions of the Board of Trade; and for the recovery by the Board of Trade of any wages which, at the time of a seaman's death, were due to him in respect of his employment in a ship registered in the United Kingdom.

(2) Regulations under this section may require the recording of particulars and the rendering of accounts and may enable the Board of Trade or any person having custody of any such property to sell it by auction or otherwise and account for the proceeds.

(3) Regulations under this section may make a contravention of any provision thereof an offence punishable on summary conviction with a fine not exceeding £100.

COMMENTS.

For 'Board of Trade' read 'Secretary of State for Trade'.

Property.

Consult the Merchant Shipping (Property of Deceased Seamen) Regulations 1972, S.I. 1972, No. 1697.

Seamen.

This term includes a master.

United Kingdom Citizen.

See the British Nationality Act, 1948.

⚓   ⚓   ⚓   ⚓

66 (1) Where, on the death of a seaman, any assets *Disposal of property of* come into the hands of the Board of Trade by virtue of section *deceased seamen.* 65 of this Act the Board may satisfy out of them any expenses incurred by the Board in respect of the seaman or his property.

(2) If the value of the residue of the assets does not exceed £500, the Board of Trade may at any time pay or deliver it to any of the persons mentioned in subsection (3) of this section or distribute it among them, unless a grant of representation, or in Scotland confirmation, has then been made and the Board of Trade know of it; and the Board shall thereby be discharged from any further liability in respect of the residue.

(3) The persons referred to in subsection (2) of this section are—

(*a*) any person appearing to the Board of Trade to be a person named as the seaman's next of kin in the crew agreement or list of the crew in which the seaman's name last appeared;

(*b*) any person appearing to the Board of Trade to be his widow or a child of his;

(*c*) any person appearing to the Board of Trade to be beneficially entitled, under a will or on intestacy, to the seaman's estate or any part of it;

(*d*) any person appearing to the Board of Trade to be a creditor of the seaman.

(4) If it appears to the Board of Trade that any of the persons to whom any assets may be paid or delivered under this section is resident in a foreign state the Board of Trade may pay or deliver them to him by paying or delivering them to a consular officer of that state for transmission to him.

(5) In this section 'child' includes an adopted child and an illegitimate child.

COMMENTS.

For 'Board of Trade' read 'Secretary of State for Trade'.

Under a Will.

A seaman while at sea may dispose of his personal property without regard to the formalities under the Wills Act of 1837. *See* section 2 of that Act. A will may be made by a seaman though the seaman is under the age of 18. *See* the Wills (Soldiers and Sailors) Act 1918, section 1. *See* also section 3 of that Act as to the disposal of real estate.

'While at Sea.'

This term is given a wide interpretation. *See* In the Goods of Lay 1840, when it was held that this term applied although the seaman was temporarily ashore during the voyage. *See* also In the Goods of McMurdo 1867, where the seaman was on board a ship in harbour. In the Goods of Newland 1952, though a seaman made a will ashore, a few days before completing a fresh voyage, it was held to come within the provisions of the Act.

Intestacy.

This term means 'without leaving a will'. Re Skeats, Thain *v* Gibbs 1936.

⚓   ⚓   ⚓   ⚓

Application of sections 62 to 66 to masters

Application
of sections
62 to 66 to
masters.

67 In sections 62 to 66 of this Act 'seaman' (notwithstanding the definition in section 742 of the Merchant Shipping Act 1894) includes the master of a ship.

⚓   ⚓   ⚓   ⚓

Documentation, reports and returns

Official log
books.

68 (1) Except as provided by regulations under this section an official log book in a form approved by the Board of Trade shall be kept in every ship registered in the United Kingdom.

(2) The Board of Trade may make regulations prescribing the particulars to be entered in official log books, the persons by whom such entries are to be made, signed or witnessed, and the procedure to be followed in the making of such entries and in their amendment or cancellation.

(3) The regulations may require the production or delivery of official log books to such persons, in such circumstances and within such times as may be specified therein.

(4) Regulations under this section may exempt ships of any description from any requirements thereof, either generally or in such circumstances as may be specified in the regulations.

(5) Regulations under this section may make a contravention of any provision thereof an offence punishable on summary conviction with a fine not exceeding £20.

(6) If a person wilfully destroys or mutilates or renders illegible any entry in an official log book he shall be liable on summary conviction to a fine not exceeding £100.

COMMENTS.

For 'Board of Trade' read 'Secretary of State for Trade'.

Regulations.

Merchant Shipping (Official Log Books) Regulations 1972, S.I. 1972, No. 1874.

Merchant Shipping (Official Log Books) (Fishing Vessels) Regulations 1972, S.I. 1972, No. 1873.

Merchant Shipping (Crew Agreements, List of Crew and Discharge of Seamen) Regulations 1972, S.I. 1972, No. 918.

Merchant Shipping (Crew Agreements, Lists of Crew and Discharge of Seamen) (Fishing Vessels) Regulations 1972, S.I. 1972, No. 919.

Merchant Shipping (Disciplinary Offences) Regulations 1972, S.I. 1972, No. 1294.

Merchant Shipping (Disciplinary Offences) (Amendment) Regulations, 1974, S.I. 1974, No. 2047.

Merchant Shipping (Repatriation) Regulations 1972, S.I. 1972, No. 1805.

⚓   ⚓   ⚓   ⚓

69 (1) Except as provided by regulations made under Lists of crew. this section the master of every ship registered in the United Kingdom shall make and maintain a list of the crew containing such particulars as may be required by the regulations.

(2) The Board of Trade may make regulations—

(*a*) specifying the particulars to be entered in a list of the crew;

(*b*) limiting the time for which a list of the crew may remain in force;

(*c*) providing for the maintenance by such persons and either in such place as may be specified in the regulations or,

if it is so specified, in the ship, of a copy or copies of each
list of a crew, and for the notification to such persons of
any changes therein;

(d) for the production of a list of the crew to such persons,
in such circumstances and within such time as may be
specified in the regulations; and

(e) for the delivery to a superintendent or proper officer or
the Registrar General of Shipping and Seamen, in such
circumstances as may be specified in the regulations, of
a list of the crew or a copy thereof maintained under the
regulations and for the notification to him of any changes
in such a list.

(3) Regulations under this section may enable a list of the
crew to be contained in the same document as a crew agreement and may treat any particulars entered in the crew agreement as forming part of the particulars entered in the list.

(4) Regulations under this section may exempt from the
requirements thereof such descriptions of ship as may be
specified in the regulations and may make different provision
for different circumstances.

(5) Regulations under this section may make a contravention of any provision thereof an offence punishable on
summary conviction with a fine not exceeding £20.

COMMENTS.
For 'Board of Trade' read 'Secretary of State for Trade'.

Regulations.
See Merchant Shipping (Crew Agreements, Lists of Crew, and Discharge of Seamen) Regulations 1972, S.I. 1972, No. 918.

Merchant Shipping (Crew Agreements, Lists of Crew, and Discharge
of Seamen) (Fishing Vessels) Regulations 1972, No. 919, as amended by
S.I. 1977, No. 45.

⚓   ⚓   ⚓   ⚓

British
seamen's cards.   **70** (1) The Board of Trade may make regulations providing—

(a) for the issue to British seamen of cards (in this section
referred to as 'British seamen's cards') in such form and
containing such particulars with respect to the holders
thereof and such other particulars (if any) as may be

prescribed by the regulations, and for requiring British
seamen to apply for such cards;

(b) for requiring the holders of British seamen's cards to
produce them to such persons and in such circumstances
as may be prescribed by the regulations;

(c) for the surrender of British seamen's cards in such circumstances as may be prescribed by the regulations;

(d) for any incidental or supplementary matters for which
the Board think it expedient for the purposes of the
regulations to provide;

and any provision of the regulations having effect by virtue
of paragraph (a) of this subsection may be so framed as to
apply to all British seamen or any description of them and as to
have effect subject to any exemptions for which provision may
be made by the regulations.

(2) Regulations under this section may make a contravention of any provision thereof an offence punishable on
summary conviction with a fine not exceeding £10.

(3) In this section 'British seamen' means persons who are
not aliens within the meaning of the British Nationality Act
1948 and are employed, or ordinarily employed, as masters
or seamen.

(4) If a person makes a statement which he knows to be
false or recklessly makes a statement which is false in a
material particular for the purpose of obtaining for himself
or another person a British seaman's card he shall be liable
on summary conviction to a fine not exceeding £100.

COMMENTS.
For 'Board of Trade', read 'Secretary of State for Trade'.
See Merchant Shipping (Seamen's Documents) Regulations 1972, S.I.
1972, No. 1295, as amended by Merchant Shipping (Seamen's Documents)
(Amendment) Regulations 1974, S.I. 1974, No. 1734; Merchant Shipping
(Fees for Seamen's Documents) Regulations 1975, S.I. 1975, No. 1692,
as amended by Statutory Instrument 1976, No. 2015.

⚓   ⚓   ⚓   ⚓

71 (1) The Board of Trade may make regulations pro- Discharge books.
viding—

(a) for the issue to persons who are or have been employed

in ships registered in the United Kingdom of discharge books in such form and containing such particulars with respect to the holders thereof and such other particulars (if any) as may be prescribed by the regulations and for requiring such persons to apply for such discharge books;

(b) for requiring the holders of discharge books to produce them to such persons and in such circumstances as may be prescribed by the regulations;

(c) for the surrender of discharge books in such circumstances as may be prescribed by the regulations;

(d) for any incidental or supplementary matters for which the Board think it expedient for the purposes of the regulations to provide;

and any provision of the regulations having effect by virtue of paragraph (a) of this subsection may be so framed as to apply to all such persons as are mentioned in that paragraph or any description of such persons and as to have effect subject to any exemptions for which provision may be made by the regulations.

(2) Regulations under this section may make a contravention of any provision thereof an offence punishable on summary conviction with a fine not exceeding £10.

COMMENTS.

See under section 70.

⚓   ⚓   ⚓   ⚓

Returns of
births and
deaths in
ships, etc.

72 (1) The Board of Trade may make regulations—

(a) requiring the master of any ship registered in the United Kingdom to make a return to a superintendent or proper officer for transmission to the Registrar General of Shipping and Seamen of any birth or death occurring in the ship and of the death, wherever occurring outside the United Kingdom, of any person employed in the ship, and to notify any such death to such person (if any) as the deceased may have named to him as his next of kin; and

(b) requiring the master of any ship not registered in the United Kingdom which calls at a port in the United Kingdom in the course of or at the end of a voyage to make a return to a superintendent for transmission to the Registrar General of Shipping and Seamen of any birth or death of a citizen of the United Kingdom and Colonies which has occurred in the ship during the voyage.

(2) Regulations under this section may require the Registrar General of Shipping and Seamen to send a certified copy of any return made thereunder to the Registrar General for England and Wales, the Registrar General of Births, Deaths and Marriages for Scotland or the Registrar General for Northern Ireland, as the case may require.

(3) The Registrar General to whom any such certified copies are sent shall record the information contained therein in a register kept by him for the purpose and to be called the marine register, and may also record in that register such additional information as appears to him desirable for the purpose of ensuring the completeness and correctness of the register; and the enactments relating to the registration of births and deaths in England, Scotland and Northern Ireland shall have effect as if the marine register were a register of births (other than still-births) or deaths or certified copies of entries in such a register and had been transmitted to the Registrar General in accordance with those enactments.

(4) Regulations under the preceding provisions of this section may make a contravention of any provision thereof an offence punishable on summary conviction with a fine not exceeding £20.

(5) Regulations under this section may contain provisions for authorising the registration of the following births and deaths occurring outside the United Kingdom in circumstances where no return is required to be made under the preceding provisions of this section—

(a) any birth or death of a citizen of the United Kingdom and Colonies which occurs in a ship not registered in the United Kingdom;

(b) any death of a citizen of the United Kingdom and Colonies who has been employed in such a ship which occurs elsewhere than in the ship; and

(c) any death of a person who has been employed in a ship registered in the United Kingdom which occurs elsewhere than in the ship.

COMMENTS.

For 'Board of Trade' read 'Secretary of State for Trade'.

Registrar General of Shipping and Seamen.

See section 80.

Regulations.

See Merchant Shipping (Returns of Births and Deaths) Regulations 1972, S.I. 1972, No. 1523.

⚓   ⚓   ⚓   ⚓

Reports of shipping casualties.

73 (1) Where any such casualty as is mentioned in section 55(1) of this Act has occurred in the case of a ship or ship's boat and, at the time it occurred, the ship was registered in the United Kingdom, the owner or master of the ship shall, as soon as practicable, and in any case not later than twenty-four hours after the ship's arrival at the next port, report the casualty to the Board of Trade, giving a brief description of it and stating the time and place where it occurred, the name and official number of the ship, its position at the time of the report and the next port of call.

(2) If the owner or master of a ship fails without reasonable cause to comply with the preceding provisions of this section he shall be liable on summary conviction to a fine not exceeding £100.

COMMENTS.

For 'Board of Trade' read 'Secretary of State for Trade'.

Boiler Explosion.

In the case of a boiler explosion, no further notice is required under the Boiler Explosion Act 1882, as long as a report is sent under this section.

⚓   ⚓   ⚓   ⚓

Handing over of documents on change of master.

74 If a person ceases to be the master of a ship registered in the United Kingdom during a voyage of the ship he shall deliver to his successor the documents relating to the ship or its crew which are in his custody; and if he fails without reasonable cause to do so he shall be liable on summary conviction to a fine not exceeding £100.

⚓   ⚓   ⚓   ⚓

Admissibility in evidence and inspection of certain documents.

75 (1) The following documents shall be admissible in evidence and, when in the custody of the Registrar General of Shipping and Seamen, shall be open to public inspection, that is to say,—

(*a*) crew agreements, lists of crews made under section 69 of this Act and notices given under this Act of additions to or changes in crew agreements and lists of crews;

(*b*) the official log book of any ship kept under section 68 of this Act and, without prejudice to section 695(2) of the Merchant Shipping Act 1894, any document purporting to be a copy of an entry therein and to be certified as a true copy by the master of the ship;

(*c*) documents purporting to be submissions to or decisions by superintendents or proper officers under section 10 of this Act;

(*d*) returns or reports under section 72 of this Act or under regulations made under section 19 of this Act.

(2) A certificate issued under section 43 of this Act shall be admissible in evidence.

Inspections

76 (1) For the purpose of seeing that the provisions of _{Inspections.} the Merchant Shipping Acts and regulations and rules made thereunder are duly complied with any of the following persons, that is to say,—

(*a*) a surveyor of ships;

(*b*) a superintendent;

(*c*) any person appointed by the Board of Trade, either generally or in a particular case, to exercise powers under this section;

may at all reasonable times go on board a ship and inspect the ship and its equipment or any part thereof, any articles on board, and any document carried in the ship in pursuance of the Merchant Shipping Acts or regulations or rules made thereunder; and if the ship is registered in the United Kingdom the powers conferred by this subsection may also be exercised outside the United Kingdom and may be so exercised by a proper officer as well as by the persons mentioned in paragraphs (*a*) to (*c*) of this subsection.

(2) A person exercising powers under this section shall not unnecessarily detain or delay a ship but may, if he considers it necessary in consequence of an accident or for any other

reason, require a ship to be taken into dock for a survey of its hull or machinery.

(3) Where any such person as is mentioned in paragaphs (*a*) to (*c*) of subsection (1) of this section has reasonable ground for believing that there are on any premises provisions or water intended for supply to a ship registered in the United Kingdom which, if provided on the ship, would not be in accordance with regulations under section 21 of this Act, he may enter the premises and inspect the provisions or water for the purpose of ascertaining whether they would be in accordance with those regulations.

(4) If any person obstructs a person in the exercise of his powers under this section, or fails to comply with a requirement made under subsection (2) thereof, he shall be liable on summary conviction to a fine not exceeding £100.

COMMENTS.

For 'Board of Trade' read 'Secretary of State for Trade'.

Reasonable Times.

See Small *v.* Bickley 1875.

For Believing.

The person must not only have reasonable grounds for believing, but actually believe. R. *v.* Harrison 1938.

Stowaways, unauthorised presence on board ship and master's power of arrest

Stowaways.

77 (1) If a person, without the consent of the master or of any other person authorised to give it, goes to sea or attempts to go to sea in a ship registered in the United Kingdom he shall be liable on summary conviction to a fine not exceeding £100 or to imprisonment for a period not exceeding three months.

(2) Nothing in section 686 of the Merchant Shipping Act 1894 shall be taken to limit the jurisdiction of any court in the United Kingdom to deal with an offence under this section which has been committed in a country outside the United Kingdom by a person who is not a British subject.

COMMENTS.

Offence—Jurisdiction.

The offence can be regarded as committed on board a ship on the high seas, thus giving jurisdiction under the Principal Act, section 686, sub-section 1, in respect of a person who is not a British subject. Robey v. Vladinier 1935.

⚓   ⚓   ⚓   ⚓

78 Where a ship registered in the United Kingdom or any other country is in a port in the United Kingdom and a person who is neither in Her Majesty's service nor authorised by law to do so— *Unauthorised presence on board ship.*

(*a*) goes on board the ship without the consent of the master or of any other person authorised to give it; or

(*b*) remains on board the ship after being requested to leave by the master, a constable, or an officer of the Board of Trade or of customs and excise;

he shall be liable on summary conviction to a fine not exceeding £20.

COMMENTS.

Constable.

This means the office and not the rank of a constable. The Police Act 1964, section 18.

⚓   ⚓   ⚓   ⚓

79 The master of any ship registered in the United Kingdom may cause any person on board the ship to be put under restraint if and for so long as it appears to him necessary or expedient in the interest of safety or for the preservation of good order or discipline on board the ship. *Master's power of arrest.*

COMMENTS.

Master's Authority.

The Master is justified in arresting and confining in a reasonable manner and for a reasonable time, any person on board his ship if he has reasonable cause to believe that such arrest or confinement is necessary for the preservation of order and discipline, or for the safety of the vessel, or the persons or the property on board. Hook v. Cunard Steamship Co. 1953.

⚓   ⚓   ⚓   ⚓

Administrative provisions

Registrar
General of
Shipping and
Seamen.

80 (1) The Board of Trade shall appoint, and may remove, an officer to be styled the Registrar General of Shipping and Seamen, who shall exercise such functions as are conferred on him by the Merchant Shipping Acts and keep such records and perform such other duties as the Board of Trade may direct.

(2) The Board of Trade may appoint and remove persons to perform on behalf of the Registrar General of Shipping and Seamen such of his functions as the Board or the Registrar General of Shipping and Seamen may direct.

COMMENTS.

For 'Board of Trade' read 'Secretary of State for Trade'.

⚓   ⚓   ⚓   ⚓

Appointment
of
superinten-
dents.

81 The Board of Trade shall appoint, and may remove, officers to be styled mercantile marine superintendents, who shall exercise the functions conferred on superintendents by the Merchant Shipping Acts.

COMMENTS.

For 'Board of Trade' read 'Secretary of State for Trade'.

⚓   ⚓   ⚓   ⚓

Appointment
of wreck
commissioners.

82 (1) The Lord Chancellor may appoint such number of persons as he thinks fit to be wreck commissioners and may remove any wreck commissioners appointed by him.

(2) Before appointing a person to act as wreck commissioner in Northern Ireland the Lord Chancellor shall consult the Lord Chief Justice of Northern Ireland.

⚓   ⚓   ⚓   ⚓

Remuneration
of wreck
commissioners
and assessors.

83 There shall be paid to any wreck commissioner or assessor appointed under this Act such remuneration, out of moneys provided by Parliament, as the Lord Chancellor may with the consent of the Treasury determine.

⚓   ⚓   ⚓   ⚓

84 The Board of Trade may with the consent of the Fees. Treasury make regulations prescribing fees to be paid in respect of the issue or recording of any certificate, licence or other document or the doing of any other thing in pursuance of this Act.

COMMENTS.

For 'Board of Trade' read 'Secretary of State for Trade'.

Regulations—Fees.

See now, the Merchant Shipping (Fees for Seamen's Documents) Regulations 1975, S.I. 1975, No. 1692, as amended by S.I. 1976, No. 2015. In operation from the 12th November, 1975, and which revoke the Merchant Shipping (Fees for Seamen's Documents) Regulations 1972, S.I. 1972, No. 1930 as amended.

⚓   ⚓   ⚓   ⚓

Miscellaneous

85 (1) For sections 3 and 6 of the Merchant Shipping Amendment of Merchant (Safety Conventions) Act 1949 there shall be substituted the Shipping sections set out in Schedule 1 to this Act. (Safety Convention) Act 1949.

(2) In section 5(2) of that Act (rules for direction finders) the words 'being ships of sixteen hundred tons gross tonnage or upwards' shall be omitted.

(3) Before making rules under any of those sections the Board of Trade shall consult with organisations in the United Kingdom appearing to them representative of persons who will be affected by the rules.

COMMENTS.

For 'Board of Trade' read 'Secretary of State for Trade'.

Rules.

See the Merchant Shipping (Radio) (Fishing Vessels) Rules 1974, S.I. 1974, No. 1919. This section came into force on the 18th November, 1974, The Merchant Shipping Act 1970 (Commencement No. 3) Order 1974, No. 1908.

86 (1) The Board of Trade may make rules specifying Nautical publications. such charts, directions or information as appear to the Board necessary or expedient for the safe operation of ships and those rules may require ships registered in the United Kingdom, or such descriptions of ships registered in the United Kingdom as may be specified in the rules, to carry, either at all times or on such voyages as may be specified in the rules, copies of the charts, directions or information so specified.

(2) If a ship goes to sea or attempts to go to sea without carrying copies of the charts, directions or information which it is required to carry by rules under this section the master or owner shall be liable on summary conviction to a fine not exceeding £100.

COMMENTS.

For 'Board of Trade' read 'Secretary of State for Trade'.

This section came into force on the 18th November, 1974, the Merchant Shipping Act 1970 (Commencement No. 3) Order 1974, S.I. 1974, No. 1908.

Rules.

See the Merchant Shipping (Carriage of Nautical Publications) Rules 1975, S.I. No. 700.

⚓   ⚓   ⚓   ⚓

The merchant navy uniform.

87 (1) The Board of Trade may make regulations prescribing a uniform, to be known as the merchant navy uniform, for the use of persons serving in ships registered in the United Kingdom, and distinguishing marks to be worn, as part of the uniform, by persons so serving in different positions or in different circumstances.

(2) Regulations under this section may prescribe the persons by whom and the circumstances in which the merchant navy uniform or any part of it may be worn.

(3) If a person wears the merchant navy uniform or any part of it, or wears anything bearing the appearance of the uniform or any part of it, when he is not authorised by regulations under this section to wear the uniform or that part he shall be liable on summary conviction to a fine not exceeding £50.

(4) Where any design, within the meaning of the Registered Designs Act 1949, which forms part of the merchant navy uniform has been registered under that Act and the Board of Trade are the registered proprietor thereof their copyright in the design shall, notwithstanding section 8 of that Act, continue so long as the design remains so registered.

(5) Nothing in this section shall prohibit or restrict the use of the merchant navy uniform or any part of it for the purposes of any stage, film or television performance, unless the use is such as to bring the uniform into disrepute.

COMMENTS.

This section is not yet in force.

For 'Board of Trade' *read* 'Secretary of State for Trade'.

⚓　　　⚓　　　⚓　　　⚓

88 In section 692(1) of the Merchant Shipping Act 1894 (enforcing detention of ship) for the words 'one hundred pounds' there shall be substituted the words 'two hundred pounds'.

Increase of penalty for sailing while ship under detention.

⚓　　　⚓　　　⚓　　　⚓

89 (1) Subject to subsection (5) of this section, this section applies to any country to which, immediately before the coming into operation of the repeal by this Act of section 238 of the Merchant Shipping Act 1894, that section applied by virtue of an Order in Council made under it or having effect as if made under it.

Dealing with deserters under reciprocal arrangements.

(2) Where a seaman deserts in the United Kingdom from a ship registered in a country to which this section applies, a justice of the peace may, on the application of a consular officer of that country and on information on oath, issue a warrant for the arrest of the seaman.

(3) Where a seaman has been arrested on a warrant issued under this section a magistrates' court may, on proof of the desertion, order him to be conveyed on board his ship.

(4) Where a seaman is liable to be arrested under this section, any person who, knowing or believing that he has

deserted, does without lawful authority or reasonable excuse any act with intent to impede his arrest shall be liable on summary conviction to a fine not exceeding £20.

(5) Her Majesty may by Order in Council direct that this section shall cease to apply to any country specified in the Order.

(6) In its application to Scotland this section shall have effect as if for the reference to a justice of the peace there were substituted a reference to a sheriff, magistrate or justice of the peace, for the reference to a magistrates' court a reference to a court of summary jurisdiction within the meaning of the Summary Jurisdiction (Scotland) Act 1954, and for the reference to information on oath a reference to evidence on oath.

(7) In its application to Northern Ireland this section shall have effect as if in subsection (3) for the reference to a magistrates' court there were substituted a reference to a court of summary jurisdiction.

COMMENTS.

Countries which have Agreed to Reciprocal Arrangements.

Belgium, 1964; Brazil, 1888; Columbia, 1866; Denmark, 1963; Estonia and Finland, 1934; Federal Republic of Germany, 1958; Greece, 1954; Italian Republic, 1958; Japan, 1911; Latvia, 1934; Mexico, 1955; Netherlands, 1854; Nicaragua, 1907; Norway, 1951; Peru, 1852; Portugal, 1934; Roumania, 1908; Spain, 1963; Turkey, 1865; Yugoslavia, 1934.

This section is not applicable to fishing vessels.

⚓   ⚓   ⚓   ⚓

Adaptation to metric units.

90 The Board of Trade may by regulations provide for such adaptations of any enactments contained in the Merchant Shipping Acts as appear to them appropriate for the purpose of replacing references therein to units other than metric units by references to metric units which are either equivalent thereto or such approximations thereto as appear to the Board desirable for the purpose of securing that the enactments as adapted are expressed in convenient terms.

COMMENTS.

For 'Board of Trade' read 'Secretary of State for Trade'.

Regulations.

Consult the Merchant Shipping (Metrication) Regulations 1973, S.I. 1973, No. 1979.

⚓   ⚓   ⚓   ⚓

91 For subsections (5) and (6) of section 1 of the Merchant Shipping Act 1965 (tonnage regulations) there shall be substituted the following subsections— Tonnage Measurement and Certificates.

'(5) Regulations under this section may make provision for the alteration (notwithstanding section 82 of the principal Act) of the particulars relating to the registered tonnage of a ship.

(6) Regulations under this section may provide for the issue by the Board of Trade or by persons appointed by such organisations as may be authorised in that behalf by the Board of Trade of certificates of the registered tonnage of any ship or of the tonnage which is to be taken for any purpose specified in the regulations as the tonnage of a ship not registered in the United Kingdom, and for the cancellation and delivery up of such certificates in such circumstances as may be prescribed by the regulations.

(6A) Regulations under this section requiring the delivery up of any certificate may make a failure to comply with the requirement an offence punishable on summary conviction with a fine not exceeding £100.'

This section is not yet in force.

⚓   ⚓   ⚓   ⚓

Unregistered ships and ships registered outside the United Kingdom

92 The Board of Trade may make regulations specifying any description of British ships which are not registered in the United Kingdom or elsewhere and directing that such of the provisions of this Act and of regulations and rules made thereunder as may be specified in the regulations shall extend to Unregistered British ships.

ships of that description and to masters and seamen employed in them, with such exceptions, adaptations or modifications as may be so specified.

COMMENTS.

For 'Board of Trade' read 'Secretary of State for Trade'.

Regulations.

Consult the Merchant Shipping (Unregistered Ships) Regulations 1972, S.I. 1972, No. 1876; The Merchant Shipping (Unregistered Fishing Vessels) Regulations 1972, No. 1877.

See also: The Merchant Shipping (Crew Accommodation) (Fishing Vessels) Regulations 1975, No. 2220, in operation as from the 1st January, 1977, as amended by S.I. 1977, No. 628.

⚓　　　　⚓　　　　⚓　　　　⚓

Ships registered in independent Commonwealth countries.

93 (1) Her Majesty may by Order in Council direct that such of the provisions of this Act and of regulations and rules made thereunder as may be specified in the Order shall extend, with such exceptions, adaptations or modifications as may be so specified, to ships registered in any independent Commonwealth country so specified and to masters and seamen employed in them.

(2) The modifications that may be made by an Order in Council under this section with respect to the ships registered in any country and the masters and seamen employed in them include the substitution, for any provision of this Act or of regulations or rules made thereunder, of a corresponding provision of the law of that country, with such exceptions, adaptations or modifications as appear to Her Majesty expedient.

(3) In this section 'independent Commonwealth country' means any country for the time being specified in section 1(3) of the British Nationality Act 1948.

COMMENTS.

This section is not applicable to fishing vessels.

⚓　　　　⚓　　　　⚓　　　　⚓

94 Her Majesty may by Order in Council give with respect to any of the following territories, that is to say—

(a) the Isle of Man;

(b) any of the Channel Islands;

(c) any colony;

(d) any territory outside Her Majesty's dominions in which for the time being Her Majesty has jurisdiction;

either or both of the following directions—

(i) that such of the provisions of this Act and of regulations and rules made thereunder as may be specified in the Order shall apply to ships registered in that territory and to masters and seamen employed in them, with such exceptions, adaptations or modifications as may be specified in the Order, as they apply to ships registered in the United Kingdom and to masters and seamen employed in them;

(ii) that such of the provisions of this Act and of any regulations and rules made thereunder as may be specified in the Order shall extend to that territory, with such exceptions, adaptations or modifications as may be specified in the Order, as part of the law of that territory.

Power to extend Act to certain territories outside the United Kingdom, and to ships registered therein.

⚓   ⚓   ⚓   ⚓

Fishing vessels and non-sea-going ships

95 (1) In the application of this Act to fishing vessels and persons serving in them—

Fishing vessels.

(a) sections 6, 29 to 32, 34 to 38, 89 and 93 do not apply and the provisions contained in Part I of Schedule 2 to this Act apply in addition to the other provisions of this Act; and

(b) sections 7 and 8 apply as set out in Part II of that Schedule; and nothing in Schedule 2 to this Act applies to fishing vessels not registered in the United Kingdom or to persons serving in them.

(2) Section 15 of this Act does not apply to so much of the wages of a seaman employed in a fishing vessel as is in any manner related to the catch.

(3) In its application to persons serving in fishing vessels, section 87 of this Act shall have effect as if for the words

'merchant navy uniform', wherever they occur, there were substituted the words 'fishing fleet uniform'.

(4) Nothing in section 11 of this Act shall affect the operation of Part II of the Administration of Justice Act 1970 in relation to wages due to a person employed in a fishing vessel; and the provisions of the Magistrates' Courts Act (Northern Ireland) 1964 and the Judgments (Enforcement) Act (Northern Ireland) 1969 relating to the attachment of wages shall apply in relation to such wages as they apply in relation to other wages.

(5) The Board of Trade may grant exemptions from any requirements of this Act or of any regulations made under this Act—

(a) with respect to any fishing vessel or to a fishing vessel of any description; or

(b) with respect to any person or a person of any description serving in a fishing vessel or in a fishing vessel of any description;

and nothing in any other provision of this Act conferring a power to provide for or grant exemptions shall be taken to restrict the power conferred by this subsection.

(6) In this Act 'fishing vessel' means a vessel which is for the time being employed in sea fishing, but does not include a vessel used otherwise than for profit.

COMMENTS.

For 'Board of Trade' read 'Secretary of State for Trade'.

Sections 29 and 31 repealed Merchant Shipping Act 1974, section 19, substitution in lieu; sections 30 and 32, *see* sub-section 1(a).

Sub-section 3, underlined, is not yet in force.

Fishing Vessel.

The definition of fishing vessel contained in the Merchant Shipping Act 1894, section 370, is amended by section 100, sub-section 3, Schedule 5 of this Act, and does no longer distinguish between those which catch fish for profit and those that do not.

⚓   ⚓   ⚓   ⚓

Non-sea-going ships.

96 (1) The preceding provisions of this Act other than sections 19, 20, 43 to 60, 88, 90 and 91 do not apply to ships which are not sea-going ships or to masters or seamen employed in ships which are not sea-going ships.

(2) In relation to ships which are not sea-going ships, section 45 of this Act shall have effect as if for the words 'goes to sea or attempts to go to sea' there were substituted the words 'plies or attempts to ply' and the words 'if in the United Kingdom' were omitted; and where such a ship may be detained in pursuance of that section, section 692 of the Merchant Shipping Act 1894 shall have effect, in relation to it, as if subsections (2) to (4) were omitted and in subsection (1) for the words 'proceeds to sea' there were substituted the word 'plies', for the words 'sends the ship to sea' there were substituted the words 'causes the ship to ply' and the words 'any British consular officer' were omitted.

⚓   ⚓   ⚓   ⚓

Supplementary

97   (1) In this Act—   Interpretation.

'crew agreement' has the meaning assigned to it by section 1(2) of this Act;

'enactment' includes an enactment of the Parliament of Northern Ireland;

'proper officer' means a consular officer appointed by Her Majesty's Government in the United Kingdom and, in relation to a port in a country outside the United Kingdom which is not a foreign country, also any officer exercising in that port functions similar to those of a superintendent;

'relief and maintenance' includes the provision of surgical or medical treatment and such dental and optical treatment (including the repair or replacement of any appliance) as cannot be postponed without impairing efficiency;

'ship's boat' includes a life-raft; and

'the Merchant Shipping Acts' means the Merchant Shipping Acts 1894 to 1967, the Fishing Vessels (Safety Provisions) Act 1970 and this Act.

(2) References in this Act to going to sea include references to going to sea from any country outside the United Kingdom.

(3) For the purposes of this Act a seaman is discharged from a ship when his employment in that ship is terminated.

(4) For the purposes of this Act a seaman discharged from a ship in any country and left there shall be deemed to be left behind in that country notwithstanding that the ship also remains there.

(5) References in this Act to dying in a ship include references to dying in a ship's boat and to being lost from a ship or ship's boat.

(6) Any power conferred by this Act to provide for or grant an exemption includes power to provide for or grant the exemption subject to conditions.

(7) If the Parliament of Northern Ireland passes provisions amending or replacing any enactment of that Parliament referred to in this Act the reference shall be construed as a reference to the enactment as so amended or, as the case may be, as a reference to those provisions.

⚓   ⚓   ⚓   ⚓

Expenses and receipts. **98** (1) Any expenses incurred by the Board of Trade under this Act shall be defrayed out of moneys provided by Parliament.

(2) Any fees received by the Board of Trade under this Act shall be paid into the Consolidated Fund.

COMMENTS.

For 'Board of Trade' read 'Secretary of State for Trade'.

⚓   ⚓   ⚓   ⚓

Regulations and rules. **99** (1) Any regulations or rules made under this Act shall be made by statutory instrument, which, except in the case of regulations made under section 36 of this Act or paragraph 2 of Schedule 2 of this Act, shall be subject to annulment in pursuance of a resolution of either House of Parliament.

(2) Before making regulations under any provision of this Act other than sections 84 and 90 the Board of Trade shall consult with organisations in the United Kingdom appearing to them representative of masters and seamen who will be

affected by the regulations and of persons employing such masters and seamen.

COMMENTS.

For 'Board of Trade' read 'Secretary of State for Trade'.

⚓   ⚓   ⚓   ⚓

100 (1) The enactments mentioned in Schedule 3 to this Act shall have effect subject to the minor and consequential amendments specified therein. *Amendments, savings, transitional provisions and repeals.*

(2) This Act shall have effect subject to the savings and transitional provisions contained in Schedule 4 to this Act.

(3) The enactments specified in Schedule 5 to this Act (which include some which are obsolete and some not affected by the preceding provisions of this Act) are hereby repealed to the extent specified in the third column of that Schedule.

COMMENTS.

See the Merchant Shipping Act 1970 (Commencement No. 2) Order 1974, S.I. 1974, No. 1194, which repeals section 200 of the Principal Act, and applies sub-section 3 so far as it relates to the provisions of Schedule 5, as from the 1st October, 1974.

See also, the Merchant Shipping Act 1970 (Commencement No. 3) Order 1974, S.I. 1974, No. 1908, which applies sub-section 1 so far as it relates to paragraph 10 of Schedule 3, and also provides for the substitution of sub-section 2 of section 10 of the Merchant Shipping Act 1964, as from the 18th November, 1974.

⚓   ⚓   ⚓   ⚓

101 (1) This Act may be cited as the Merchant Shipping Act 1970. *Citation, construction and commencement.*

(2) This Act, the Merchant Shipping Acts 1894 to 1967 and the Fishing Vessels (Safety Provisions) Act 1970 may be cited together as the Merchant Shipping Acts 1894 to 1970.

(3) This Act shall be construed as one with the Merchant Shipping Acts 1894 to 1967 and the Fishing Vessels (Safety Provisions) Act 1970.

(4) This Act shall come into force on such date as the Board of Trade may by order made by statutory instrument

appoint, and different days may be so appointed for different provisions of this Act.

COMMENTS.

For 'Board of Trade' read 'Secretary of State for Trade'.

Different Provisions of this Act.

See the following Statutory Orders:

(1) The Merchant Shipping Act 1970 (Commencement No. 1) Order 1972, S.I. 1972, No. 1977.

(2) The Merchant Shipping Act 1970 (Commencement No. 2) Order, 1974, S.I. 1974, No. 1194.

(3) The Merchant Shipping Act 1970 (Commencement No. 3) Order, 1974, S.I. 1974, No. 1908.

(4) The Merchant Shipping Act 1970 (Commencement No. 4) Order, 1975, S.I. 1975, No. 2156.

⚓   ⚓   ⚓   ⚓

SCHEDULES

SCHEDULE 1

SECTIONS SUBSTITUTED FOR SECTIONS 3 AND 6 OF MERCHANT SHIPPING (SAFETY CONVENTION) ACT 1949

Section 85.
Radio rules.

3. (1) The Board of Trade may make rules (in this Act called 'radio rules') requiring ships to which this section applies to be provided with radio equipment of such a nature (but not including a radio navigational aid) as may be prescribed by the rules and to maintain such a radio service and to carry such number of radio officers or operators, of such grades and possessing such qualifications, as may be so prescribed; and the rules may contain provisions for preventing so far as practicable electrical interference by other apparatus on board with the equipment provided under the rules.

(2) This section applies to—

(a) sea-going ships registered in the United Kingdom;

(b) other sea-going ships while they are in the United Kingdom or the territorial waters thereof.

(3) Radio rules shall include such requirements as appear to the Board of Trade to implement the provisions of the Convention for the Safety of Life at Sea signed in London on 17th June, 1960 as from time to time amended, so far as those provisions relate to radio telegraphy and radio telephony.

(4) Without prejudice to the generality of the preceding provisions of this section, radio rules may—

(a) prescribe the duties of radio officers and operators, including the duty of keeping a radio log-book;

(b) apply to any radio log-book required to be kept under the rules any of the provisions of any regulations with respect to official log-books made under section 68 of the Merchant Shipping Act 1970.

(5) If any radio officer or operator contravenes any rules made in pursuance of subsection (4)(a) of this section, he shall be liable to a fine not exceeding £10; and if radio rules are contravened in any other respect in relation to any ship, the owner or master of the ship shall be liable on conviction on indictment to a fine not exceeding £500, or on summary conviction to a fine not exceeding £100.

(6) If a ship to which this section applies is not provided with radio equipment or radio officers or operators in conformity with radio rules the ship, if in the United Kingdom, may be detained.

6 (1) The Board of Trade may make rules—

(a) requiring ships to which this section applies to be provided with such radio navigational aids, other than direction-finders, as may be specified in the rules and prescribing requirements which such radio navigational aids are to comply with;

(b) prescribing requirements which radio navigational aids, other than direction-finders and other than such as are provided in pursuance of rules made under the preceding paragraph, are to comply with when carried in ships to which this section applies;

(c) prescribing requirements which apparatus designed for the purpose of transmitting or reflecting signals to or from radio navigational aids is to comply with if it is apparatus in the United Kingdom or apparatus off the shores of the United Kingdom but maintained from the United Kingdom;

and the requirements prescribed under paragraph (a) or (b) of this subsection may include requirements relating to the position and method of fitting of the radio navigational aids.

(2) This section applies to—

(a) ships registered in the United Kingdom;

(b) other ships while they are within any port in the United Kingdom.

(3) If a ship to which this section applies proceeds, or attempts to proceed, to sea without carrying such navigational aids as it is required to carry by rules made under subsection(1) of this section or carrying radio navigational aids not complying with rules made under that subsection, the owner or master of the ship shall be liable on summary conviction to a fine not exceeding £100.

(4) If any person establishes or operates any such apparatus as is mentioned in subsection (1)(c) of this section and the apparatus does not comply with rules made thereunder, he shall be liable on summary conviction to a fine not exceeding £100.

COMMENTS.

For 'Board of Trade' read 'Secretary of State for Trade'.

See the Merchant Shipping Act 1970 (Commencement No. 3) Order 1974, which brought this Schedule into force as from 18th November, 1974.

⚓   ⚓   ⚓   ⚓

O

SCHEDULE 2

FISHING VESSELS
PART I
ADDITIONAL PROVISIONS

Regulations relating to crew agreements

1   (1) The Board of Trade may make regulations prescribing the procedure to be followed in connection with the making of crew agreements between persons employed in fishing vessels and persons employing them and prescribing the places where such crew agreements are to be made or where an agreement with any person may be added to those contained in such a crew agreement.

(2) Regulations under this paragraph may make a contravention of any provision thereof an offence punishable on summary conviction with a fine not exceeding £50 or such less amount as may be specified in the regulations.

Offences

2   (1) For the purpose of maintaining discipline on board fishing vessels and ensuring the safe and efficient operation of such vessels the Board of Trade may by regulations specify any misconduct on board of or in relation to a fishing vessel which, but for section 95(1)(a) of this Act, would be an offence under section 29, 30 or 31 thereof, and provide for its being an offence punishable on summary conviction with a fine not exceeding £100 or such less amount as may be specified in the regulations.

(2) Regulations under this paragraph may apply section 32 of this Act with such modifications as may be required to substitute in it for the reference to section 29, 30(b) and 30(c) of this Act a reference to the corresponding provisions of the regulations.

(3) Regulations under this paragraph may make different

provision for different descriptions of fishing vessel or fishing vessels of the same description in different circumstances.

(4) No regulations shall be made under this paragraph unless a draft thereof has been laid before Parliament and approved by resolution of each House of Parliament.

Production of certificates and other documents of qualification

3. Any person serving or engaged to serve in a fishing vessel and holding any certificate or other document which is evidence that he is qualified for the purposes of section 43 of this Act shall on demand produce it to any person who is a British sea-fishery officer for the purposes of the Sea Fisheries Acts (within the meaning of the Sea Fisheries Act 1968); and if he fails to do so without reasonable cause he shall be liable on summary conviction to a fine not exceeding £20.

Hours of work

4. (1) The Board of Trade may make regulations prescribing maximum periods of duty and minimum periods of rest for seamen employed in fishing vessels, and such regulations may make different provision for different descriptions of fishing vessels or seamen employed in them or for fishing vessels and seamen of the same description in different circumstances.

(2) If any provision of regulations made under this paragraph is contravened in the case of any seaman employed in a fishing vessel the persons employing him and the master shall each be liable on summary conviction to a fine not exceeding £100.

Reports of and inquiries into injuries

5 (1) Where the master or a member of the crew of a fishing vessel is injured during a voyage, an inquiry into the cause and nature of the injury may be held by a superintendent or proper officer.

(2) The superintendent or proper officer holding an inquiry under this section shall for the purposes of the inquiry have the powers conferred on an inspector by section 729 of the Merchant Shipping Act 1894 and shall make a report of his findings to the Board of Trade.

COMMENTS.

Paragraphs 2 to 5, inclusive, underlined above, are not yet in force. *For* 'Board of Trade' *read* 'Secretary of State for Trade'.

Paragraph 1.

See The Merchant Shipping (Crew Agreements, Lists of Crew and Discharge of Seamen) Regulations 1972, S.I. 1972, No. 918. For Fishing Vessels, S.I. 1972, No. 919. Both as amended by S.I. 1977, No. 45.

⚓   ⚓   ⚓   ⚓

PART II

SECTIONS 7 AND 8 SET OUT AS THEY APPLY TO FISHING VESSELS AND PERSONS EMPLOYED IN THEM

Payment of seamen's wages.

7. Except as provided by or under this Act or any other enactment, the wages due to a seaman under a crew agreement relating to a fishing vessel shall be paid to him in full.

Accounts of Wages and Catch.

8. (1) Subject to regulations made under section 9 or 62 of this Act, the persons employing any seaman under a crew agreement relating to a fishing vessel shall deliver to him at a time prescribed by regulations under this section an account of the wages due to him under that crew agreement and of the deductions subject to which the wages are payable.

(2) Where the wages of any person employed in a fishing vessel are in any manner related to the catch the persons employing him shall at a time prescribed by regulations under this section deliver to the master an account (or, if the master is the person employing him, make out an account) showing how those wages (or any part thereof related to the catch) are arrived at and shall make the account available to the crew in such manner as may be prescribed by the regulations.

(3) Where there is a partnership between the master and any members of the crew of a fishing vessel the owner of the vessel shall at a time prescribed by regulations under this

section make out an account showing the sums due to each partner in respect of his share and shall make the account available to the partners.

(4) The Board of Trade may make regulations prescribing the time at which any account required by this section is to be delivered or made out and the manner in which the account required by subsection (2) or (3) of this section is to be made available.

(5) If a person fails without reasonable cause to comply with the preceding provisions of this section he shall be liable on summary conviction to a fine not exceeding £20.

COMMENTS.

For 'Board of Trade' read 'Secretary of State for Trade'.

SCHEDULE 3

MINOR AND CONSEQUENTIAL AMENDMENTS

The Conspiracy and Protection of Property Act 1875

1. For section 16 of the Conspiracy and Protection of Property Act 1875 there shall be substituted the following section:—

'16. Section 5 of this Act does not apply to seamen.'

The Merchant Shipping Act 1894

2. In subsection (1) of section 689 of the Merchant Shipping Act 1894 for the words 'seaman or apprentice', in both places, there shall be substituted the words 'or seaman'.

3. In subsection (1) of section 695 of that Act, after the words 'shall be evidence' there shall be inserted the words 'and in Scotland sufficient evidence'; and in subsection (2) of that section, after the words 'admissible in evidence' there shall be inserted the words 'and be evidence, and in Scotland sufficient evidence, of those matters'.

4. In section 742 of that Act, in the definition of 'seaman', for the words 'masters, pilots and apprentices duly indentured and registered, there shall be substituted the words 'masters and pilots'.

The Pilotage Act 1913

5. In section 17(1)(*l*) of the Pilotage Act 1913 for the words from 'a mate's certificate' to '1894' there shall be substituted the words 'such certificate issued under the Merchant Shipping Act 1970 as may be specified in the byelaws'.

6. In paragraph (*b*) of the proviso to section 23(1) of that Act for the words from 'a mate's certificate' to '1894' there shall be substituted the words 'such certificate issued under the Merchant Shipping Act 1970 as is specified in the byelaw' and for the words 'such a certificate of competency' there shall be substituted the words 'a certificate so specified'.

7. In section 25 of that Act for the words 'certificates of

competency recognised under Part II of the Merchant Shipping
Act 1894' there shall be substituted the words 'certificates
issued under the Merchant Shipping Act 1970'.

The Illegal Trawling (Scotland) Act 1934

8. In section 1(6) of the Illegal Trawling (Scotland) Act
1934 for the words 'at each mercantile marine office' there
shall be substituted the words 'at the office of each mercantile
marine superintendent'.

The Pensions (Navy, Army, Air Force and Mercantile Marine) Act 1939

9. In section 6(3) of the Pensions (Navy, Army, Air Force
and Mercantile Marine) Act 1939, for the words from 'section
one hundred and seventy-six' to 'deceased seamen' there shall
be substituted the words 'section 66 of the Merchant Shipping
Act 1970 (disposal of property of deceased seamen)'.

The Merchant Shipping Act 1964

10. For subsection (2) of section 10 of the Merchant
Shipping Act 1964 there shall be substituted the following
subsection—

'(2) Subsection (6) of section 3 of the Act of 1949
(detention of ships not conforming with radio rules)
shall apply in relation to the portable radio apparatus
so required to be carried by the boats or life rafts on
any ship as it applies in relation to the radio equipment of the ship.'

The Administration of Estates (Small Payments) Act 1965

11. In section 6 of the Administration of Estates (Small
Payments) Act 1965 there shall be added at the end of sub-
section (1)(b) the words 'and

(c) section 66(2) of the Merchant Shipping Act 1970'.

The Merchant Shipping (Load Lines) Act 1967

12. In section 10(2) of the Merchant Shipping (Load
Lines) Act 1967, paragraph (a) shall be omitted, and in
paragraph (b) for the words from 'in such form' to the end of
the paragraph there shall be substituted the words 'to be
posted up in some conspicuous place on board the ship,
which shall be in such form and containing such particulars

relating to the depth to which the ship is for the time being loaded as may be specified in regulations made by the Board of Trade under this Act;'.

The Hovercraft Act 1968

13. The enactments and instruments with respect to which provision may be made by an Order in Council under section 1(1)(*h*) of the Hovercraft Act 1968 shall include this Act and any instrument made under it.

The Income and Corporation Taxes Act 1970

14. In section 414(1) of the Income and Corporation Taxes Act 1970 the word 'or' shall be added at the end of paragraph (*a*), and paragraph (*c*) and the word 'or' preceding it shall be omitted.

COMMENTS.

Paragraphs 5, 6, and 7, underlined above, are not yet in force.

⚓   ⚓   ⚓   ⚓

SCHEDULE 4

SAVINGS AND TRANSITIONAL PROVISIONS

1. The repeals made by this Act shall not be taken to extend to any country outside the United Kingdom and shall not affect any Order in Council providing for the extension of any enactments to any country outside the United Kingdom or any power to vary or revoke such an Order in Council.

2. The repeal by this Act of sections 145 and 146 of the Merchant Shipping Act 1894 shall not affect the operation, in relation to a seaman's money order issued before the coming into force of the repeal, of regulations under section 145(2) or of section 146.

3. The repeal by this Act of sections 148 to 153 of the Merchant Shipping Act 1894 shall not affect the operation of those sections in relation to any deposit received under section 148 before the coming into force of the repeal; but the Board of Trade may by regulations make provision for the repayment of such deposits within such period as may be specified by or under the regulations and for the transfer to the National Savings Bank of any deposit not repaid before the end of that period.

4. The repeal by this Act of section 254 of the Merchant Shipping Act 1894 shall not affect the operation of that section in relation to any return made under it and any marine register book kept under that section shall be treated as part of a marine register kept under section 72 of this Act.

5. Any licence granted under section 110 of the Merchant Shipping Act 1894 shall have effect as if granted under section 6 of this Act.

6. Any regulations made under section 1 of the Merchant Shipping Act 1948 shall have effect as if made under section 20 of this Act.

7. Any reference in regulations made under section 1 of the Merchant Shipping Act 1965 to regulations made under section 1 of the Merchant Shipping Act 1948 shall be construed

as including a reference to regulations made under section 20 of this Act.

8. The references in section 57 of this Act to an inquiry or formal investigation held under this Act shall be construed as including references to an inquiry or formal investigation held under section 466, 468 or 471 of the Merchant Shipping Act 1894.

9. The references in section 60 of this Act to a certificate which has been cancelled or suspended under this Act shall be construed as including references to a certificate which has been cancelled or suspended under the provisions repealed by this Act.

10. For the purposes of section 87 of this Act the registration of any design under Part II of the Patents and Designs Act 1907 shall be deemed to be a registration under the Registered Designs Act 1949.

COMMENTS.

Paragraphs 5–10 of this Schedule are not yet in force.

⚓   ⚓   ⚓   ⚓

SCHEDULE 5

ENACTMENTS REPEALED

COMMENTS.

The repeals contained in this Schedule relating to the Merchant Shipping Acts, which have been made effective are contained and noted in the relevant parts of the text. *See* also, future supplements to *A Guide to the Merchant Shipping Acts*, Volumes 1 and 2, for further notice of repeals, not yet made effective.

⚓   ⚓   ⚓   ⚓

Merchant Shipping (Oil Pollution) Act 1971

An Act to make provision with respect to Civil Liability for Oil Pollution by Merchant Ships; and for Connected Purposes.

GENERAL COMMENTS

The following sections of the Merchant Shipping (Oil Pollution) Act 1971, came into operation as from the 9th September, 1971:

Section 1 (Excluding sub-section 2).
Section 2; Section 3; Section 9.
Section 13, sub-section (1).
Section 14; sub-section (1).
Section 15; Section 16.
Section 17; Section 18; Section 20 and Section 21.

See the Merchant Shipping (Oil Pollution) Act 1971 (Commencement) Order 1971, S.I. 1971, No. 1423.

The remainder of the Act came into force on the 19th June, 1975.

See the Merchant Shipping (Oil Pollution) Act 1971 (Commencement No. 2) Order 1965, S.I. 1975, No. 867.

See also the Merchant Shipping Act 1974, section 9. The Merchant Shipping Act 1974 (Commencement No. 2) Order 1975, S.I. 1975, No. 866.

⚓ ⚓ ⚓ ⚓

Liability for oil pollution.

1 (1) Where, as a result of any occurrence taking place while a ship is carrying a cargo of persistent oil in bulk, any persistent oil carried by the ship (whether as part of the cargo or otherwise) is discharged or escapes from the ship, the owner of the ship shall be liable, except as otherwise provided by this Act,—

(*a*) for any damage caused in the area of the United Kingdom by contamination resulting from the discharge or escape; and

(*b*) for the cost of any measures reasonably taken after the discharge or escape for the purpose of preventing or reducing any such damage in the area of the United Kingdom; and

(c) for any damage caused in the area of the United Kingdom
by any measures so taken.

(2) Where a person incurs a liability under subsection (1)
of this section he shall also be liable for any damage or cost
for which he would be liable under that subsection if the
references therein to the area of the United Kingdom included
the area of any other Convention country.

(3) Where persistent oil is discharged or escapes from two
or more ships and—

(a) a liability is incurred under this section by the owner of
each of them; but

(b) the damage or cost for which each of the owners would be
liable cannot reasonably be separated from that for which
the other or others would be liable;

each of the owners shall be liable, jointly with the other or
others, for the whole of the damage or cost for which the
owners together would be liable under this section.

(4) For the purposes of this Act, where more than one
discharge or escape results from the same occurrence or from
a series of occurrences having the same origin, they shall be
treated as one; but any measures taken after the first of them
shall be deemed to have been taken after the discharge or
escape.

(5) The Law Reform (Contributory Negligence) Act 1945
and, in Northern Ireland, the Law Reform (Miscellaneous
Provisions) Act (Northern Ireland) 1948 shall apply in relation
to any damage or cost for which a person is liable under this
section, but which is not due to his fault, as if it were due to
his fault.

COMMENTS.

Persistent Oil.

See The Oil Pollution (Compulsory Insurance) Regulations 1977, S.I.
1977 No. 85, as amended by S.I. 1977, No. 497.

⚓   ⚓   ⚓   ⚓

2   The owner of a ship from which persistent oil has been Exceptions
discharged or has escaped shall not incur any liability under from liability
section 1 of this Act if he proves that the discharge or escape— under s. 1.

(a) resulted from an act of war, hostilities, civil war, insurrection or an exceptional, inevitable and irresistible natural phenomenon; or

(b) was due wholly to anything done or left undone by another person, not being a servant or agent of the owner, with intent to do damage; or

(c) was due wholly to the negligence or wrongful act of a government or other authority in exercising its function of maintaining lights or other navigational aids for the maintenance of which it was responsible.

⚓   ⚓   ⚓   ⚓

Restriction of liability for oil pollution.

3   Where, as a result of any occurrence taking place while a ship is carrying a cargo of persistent oil in bulk, any persistent oil carried by the ship is discharged or escapes then, whether or not the owner incurs a liability under section 1 of this Act,—

(a) he shall not be liable otherwise than under that section for any such damage or cost as is mentioned therein; and

(b) no servant or agent of the owner nor any person performing salvage operations with the agreement of the owner shall be liable for any such damage or cost.

⚓   ⚓   ⚓   ⚓

Limitation of liability under s. 1.

4   (1) Where the owner of a ship incurs a liability under section 1 of this Act by reason of a discharge or escape which occurred without his actual fault or privity—

(a) section 503 of the Merchant Shipping Act 1894 (limitation of liability) shall not apply in relation to that liability; but

(b) he may limit that liability in accordance with the provisions of this Act, and if he does so his liability (that is to say, the aggregate of his liabilities under section 1 resulting from the discharge or escape) shall not exceed 2,000 gold francs for each ton of the ship's tonnage nor (where that tonnage would result in a greater amount) 210 million gold francs.

(2) For the purposes of this section the tonnage of a ship shall be ascertained as follows:—

(a) if the ship is a British ship (whether registered in the United Kingdom or elsewhere) or a ship to which an Order under section 84 of the Merchant Shipping Act 1894 applies, its tonnage shall be taken to be its registered tonnage increased, where a deduction has been made for engine room space in arriving at that tonnage, by the amount of that deduction;

(b) if the ship is not such a ship as is mentioned in the preceding paragraph and it is possible to ascertain what would be its registered tonnage if it were registered in the United Kingdom, that paragraph shall apply (with the necessary modifications) as if the ship were so registered;

(c) if the ship is not such a ship as is mentioned in paragraph (a) of this subsection and is of a description with respect to which no provision is for the time being made by regulations under section 1 of the Merchant Shipping Act 1965 (tonnage regulations) its tonnage shall be taken to be 40 per cent of the weight (expressed in tons of 2,240 lbs.) of oil which the ship is capable of carrying;

(d) if the tonnage of the ship cannot be ascertained in accordance with the preceding paragraphs the Chief Ship Surveyor of the Department of Trade and Industry shall, if so directed by the court, certify what, on the evidence specified in the direction, would in his opinion be the tonnage of the ship if ascertained in accordance with those paragraphs, and the tonnage stated in his certificate shall be taken to be the tonnage of the ship.

(3) For the purposes of this section a gold franc shall be taken to be a unit of sixty-five and a half milligrams of gold of millesimal fineness nine hundred.

(4) The Secretary of State may from time to time by order made by statutory instrument specify the amounts which for the purposes of this section are to be taken as equivalent to 2,000 gold francs and 210 million gold francs respectively.

(5) Where the amounts specified by an order under the preceding subsection are varied by a subsequent order the variation shall not affect the limit of any liability under section 1 of this Act if, before the variation comes into force, an amount not less than that limit (ascertained in accordance with the order then in force) has been paid into court (or, in Scotland, consigned in court) in proceedings for the limitation of that liability in accordance with this Act.

COMMENTS.

See general comments at the beginning of this Act, as to time of coming into force.

Tonnage Regulations.

Consult Merchant Shipping (Tonnage) Regulations 1967, S.I. 1967, No. 173 as amended by Merchant Shipping (Tonnage) Regulations 1967, No. 1093.

The Merchant Shipping (Tonnage) Regulations 1972, No. 656 and the Merchant Shipping (Tonnage) (Amendment) Regulations 1975, No. 594.

2,000 Gold Francs; 210 Million Gold Francs.

For sterling equivalents, *see* now The Merchant Shipping (Sterling Equivalents) (Various Enactments) Order 1978, S.I. 1978 No. 54.

The specified amounts in accordance with this Order is £86·23 and £9,054,122·94 respectively.

⚓   ⚓   ⚓   ⚓

Limitation actions.

5 (1) Where the owner of a ship has or is alleged to have incurred a liability under section 1 of this Act he may apply to the court for the limitation of that liability to an amount determined in accordance with section 4 of this Act.

(2) If on such an application the court finds that the applicant has incurred such a liability and is entitled to limit it, the court shall, after determining the limit of the liability and directing payment into court of the amount of that limit,—

(*a*) determine the amounts that would, apart from the limit, be due in respect of the liability to the several persons making claims in the proceedings; and

(*b*) direct the distribution of the amount paid into court (or, as the case may be, so much of it as does not exceed the liability) among those persons in proportion to their claims, subject to the following provisions of this section.

(3) No claim shall be admitted in proceedings under this section unless it is made within such time as the court may direct or such further time as the court may allow.

(4) Where any sum has been paid in or towards satisfaction of any claim in respect of the damage or cost to which the liability extends,—

(*a*) by the owner or the person referred to in section 12 of this Act as 'the insurer'; or

(*b*) by a person who has or is alleged to have incurred a liability, otherwise than under section 1 of this Act, for the damage or cost and who is entitled to limit his liability in connection with the ship by virtue of the Merchant

Shipping (Liability of Shipowners and Others) Act 1958; the person who paid the sum shall, to the extent of that sum, be in the same position with respect to any distribution made in proceedings under this section as the person to whom it was paid would have been.

(5) Where the person who incurred the liability has voluntarily made any reasonable sacrifice or taken any other reasonable measures to prevent or reduce damage to which the liability extends or might have extended he shall be in the same position with respect to any distribution made in proceedings under this section as if he had a claim in respect of the liability equal to the cost of the sacrifice or other measures.

(6) The court may, if it thinks fit, postpone the distribution of such part of the amount to be distributed as it deems appropriate having regard to any claims that may later be established before a court of any country outside the United Kingdom.

COMMENTS.

See general comments at the beginning of this Act as to the time of coming into force.

Person who has or is alleged to have Incurred a Liability.

See section 3 of the Merchant Shipping (Liability of Shipowners and Others) Act 1958.

⚓   ⚓   ⚓   ⚓

6 (1) Where the court has found that a person who has incurred a liability under section 1 of this Act is entitled to limit that liability to any amount and he has paid into court a sum not less than that amount— *(Restrictions on enforcement of claims after establishment of limitation fund.)*

(*a*) the court shall order the release of any ship or other property arrested in connection with a claim in respect of that liability or any security given to prevent or obtain release from such an arrest; and

(*b*) no judgment or decree for any such claim shall be enforced, except so far as it is for costs (or, in Scotland, expenses);

if the sum paid into court, or such part thereof as corresponds to the claim, will be actually available to the claimant or would have been available to him if the proper steps in the proceedings under section 5 of this Act had been taken.

(2) In the application of this section to Scotland, any reference (however expressed) to release from arrest shall be construed as a reference to the recall of an arrestment.

COMMENTS.

See general comments at the beginning of this Act as to time of coming into force.

⚓   ⚓   ⚓   ⚓

Concurrent liabilities of owners and others.

7 Where, as a result of any discharge or escape of persistent oil from a ship, the owner of the ship incurs a liability under section 1 of this Act and any other person incurs a liability, otherwise than under that section, for any such damage or cost as is mentioned in subsection (1) of that section, then, if—

(*a*) the owner has been found, in proceedings under section 5 of this Act, to be entitled to limit his liability to any amount and has paid into court a sum not less than that amount; and

(*b*) the other person is entitled to limit his liability in connection with the ship by virtue of the Merchant Shipping (Liability of Shipowners and Others) Act 1958;

no proceedings shall be taken against the other person in respect of his liability, and if any such proceedings were commenced before the owner paid the sum into court, no further steps shall be taken in the proceedings except in relation to costs.

COMMENTS.

See general comments at the beginning of this Act as to time of coming into force.

⚓   ⚓   ⚓   ⚓

Establishment of limitation fund outside United Kingdom.

8 Where the events resulting in the liability of any person under section 1 of this Act also resulted in a corresponding liability under the law of another Convention country, sections 6 and 7 of this Act shall apply as if the references to sections 1 and 5 of this Act included references to the corresponding provisions of that law and the references to sums paid into court included references to any sums secured under those provisions in respect of the liability.

Comments.

See general comments at the beginning of this Act as to time of coming into force.

See also section 9 of the Merchant Shipping Act 1974, which modifies the limitation of liability in this Act. The Merchant Shipping Act 1974 (Commencement No. 2) Order 1975, S.I. 1975, No. 866.

States which are Parties to the 1969 Convention.

See The Merchant Shipping (Oil Pollution) (Parties to the Conventions) Order 1975, S.I. 1975, No. 1036, as amended by The Merchant Shipping (Oil Pollution) (Parties to Conventions) (Amendment) (No. 2) Order 1977, S.I. 1977, No. 826.

⚓   ⚓   ⚓   ⚓

9 No action to enforce a claim in respect of a liability incurred under section 1 of this Act shall be entertained by any court in the United Kingdom unless the action is commenced not later than three years after the claim arose nor later than six years after the occurrence or first of the occurrences resulting in the discharge by escape by reason of which the liability was incurred.

Extinguishment of claims.

⚓   ⚓   ⚓   ⚓

10 (1) Subject to the provisions of this Act relating to Government ships, subsection (2) of this section shall apply to any ship carrying in bulk a cargo of more than 2000 tons of persistent oil of a description specified in regulations made by the Secretary of State.

Compulsory insurance against liability for pollution.

(2) The ship shall not enter or leave a port in the United Kingdom or arrive at or leave a terminal in the territorial sea of the United Kingdom nor, if the ship is registered in the United Kingdom, a port in any other country or a terminal in the territorial sea of any other country, unless there is in force a certificate complying with the provisions of subsection (3) of this section and showing that there is in force in respect of the ship a contract of insurance or other security satisfying the requirements of Article VII of the Convention (cover for owner's liability).

(3) The certificate must be—

(*a*) if the ship is registered in the United Kingdom, a certificate issued by the Secretary of State;

(*b*) if the ship is registered in a Convention country other than the United Kingdom, a certificate issued by or under the authority of the government of the other Convention country; and

(*c*) if the ship is registered in a country which is not a Convention country, a certificate issued by the Secretary of State or a certificate recognised for the purposes of this paragraph by regulations made under this section.

(4) The Secretary of State may by regulations provide that certificates in respect of ships registered in any, or any specified, country which is not a Convention country shall, in such circumstances as may be specified in the regulations, be recognised for the purposes of subsection (3)(*c*) of this section if issued by or under the authority of the government of the country designated in the regulations in that behalf; and the country that may be so designated may be either or both of the following, that is to say—

(*a*) the country in which the ship is registered; and

(*b*) any country specified in the regulations for the purposes of this paragraph.

(5) Any certificate required by this section to be in force in respect of a ship shall be carried in the ship and shall, on demand, be produced by the master to any officer of customs or of the Department of Trade and Industry and, if the ship is registered in the United Kingdom, to any proper officer within the meaning of section 97(1) of the Merchant Shipping Act 1970.

(6) If a ship enters or leaves, or attempts to enter or leave, a port or arrives at or leaves, or attempts to arrive at or leave, a terminal in contravention of subsection (2) of this section, the master or owner shall be liable on conviction on indictment to a fine, or on summary conviction to a fine not exceeding £35,000.

(7) If a ship fails to carry, or the master of a ship fails to produce, a certificate as required by subsection (5) of this section the master shall be liable on summary conviction to a fine not exceeding £400.

(8) If a ship attempts to leave a port in the United Kingdom in contravention of this section the ship may be detained.

(9) Regulations under this section shall be made by

statutory instrument, which shall be subject to annulment in pursuance of a resolution of either House of Parliament.

COMMENTS.

See general comments at the beginning of this Act, as to the time of coming into force.

Regulations.

See now Oil Pollution (Compulsory Insurance) Amendment Regulations 1977, S.I. 1977, No. 85, as amended by S.I. 1977, No. 497.

⚓   ⚓   ⚓   ⚓

11 (1) Subject to subsection (2) of this section, if the Secretary of State is satisfied, on an application for such a certificate as is mentioned in section 10 of this Act in respect of a ship registered in the United Kingdom or any country which is not a Convention country, that there will be in force in respect of the ship, throughout the period for which the certificate is to be issued, a contract of insurance or other security satisfying the requirements of Article VII of the Convention, the Secretary of State shall issue such a certificate to the owner.

Issue of certificate by Secretary of State.

(2) If the Secretary of State is of opinion that there is a doubt whether the person providing the insurance or other security will be able to meet his obligations thereunder, or whether the insurance or other security will cover the owner's liability under section 1 of this Act in all circumstances, he may refuse the certificate.

(3) The Secretary of State may make regulations—

(*a*) prescribing the fee to be paid on an application for a certificate to be issued by him under this section; and

(*b*) providing for the cancellation and delivery up of such a certificate in such circumstances as may be prescribed by the regulations.

(4) If a person required by regulations under subsection (3)(*b*) of this section to deliver up a certificate fails to do so he shall be liable on summary conviction to a fine not exceeding £200.

(5) The Secretary of State shall send a copy of any certificate issued by him under this section in respect of a ship

registered in the United Kingdom to the Registrar General of Shipping and Seamen, and the Registrar shall make the copy available for public inspection.

(6) Regulations under this section shall be made by statutory instrument, which shall be subject to annulment in pursuance of a resolution of either House of Parliament.

COMMENTS.

See general comments at the beginning of this Act as to the time of coming into force.

Regulations.

See Oil Pollution (Compulsory Insurance) Regulations 1977, S.I. 1977, No. 85, as amended by S.I. 1977, No. 497.

⚓   ⚓   ⚓   ⚓

Rights of
third parties
against
insurers.

12 (1) Where it is alleged that the owner of a ship has incurred a liability under section 1 of this Act as a result of any discharge or escape of oil occurring while there was in force a contract of insurance or other security to which such a certificate as is mentioned in section 10 of this Act related, proceedings to enforce a claim in respect of the liability may be brought against the person who provided the insurance or other security (in the following provisions of this section referred to as 'the insurer').

(2) In any proceedings brought against the insurer by virtue of this section it shall be a defence (in addition to any defence affecting the owner's liability) to prove that the discharge or escape was due to the wilful misconduct of the owner himself.

(3) The insurer may limit his liability in respect of claims made against him by virtue of this section in like manner and to the same extent as the owner may limit his liability but the insurer may do so whether or not the discharge or escape occurred without the owner's actual fault or privity.

(4) Where the owner and the insurer each apply to the court for the limitation of his liability any sum paid into court in pursuance of either application shall be treated as paid also in pursuance of the other.

(5) The Third Parties (Rights against Insurers) Act 1930 and the Third Parties (Rights against Insurers) Act (Northern

Ireland) 1930 shall not apply in relation to any contract of insurance to which such a certificate as is mentioned in section 10 of this Act relates.

COMMENTS.

See generally, comments at the beginning of this Act as to the time of coming into force.

⚓   ⚓   ⚓   ⚓

13 (1) Paragraph (*d*) of section 1(1) of the Administra- tion of Justice Act 1956 and paragraph 1(1)(*d*) of Schedule 1 to that Act (Admiralty jurisdiction in claims for damage done by ships) shall be construed as extending to any claim in respect of a liability incurred under this Act, and the Admiralty jurisdiction of the Court of Session shall extend to any case arising out of any such claim.

Jurisdiction of United Kingdom courts and registration of foreign judgments.

(2) Where any persistent oil is discharged or escapes from a ship but does not result in any damage caused by contamination in the area of the United Kingdom and no measures are reasonably taken to prevent or reduce such damage in that area, no court in the United Kingdom shall entertain an action (whether *in rem* or *in personam*) to enforce a claim arising from—

(*a*) any damage caused in the area of another Convention country by contamination resulting from the discharge or escape;

(*b*) any cost incurred in taking measures to prevent or reduce such damage in the area of another Convention country; or

(*c*) any damage caused by any measures so taken.

(3) Part I of the Foreign Judgments (Reciprocal Enforcement) Act 1933 shall apply, whether or not it would so apply apart from this section, to any judgment given by a court in a Convention country to enforce a claim in respect of a liability incurred under any provision corresponding to section 1 of this Act; and in its application to such a judgment that Part shall have effect with the omission of subsections (2) and (3) of section 4 of that Act.

COMMENTS.

See general comments at the beginning of this Act as to the time of coming into force.

⚓   ⚓   ⚓   ⚓

Government ships.

14 (1) Nothing in the preceding provisions of this Act applies in relation to any warship or any ship for the time being used by the government of any State for other than commercial purposes.

(2) In relation to a ship owned by a State and for the time being used for commercial purposes it shall be a sufficient compliance with subsection (2) of section 10 of this Act if there is in force a certificate issued by the government of that State and showing that the ship is owned by that State and that any liability for pollution damage as defined in Article I of the Convention will be met up to the limit prescribed by Article V thereof.

(3) Every Convention State shall, for the purposes of any proceedings brought in a court in the United Kingdom to enforce a claim in respect of a liability incurred under section 1 of this Act, be deemed to have submitted to the jurisdiction of that court, and accordingly rules of court may provide for the manner in which such proceedings are to be commenced and carried on; but nothing in this subsection shall authorise the issue of execution, or in Scotland the execution of diligence, against the property of any State.

COMMENTS.

See general comments at the beginning of this Act as to the time of coming into force.

⚓   ⚓   ⚓   ⚓

Liability for cost of preventive measures where s. 1 does not apply.

15 (1) Where,—

(a) after an escape or discharge of persistent oil from a ship, measures are reasonably taken for the purpose of preventing or reducing damage in the area of the United Kingdom which may be caused by contamination resulting from the discharge or escape; and

(b) any person incurs, or might but for the measures have incurred, a liability, otherwise than under section 1 of this Act, for any such damage;

then, notwithstanding that subsection (1)(b) of that section does not apply, he shall be liable for the cost of the measures, whether or not the person taking them does so for the protection of his interests or in the performance of a duty.

(2) For the purposes of section 503 of the Merchant Ship-

ping Act 1894 (limitation of liability) any liability incurred under this section shall be deemed to be a liability to damages in respect of such loss, damage or infringement as is mentioned in subsection (1)(*d*) of that section.

COMMENTS.

Preventing or Minimising Damage Caused by Contamination.

Sub-section 1 of this section appears to have come into being as the result of the stranding of the m.v. *Torrey Canyon* in 1967, with the result that a large amount of her crude oil cargo contaminated the shores and the waters of the United Kingdom, particularly in the vicinity of the Cornish coast. It cost the British Government a huge sum in endeavouring to minimise the effects of pollution.

⚓   ⚓   ⚓   ⚓

16 Nothing in this Act shall prejudice any claim, or the enforcement of any claim, a person incurring any liability under this Act may have against another person in respect of that liability. *Saving for recourse actions.*

⚓   ⚓   ⚓   ⚓

17 The enactments and instruments with respect to which provision may be made by an Order in Council under section 1(1)(*h*) of the Hovercraft Act 1968 shall include this Act and any instrument made under it. *Application to hovercraft.*

COMMENTS.

No Order in Council has yet been made under this section.

⚓   ⚓   ⚓   ⚓

18 (1) Her Majesty may by Order in Council direct that this Act shall extend, subject to such exemptions, modifications or adaptations as may be specified in the Order, to any of the following countries, that is to say— *Extension to British possessions, etc.*

(*a*) the Isle of Man;

(*b*) any of the Channel Islands;

(*c*) any colony other than one for whose external relations a country other than the United Kingdom is responsible;

(*d*) any country outside Her Majesty's dominions in which Her Majesty has jurisdiction in right of Her Majesty's Government of the United Kingdom.

(2) Her Majesty may by Order in Council provide that this Act shall have effect as if any reference therein to the United Kingdom included a reference to any of the countries mentioned in the preceding subsection.

(3) Any statutory instrument made by virtue of subsection (2) of this section shall be subject to annulment in pursuance of a resolution of either House of Parliament.

COMMENTS:

The following Orders have been made under this section: In respect of these Orders, *see* also the Merchant Shipping Act 1974, section 20, sub-section 1.

The Merchant Shipping (Oil Pollution) (Belize) Order 1975, S.I. 1975, No. 2164.

The Merchant Shipping (Oil Pollution) (Bermuda) Order 1975, S.I. 1975, No. 2165.

The Merchant Shipping (Oil Pollution) (Cayman Islands) Order 1975, S.I. 1975, No. 2166.

The Merchant Shipping (Oil Pollution) (Falkland Islands) Order 1975, S.I. 1975, No. 2167.

The Merchant Shipping (Oil Pollution) (Gilbert Islands) Order 1975, S.I. 1975, No. 2168.

The Merchant Shipping (Oil Pollution) (Hong Kong) Order 1975, S.I. 1975, No. 2169.

The Merchant Shipping (Oil Pollution) (Montserrat) Order 1975, S.I. 1975, No. 2170.

The Merchant Shipping (Oil Pollution) (Overseas Territories) Order 1975, S.I. 1975, No. 2171.

The Merchant Shipping (Oil Pollution) (Seychelles) Order 1975, S.I. 1975, No. 2172.

The Merchant Shipping (Oil Pollution) (Solomon Islands) Order 1975, S.I. 1975, No. 2173.

The Merchant Shipping (Oil Pollution) (Tuvalu) Order 1975, S.I. 1975, No. 2174.

The Merchant Shipping (Oil Pollution) (Virgin Islands) Order 1975, S.I. 1975, No. 2175.

The Merchant Shipping (Oil Pollution) (Jersey) Order 1975, S.I. 1975, No. 2184.

The Merchant Shipping (Oil Pollution) (Guernsey) Order 1975, S.I. 1975, No. 2185.

The Merchant Shipping (Oil Pollution) (Isle of Man) Order 1975, S.I. 1975, No. 2186.

The Merchant Shipping (Oil Pollution) .Turks and Caicos Islands) Order 1975, S.I. 1976, No. 223.

⚓   ⚓   ⚓   ⚓

19 (1) In this Act—

'the Convention' means the International Convention on Civil Liability for Oil Pollution Damage signed in Brussels in 1969;

'Convention country' means a country in respect of which the Convention is in force; and

'Convention State' means a State which is a party to the Convention.

Meaning of 'the Convention'. 'Convention country' and 'Convention State'.

(2) If Her Majesty by Order in Council declares that any State specified in the Order is a party to the Convention in respect of any country so specified the Order shall, while in force, be conclusive evidence that that State is a party to the Convention in respect of that country.

COMMENTS.

See general comments at the beginning of this Act as to the time of coming into force.

⚓   ⚓   ⚓   ⚓

20 (1) In this Act—

'damage' includes loss;

'owner', in relation to a registered ship, means the person registered as its owner, except that in relation to a ship owned by a State which is operated by a person registered as the ship's operator, it means the person registered as its operator;

'the court' means the High Court in England and Wales, the Court of Session or the High Court in Northern Ireland or a judge thereof.

Interpretation of other expressions.

(2) In relation to any damage or cost resulting from the discharge or escape of any oil carried in a ship references in this Act to the owner of the ship are references to the owner

at the time of the occurrence or first of the occurrences resulting in the discharge or escape.

(3) References in this Act to the area of any country include the territorial sea of that country.

⚓   ⚓   ⚓   ⚓

Citation,
construction,
commence-
ment and
extent.

21 (1) This Act may be cited as the Merchant Shipping (Oil Pollution) Act 1971, and this Act and the Merchant Shipping Acts 1894 to 1970 may be cited together as the Merchant Shipping Acts 1894 to 1971.

(2) This Act shall be construed as one with the Merchant Shipping Acts 1894 to 1970.

(3) This Act shall come into force on such day as the Secretary of State may by order made by statutory instrument appoint, and different days may be so appointed for different provisions of this Act.

(4) This Act extends to Northern Ireland.

⚓   ⚓   ⚓   ⚓

Prevention of Oil Pollution Act 1971

INTRODUCTORY COMMENTS

The prevention of Oil Pollution Act 1971, consolidates the Oil in Navigable Waters Act 1955 to 1971, and section 5 of the Continental Shelf Act 1964.

The various Acts and sections of Acts repealed by this enactment are contained in the Schedule to this Act q.v.

The Act came into force on the 1st March, 1973. *See* the Prevention of Oil Pollution Act 1971 (Commencement) Order 1973, S.I. 1973, No. 203.

General provisions for preventing oil pollution

1 (1) If any oil to which this section applies or any mixture containing such oil is discharged from a ship registered in the United Kingdom into any part of the sea outside the territorial waters of the United Kingdom, the owner or master of the ship shall, subject to the provisions of this Act, be guilty of an offence.

Discharge of certain oils into sea outside territorial waters.

(2) This section applies—

(*a*) to crude oil, fuel oil and lubricating oil; and

(*b*) to heavy diesel oil, as defined by regulations made under this section by the Secretary of State;

and shall also apply to any other description of oil which may be specified by regulations made by the Secretary of State, having regard to the provisions of any Convention accepted by Her Majesty's Government in the United Kingdom in so far as it relates to the prevention of pollution of the sea by oil, or having regard to the persistent character of oil of that description and the likelihood that it would cause pollution if discharged from a ship into any part of the sea outside the territorial waters of the United Kingdom.

(3) Regulations made by the Secretary of State may make exceptions from the operation of subsection (1) of this section, either generally or with respect to particular classes of ships, particular descriptions of oil or mixtures containing oil or the discharge of oil or mixtures in particular circumstances or into particular areas of the sea, and may do so either absolutely or subject to any specified conditions.

(4) A person guilty of an offence under this section shall be liable on summary conviction to a fine not exceeding £50,000 or on conviction on indictment to a fine.

COMMENTS.

Owner or Master.

Both may be prosecuted and if guilty be convicted of an offence arising out of the same facts.

Compare R. *v.* Federal Steam Navigation Co. 1973 and R. *v.* Moran 1973.

Regulations (Exceptions).

Consult the Oil in Navigable Waters (Exceptions) Regulations 1972, S.I. 1972, No. 1928.

Territorial Waters.

These extend for 3 miles from the low-water mark. *See* section 7 of the Territorial Waters Jurisdiction Act 1878.

In the event of dispute the court will accept as conclusive evidence the statement of an appropriate officer of the Crown the *Fagerives* 1927.

Heavy Diesel Oil.

See the Oil in Navigable Waters (Heavy Diesel Oil) Regulations 1967, S.I. 1967, No. 710.

Discharge of oil into United Kingdom waters.

2 (1) If any oil or mixture containing oil is discharged as mentioned in the following paragraphs into waters to which this section applies, then, subject to the provisions of this Act, the following shall be guilty of an offence, that is to say—

(*a*) if the discharge is from a vessel, the owner or master of the vessel, unless he proves that the discharge took place and was caused as mentioned in paragraph (*b*) of this subsection;

(*b*) if the discharge is from a vessel but takes place in the course of a transfer of oil to or from another vessel or a place on land and is caused by the act or omission of any person in charge of any apparatus in that other vessel or that place, the owner or master of that other vessel or, as the case may be, the occupier of that place;

(*c*) if the discharge is from a place on land, the occupier of that place, unless he proves that the discharge was caused as mentioned in paragraph (*d*) of this subsection;

(*d*) if the discharge is from a place on land and is caused by the act of a person who is in that place without the permission (express or implied) of the occupier, that person;

(e) if the discharge takes place otherwise than as mentioned in the preceding paragraphs and is the result of any operations for the exploration of the sea-bed and sub-soil or the exploitation of their natural resources, the person carrying on the operations.

(2) This section applies to the following waters, that is to say,—

(a) the whole of the sea within the seaward limits of the territorial waters of the United Kingdom; and

(b) all other waters (including inland waters) which are within those limits and are navigable by sea-going ships.

(3) In this Act 'place on land' includes anything resting on the bed or shore of the sea, or of any other waters to which this section applies, and also includes anything afloat (other than a vessel) if it is anchored or attached to the bed or shore of the sea or of any such waters; and 'occupier', in relation to any such thing as is mentioned in the preceding provisions of this subsection, if it has no occupier, means the owner thereof, and, in relation to a railway wagon or road vehicle, means the person in charge of the wagon or vehicle and not the occupier of the land on which the wagon or vehicle stands.

(4) A person guilty of an offence under this section shall be liable on summary conviction to a fine not exceeding £50,000 or on conviction on indictment to a fine.

COMMENTS.

Oil or Mixture.

See section 29, sub-sections 1 and 2 of this Act for definitions.

Navigable by Sea-going Ships.

It has been held that a dry-dock may be 'navigable by sea-going ships' although the water in the dry dock has been so emptied that the vessel is on the blocks. Compare and *see* Rankin *v.* De Coster, 1975.

In Charge.

For the meaning of this term *see* and compare: Leach *v.* Evans, 1952; Haines *v.* Roberts, 1953; Ellis *v.* Smith, 1962.

⚓   ⚓   ⚓   ⚓

Discharge of certain oils from pipe-lines or as the result of exploration etc., in designated areas.

3 (1) If any oil to which section 1 of this Act applies, or any mixture containing such oil, is discharged into any part of the sea—

(*a*) from a pipe-line; or

(*b*) (otherwise than from a ship) as the result of any operation for the exploration of the sea-bed and subsoil or the exploitation of their natural resources in a designated area.

then, subject to the following provisions of this Act, the owner of the pipe-line or, as the case may be, the person carrying on the operations shall be guilty of an offence unless the discharge was from a place in his occupation and he proves that it was due to the act of a person who was there without his permission (express or implied).

(2) In this section 'designated area' means an area for the time being designated by an Order made under section 1 of the Continental Shelf Act 1964.

(3) A person guilty of an offence under this section shall be liable on summary conviction to a fine not exceeding £50,000 or on conviction on indictment to a fine.

COMMENTS.

'Mixture', 'oil', 'any part of the sea'. *See* generally, for definitions, section 29 of this Act.

Designated Area—Continental Shelf Act 1964.

Consult the following Orders:

Continental Shelf (Designation of Areas) Order 1964, S.I. 1964, No. 697.

Continental Shelf (Designation of Additional Areas) Order 1965, S.I. 1965, No. 1531.

Continental Shelf (Designation of Additional Areas) Order 1968, S.I. 1968, No. 891.

Continental Shelf (Designation of Additional Areas) Order 1971, S.I. 1971, No. 594.

⚓   ⚓   ⚓   ⚓

Equipment in ships to prevent oil pollution.

4 (1) For the purpose of preventing or reducing discharges of oil and mixtures containing oil into the sea, the Secretary of State may make regulations requiring ships registered in the United Kingdom to be fitted with such equipment and to comply with such other requirements as may be specified in the regulations.

(2) Without prejudice to the generality of subsection (1) of this section, where any regulations made thereunder require ships to be fitted with equipment of a specified description, the regulations may provide that equipment of that description—

(a) shall not be installed in a ship to which the regulations apply unless it is of a type tested and approved by a person appointed by the Secretary of State;

(b) while installed in such a ship, shall not be treated as satisfying the requirements of the regulations unless, at such times as may be specified in the regulations, it is submitted for testing and approval by a person so appointed.

(3) The Secretary of State may appoint persons to carry out tests for the purposes of any regulations made under this section, and, in respect of the carrying out of such tests, may charge such fees as, with the approval of the Treasury, may be prescribed by the regulations.

(4) Every surveyor of ships shall be taken to be a person appointed by the Secretary of State to carry out tests for the purposes of any regulations made under this section, in so far as they relate to tests required in accordance with paragraph (b) of subsection (2) of this section.

(5) If, in the case of any ship, the provisions of any regulations made under this section which apply to that ship are contravened, the owner or master of the ship shall be guilty of an offence.

(6) A person guilty of an offence under this section shall be liable on summary conviction to a fine not exceeding £1,000 or on conviction on indictment to a fine.

COMMENTS.

Oil and Mixtures.

See generally section 29 for definitions.

Regulations.

Consult:

Oil in Navigable Water (Ships Equipment) (No. 1) Regulations, 1956, S.I. 1956 No. 1423.

Oil in Navigable Waters (Ships Equipment) Regulations 1957, S.I. 1957 No. 1424 and the saving of these Regulations by section 33, sub-section 2 of this Act.

P

Regulations made under this section can be extended to include vessels registered outside the United Kingdom. Consult section 22, sub-section 1 of this Act.

⚓   ⚓   ⚓   ⚓

5 (1) Where a person is charged with an offence under section 1 of this Act, or is charged with an offence under section 2 of this Act as the owner or master of a vessel, it shall be a defence to prove that the oil or mixture was discharged for the purpose of securing the safety of any vessel, or of preventing damage to any vessel or cargo, or of saving life, unless the court is satisfied that the discharge of the oil or mixture was not necessary for that purpose or was not a reasonable step to take in the circumstances.

(2) Where a person is charged as mentioned in subsection (1) of this section, it shall also be a defence to prove—

(a) that the oil or mixture escaped in consequence of damage to the vessel, and that as soon as practicable after the damage occurred all reasonable steps were taken for preventing, or (if it could not be prevented) for stopping or reducing, the escape of the oil or mixture, or

(b) that the oil or mixture escaped by reason of leakage, that neither the leakage nor any delay in discovering it was due to any want of reasonable care, and that as soon as practicable after the escape was discovered all reasonable steps were taken for stopping or reducing it.

COMMENTS.

Oil: Mixture.

See generally section 29 for definitions of these and other terms.

Leakage.

An escape of oil brought about by some physical force, such as air pressure, does not come within this term. *See* Nicholson *v.* Freemantle Port Authority 1970.

As Soon as Practicable.

For meaning, *see* Marshall *v.* Gotlam Ltd. 1954; Moorcraft *v.* Powles & Son Ltd. 1962; Jayne *v.* National Coal Board 1963.

⚓   ⚓   ⚓   ⚓

6 (1) Where a person is charged, in respect of the escape Defences of
other persons of any oil or mixture containing oil, with an offence under charged with
offences under section 2 or 3 of this Act— s. 2 or s. 3.

(*a*) as the occupier of a place on land; or

(*b*) as a person carrying on operations for the exploration of the sea-bed and subsoil or the exploitation of their natural resources; or

(*c*) as the owner of a pipe-line,

it shall be a defence to prove that neither the escape nor any delay in discovering it was due to any want of reasonable care and that as soon as practicable after it was discovered all reasonable steps were taken for stopping or reducing it.

(2) Where a person is charged with an offence under section 2 of this Act in respect of the discharge of a mixture containing oil from a place on land, it shall also, subject to subsection (3) of this section, be a defence to prove—

(*a*) that the oil was contained in an effluent produced by operations for the refining of oil;

(*b*) that it was not reasonably practicable to dispose of the effluent otherwise than by discharging it into waters to which that section applies; and

(*c*) that all reasonably practicable steps had been taken for eliminating oil from the effluent.

(3) If it is proved that, at a time to which the charge relates, the surface of the waters into which the mixture was discharged from the place on land, or land adjacent to those waters, was fouled by oil, subsection (2) of this section shall not apply unless the court is satisfied that the fouling was not caused, or contributed to, by oil contained in any effluent discharged at or before that time from that place.

COMMENTS.

Oil: Mixture: Discharge.

See generally, section 29 of this Act for definitions of these and other terms.

Practicable.

See comments to preceding section.

⚓   ⚓   ⚓   ⚓

Protection of
acts done in
exercise of
certain powers
of harbour
authorities, etc.

7 (1) Where any oil, or mixture containing oil, is discharged in consequence of—

(a) the exercise of any power conferred by sections 530 to 532 of the Merchant Shipping Act 1894 (which relate to the removal of wrecks by harbour, conservancy and lighthouse authorities); or

(b) the exercise, for the purpose of preventing an obstruction or danger to navigation, of any power to dispose of sunk, stranded or abandoned vessels which is exercisable by a harbour authority under any local enactment;

and apart from this subsection the authority exercising the power, or a person employed by or acting on behalf of the authority, would be guilty of an offence under section 1 or section 2 of this Act in respect of that discharge, the authority or person shall not be convicted of that offence unless it is shown that they or he failed to take such steps (if any) as were reasonable in the circumstances for preventing, stopping or reducing the discharge.

(2) Subsection (1) of this section shall apply to the exercise of any power conferred by section 13 of the Dockyard Ports Regulation Act 1865 (which relates to the removal of obstructions to dockyard ports) as it applies to the exercise of any such power as is mentioned in paragraph (a) of that subsection, and shall, as so applying, have effect as if references to the authority exercising the power were references to the Queen's harbour master for the port in question.

COMMENTS.

For definitions of the various terms used in this section, consult generally section 29.

Harbour Authority.

Is defined in section 8, sub-section 2 of this Act.

⚓   ⚓   ⚓   ⚓

Discharge of
certain ballast
water into
harbours.

8 (1) A harbour authority may appoint a place within their jurisdiction where the ballast water of vessels in which a cargo of petroleum-spirit has been carried may be discharged into the waters of the harbour, at such times, and subject to such conditions, as the authority may determine; and, where a place is so appointed, the discharge of ballast water from such a vessel shall not constitute an offence under section 2 of this

Act, if the ballast water is discharged at that place, and at a time and in accordance with the conditions so determined, and the ballast water contains no oil other than petroleum-spirit.

(2) In this Act—

'harbour authority' means a person or body of persons empowered by an enactment to make charges in respect of vessels entering a harbour in the United Kingdom or using facilities therein;

'harbour in the United Kingdom' means a port, estuary, haven, dock, or other place which fulfils the following conditions, that is to say,—

(*a*) that it contains waters to which section 2 of this Act applies, and

(*b*) that a person or body of persons is empowered by an enactment to make charges in respect of vessels entering that place or using facilities therein.

In this subsection 'enactment' includes a local enactment, and 'charges' means any charges with the exception of light dues, local lightdues any any other charges payable in respect of lighthouses, buoys or beacons, and of charges in respect of pilotage.

COMMENTS.

Cases Excluded from the Preceding Sections, 4–8 inclusive.

See Merchant Shipping Act 1974, section 9, which includes a new section to this Act, viz.: Section 8 (*a*).

⚓   ⚓   ⚓   ⚓

9 (1) The powers exercisable by a harbour authority in respect of any harbour in the United Kingdom shall include power to provide facilities for enabling vessels using the harbour to discharge or deposit oil residues (in this Act referred to as 'oil reception facilities'). _{Facilities in harbour for disposal of oil residues.}

(2) Any power of a harbour authority to provide oil reception facilities shall include power to join with any other person in providing them, and references in this section to the provision of oil reception facilities by a harbour authority shall be construed accordingly; and any such power shall also include power to arrange for the provision of such facilities by any other person.

(3) A harbour authority providing oil reception facilities, or a person providing such facilities by arrangement with a

harbour authority, may make reasonable charges for the use of the facilities, and may impose reasonable conditions in respect of the use thereof.

(4) Subject to the following provisions of this section, any oil reception facilities provided by, or by arrangement with, a harbour authority shall be open to all vessels using the harbour on payment of any charges, and subject to compliance with any conditions, imposed in accordance with subsection (3) of this section.

(5) Where in the case of any harbour in the United Kingdom it appears to the Secretary of State, after consultation with the harbour authority and with any organisation appearing to the Secretary of State to be representative of owners of ships registered in the United Kingdom,—

(a) if the harbour has oil reception facilities, that those facilities are inadequate, or

(b) if the harbour has no such facilities, that the harbour has need of such facilities,

the Secretary of State may direct the harbour authority to provide, or arrange for the provision of, such oil reception facilities as may be specified in the direction.

(6) Notwithstanding the provisions of subsection (4) of this section, a harbour authority providing oil reception facilities, or a person providing such facilities by arrangement with a harbour authority, shall not be obliged to make those facilities available for use by tankers, or for the reception of oil residues discharged for the purpose of enabling a vessel to undergo repairs; and the requirements of tankers, and the reception of oil residues so discharged, shall be disregarded by the Secretary of State in exercising his powers under subsection (5) of this section.

(7) Nothing in this section shall be construed as requiring a harbour authority to allow untreated ballast water (that is to say, ballast water which contains oil and has not been subjected to an effective process for separating the oil from the water) to be discharged into any oil reception facilities provided by, or by arrangement with, the authority; and the Secretary of State shall exercise his powers under subsection (5) of this section accordingly.

(8) Any harbour authority failing to comply with any direction given under subsection (5) of this section within the

period specified in the direction, or within any extended period allowed by the Secretary of State (whether before or after the end of the period so specified), shall be guilty of an offence, and liable on summary conviction to a fine not exceeding £10 for each day during which the default continues, from the day after the end of the period specified in the direction, or any extended period allowed by the Secretary of State, as the case may be, until the last day before that on which the facilities are provided in accordance with the direction.

(9) Subsections (1), (2), (5) and (8) of this section shall have effect in relation to arrangements for disposing of oil residues discharged or deposited by vessels using a harbour's oil reception facilities, and to the making of such arrangements, as those subsections have effect in relation to oil reception facilities and the provision of such facilities.

⚓   ⚓   ⚓   ⚓

10 (1) No oil shall be transferred between sunset and sunrise to or from a vessel in any harbour in the United Kingdom unless the requisite notice has been given in accordance with this section or the transfer is for the purposes of a fire brigade. *Restrictions on transfer of oil at night.*

(2) A general notice may be given to the harbour master of a harbour that transfers of oil between sunset and sunrise will be frequently carried out at a place in the harbour within such period, not ending later than twelve months after the date on which the notice is given, as is specified in the notice; and if such a notice is given it shall be the requisite notice for the purposes of this section as regards transfers of oil at that place within the period specified in the notice.

(3) Subject to subsection (2) of this section, the requisite notice for the purposes of this section shall be a notice given to the harbour master not less than three hours nor more than ninety-six hours before the transfer of oil begins.

(4) In the case of a harbour which has no harbour master, references in this section to the harbour master shall be construed as references to the harbour authority.

(5) If any oil is transferred to or from a vessel in contravention of this section, the master of the vessel, and, if the oil

is transferred from or to a place on land, the occupier of that place, shall be liable on summary conviction to a fine not exceeding £100.

COMMENTS.

No Oil Shall be Transferred.

See generally section 29 for definitions.

Harbour Authority.

See section 8, sub-section 2 for definition.

⚓   ⚓   ⚓   ⚓

Duty to report discharge of oil into waters of harbours.

11 (1) If any oil or mixture containing oil—

(*a*) is discharged from a vessel into the waters of a harbour in the United Kingdom; or

(*b*) is found to be escaping or to have escaped from a vessel into any such waters; or

(*c*) is found to be escaping or to have escaped into any such waters from a place on land;

the owner or master of the vessel, or the occupier of the place on land, as the case may be, shall forthwith report the occurrence to the harbour master, or, if the harbour has no harbour master, to the harbour authority.

(2) A report made under subsection (1) of this section by the owner or master of a vessel shall state whether the occurrence falls within paragraph (*a*) or paragraph (*b*) of that sub-section.

(3) If a person fails to make a report as required by this section he shall be liable on summary conviction to a fine not exceeding £200.

COMMENTS.

Oil: Mixture, etc.

For the definitions of these terms and others, *see* generally, section 29.

Harbour Authority.

See section 8, sub-section 2 for definition.

⚓   ⚓   ⚓   ⚓

Shipping Casualties

12 (1) The powers conferred by this section shall be Shipping casualties. exercisable where—

(*a*) an accident has occurred to or in a ship; and

(*b*) in the opinion of the Secretary of State oil from the ship will or may cause pollution on a large scale in the United Kingdom or in the waters in or adjacent to the United Kingdom up to the seaward limits of territorial waters; and

(*c*) in the opinion of the Secretary of State the use of the powers conferred by this section is urgently needed.

(2) For the purpose of preventing or reducing oil pollution, or the risk of oil pollution, the Secretary of State may give directions as respects the ship or its cargo—

(*a*) to the owner of the ship, or to any person in possession of the ship; or

(*b*) to the master of the ship; or

(*c*) to any salvor in possession of the ship, or to any person who is the servant or agent of any salvor in possession of the ship, and who is in charge of the salvage operation.

(3) Directions under subsection (2) of this section may require the person to whom they are given to take, or refrain from taking, any action of any kind whatsoever, and without prejudice to the generality of the preceding provisions of this subsection the directions may require—

(*a*) that the ship is to be, or is not to be, moved, or is to be moved to a specified place, or is to be removed from a specified area or locality; or

(*b*) that the ship is not to be moved to a specified place or area, or over a specified route; or

(*c*) that any oil or other cargo is to be, or is not to be, unloaded or discharged; or

(*d*) that specified salvage measures are to be, or are not to be, taken.

(4) If in the opinion of the Secretary of State the powers conferred by subsection (2) of this section are, or have proved to be, inadequate for the purpose, the Secretary of State may, for the purpose of preventing or reducing oil pollution, or the risk of oil pollution, take, as respects the ship or its cargo,

any action of any kind whatsoever, and without prejudice to the generality of the preceding provisions of this subsection the Secretary of State may—

(*a*) take any such action as he has power to require to be taken by a direction under this section;

(*b*) undertake operations for the sinking or destruction of the ship, or any part of it, of a kind which is not within the means of any person to whom he can give directions;

(*c*) undertake operations which involve the taking over of control of the ship.

(5) The powers of the Secretary of State under subsection (4) of this section shall also be exercisable by such persons as may be authorised in that behalf by the Secretary of State.

(6) Every person concerned with compliance with directions given, or with action taken, under this section shall use his best endeavours to avoid any risk to human life.

(7) The provisions of this section and of section 16 of this Act are without prejudice to any rights or powers of Her Majesty's Government in the United Kingdom exercisable apart from those sections whether under international law or otherwise.

(8) It is hereby declared that any action taken as respects a ship which is under arrest or as respects the cargo of such a ship, being action duly taken in pursuance of a direction given under this section, or being any action taken under subsection (4) or (5) of this section—

(*a*) does not constitute contempt of court; and

(*b*) does not in any circumstances make the Admiralty Marshal liable in any civil proceedings.

(9) In this section, unless the context otherwise requires—

'accident' includes the loss, stranding, abandonment of or damage to a ship; and

'specified', in relation to a direction under this section, means specified by the direction;

and the reference in subsection (8) of this section to the Admiralty Marshal includes a reference to the Admiralty Marshal of the Supreme Court of Northern Ireland.

Comments.

Accident.

See sub-section 9 of this section for meaning.

Unloaded or Discharged.

See section 29 of this Act for definition.

⚓   ⚓   ⚓   ⚓

13 (1) If any action duly taken by a person in pursuance of a direction given to him under section 12 of this Act, or any action taken under subsection (4) or (5) of that section— *Right to recover in respect of unreasonable loss or damage.*

(*a*) was not reasonably necessary to prevent or reduce oil pollution, or risk of oil pollution; or

(*b*) was such that the good it did or was likely to do was disproportionately less than the expense incurred, or damage suffered, as a result of the action,

a person incurring expense or suffering damage as a result of, or by himself taking, the action shall be entitled to recover compensation from the Secretary of State.

(2) In considering whether subsection (1) of this section applies, account shall be taken of—

(*a*) the extent and risk of oil pollution if the action had not been taken;

(*b*) the likelihood of the action being effective; and

(*c*) the extent of the damage which has been caused by the action.

(3) Any reference in this section to the taking of any action includes a reference to a compliance with a direction not to take some specified action.

(4) The Admiralty jurisdiction of the High Court, of the Court of Session and of the Supreme Court of Northern Ireland shall include jurisdiction to hear and determine any claim arising under this section.

Comments.

See section 16 of this Act for application of this section to certain foreign and other ships.

⚓   ⚓   ⚓   ⚓

14 (1) If the person to whom a direction is duly given under section 12 of this Act contravenes, or fails to comply with, any requirement of the direction, he shall be guilty of an offence.

(2) if a person wilfully obstructs any person who is—

(*a*) acting on behalf of the Secretary of State in connection with the giving or service of a direction under section 12 of this Act;

(*b*) acting in compliance with a direction under that section; or

(*c*) acting under subsection (4) or (5) of that section;

he shall be guilty of an offence.

(3) In proceedings for an offence under subsection (1) of this section, it shall be a defence for the accused to prove that he has used all due diligence to ensure compliance with the direction, or that he had reasonable cause for believing that compliance with the direction would have involved a serious risk to human life.

(4) A person guilty of an offence under this section shall be liable on summary conviction to a fine not exceeding £50,000, or on conviction on indictment to a fine.

⚓   ⚓   ⚓   ⚓

15 (1) If the Secretary of State is satisfied that a company or other body is not one to whom section 412 or section 437 of the Companies Act 1948 (service of notices) applies so as to authorise the service of a direction on that body under either of those sections, he may give a direction under section 12 of this Act—

(*a*) to that body, as the owner of, or the person in possession of, a ship, by serving the direction on the master of the ship; or

(*b*) to that body, as a salvor, by serving the direction on the person in charge of the salvage operations.

(2) For the purpose of giving or serving a direction under section 12 of this Act to or on any person on a ship, a person acting on behalf of the Secretary of State shall have the right to go on board the ship.

(3) In the application of subsection (1) of this section to

Northern Ireland, for references to sections 412 and 437 of the Companies Act 1948 there shall be substituted references to sections 361 and 385 of the Companies Act (Northern Ireland) 1960.

COMMENTS.

See section 16 of this Act for application of the section to certain foreign and other ships.

⚓   ⚓   ⚓   ⚓

16 (1) Her Majesty may by Order in Council provide that sections 12 to 15 of this Act, together with any other provisions of this Act, shall apply to a ship— *(Application of ss. 12 to 15 to certain foreign and other ships.)*

(a) which is not a ship registered in the United Kingdom; and

(b) which is for the time being outside the territorial waters of the United Kingdom;

in such cases and circumstances as may be specified in the Order, and subject to such exceptions, adaptations and modifications, if any, as may be so specified.

(2) An Order in Council under subsection (1) of this section may contain such transitional and other consequential provisions as appear to Her Majesty to be expedient.

(3) Except as provided by an Order in Council under subsection (1) of this section, no direction under section 12 of this Act shall apply to a ship which is not registered in the United Kingdom and which is for the time being outside the territorial waters of the United Kingdom, and no action shall be taken under subsection (4) or (5) of section 12 of this Act as respects any such ship.

(4) No direction under section 12 of this Act shall apply to any vessel of Her Majesty's navy or to any Government ship (within the meaning of section 80 of the Merchant Shipping Act 1906) and no action shall be taken under subsection (4) or (5) of that section as respects any such vessel or ship.

COMMENTS.

Order in Council.

Consult the Oil in Navigable Water (Shipping Casualties) Order 1971, S.I. 1971, No. 1736 saved by virtue of section 33, sub-section 2 of this Act.

⚓   ⚓   ⚓   ⚓

Enforcement

17 (1) The Secretary of State may make regulations requiring oil record books to be carried in ships registered in the United Kingdom and requiring the master of any such ship to record in the oil record book carried by it—

(*a*) the carrying out, on board or in connection with the ship, of such of the following operations as may be prescribed, that is to say, operations relating to—

(i) the loading of oil cargo, or

(ii) the transfer of oil cargo during a voyage, or

(iii) the discharge of oil cargo, or

(iv) the ballasting of oil tanks (whether cargo or bunker fuel tanks) and the discharge of ballast from, and cleaning of, such tanks, or

(v) the separation of oil from water, or from other substances, in any mixture containing oil, or

(vi) the disposal of any oil or water, or any other substance, arising from operations relating to any of the matters specified in the preceding sub-paragraphs, or

(vii) the disposal of any other oil residues;

(*b*) any occasion on which oil or a mixture containing oil is discharged from the ship for the purpose of securing the safety of any vessel, or of preventing damage to any vessel or cargo, or of saving life;

(*c*) any occasion on which oil or a mixture containing oil is found to be escaping, or to have escaped, from the ship in consequence of damage to the ship, or by reason of leakage.

(2) The Secretary of State may make regulations requiring the keeping of records relating to the transfer of oil to and from vessels while they are within the seaward limits of the territorial waters of the United Kingdom; and the requirements of any regulations made under this subsection shall be in addition to the requirements of any regulations made under subsection (1) of this section.

(3) Any records required to be kept by regulations made under subsection (2) of this section shall, unless the vessel is a barge, be kept by the master of the vessel, and shall, if the vessel is a barge, be kept, in so far as they relate to the transfer

of oil to the barge, by the person supplying the oil and, in so
far as they relate to the transfer of oil from the barge, by the
person to whom the oil is delivered.

(4) Regulations under this section requiring the carrying of
oil record books or the keeping of records may—

(a) prescribe the form of the oil record books or records
and the nature of the entries to be made in them;

(b) require the person providing or keeping the books or
records to retain them for a prescribed period;

(c) require that person, at the end of the prescribed period,
to transmit the books or records to a place or person
determined by or under the regulations;

(d) provide for the custody or disposal of the books or
records after their transmission to such a place or person.

(5) If any ship fails to carry such an oil record book as it
is required to carry under this section the owner or master
shall be liable on summary conviction to a fine not exceeding
£500; if any person fails to comply with any requirements
imposed on him by or under this section, he shall be liable on
summary conviction to a fine not exceeding £500; and if any
person makes an entry in any oil record book carried or
record kept under this section which is to his knowledge false
or misleading in any material particular, he shall be liable on
summary conviction to a fine not exceeding £500, or imprisonment for a term not exceeding six months, or both, or on
conviction on indictment to a fine or to imprisonment for a
term not exceeding two years or both.

(6) In any proceedings under this Act—

(a) any oil record book carried or record kept in pursuance
of regulations made under this section shall be admissible
as evidence, and in Scotland shall be sufficient evidence,
of the facts stated in it;

(b) any copy of an entry in such an oil record book or record
which is certified by the master of the ship in which the
book is carried or by the person by whom the record is
required to be kept to be a true copy of the entry shall be
admissible as evidence, and in Scotland shall be sufficient
evidence, of the facts stated in the entry;

(c) any document purporting to be an oil record book carried
or record kept in pursuance of regulations made under
this section, or purporting to be such a certified copy as is

mentioned in the preceding paragraph, shall, unless the contrary is proved, be presumed to be such a book, record or copy, as the case may be.

COMMENTS.

Regulations.

Consult the Oil in Navigable Waters (Transfer Records) Regulations 1957, S.I. 1957, No. 358, saved by virtue of section 33, sub-section 2 of this Act.

Loading of Oil and Other Terms.

See generally, section 29 for definition of this and other terms.

⚓   ⚓   ⚓   ⚓

Powers of inspection.

18 (1) The Secretary of State may appoint any person as an inspector to report to him—

(*a*) whether the prohibitions, restrictions and obligations imposed by virtue of this Act (including prohibitions so imposed by the creation of offences under any provision of this Act other than section 3) have been complied with;

(*b*) what measures (other than measures made obligatory by regulations made under section 4 of this Act) have been taken to prevent the escape of oil and mixtures containing oil;

(*c*) whether the oil reception facilities provided in harbours are adequate;

and any such inspector may be so appointed to report either in a particular case or in a class of cases specified in his appointment.

(2) Every surveyor of ships shall be taken to be a person appointed generally under the preceding subsection to report to the Secretary of State in every kind of case falling within that subsection.

(3) Section 729 of the Merchant Shipping Act 1894 (powers of inspectors) shall apply to persons appointed or taken to be appointed under subsection (1) of this section as it applies to the inspectors referred to in that section and shall, as so applying, have effect as if—

(*a*) in paragraph (*a*) of subsection (1) of that section, the reference to a ship included any vessel, and the reference to that Act were a reference to this Act and any regulations made under this Act; and

(b) any power under that section to inspect premises included power to inspect any apparatus used for transferring oil.

(4) Any power of an inspector, under section 729 as applied by the preceding subsection, to inspect a vessel shall include power to test any equipment with which the vessel is required to be fitted in pursuance of regulations made under section 4 of this Act.

(5) Any power of an inspector, under section 729 as so applied, to require the production of any oil record book required to be carried or records required to be kept in pursuance of regulations made under section 17 of this Act shall include power to copy any entry therein and require the master to certify the copy as a true copy of the entry; and in subsection (3) of section 729, as so applied, the reference to making a declaration shall be construed as a reference to the certification of such a copy.

(6) Without prejudice to any powers exercisable by virtue of the preceding provisions of this section, in the case of a vessel which is for the time being in a harbour in the United Kingdom the harbour master, and any other person appointed by the Secretary of State under this subsection (either generally or in relation to a particular vessel), shall have power—

(a) to go on board and inspect the vessel or any part thereof, or any of the machinery, boats, equipment or articles on board the vessel, for the purpose of ascertaining the circumstances relating to an alleged discharge of oil or a mixture containing oil from the vessel into the waters of the harbour;

(b) to require the production of any oil record book required to be carried or records required to be kept in pursuance of regulations made under section 17 of this Act; and

(c) to copy any entry in any such book or record and require the master to certify the copy as a true copy of the entry.

(7) A person exercising any powers conferred by subsection (6) of this section shall not unnecessarily detain or delay the vessel from proceeding on any voyage.

(8) If any person fails to comply with any requirement duly made in pursuance of paragraph (b) or paragraph (c) of subsection (6) of this section, he shall be liable on summary conviction to a fine not exceeding £10; and if any person wilfully obstructs a person acting in the exercise of any power con-

ferred by virtue of this section, he shall be liable on summary conviction to a fine not exceeding £100.

COMMENTS.

See generally, section 29 of this Act for definition of various terms used in this section.

Oil Reception Facilities.

See section 9, sub-section 1 of this Act.

Oil Record Book.

See section 17 of this Act.

Harbour.

See section 8, sub-section 2 of this Act.

⚓ ⚓ ⚓ ⚓

Prosecutions. **19** (1) Proceedings for an offence under this Act may, in England or Wales, be brought only—

(*a*) by or with the consent of the Attorney General, or

(*b*) if the offence is one to which subsection (2) of this section applies, by the harbour authority, or

(*c*) unless the offence is one mentioned in paragraph (*b*), (*c*) or (*d*) of subsection (2) of this section, by the Secretary of State or a person authorised by any general or special direction of the Secretary of State.

(2) This subsection applies to the following offences—

(*a*) any offence under section 2 of this Act which is alleged to have been committed by the discharge of oil, or a mixture containing oil, into the waters of a harbour in the United Kingdom;

(*b*) any offence in relation to such a harbour under section 10 or section 11 of this Act;

(*c*) any offence under section 17 of this Act relating to the keeping of records of the transfer of oil within such a harbour; and

(*d*) any offence under section 18 of this Act in respect of a failure to comply with a requirement of a harbour master, or in respect of obstruction of a harbour master acting in the exercise of any power conferred by virtue of that section.

(3) The preceding provisions of this section shall apply in

relation to any part of a dockyard port within the meaning of the Dockyard Ports Regulation Act 1865 as follows, that is to say—

(a) if that part is comprised in a harbour in the United Kingdom, the reference to the harbour authority shall be construed as including a reference to the Queen's harbour master for the port;

(b) if that part is not comprised in a harbour in the United Kingdom, the references to such a harbour shall be construed as references to such a dockyard port and the reference to the harbour authority as a reference to the Queen's harbour master for the port.

(4) Where, immediately before the date on which (apart from this subsection) the time for bringing summary proceedings for an offence under this Act would expire, the person to be charged is outside the United Kingdom, the time for bringing the proceedings shall be extended until the end of the period of two months beginning with the date on which he next enters the United Kingdom.

(5) Proceedings for any offence under this Act may (without prejudice to any jurisdiction exercisable apart from this sub-section) be taken against a person at any place at which he is for the time being.

(6) If a local fisheries committee constituted by an order made, or having effect as if made, under section 1 of the Sea Fisheries Regulation Act 1966 or any of its officers is authorised in that behalf under subsection (1) of this section, the committee may institute proceedings for any offence under this Act committed within the district of the committee.

(7) The preceding provisions of this section do not apply in relation to an offence under section 3 of this Act, but proceedings for such an offence may—

(a) in England and Wales, be brought only by or with the consent of the Director of Public Prosecutions; and

(b) in Northern Ireland, be brought only by or with the consent of the Attorney General for Northern Ireland; and any such proceedings may be taken, and the offence may for all incidental purposes be treated as having been committed, in any place in the United Kingdom.

(8) Where a body corporate is guilty of an offence under section 3 of this Act and the offence is proved to have been

committed with the consent or connivance of, or to be attributable to any neglect on the part of, any director, manager, secretary or other similar officer of the body corporate or any person who was purporting to act in any such capacity he, as well as the body corporate, shall be guilty of the offence and shall be liable to be proceeded against and punished accordingly.

In this subsection, 'director' in relation to a body corporate established for the purpose of carrying on under national ownership any industry or part of an industry or undertaking, being a body corporate whose affairs are managed by its members, means a member of that body corporate.

COMMENTS.

See generally, section 29 of this Act for definition of various terms used in this section.

Harbour Authority

See section 8, sub-section 2 of this Act.

⚓   ⚓   ⚓   ⚓

Enforcement and application of fines.

20 (1) Where a fine imposed by a court in proceedings against the owner or master of a vessel for an offence under this Act is not paid at the time ordered by the court, the court shall, in addition to any other powers for enforcing payment, have power to direct the amount remaining unpaid to be levied by distress or poinding and sale of the vessel, her tackle, furniture and apparel.

(2) Where a person is convicted of an offence under section 1 or section 2 of this Act, and the court imposes a fine in respect of the offence, then if it appears to the court that any person has incurred, or will incur, expenses in removing any pollution, or making good any damage, which is attributable to the offence, the court may order the whole or part of the fine to be paid to that person for or towards defraying those expenses.

⚓   ⚓   ⚓   ⚓

Enforcement of Conventions relating to oil pollution.

21 (1) Her Majesty may by Order in Council empower such persons as may be designated by or under the Order to go on board any Convention ship while the ship is within a harbour in the United Kingdom, and to require production of any oil record book required to be carried in accordance with the Convention.

(2) An Order in Council under this section may, for the purposes of the Order, and with any necessary modifications, apply any of the provisions of this Act relating to the production and inspection of oil record books and the taking of copies of entries therein, and to the admissibility in evidence of such oil record books and copies, including any provisions of the Merchant Shipping Act 1894 applied by those provisions, and including any penal provisions of this Act in so far as they relate to those matters.

(3) Her Majesty, if satisfied that the government of any country has accepted, or denounced, the Convention, or that the Convention extends, or has ceased to extend, to any territory, may by Order in Council make a declaration to that effect.

(4) In this section 'the Convention' means any Convention accepted by Her Majesty's Government in the United Kingdom in so far as it relates to the prevention of pollution of the sea by oil; and 'Convention ship' means a ship registered in—

(a) a country the government of which has been declared by an Order in Council under the preceding subsection to have accepted the Convention, and has not been so declared to have denounced it; or

(b) a territory to which it has been so declared that the Convention extends, not being a territory to which it has been so declared that the Convention has ceased to extend.

COMMENTS.

Order in Council.

(Relating to the acceptance by Her Majesty's Government of the various countries whose governments have accepted any Convention as far is it relates to the prevention of pollution of the sea by Oil.)

These Orders have been saved by virtue of section 33, sub-section 2 of this Act.

S.I. 1958, No. 1527—Belgium, Canada, Denmark, Germany, France, Ireland, Mexico, Netherlands, Norway, Sweden, United Kingdom.

S.I. 1959, No. 869— Finland.

S.I. 1961, No. 1008—Poland.
S.I. 1961, No. 2277—United States of America.
S.I. 1962, No. 174— Kuwait.
S.I. 1962, No. 1092—Iceland.
S.I. 1962, No. 1345—Liberia.
S.I. 1962, No. 1657—Ghana.
S.I. 1962, No. 2189—Netherlands Antilles.
S.I. 1962, No. 2354—Australia.
S.I. 1963, No. 1149—Jordan.
S.I. 1963, No. 1150—U.A.R.
S.I. 1963, No. 1317—Dominican Republic.
S.I. 1963, No. 1931—Panama.
S.I. 1964, No. 60— Philippines.
S.I. 1964, No. 64— Venezuela.
S.I. 1964, No. 280— Algeria.
S.I. 1964, No. 281— Spain.
S.I. 1964, No. 931— Italy.
S.I. 1965, No. 976— Malagasy.
S.I. 1966, No. 189— Israel.
S.I. 1966, No. 392— Switzerland.
S.I. 1967, No. 814— Greece, Ivory Coast.
S.I. 1967, No. 1153—Lebanon.
S.I. 1967, No. 1680—Portugal, Japan.
S.I. 1968, No. 468— Nigeria.
S.I. 1968, No. 730— Morocco.
S.I. 1969, No. 387— Syria.
S.I. 1969, No. 1085—South Yemen.
S.I. 1970, No. 638— U.S.S.R.
S.I. 1970, No. 824— Monaco.
S.I. 1971, No. 1735—New Zealand.
S.I. 1972, No. 1591—Libya, Senegal.
S.I. 1973, No. 613— Fiji.
S.I. 1973, No. 1752—Tunisia.
S.I. 1976, No. 1160—Austria, India, Kenya, Malta, Uruguay, Yugo-
slavia.

Order in Council (empowering certain persons to go on board).

See the Oil in Navigable Waters (Enforcement of Convention) Order, 1958, S.I. 1958, No. 1526, saved by virtue of section 33, sub-section 2 of this Act.

⚓   ⚓   ⚓   ⚓

Miscellaneous and Supplementary

22 (1) Her Majesty may by Order in Council direct that, subject to such exceptions and modifications as may be specified in the Order, any regulations made under section 4 or section 17(1) of this Act shall apply to ships registered in countries and territories other than the United Kingdom at any time when they are in a harbour in the United Kingdom, or are within the seaward limits of the territorial waters of the United Kingdom while on their way to or from a harbour in the United Kingdom.

(2) An Order in Council under subsection (1) of this section shall not be made so as to impose different requirements in respect of ships of different countries or territories; but if Her Majesty is satisfied, as respects any country or territory, that ships registered there are required, by the law of that country or territory, to comply with provisions which are substantially the same as, or equally effective with, the requirements imposed by virtue of the Order, Her Majesty may by Order in Council direct that those requirements shall not apply to any ship registered in that country or territory if the ship complies with such of those provisions as are applicable thereto under the law of that country or territory.

(3) No regulation shall by virtue of an Order in Council under this section apply to any ship as being within a harbour in the United Kingdom, or on her way to or from such a harbour, if the ship would not have been within the harbour, or, as the case may be, on her way to or from the harbour, but for stress of weather or any other circumstances which neither the master nor the owner nor the charterer (if any) of the ship could have prevented or forestalled.

COMMENTS.

Order in Council.

At the time of going to print, no such Order has been made.

⚓   ⚓   ⚓   ⚓

23 The Secretary of State may exempt any vessels or classes of vessels from any of the provisions of this Act or of any regulations made thereunder, either absolutely or subject to such conditions as he thinks fit.

⚓   ⚓   ⚓   ⚓

24 (1) The provisions of this Act do not apply to vessels of Her Majesty's navy, nor to Government ships in the service of the Secretary of State while employed for the purposes of Her Majesty's navy.

(2) Subject to subsection (1) of this section and subsection (4) of section 16 of this Act—

(*a*) provisions of this Act which are expressed to apply only to ships registered in the United Kingdom apply to Government ships so registered and also to Government ships not so registered but held for the purposes of Her Majesty's Government in the United Kingdom;

(*b*) provisions of this Act which are expressed to apply to vessels generally apply to Government ships.

(3) In this section 'Government ships' has the same meaning as in section 80 of the Merchant Shipping Act 1906.

⚓   ⚓   ⚓   ⚓

Provisions
as to Isle of
Man, Channel
Islands,
colonies and
dependencies.

25 (1) Her Majesty may by Order in Council direct that such of the provisions of this Act, other than section 3, or of any enactment for the time being in force amending or replacing them, as may be specified in the Order shall extend, with such exceptions and modifications, if any, as may be specified in the Order, to the Isle of Man, any of the Channel Islands, or any colony.

(2) The Foreign Jurisdiction Act 1890 shall have effect as if the provisions of this Act, other than section 3, were included among the enactments which, by virtue of section 5 of that Act, may be extended by Order in Council to foreign countries in which for the time being Her Majesty has jurisdiction.

(3) Her Majesty may by Order in Council direct that, subject to such exceptions and modifications as may be specified in the Order, the provisions of this Act which (apart from sections 22 and 24 of this Act) apply only to ships registered in the United Kingdom shall apply also to ships registered in any country or territory specified in the Order, being a country or territory to which the provisions of this Act can be extended by virtue of either of the preceding subsections.

COMMENTS.

Order in Council.

Consult the following Orders and Regulations:

1963 S.I. 1963, No. 788.
     S.I. 1963, No. 848—Hong Kong.
1966 S.I. 1966, No. 393—Guernsey.
     S.I. 1966, No. 425.
     S.I. 1966, No. 394—Isle of Man.
     S.I. 1966, No. 426.
     S.I. 1966, No. 395—Jersey.
     S.I. 1966, No. 427.

⚓   ⚓   ⚓   ⚓

26 The Secretary of State shall, as soon as possible after the end of each calendar year, make a report on the exercise and performance of his functions under this Act during that year, which shall include such observations as he may think fit to make on the operation during that year of this Act and of any Convention accepted by Her Majesty's Government in the United Kingdom in so far as it relates to the prevention of pollution of the sea by oil, and the Secretary of State shall lay a copy of every such report before each House of Parliament. *Annual report.*

⚓   ⚓   ⚓   ⚓

27 (1) Any power to make regulations or an order under this Act shall be exercisable by statutory instrument. *General provisions as to Orders in Council, regulations and orders.*

(2) Any statutory instrument made by virtue of this Act, other than an Order in Council under section 25 or an order under section 34 of this Act, shall be subject to annulment in pursuance of a resolution of either House of Parliament.

(3) Any Order in Council, or other order, made under any provision of this Act may be varied or revoked by a subsequent Order in Council or order made thereunder.

(4) Where a power to make regulations is conferred by any provision of this Act, regulations made under that power may be made with respect to all or with respect to any one or more of the classses of vessel or other matters to which the provision relates, and different provision may be made by any such regulations for different classes of vessel or otherwise for different classes of case or different circumstances.

⚓   ⚓   ⚓   ⚓

28 (1) There shall be defrayed out of moneys provided by Parliament any administrative expenses of the Secretary of State under this Act.

(2) Any fees received by the Secretary of State under this Act shall be paid into the Consolidated Fund.

⚓   ⚓   ⚓   ⚓

29 (1) In this Act—
    'barge' includes a lighter and any similar vessel;
    'harbour authority' and 'harbour in the United Kingdom' have the meanings assigned to them by section 8(2) of this Act;
    'harbour master' includes a dock master or pier master, and any person specially appointed by a harbour authority for the purpose of enforcing the provisions of this Act in relation to the harbour;
    'local enactment' means a local or private Act, or an order confirmed by Parliament or brought into operation in accordance with special parliamentary procedure;
    'oil' means oil of any description and includes spirit produced from oil of any description, and also includes coal tar;
    'oil reception facilities' has the meaning assigned to it by section 9(1) of this Act;
    'oil residues means any waste consisting of, or arising from, oil or a mixture containing oil;
    'outside the territorial waters of the United Kingdom' means outside the seaward limits of those waters;
    'petroleum-spirit' has the same meaning as in the Petroleum (Consolidation) Act 1928;
    'place on land' has the meaning assigned to it by section 2(3) of this Act;
    'sea' includes any estuary or arm of the sea;
    'transfer', in relation to oil, means transfer in bulk.

(2) Any reference in any provision of this Act to a mixture containing oil shall be construed as a reference to any mixture of oil (or, as the case may be, of oil of a description referred to in that provision) with water or with any other substance.

(3) Any reference in the provisions of this Act other than

section 11 to the discharge of oil or a mixture containing oil, or to its being discharged, from a vessel, place or thing, except where the reference is to its being discharged for a specified purpose, includes a reference to the escape of the oil or mixture, or (as the case may be) to its escaping, from that vessel, place or thing.

(4) For the purposes of any provision of this Act relating to the discharge of oil or a mixture containing oil from a vessel, any floating craft (other than a vessel) which is attached to a vessel shall be treated as part of the vessel.

(5) Any power conferred by this Act to test any equipment on board a vessel shall be construed as including a power to require persons on board the vessel to carry out such work as may be requisite for the purpose of testing the equipment; and any provisions of this Act as to submitting equipment for testing shall be construed accordingly.

(6) Subject to the preceding subsections, expressions used in this Act and in the Merchant Shipping Act 1894, have the same meanings in this Act as in that Act.

(7) Except in so far as the context otherwise requires, any reference in this Act to an enactment shall be construed as a reference to that enactment as amended by or under any other enactment.

COMMENTS.

Oil of Any Description.

This term includes vegetable oil as well as mineral oils. Cosh *v.* Larsen 1971. Merchant Shipping Act 1894. *See* definitions contained in section 742 of that Act.

⚓   ⚓   ⚓   ⚓

30 (1) This Act extends to Northern Ireland and the following provisions of this section shall have effect with respect to the application of this Act to Northern Ireland. *Provisions as to Northern Ireland.*

(2) References in section 9 of this Act to the Secretary of State shall be construed as references to the Ministry of Commerce for Northern Ireland (in this section referred to as 'the Ministry of Commerce').

(3) In relation to places on land in Northern Ireland and to apparatus located in Northern Ireland, otherwise than on board a vessel,—

(a) persons appointed by the Secretary of State as inspectors under section 18 of this Act, and surveyors of ships in their capacity as persons so appointed, shall have no powers of entry or inspection; but

(b) persons appointed by the Ministry of Commerce shall have the like powers as (but for the preceding paragraph) persons appointed by the Secretary of State would have by virtue of that section, and the provisions of that section shall have effect in relation to persons appointed by the Ministry of Commerce as, in England and Wales, they have effect in relation to persons appointed by the Secretary of State.

(4) Subsection (1) of section 19 of this Act shall apply to proceedings in Northern Ireland as it applies to proceedings in England and Wales, but with the substitution, for references to the Attorney General, of references to the Attorney General for Northern Ireland; except that, in relation to proceedings for an offence under section 2 of this Act—

(a) if the alleged offence relates to the discharge of oil or a mixture containing oil from a vessel in a harbour or inland waterway in Northern Ireland, the references in that subsection to the Secretary of State shall be construed as references to the Secretary of State or the Ministry of Commerce;

(b) if the alleged offence relates to the discharge of oil or a mixture containing oil from a place on land in Northern Ireland, or from apparatus located in Northern Ireland otherwise than on board a vessel, the references in that subsection to the Secretary of State shall be construed as references to the Ministry of Commerce.

(5) In the definition of 'local enactment' in subsection (1) of section 29 of this Act the reference to a local or private Act includes a reference to a local or private Act of the Parliament of Northern Ireland, and the reference to an order confirmed by Parliament includes a reference to an order confirmed by that Parliament; and the reference in that subsection to the Petroleum (Consolidation) Act 1928 shall be construed as a reference to the Petroleum (Consolidation) Act (Northern Ireland) 1929.

(6) The provisions of this Act, so far as they relate to matters with respect to which the Parliament of Northern Ireland has power to make laws, shall not be taken to restrict that power, and any laws made by that Parliament in the

exercise of that power shall have effect notwithstanding anything in those provisions.

COMMENTS.

Definitions.

See generally, section 29 of this Act.

⚓   ⚓   ⚓   ⚓

31   The enactments and instruments with respect to   Application to hovercraft.
which provision may be made by an Order in Council under
section 1(1)(*h*) of the Hovercraft Act 1968 shall include this
Act and any instrument made under it.

COMMENTS.

Order in Council.

At the time of going to Press no such Order has been made.

⚓   ⚓   ⚓   ⚓

32   Subject to section 33 of the Interpretation Act 1889   Saving for other
(offence under two or more laws) nothing in this Act shall   restrictions,
affect any restriction imposed by or under any other enact-   rights of action, etc.
ment, whether contained in a public general Act or in a local
or private Act, or shall derogate from any right of action or
other remedy (whether civil or criminal) in proceedings
instituted otherwise than under this Act.

⚓   ⚓   ⚓   ⚓

33   (1) The enactments specified in the Schedule to this   Repeals and savings.
Act are hereby repealed to the extent specified in the third
column of that Schedule.

(2) In so far as any instrument made or other thing done
under any enactment repealed by this Act could have been
made or done under any provision of this Act it shall have
effect as if made or done under that provision; and references
in any such instrument to any such enactment shall be construed as referring to the corresponding provision of this Act
or, as the case may be, to this Act.

(3) Nothing in the foregoing provisions of this section shall

be taken as prejudicing the operation of section 38 of the
Interpretation Act 1889 (which relates to the effect of repeals).

⚓   ⚓   ⚓   ⚓

Short title and
commence-
ment.

34 (1) This Act may be cited as the Prevention of Oil
Pollution Act 1971.

(2) This Act shall come into force on such day as the
Secretary of State may by order appoint; but the day so
appointed shall not be earlier than the day or, if more than one,
the latest day, appointed under section 12(3) of the Oil in
Navigable Waters Act 1971 for the coming into force of the
provisions of that Act.

COMMENTS.

The Day Appointed.

This Act came into force on the 11th of March, 1973. Prevention of
Oil Pollution Act, 1971 (Commencement) Order, 1973, S.I. 1973, No. 203.

⚓   ⚓   ⚓   ⚓

Schedule

Enactments Repealed

Short Title:	*Extent of Repeal*:
The Oil in Navigable Waters Act 1955	The Whole Act.
The Oil in Navigable Waters Act 1963	The Whole Act.
The Continental Shelf Act 1964	Section 5.
The Sea Fisheries Regulations Act 1966	Section 21, sub-section 7
The Oil in Navigable Waters Act 1971	The Whole Act.
The Mineral Workings (Offshore Installations) Act 1971	Section 10, sub-section 1, paragraph (*c*).

⚓   ⚓   ⚓   ⚓

The Merchant Shipping Act 1974

(*See* Introduction for the sections now in force)

INTRODUCTION

The Merchant Shipping Act 1974 (Commencement No. 1) Order 1974, S.I. 1974, No. 1792 came into effect as from the 1st November, 1974. The Act of 1974 is to a certain extent an 'enabling' Act, and whilst the Order above has brought into force certain sections listed in accordance with the schedule, other regulations will be required to bring in other provisions of the Act.

The provisions of the 1974 Act, specified in the Schedule to the Order.

Section 3, Section 10, Section 11, in Schedule 2

Paragraphs 1, 2, 5 and 6, Part IV;

Schedule 5, Section 18, Section 19; Section 20;

Section 21; Section 22; Section 23; Section 24, except subsection 4.

See also the Merchant Shipping Act 1974 (Commencement No. 2) Order, S.I. 1975, No. 866.

The main sections contained in the Act are those relating to providing compensation for victims of oil pollution who have been unable to obtain adequate recompense under the Merchant Shipping (Oil Pollution) Act 1971; to regulate the design and construction of oil tankers, particularly the size of individual tanks in tankers; to give power to protect shipping and trading interests against foreign action concerning or affecting carriage of goods by sea; to make provision relating to the operation of submersible apparatus, and the welfare of those using them. The regulations made are contained in the Merchant Shipping (Diving Operations) Regulations 1975, S.I. 1975, No. 116, as amended by the Merchant Shipping (Diving Operations) (Amendment) Regulations 1975, S.I. 1975, No. 2062. *See* also the provisions of Part VI of the principal Act, and section 66 of the 1906 Act, relating to diving operations. Section 19 deals with disciplinary provisions and amends certain sections of the Merchant Shipping Act 1970.

In regard to Regulation of Submersible Craft, *see* S.I. 1976, No. 940.

Submarine Pipelines.
In relation to diving operations in respect of submarine pipelines in areas designated pursuant to the Continental Shelf Act 1964, *see* the Submarine Pipelines (Diving Operations) Regulations 1976, S.I. 1976, No. 923.

PART I

THE INTERNATIONAL OIL POLLUTION COMPENSATION FUND

Interpretation of Part I.

1 (1) In this Part of this Act—

(*a*) the 'Liability Convention' means the International Convention on Civil Liability for Oil Pollution Damage opened for signature in Brussels on 29th November, 1969.

(*b*) the 'Fund Convention' means the International Convention on the Establishment of an International Fund for Compensation for Oil Pollution Damage opened for signature in Brussels on 18th December, 1971;

(*c*) 'the Fund' means the International Fund established by the Fund Convention; and

(*d*) 'Fund Convention country' means a country in respect of which the Fund Convention is in force.

(2) If Her Majesty by Order in Council declares that any State specified in the Order is a party to the Fund Convention in respect of any country so specified the Order shall, while in force, be conclusive evidence that that State is a party to the Convention in respect of that country.

(3) In this Part of this Act, unless the context otherwise requires—

the 'Act of 1971' means the Merchant Shipping (Oil Pollution) Act 1971,

'damage' includes loss,

'discharge or escape', in relation to pollution damage, means the discharge or escape of oil carried by the ship,

'guarantor' means any person providing insurance or other financial security to cover the owner's liability of the kind described in section 10 of the Act of 1971, 'oil', except in sections 2 and 3, means persistent hydro-carbon mineral oil,

'owner' means the person or persons registered as the owner of the ship or, in the absence of registration, the person or persons owning the ship, except that in relation to a ship owned by a State which is operated by a person registered as the ship's operator, it means the person registered as its operator,

'pollution damage' means damage caused outside the ship carrying oil by contamination resulting from the escape or discharge of oil from the ship, wherever the escape or discharge may occur, and includes the cost of preventive measures and further damage caused by preventive measures,

'preventive measures' means any reasonable measures taken by any person after the occurrence to prevent or minimise pollution damage,

'ship' means any sea-going vessel and any seaborne craft of any type whatsoever carrying oil in bulk as cargo.

(4) For the purposes of this Part of this Act a ship's tonnage shall be the net tonnage of the ship with the addition of the amount deducted from the gross tonnage on account of engine room space for the purpose of ascertaining the net tonnage.

If the ship cannot be measured in accordance with the normal rules, its tonnage shall be deemed to be 40 per cent of the weight in tons (of 2240 lbs.) of oil which the ship is capable of carrying.

(5) For the purposes of this Part of this Act, where more than one discharge or escape results from the same occurrence or from a series of occurrences having the same origin, they shall be treated as one.

(6) In this Part of this Act a franc shall be taken to be a unit of $65\frac{1}{2}$ milligrammes of gold of millesimal fineness 900.

(7) The Secretary of State may from time to time by order made by statutory instrument specify the amounts which for the purposes of this Part of this Act are to be taken as equivalent to any specified number of francs.

⚓   ⚓   ⚓   ⚓

Q

Contributions to Fund

2 (1) Contributions shall be payable to the Fund in respect of oil carried by sea to ports or terminal installations in the United Kingdom.

(2) Subsection (1) above applies whether or not the oil is being imported, and applies even if contributions are payable in respect of carriage of the same oil on a previous voyage.

(3) Contributions shall also be payable to the Fund in respect of oil when first received in any installation in the United Kingdom after having been carried by sea and discharged in a port or terminal installation in a country which is not a Fund Convention country.

(4) The person liable to pay contributions is—

(*a*) in the case of oil which is being imported into the United Kingdom, the importer, and

(*b*) otherwise, the person by whom the oil is received.

(5) A person shall not be liable to make contributions in respect of the oil imported or received by him in any year if the oil so imported or received in the year does not exceed 150,000 tonnes.

(6) For the purpose of subsection (5) above—

(*a*) all the members of a group of companies shall be treated as a single person, and

(*b*) any two or more companies which have been amalgamated into a single company shall be treated as the same person as that single company.

(7) The contributions payable by a person for any year shall—

(*a*) be of such amount as may be determined by the Assembly of the Fund under Articles 11 and 12 of the Fund Convention and notified to him by the Fund;

(*b*) be payable in such instalments, becoming due at such times, as may be so notified to him;

and if any amount due from him remains unpaid after the date on which it became due, it shall from then on bear interest, at a rate determined from time to time by the said Assembly, until it is paid.

(8) The Secretary of State may by regulations contained

in a statutory instrument impose on persons who are or may be liable to pay contributions under this section obligations to give security for payment to the Secretary of State, or to the Fund.

Regulations under this subsection—

(a) may contain such supplemental or incidental provisions as appear to the Secretary of State expedient,

(b) may impose penalties for contravention of the regulations punishable on summary conviction by a fine not exceeding £400, or such lower limit as may be specified in the regulations, and

(c) shall be subject to annulment in pursuance of a resolution of either House of Parliament.

(9) In this and the next following section, unless the context otherwise requires—

'company' means a body incorporated under the law of the United Kingdom, or of any other country;

'group' in relation to companies, means a holding company and its subsidiaries as defined by section 154 of the Companies Act 1948 (or for companies in Northern Ireland section 148 of the Companies Act (Northern Ireland) 1960), subject, in the case of a company incorporated outside the United Kingdom, to any necessary modifications of those definitions;

'importer' means the person by whom or on whose behalf the oil in question is entered for customs purposes on importation, and 'import' shall be construed accordingly;

'oil' means crude oil and fuel oil, and

(a) 'crude oil' means any liquid hydrocarbon mixture occurring naturally in the earth whether or not treated to render it suitable for transportation, and includes—

(i) crude oils from which distillate fractions have been removed, and

(ii) crude oils to which distillate fractions have been added,

(b) 'fuel oil' means heavy distillates or residues from crude oil or blends of such materials intended for use as a fuel for the production of heat or power of a quality equivalent to the 'American Society for Testing and Materials' Specification for Number Four Fuel Oil (Designation D 396–69)', or heavier.

'terminal installation' means any site for the storage of oil in bulk which is capable of receiving oil from waterborne transportation, including any facility situated offshore and linked to any such site.

(10) In this section 'sea' does not include any waters on the landward side of the baselines from which the territorial sea of the United Kingdom is measured.

⚓   ⚓   ⚓   ⚓

Power to obtain information.

3 (1) For the purpose of transmitting to the Fund the names and addresses of the persons who under the last preceding section are liable to make contributions to the Fund for any year, and the quantity of oil in respect of which they are so liable, the Secretary of State may by notice require any person engaged in producing, treating, distributing or transporting oil to furnish such information as may be specified in the notice.

(2) A notice under this section may require a company to give such information as may be required to ascertain whether its liability is affected by subsection (6) of the last preceding section.

(3) A notice under this section may specify the way in which, and the time within which, it is to be complied with.

(4) In proceedings by the Fund against any person to recover any amount due under the last preceding section, particulars contained in any list transmitted by the Secretary of State to the Fund shall, so far as those particulars are based on information obtained under this section, be admissible as evidence of the facts stated in the list; and so far as particulars which are so admissible are based on information given by the person against whom the proceedings are brought, those particulars shall be presumed to be accurate until the contrary is proved.

(5) If a person discloses any information which has been furnished to or obtained by him under this section, or in connection with the execution of this section, he shall, unless the disclosure is made—

(*a*) with the consent of the person from whom the information was obtained, or

(*b*) in connection with the execution of this section, or

(*c*) for the purposes of any legal proceedings arising out of this section or of any report of such proceedings,

be liable on summary conviction to a fine not exceeding £400.

(6) A person who—

(*a*) refuses or wilfully neglects to comply with a notice under this section, or

(*b*) in furnishing any information in compliance with a notice under this section makes any statement which he knows to be false in a material particular, or recklessly makes any statement which is false in a material particular,

shall be liable—

(i) on summary conviction to a fine not exceeding £400, and

(ii) on conviction on indictment to a fine, or to imprisonment for a term not exceeding twelve months, or to both.

COMMENTS.

See introduction as to the coming into force of this section.

⚓   ⚓   ⚓   ⚓

Compensation for persons suffering pollution damage

4 (1) The Fund shall be liable for pollution damage in the United Kingdom if the person suffering the damage has been unable to obtain full compensation under section 1 of the Act of 1971 (which gives effect to the Liability Convention)— Liability of the Fund.

(*a*) because the discharge or escape causing the damage—

(i) resulted from an exceptional, inevitable and irresistible phenomenon, or

(ii) was due wholly to anything done or left undone by another person (not being a servant or agent of the owner) with intent to do damage, or

(iii) was due wholly to the negligence or wrongful act of a government or other authority in exercising its function of maintaining lights or other navigational aids

for the maintenance of which it was responsible,
(and because liability is accordingly wholly displaced by
section 2 of the Act of 1971), or

(b) because the owner or guarantor liable for the damage
cannot meet his obligations in full, or

(c) because the damage exceeds the liability under section 1
of the Act of 1971 as limited—

(i) by section 4 of the Act of 1971, or

(ii) (where the said section 4 is displaced by section 9
of this Act) by section 503 of the Merchant Shipping Act
1894.

(2) Subsection (1) above shall apply with the substitution
for the words 'the United Kingdom' of the words 'a Fund
Convention country' where—

(a) the headquarters of the Fund is for the time being in the
United Kingdom, and proceedings under the Liability
Convention for compensation for the pollution damage
have been brought in a country which is not a Fund
Convention country, or

(b) the incident has caused pollution damage both in the
United Kingdom and in another Fund Convention
country, and proceedings under the Liability Convention
for compensation for the pollution damage have been
brought in a country which is not a Fund Convention
country or in the United Kingdom.

(3) Where the incident has caused pollution damage both
in the United Kingdom and in another country in respect of
which the Liability Convention is in force, reference in this
section to the provisions of the Act of 1971 shall include
references to the corresponding provisions of the law of any
country giving effect to the Liability Convention.

(4) Where proceedings under the Liability Convention for
compensation for pollution damage have been brought in a
country which is not a Fund Convention country and the Fund
is liable for that pollution damage by virtue of subsection (2)(a)
above, references in this section to the provisions of the Act
of 1971 shall be treated as references to the corresponding
provisions of the law of the country in which those proceedings were brought.

(5) For the purposes of this section an owner or guarantor
is to be treated as incapable of meeting his obligations if the

obligations have not been met after all reasonable steps to pursue the legal remedies available have been taken.

(6) Expenses reasonably incurred, and sacrifices reasonably made, by the owner voluntarily to prevent or minimise pollution damage shall be treated as pollution damage for the purposes of this section, and accordingly he shall be in the same position with respect to claims against the Fund under this section as if he had a claim in respect of liability under section 1 of the Act of 1971.

(7) The Fund shall incur no obligation under this section if—

(a) it proves that the pollution damage—

    (i) resulted from an act of war, hostilities, civil war or insurrection, or

    (ii) was caused by oil which has escaped or been discharged from a warship or other ship owned or operated by a State and used, at the time of the occurrence, only on Government non-commercial service, or

(b) the claimant cannot prove that the damage resulted from an occurrence involving a ship identified by him, or involving two or more ships one of which is identified by him.

(8) If the Fund proves that the pollution damage resulted wholly or partly—

(a) from an act or omission done with intent to cause damage by the person who suffered the damage, or

(b) from the negligence of that person,

the Fund may be exonerated wholly or partly from its obligation to pay compensation to that person:

Provided that this subsection shall not apply to a claim in respect of expenses or sacrifices made voluntarily to prevent or minimise pollution damage.

(9) Where the liability under section 1 of the Act of 1971 is limited to any extent by subsection (5) of that section (contributory negligence), the Fund shall be exonerated to the same extent.

(10) The Fund's liability under this section shall be subject to the limits imposed by paragraphs 4, 5 and 6 of Article 4 of the Fund Convention which impose an overall liability on

the liabilities of the owner and of the Fund, and the text of which is set out in Schedule 1 to this Act.

(11) Evidence of any instrument issued by any organ of the Fund or of any document in the custody of the Fund, or any entry in or extract from such a document, may be given in any legal proceedings by production of a copy certified as a true copy by an official of the Fund; and any document purporting to be such a copy shall be received in evidence without proof of the official position or handwriting of the person signing the certificate.

(12) For the purpose of giving effect to the said provisions of Article 4 of the Fund Convention a court giving judgment against the Fund in proceedings under this section shall notify the Fund, and—

(a) no steps shall be taken to enforce the judgment unless and until the court gives leave to enforce it,

(b) that leave shall not be given unless and until the Fund notifies the court either that the amount of the claim is not to be reduced under the said provisions of Article 4 of the Fund Convention, or that it is to be reduced to a specified amount, and

(c) in the latter case the judgment shall be enforceable only for the reduced amount.

⚓   ⚓   ⚓   ⚓

Indemnification of Shipowners

PART I

Indemnification where damage is caused by ship registered in Fund Convention country.

5 (1) Where a liability is incurred under section 1 of the Act of 1971 in respect of a ship registered in a Fund Convention country the Fund shall indemnify the owner and his guarantor for that portion of the aggregate amount of the liability which—

(a) is in excess of an amount equivalent to 1500 francs for each ton of the ship's tonnage or of an amount of 125 million francs, whichever is the less, and

(b) is not in excess of an amount equivalent to 2000 francs for each ton of the said tonnage or an amount of 210 million francs, whichever is the less.

(2) Where proceedings under the Liability Convention for compensation for pollution damage have been brought in a country which is not a Fund Convention country (but is a

country in respect of which the Liability Convention is in force), and either—

(a) the incident has caused pollution damage in the United Kingdom (as well as in that other country); or

(b) the headquarters of the Fund is for the time being in the United Kingdom,

subsection (1) above shall apply with the omission of the words 'under section 1 of the Act of 1971'.

(3) The Fund shall not incur an obligation under this section where the pollution damage resulted from the wilful misconduct of the owner.

(4) In proceedings to enforce the Fund's obligation under this section the court may exonerate the Fund wholly or partly if it is proved that, as a result of the actual fault or privity of the owner—

(a) the ship did not comply with such requirements as the Secretary of State may by order prescribe for the purposes of this section, and

(b) the occurrence or damage was caused wholly or partly by that non-compliance.

(5) The requirements referred to in subsection (4) above are such requirements as appear to the Secretary of State appropriate to implement the provisions of—

(a) article 5(3) of the Fund Convention (marine safety conventions), and

(b) article 5(4) of the Fund Convention (which enables the Assembly of the Fund to substitute new conventions).

(6) An order made under subsection (4) above—

(a) may be varied or revoked by a subsequent order so made, or

(b) may contain such transitional or other supplemental provisions as appear to the Secretary of State to be expedient, and

(c) shall be contained in a statutory instrument subject to annulment in pursuance of a resolution of either House of Parliament.

(7) Expenses reasonably incurred, and sacrifices reasonably made, by the owner voluntarily to prevent or minimise the

pollution damage shall be treated as included in the owner's liability for the purposes of this section.

COMMENTS.

Incident.

This is not defined in the Act, but consult the Convention, Brussels 1971—'any occurrence or series of occurrences, having the same origin which causes pollution damage'.

⚓   ⚓   ⚓   ⚓

Supplemental

Jurisdiction and effect of judgments.

6 (1) Paragraph (*d*) of section 1(1) of the Administration of Justice Act 1956 and paragraph 1(1)(*d*) of Schedule 1 to that Act (Admiralty jurisdiction in claims for damage done by ships) shall be construed as extending to any claim in respect of a liability falling on the Fund under this Part of this Act; and the Admiralty jurisdiction of the Court of Session shall extend to any case arising out of any such claim.

(2) Where in accordance with rules of court made for the purposes of this subsection the Fund has been given notice of proceedings brought against an owner or guarantor in respect of liability under section 1 of the Act of 1971, any judgment given in the proceedings shall, after it has become final and enforceable, become binding upon the Fund in the sense that the facts and evidence in the judgment may not be disputed by the Fund even if the Fund has not intervened in the proceedings.

(3) Where a person incurs a liability under the law of a Fund Convention country corresponding to the Act of 1971 for damage which is partly in the area of the United Kingdom, subsection (2) above shall, for the purpose of proceedings under this Part of this Act, apply with any necessary modifications to a judgment in proceedings under that law of the said country.

(4) Subject to subsection (5) below, Part I of the Foreign Judgments (Reciprocal Enforcement) Act 1933 shall apply, whether or not it would so apply apart from this subsection, to any judgment given by a court in a Fund Convention country to enforce a claim in respect of liability incurred under any provision corresponding to section 4 or 5 of this Act and in its application to such a judgment the said Part I shall have effect with the omission of subsections (2) and (3) of section 4 of the Act of 1933.

(5) No steps shall be taken to enforce such a judgment unless and until the court in which it is registered under Part I of the Act of 1933 gives leave to enforce it: and—

(*a*) that leave shall not be given unless and until the Fund notifies the court either that the amount of the claim is not to be reduced under paragraph 4 of Article 4 of the Fund Convention (as set out in Schedule 1 to this Act) or that it is to be reduced to a specified amount; and

(*b*) in the latter case, the judgment shall be enforceable only for the reduced amount.

⚓   ⚓   ⚓   ⚓

7 (1) No action to enforce a claim against the Fund under this Part of this Act shall be entertained by a court in the United Kingdom unless—

Extinguishment of claims.

(*a*) the action is commenced, or

(*b*) a third-party notice of an action to enforce a claim against the owner or his guarantor in respect of the same damage is given to the Fund,

not later than three years after the claim against the Fund arose.

In this subsection 'third party notice' means a notice of the kind described in subsections (2) and (3) of the last preceding section.

(2) No action to enforce a claim against the Fund under this Part of this Act shall be entertained by a court in the United Kingdom unless the action is commenced not later than six years after the occurrence, or first of the occurrences, resulting in the discharge or escape by reason of which the claim against the Fund arose.

(3) Notwithstanding the preceding provisions of this section, a person's right to bring an action under section 5 of this Act shall not be extinguished before six months from the date when that person first acquired knowledge of the bringing of an action against him under the Act of 1971 (that is to say an action to enforce a liability against which he seeks indemnity), or under the corresponding provisions of the law of any country outside the United Kingdom giving effect to the Liability Convention.

⚓   ⚓   ⚓   ⚓

Subrogation
and rights of
recourse.

8 (1) In respect of any sum paid under section 4(1)(*b*) of this Act (default by owner or guarantor on liability for pollution damage) the Fund shall acquire by subrogation the rights of the recipient against the owner or guarantor.

(2) The right of the Fund under subsection (1) above is subject to any obligation of the Fund under section 5 of this Act to indemnify the owner or guarantor for any part of the liability on which he has defaulted.

(3) In respect of any sum paid—

(*a*) under paragraph (*a*) or paragraph (*c*) of section 4(1); or

(*b*) under section 5,

the Fund shall acquire by subrogation any rights of recourse or subrogation which the owner or guarantor or any other person has in respect of his liability for the damage in question.

(4) In respect of any sum paid by a public authority in the United Kingdom as compensation for pollution damage, that authority shall acquire by subrogation any rights which the recipient has against the Fund under this Part of this Act.

⚓   ⚓   ⚓   ⚓

Modification
of limitation
of liability
under Act of
1971.

9 In the Act of 1971 after section 8 there shall be inserted the following section—

Cases
excluded
from sections
4 to 8.

'**8A.** (1) Sections 4 to 8 of this Act shall not apply to a ship which at the time of the discharge or escape was registered in a country—

(*a*) which was not a Convention country, and

(*b*) which was a country in respect of which the 1957 Convention was in force.

(2) In this section 'the 1957 Convention' means the International Convention relating to the Limitation of the Liability of Owners of Seagoing Ships signed in Brussels on 10th October, 1957.

(3) If Her Majesty by Order in Council declares that any country—

(*a*) is not a Convention country within the meaning of this Act, and

(*b*) is a country in respect of which the 1957
Convention is in force,

or that it was such a country at a time specified
in the Order, the Order shall, while in force, be
conclusive evidence of the facts stated in the Order.'

COMMENTS.

Consult the Merchant Shipping Act 1974 (Commencement No. 2)
Order 1975, S.I. 1975, No. 866, which brings this section into force as
from the 19th June, 1975.

States which are Parties to the 1957 Convention.

See The Merchant Shipping (Oil Pollution) (Parties to the Conventions) Order 1975, No. 1036, as amended by The Merchant Shipping (Oil Pollution) (Parties to Conventions) (Amendment) (No. 2) Order 1977, S.I. 1977, No. 826.

⚓   ⚓   ⚓   ⚓

PART II

OIL TANKERS

10 (1) In this Part of this Act 'the Conventions' means— _{Interpretation of Part II.}

(*a*) Article VI bis and Annex C of the International Convention, signed in London on 12th May, 1954, for the Prevention of Pollution of the Sea by Oil, which Article and Annex were added on 15th October, 1971 by resolution of the Assembly of the Inter-governmental Maritime Consultative Organisation; and

(*b*) any other international convention, or amendment of an international convention, which relates in whole or in part to prevention of pollution of the sea by oil, and which has been signed for the United Kingdom before the passing of this Act, or later.

(2) In this Part of this Act 'Convention country' means a country in respect of which a State is a party to any of the Conventions.

(3) If Her Majesty by Order in Council declares that any State specified in the Order is a party to any of the Conventions in respect of any country so specified, the Order shall,

while in force, be conclusive evidence that that State is a party to the Convention in respect of that country.

(4) In this Part of this Act—

'oil tanker' means a ship which is constructed or adapted primarily to carry oil in bulk in its cargo spaces (whether or not it is also so constructed or adapted as to be capable of carrying other cargoes in those spaces),

'United Kingdom oil tanker' means an oil tanker registered in the United Kingdom,

'oil' means crude oil, fuel oil (including diesel oil) and lubricating oil.

'port' includes an offshore terminal, and references to entering or leaving a port shall include references to using or ceasing to use an offshore terminal.

COMMENTS.

See introduction as to the time of coming into force of this section.

⚓   ⚓   ⚓   ⚓

Design and construction of oil tankers.

11 (1) For the purpose of preventing pollution of the sea by oil, the Secretary of State may make rules (called 'oil tanker construction rules') prescribing requirements to be complied with by United Kingdom oil tankers in respect of their design and construction.

(2) The said rules may include such requirements as appear to the Secretary of State to implement any of the provisions of the Conventions, so far as they relate to prevention of pollution of the sea by oil.

This subsection applies whether or not the said provisions are for the time being binding on Her Majesty's Government in the United Kingdom.

(3) Oil tanker construction rules may provide—

(*a*) for oil tankers to be surveyed and inspected with a view to determining whether they comply with the rules,

(*b*) for a tanker which on a survey is found to comply to be issued with a certificate called a 'tanker construction certificate', and

(*c*) for a tanker which is not required to comply with the rules to be issued with a certificate called a 'tanker exemption certificate'.

(4) Schedule 2 to this Act shall have effect for supplementing this Part of this Act.

(5) It is hereby declared that the oil tankers to which rules under this section may be applied include those designed or constructed before the rules come into force, and that the following provisions of this Part of this Act apply whether the oil tanker in question was designed or constructed before or after the relevant requirements as to design or construction came into force.

(6) Oil tanker construction rules shall be contained in a statutory instrument subject to annulment in pursuance of a resolution of either House of Parliament.

COMMENTS.

See introduction as to the time of coming into force of this section.

⚓   ⚓   ⚓   ⚓

12 (1) No oil tanker shall proceed, or attempt to proceed, to sea unless— *Restrictions on tankers sailing from United Kingdom ports.*

(a) it is a certificated oil tanker (within the meaning of Schedule 3 to this Act), or

(b) it is not registered in the United Kingdom, and—

(i) if it were a United Kingdom oil tanker, it would qualify for the issue of a tanker exemption certificate, or

(ii) its gross tonnage is less than 150 tons, or

(c) the Secretary of State has issued it with leave to sail.

(2) Where an application is made for leave to sail to be issued to an oil tanker, then—

(a) if the tanker is registered in the United Kingdom, the Secretary of State may issue it with leave to sail where he considers it appropriate to do so;

(b) if the tanker is not registered in the United Kingdom, the Secretary of State—

(i) shall issue it with leave to sail if he is satisfied that it would qualify for the issue of a tanker construction certificate if it were a United Kingdom oil tanker; and

(ii) may, if he is not so satisfied, issue it with leave to sail where he considers it appropriate to do so.

(3) Leave to sail issued under paragraph (*a*) or (*b*)(ii) of subsection (2) above may be issued subject to conditions imposed with a view to preventing or limiting the danger of oil pollution, including—

(*a*) conditions as to the cargo with which the tanker may sail;

(*b*) a condition that the tanker sails only to a specified port in the United Kingdom or elsewhere.

(4) Subject to subsection (5) below, if—

(*a*) an oil tanker proceeds, or attempts to proceed, to sea in contravention of subsection (1) above; or

(*b*) leave to sail having been issued to an oil tanker under this section subject to conditions, it proceeds to sea but the conditions are not complied with,

the owner and master of the tanker shall each be liable on summary conviction to a fine of not more than £10,000, or on conviction on indictment to a fine.

(5) In proceedings under subsection (4) above, it shall be a defence to prove that in order—

(*a*) to ensure the safety of the oil tanker, or

(*b*) to reduce the risk of damage to any other vessel or property,

it was necessary for the tanker to proceed to sea in contravention of subsection (1) above or, as the case may be, without complying with the conditions mentioned in paragraph (*b*) of subsection (4).

In this section 'damage' does not include damage caused by contamination resulting from the escape or discharge of oil from a tanker.

⚓   ⚓   ⚓   ⚓

Restrictions on uncertificated tankers.

13 (1) If it appears to the Secretary of State that an oil tanker is not certificated (within the meaning of Schedule 3 to this Act) he may direct the oil tanker—

(*a*) not to enter any port in the United Kingdom (or not to enter one or more specified ports in the United Kingdom); or

(*b*) not to enter all or any ports in the United Kingdom except subject to specified conditions.

(2) A direction may be given under this section in respect of an oil tanker which is for the time being in a port in the United Kingdom, so as to apply after it leaves that port.

(3) Directions under this section shall be addressed to the master or owner of the tanker, or to both, and may be communicated by any means which appear to the Secretary of State suitable for the purpose.

(4) Subject to subsection (5) below, if an oil tanker enters a port in the United Kingdom in contravention of a direction under this section, or without complying with any conditions imposed under this section, the owner and the master of the tanker shall each be liable on summary conviction to a fine not exceeding £15,000, or on conviction on indictment to a fine.

(5) In proceedings under subsection (4) above, it shall be a defence to prove that the tanker entered the port out of necessity due—

(*a*) to an emergency involving a threat to any person's life or the safety of the tanker, or

(*b*) to circumstances outside the control of the tanker's master.

⚓   ⚓   ⚓   ⚓

Part III

Protection of Shipping and Trading Interests

14 (1) The Secretary of State may exercise the powers conferred by this section if he is satisfied that a foreign government, or any agency or authority of a foreign government, have adopted, or propose to adopt, measures or practices concerning or affecting the carriage of goods by sea which— *Foreign action affecting shipping.*

(*a*) are damaging or threaten to damage the shipping or trading interests of the United Kingdom, or

(*b*) are damaging or threaten to damage the shipping or trading interests of another country, and the Secretary of State is satisfied that action under this section would be in fulfilment of the international obligations of Her Majesty's Government to that other country.

(2) The Secretary of State may by order make provision for requiring persons in the United Kingdom carrying on any trade or business to provide the Secretary of State with all such information as he may require for the purpose of enabling him—

(*a*) to determine what further action to take under this section, and

(*b*) to ensure compliance with any orders or directions made or given under this section.

(3) The Secretary of State may by order provide for—

(*a*) regulating the carriage of goods in ships and the rates which may or must be charged for carrying them;

(*b*) regulating the admission and departure of ships to and from United Kingdom ports, the cargoes they may carry, and the loading or unloading of cargoes;

(*c*) regulating the making and implementation of agreements (including charter-parties) whose subject matter relates directly or indirectly to the carriage of goods by sea, and requiring such agreements to be subject to the Secretary of State's approval in such cases as he may specify;

(*d*) imposing charges in respect of ships which enter United Kingdom ports to load or unload cargo.

(4) In a case falling within subsection (1)(*a*) above, an order under subsection (3) above shall specify the measures or practices which in the opinion of the Secretary of State are damaging or threaten to damage shipping or trading interests of the United Kingdom.

(5) An order under this section may authorise the Secretary of State to give directions to any person for the purposes of the order:

Provided that this subsection shall not apply for the purpose of recovering charges imposed under subsection (3)(*d*) above.

(6) Any order or direction made or given under this section—

(*a*) may be either general or special, and may be subject to such conditions or exceptions as the Secretary of State specifies (including conditions and exceptions operating by reference to the giving or withholding of his approval for any course of action);

(b) may be in terms that require compliance either generally or only in specified cases;

(c) may be varied or revoked by a subsequent order, or as the case may be, a subsequent direction, so made or given,

and an order made pursuant to this section shall be contained in a statutory instrument.

(7) Before the Secretary of State makes an order under this section he shall consult such representatives of the shipping or trading interests of the United Kingdom, and such other persons, as appear to him appropriate.

(8) If a person discloses any information which has been furnished to or obtained by him under this section, or in connection with the execution of this section, he shall, unless the disclosure is made—

(a) with the consent of the person from whom the information was obtained, or

(b) in connection with the execution of this section, or

(c) for the purposes of any legal proceedings arising out of this section or of any report of such proceedings,

be liable on summary conviction to a fine not exceeding £400.

(9) A person who—

(a) refuses or wilfully neglects to furnish any information which he is required to furnish under this section, or

(b) in furnishing any such information makes any statement which he knows to be false in a material particular, or recklessly makes any statement which is false in a material particular,

shall be liable on summary conviction to a fine not exceeding £400.

(10) A person who wilfully contravenes or fails to comply with any provision of an order or direction made or given pursuant to this section, other than a provision requiring him to give any information, shall be liable—

(a) on summary conviction to a fine of not more than £5,000;

(b) on conviction on indictment to a fine;

and where the order or direction requires anything to be done, or not to be done, by, to or on a ship, and the requirement is not complied with, the owner and master of the ship are each to be regarded as wilfully failing to comply, without prejudice to the liability of anyone else.

(11) In this section 'foreign government' means the government of any country outside the United Kingdom; and references to ships are to ships of any registration.

(12) Schedule 4 to this Act shall have effect for supplementing this section, which in that Schedule is called 'the principal section'.

⚓   ⚓   ⚓   ⚓

Parliamentary control of orders under Part III.

15 (1) No order shall be made in exercise of the powers conferred by subsection (3) of the last preceding section unless—

(*a*) a draft has been approved by resolution of each House of Parliament, or

(*b*) it is declared in the order that it appears to the Secretary of State that by reason of urgency it is necessary to make the order without a draft having been so approved.

(2) An order made in exercise of the powers conferred by the said subsection (3) without a draft having been approved by resolution of each House of Parliament shall cease to have effect at the expiration of a period of 28 days beginning with the date on which it was made unless before the expiration of that period it has been approved by resolution of each House of Parliament, but without prejudice to anything previously done, or to the making of a new order.

In reckoning for the purposes of this subsection any period of 28 days, no account shall be taken of any period during which Parliament is dissolved or prorogued or during which both Houses are adjourned for more than four days.

(3) An order under the last preceding section which is not made in exercise of the powers conferred by subsection (3) of that section shall be subject to annulment in pursuance of a resolution of either House of Parliament.

(4) If an order under that section recites that it is not made in exercise of the powers conferred by the said subsection (3), the recital shall be conclusive.

⚓   ⚓   ⚓   ⚓

Part IV

Submersible Apparatus

16 (1) This Part of this Act applies to any submersible or supporting apparatus— *Apparatus to which Part IV applies.*

(a) operated within waters which are in the United Kingdom or which are adjacent thereto and within the seaward limits of territorial waters, or

(b) launched or operated from, or comprising, a ship registered in the United Kingdom or a British ship of a specified description (being a British ship which is not registered in the United Kingdom).

(2) In this section—

'apparatus' includes any vessel, vehicle or hovercraft, any structure, any diving plant or equipment and any other form of equipment,

'specified' means specified in regulations made by the Secretary of State for the purposes of this section,

'submersible apparatus' means any apparatus used, or designed for use, in supporting human life on or under the bed of any waters or elsewhere under the surface of any waters, and

'supporting apparatus' means any apparatus used or designed for use, in connection with the operation f any submersible apparatus.

Comments.

Regulations.

As from the 1st January, 1976 the Merchant Shipping (Diving Operations) Regulations 1975, S.I. 1975, No. 116 is amended by The Merchant Shipping (Diving Operations) (Amendment Regulations) 1975, S.I. 1975, No. 2062.

See also the Merchant Shipping (Registration of Submersible Craft) Regulations 1976, S.I. 1976, No. 940.

⚓   ⚓   ⚓   ⚓

Safety of
submersible
and supporting
apparatus.

17 (1) The Secretary of State may make regulations—

(a) for the safety of submersible and supporting apparatus;

(b) for the prevention of accidents in or near submersible or supporting apparatus;

(c) for the safety, health and welfare of persons on or in submersible and supporting apparatus;

(d) for prohibiting or otherwise restricting the operation of any submersible apparatus except in accordance with the conditions of a licence granted under the regulations; and

(e) for the registration of submersible apparatus.

(2) Regulations made under this section shall be contained in a statutory instrument subject to annulment in pursuance of a resolution of either House of Parliament.

(3) Schedule 5 to this Act shall have effect for supplementing the provisions of this section.

COMMENTS.

Consult the Merchant Shipping (Diving Operations) Regulations 1975, S.I. 1975, No. 116 as amended by the Merchant Shipping (Diving Operations) (Amendment) Regulations 1975, S.I. 1975, No. 2062. *See* also the provisions of Part VI of the principal Act and section 66 of the 1906 Act relating to diving operations.

COMMENTS.

Registration of Submersible Craft.

See S.I. 1976, No. 940.

⚓   ⚓   ⚓   ⚓

PART V

MISCELLANEOUS AND SUPPLEMENTAL

Miscellaneous

Commis-
sioners of
Northern
Lighthouses.

18 (1) Section 668 of the Merchant Shipping Act 1894 (constitution of Commissioners of Northern Lighthouses) shall be amended as follows.

(2) After paragraph (d) of subsection (1) there shall be inserted—

'(dd) a person nominated by the Lieutenant-Governor of the Isle of Man and appointed by the Secretary of State'.

(3) At the end of the said section 668 there shall be added—

'(4) The Commissioners may elect, as members of their body, not more than four other persons.

(5) A person appointed by the Secretary of State under subsection (1)(*dd*) above, or a person appointed by the Commissioners under subsection (4) above, shall hold office for three years, but shall be eligible for re-appointment.'

COMMENTS.

See introduction as to the time of the coming into force of this section.

⚓   ⚓   ⚓   ⚓

19 (1) The Merchant Shipping Act 1970 shall be amended in accordance with the following provisions of this section.   *Offences by seamen.*

(2) In section 27 (which creates an offence in relation to misconduct endangering a ship or persons on board, punishable on summary conviction with a fine not exceeding £200) for the words '£200' there shall be substituted the words '£400'.

(3) Section 29 (which makes it an offence wilfully to disobey a lawful command relating to, or likely to affect, the operation of a ship or of its equipment) and section 31 (which makes it an offence in certain circumstances for a seaman to be absent without leave at the time of sailing) are hereby repealed.

(4) In section 30 (continued or concerted disobedience, neglect of duty, etc.) for the words from the beginning of paragraph (*c*) to the end there shall be substituted:

'(*c*) combines with other seamen employed in that ship—

(i) to disobey lawful commands which are required to be obeyed at a time while the ship is at sea;

(ii) to neglect any duty which is required to be discharged at such a time; or

(iii) to impede, at such a time, the progress of a voyage or the navigation of the ship,

he shall be liable on summary conviction to a fine not exceeding £100.

For the purposes of this section a ship shall be treated as being at sea at any time when it is not securely moored in a safe berth.'

(5) In section 34(2) (which imposes a limit of £10 on the amount of any fine which may be imposed on a seaman for a 'disciplinary offence') for the words '£10' there shall be substituted the words '£20'.

(6) The following provisions referring to sections repealed by subsection (3) above shall be amended, that is to say—

(a) in section 32 the words '29' shall be omitted;

(b) in paragraph 2 of Schedule 2 the words '29', in both places, and the words 'or 31' shall be omitted;

(c) in section 95(1)(a) for the words '29 to' there shall be substituted the words '30 and'.

COMMENTS.

See introduction as to the time of the coming into force of this section.

⚓   ⚓   ⚓   ⚓

Supplemental

Extension to British possessions, etc.

20 (1) Her Majesty may by Order in Council direct that specified provisions of this Act shall extend, subject to specified exceptions, modifications or adaptations, to any of the following countries, that is to say—

(a) the Isle of Man;

(b) any of the Channel Islands;

(c) any colony other than one for whose external relations a country other than the United Kingdom is responsible;

(d) any country outside Her Majesty's dominions in which Her Majesty has jurisdiction in right of Her Majesty's Government in the United Kingdom.

(2) In respect of any country falling within any of paragraphs (a) to (d) of subsection (1) above, Her Majesty may by Order in Council, specifying that country, direct that, with specified exceptions, adaptations or modifications, specified provisions of this Act shall have effect as if references therein to the United Kingdom included references to that country.

(3) In subsections (1) and (2) above 'specified' means specified by an Order under this section.

(4) Any Order made under subsection (2) above shall be subject to annulment in pursuance of a resolution of either House of Parliament.

COMMENTS.

See introduction as to the time of the coming into force of this section.

For extension of Part 1, part of Part V and Schedule 1 to the Isle of Man, Jersey, and Guernsey, as from the 1st of February, 1976, *see*:—

The Merchant Shipping Act 1974 (Jersey) Order 1975, S.I. 1975, No. 2181, as amended by S.I. 1977, No. 1242.

The Merchant Shipping Act 1974 (Guernsey) Order 1975, S.I. 1975, No. 2182, as amended by S.I. 1977, No. 1241.

The Merchant Shipping Act 1974 (Isle of Man) Order 1975, S.I. 1975, No. 2183.

⚓ ⚓ ⚓ ⚓

21 Any sum received by a Minister under this Act shall be paid into the Consolidated Fund. *Financial provisions.*

COMMENTS.

See introduction as to the coming into force of this section.

⚓ ⚓ ⚓ ⚓

22 Where an offence under this Act, or under regulations made under any of its provisions, which has been committed by a body corporate is proved to have been committed with the consent or connivance of, or to be attributable to any neglect on the part of, a director, manager, secretary or other similar officer of the body corporate, or any person who was purporting to act in any such capacity, he, as well as the body corporate, shall be guilty of that offence and shall be liable to be proceeded against and punished accordingly. *Offences by bodies corporate.*

In this section 'director', in relation to a body corporate established by or under any enactment for the purpose of carrying on under public ownership any industry or part of an industry or undertaking, being a body corporate whose affairs are managed by its members, means a member of that body corporate.

COMMENTS.

See introduction as to the time of the coming into force of this section.

⚓ ⚓ ⚓ ⚓

23 (1) This Act shall be construed as one with the Merchant Shipping Acts 1894 to 1971, and without prejudice to the generality of this provision, references in those Acts to the Merchant Shipping Acts shall be construed as including references to this Act. *Construction and interpretation.*

(2) References in this Act to the area of any country include the territorial sea of that country, and references to pollution damage in the United Kingdom shall be construed accordingly.

(3) It is hereby declared that any power to give directions conferred by this Act includes a power to vary or revoke directions so given.

(4) Except so far as the context otherwise requires, any reference in this Act to an enactment shall be construed as a reference to that enactment as amended or extended by or under any other enactment.

COMMENTS.

See introduction as to the time of the coming into force of this section.

⚓   ⚓   ⚓   ⚓

Citation, commencement, repeals and extent.

24 (1) This Act may be cited as the Merchant Shipping Act 1974; and this Act and the Merchant Shipping Acts 1894 to 1971 may be cited together as the Merchant Shipping Acts 1894 to 1974.

(2) This Act shall come into force on such day as the Secretary of State may appoint by order made by statutory instrument; and different days may be appointed for different provisions, or for different purposes.

(3) An order under subsection (2) above may make such transitional provision as appears to the Secretary of State to be necessary or expedient in connection with the provisions thereby brought into force, including such adaptations of those provisions, or any provisions of this Act then in force, as appear to him to be necessary or expedient in consequence of the partial operation of this Act (whether before or after the day appointed by the order).

(4) Sections 324 to 326 and sections 330 and 331 of the Customs Consolidation Act 1853 (which relate to reciprocity in international commerce) are hereby repealed.

(5) This Act extends to Northern Ireland.

COMMENTS.

Merchant Shipping Act 1974.

Certain sections are in force by virtue of The Merchant Shipping Act 1974 (Commencement No. 1) Order 1974, S.I. 1974, No. 1792.

The Merchant Shipping Act 1974 (Commencement No. 2) Order 1975, S.I. 1975, No. 866 q.v.   *See* also introduction.

⚓   ⚓   ⚓   ⚓

SCHEDULES

SCHEDULE 1

OVERALL LIMIT ON LIABILITY OF FUND

Article 4—paragraphs 4, 5 and 6

4. (*a*) Except as otherwise provided in sub-paragraph (*b*) of this paragraph, the aggregate amount of compensation payable by the Fund under this Article shall in respect of any one incident be limited, so that the total sum of that amount and the amount of compensation actually paid under the Liability Convention for pollution damage caused in the territory of the Contracting States, including any sums in respect of which the Fund is under an obligation to indemnify the owner pursuant to Article 5, paragraph 1, of this Convention, shall not exceed 450 million francs.

   (*b*) The aggregate amount of compensation payable by the Fund under this Article for pollution damage resulting from a natural phenomenon of an exceptional, inevitable and irresistible character shall not exceed 450 million francs.

5. Where the amount of established claims against the Fund exceeds the aggregate amount of compensation payable under paragraph 4, the amount available shall be distributed in such a manner that the proportion between any established claim and the amount of compensation actually recovered by the claimant under the Liability Convention and this Convention shall be the same for all claimants.

6. The Assembly of the Fund (hereinafter referred to as 'the Assembly') may, having regard to the experience of incidents which have occurred and in particular the amount of damage resulting therefrom and to changes in the monetary values, decide that the amount of 450 million francs referred to in paragraph 4, sub-paragraph (*a*) and (*b*), shall be changed; provided, however, that this amount shall in no case exceed 900 million francs or be lower than 450 million francs. The changed amount shall apply to incidents which occur after the date of the decision effecting the change.

SCHEDULE 2

Oil Tankers

Surveys, inspections and certificates

1.—(1) Oil tanker construction rules may provide for any surveys or inspections under the rules to be undertaken, and certificates to be issued, in such circumstances as may be specified in the rules, by persons appointed by such organisations as may be authorised for the purpose by the Secretary of State.

(2) Sub-paragraph (1) above shall have effect notwithstanding section 86 of the Merchant Shipping Act 1894 (which requires certain surveys and measurements to be carried out by officers of the Secretary of State).

(3) The rules may apply any of the following provisions of the Merchant Shipping Act 1894 with such exceptions or modifications as may be prescribed by the rules, that is—

- (*a*) section 272(2) (surveyor to deliver declaration of survey to owner),
- (*b*) section 273 (owner to deliver declaration to Secretary of State),
- (*c*) section 275 (appeal to court of survey),
- (*d*) section 276 and sections 278 to 281 (provisions about certificates),
- (*e*) section 282 (forgery of certificate or declaration of survey).

Duty to notify alterations

2.—(1) The rules may require the owner of a United Kingdom oil tanker to notify the Secretary of State of any alteration to the tanker which may affect the question of its qualification or continued qualification for a tanker construction certificate or a tanker exemption certificate.

(2) If any person contravenes the rules by failing to notify such an alteration, he shall be guilty of an offence and liable on summary conviction to a fine not exceeding £1,000.

Clearance of outgoing tanker

3.—(1) Before a certificated oil tanker proceeds to sea, the master of the tanker shall produce the certificate to the officer of customs from whom a clearance for the ship is demanded.

(2) Before any oil tanker which is not certificated proceeds to sea, the master of the tanker shall produce to the officer of customs from whom a clearance for the ship is demanded evidence to the satisfaction of the officer that the departure will not be in contravention of section 12 of this Act.

(3) A clearance shall not be granted, and the tanker may be detained, until the certificate or other evidence is so produced.

Inspection of foreign tanker

4.—(1) For the purpose of determining whether an oil tanker not registered in the United Kingdom is certificated, or whether, if it were a United Kingdom oil tanker, it would qualify for the issue of a tanker construction certificate or a tanker exemption certificate, a competent officer may at all reasonable times go on board the tanker and inspect any part of it, and call for the production of any document carried in the tanker.

(2) An officer exercising powers under this paragraph shall not unnecessarily detain or delay a tanker but may, if he considers it necessary in order to determine—

(a) whether the tanker should be issued with leave to sail under section 12 of this Act, or whether leave to sail should be issued subject to any conditions under subsection (3) of that section, or

(b) whether an order should be issued in respect of the tanker under section 13 of this Act,

require the tanker to be taken into dock for a survey of its hull, cargo-spaces or fuel-tanks.

(3) If any person obstructs an officer acting under this paragraph, or fails to comply with a requirement made under sub-paragraph (2) above, or fails to produce a document carried in the tanker when called on by the officer to produce it, he shall be guilty of an offence and liable on summary conviction to a fine of not more than £100.

(4) In this paragraph 'competent officer' means an officer of the Secretary of State authorised by him to act thereunder.

(5) Nothing in this paragraph prejudices section 76 of the Merchant Shipping Act 1970 (general powers of inspection).

Offences

5.—(1) Oil tanker construction rules may provide for the punishment of any contravention of or failure to comply with the rules by making a person liable on summary conviction to a fine not exceeding £100, or such lower limit as may be specified in the rules.

(2) This paragraph is without prejudice to liability for any offence against the rules for which a punishment is provided by some other provision of this Act.

Fees

6. Oil tanker construction rules—

  (a) may, with the approval of the Treasury, prescribe the fees payable in respect of surveys and inspections carried out, and certificates issued, under the rules)

  (b) shall, subject to sub-paragraph (c) below, provide for all fees payable under the rules to be paid to the Secretary of State; and

  (c) may, in the case of surveys and inspections carried out, and certificates issued, by persons appointed by organisations authorised under paragraph 1 above, provide for fees to be payable to those persons or organisations.

COMMENTS.

See introduction of this Act as to the time of coming into force.

⚓   ⚓   ⚓   ⚓

SCHEDULE 3

CERTIFICATED OIL TANKERS

1. In Part II of this Act a 'certificated oil tanker' means one falling within paragraphs 2, 3 or 4 below.

2. An oil tanker is certificated if it is a United Kingdom oil tanker in respect of which a tanker construction certificate or a tanker exemption certificate is in force.

3.—(1) An oil tanker registered in a Convention country (other than the United Kingdom) is certificated if a certificate corresponding to a tanker construction certificate or tanker exemption certificate duly issued under the law of that country is in force in respect of the tanker.

(2) The Secretary of State may by order in a statutoryinstrument declare that for the purposes of this paragraph a certificate of a kind specified in the order is one which corresponds to a tanker construction certificate or tanker exemption certificate, and is of a kind which is issued under the law of a Convention country so specified.

(3) An order under this paragraph shall, while the order is in force, be conclusive evidence of the facts stated in the order.

4.—(1) An oil tanker is certificated if a certificate of a prescribed kind issued under the law of a country which is not a Convention country is in force as respects the oil tanker.

(2) In this paragraph 'prescribed' means prescribed by order of the Secretary of State contained in a statutory instrument.

5. An order made under this Schedule may be varied or revoked by a subsequent order so made.

⚓   ⚓   ⚓   ⚓

SCHEDULE 4

PROTECTION OF SHIPPING AND TRADING INTERESTS

Customs powers

1.—(1) An order made under the principal section with the consent of the Commissioners of Customs and Excise may provide for the enforcement and execution of any order or direction under the principal section by officers of customs and excise.

(2) Officers of customs and excise acting under any provision made under sub-paragraph (1) above shall have power to enter any premises or vessel.

(3) Section 53 of the Customs and Excise Act 1952 (power to refuse or cancel clearance of ship or aircraft) shall apply as if the principal section and this Schedule were contained in that Act.

Orders imposing charges

2.—(1) An order under subsection (3)(*d*) of the principal section—

    (*a*) may apply to ships of any description specified in the order, and may apply in particular to ships registered in a specified country, or ships carrying specified goods or cargoes, and

    (*b*) may contain such provisions as appear to the Secretary of State expedient to enable the Commissioners of Customs and Excise to collect any charge imposed by the order, and

R

(*c*) may apply any of the provisions of the customs Acts which relate to duties of customs, subject to any modifications or exceptions specified in the order.

(2) The charge so imposed may be a fixed amount, or may be an amount depending on the tonnage of the ship.

(3) Any such charge shall be payable to the Secretary of State.

Criminal proceedings

3. A person shall not be guilty of an offence against any provision contained in or having effect under the principal section or this Schedule by reason only of something done by that person wholly outside the area of the United Kingdom unless that person is a British subject or a company incorporated under the law of any part of the United Kingdom.

Interpretation

4. In the principal section 'port' includes an off-shore terminal, and references to entering or leaving a port shall include references to using or ceasing to use an off-shore terminal.

⚓ ⚓ ⚓ ⚓

SCHEDULE 5

REGULATIONS RELATING TO SUBMERSIBLE AND SUPPORTING APPARATUS

1.—(1) In this Schedule 'regulations' means regulations made under section 17 of this Act, and 'prescribed' means prescribed by regulations.

(2) Nothing in this Schedule shall be taken to prejudice the generality of section 17 of this Act.

Registration of submersible apparatus

2. Regulations made by virtue of section 17(1)(*e*) of this Act may make provision—

(*a*) for all matters relevant to the maintenance of a register of submersible apparatus,

(*b*) without prejudice to sub-paragraph (*a*) above, for the period for which any registration or exemption is to remain effective without renewal, the alteration or cancellation in any prescribed circumstances of registration or exemption or of any conditions attached thereto, the person by whom and manner in which applications in connection with any registration or exemption are to be made, and information and evidence to be furnished in connection with any such application,

(c) for the marking or other means of identification of any submersible apparatus,

(d) for the issue of certificates of registration or exemption, and the custody, surrender, production or disolay of the certificates or copies of them,

(e) for matters arising out of the termination of any registration or exemption, or any conditions attached thereto.

Offences

3.—(1) Subject to sub-paragraph (2) below, regulations—

(a) may provide for the creation of offences and for their punishment on summary conviction or on conviction on indictment, and

(b) may afford, in respect of any description of offence created by the regulations, such defence (if any) as may be prescribed.

(2) The punishment for an offence created by regulations shall be—

(a) on summary conviction a fine not exceeding £400.

(b) on conviction on indictment imprisonment for a term not exceeding 2 years, or a fine, or both,

but without prejudice to any further restriction contained in the regulations on the punishments which can be awarded and without prejudice to the exclusion by the regulations of proceedings on indictment.

Exemptions from regulations

4.—(1) The operation of any regulations may be excluded in whole or in part in relation to any class or description of submersible or supporting apparatus by regulations, or in relation to any particular apparatus by the direction of the Secretary of State given in such manner as he thinks appropriate.

(2) Any exemption or exclusion by regulations or by directions of the Secretary of State under this paragraph may be made subject

R*

to the imposition of conditions specified by the regulations or directions.

(3) Where, in pursuance of this paragraph, a person is exempted or excluded from the requirements of the provisions of regulations but, subject to a condition, and the condition is not observed, the exemption or exclusion shall not have effect, and accordingly proceedings may be brought in respect of any offence created by the regulations.

General

5. Regulations—

    (*a*) may provide for their operation anywhere outside the United Kingdom and for their application to persons, whether or not British subjects, and to companies, whether or not incorporated under the law of any part of the United Kingdom,

    (*b*) may provide that in any proceedings for an offence under the regulations an averment in any process of the fact that anything was done or situated within waters to which this Act applies shall, until the contrary is proved, be sufficient evidence of that fact as stated in the averment,

    (*c*) may provide that proceedings for any offence under the regulations may be taken, and the offence be treated for all incidental purposes as having been committed, in any place in the United Kingdom,

    (*d*) may provide for any provisions of the Merchant Shipping Acts 1894 to 1970 relating to inquiries and investigations into shipping casualties to apply (with such modifications as may be specified) in relation to casualties involving any submersible apparatus which is not a ship as they apply to ships,

    (*e*) may provide that specified provisions of any enactment (other than this Act) shall, in such circumstances as may be prescribed, not have effect in relation to such class or description of, or to such particular, submersible or supporting apparatus as may be prescribed;

    (*f*) may make different provision for different classes or descriptions of submersible or supporting apparatus and for different circumstances,

    (*g*) may contain such supplemental, and incidental provisions as appear to the Secretary of State to be expedient, including provision for requiring the payment of fees in connection with the making of applications and the granting of licences or issue of certificates, or other matters.

COMMENTS.

Consult the introduction to this Act, and *see* the Merchant Shipping (Diving Operations) Regulations 1975, S.I. 1975, No. 116 as amended by The Merchant Shipping (Diving Operations) (Amendment) Regulations 1975, S.I. 1975, No. 2062.

Registration.

Consult S.I. 1976, No. 940.

⚓ ⚓ ⚓ ⚓

INDEX

INDEX

A